ISSN 1532-2734

ENDANGERED SPECIES

MUST THEY DISAPPEAR?

Jennifer Yeh

INFORMATION PLUS® REFERENCE SERIES
Formerly published by Information Plus, Wylie, Texas

GALE®

THOMSON

GALE

Detroit • New York • San Diego • San Francisco • Cleveland • New Haven, Conn. • Waterville, Maine • London • Munich

Endangered Species: Must They Disappear?

Jennifer Yeh

Project Editor
Ellice Engdahl

Editorial
Paula Cutcher-Jackson, Kathleen Edgar,
Christy Justice, Debra Kirby, Prindle LaBarge,
Elizabeth Manar, Kathleen Meek,
Charles B. Montney, Heather Price

Permissions
Shalice Shah-Caldwell

Imaging and Multimedia
Lezlie Light, Dan Newell, Dave Oblender,
Kelly A. Quin

Product Design
Michael Logusz

Composition and Electronic Prepress
Evi Seoud

Manufacturing
Keith Helmling

LIBRARY OF CONGRESS CATALOGING-IN-PUBLICATION DATA

ISBN 0-7876-5103-6 (set)
ISBN 0-7876-6064-7
ISSN 1532-2734

Printed in the United States of America
10 9 8 7 6 5 4 3 2 1

TABLE OF CONTENTS

ecotourism, hunting, fishing, and wildlife watching. This chapter examines the trends and expenditures associated with these types of recreation.

PREFACE

Endangered Species: Must They Disappear? is one of the latest volumes in the Information Plus Reference Series. Previously published by the Information Plus company of Wylie, Texas, the Information Plus Reference Series (and its companion set, the Information Plus Compact Series) became a Gale Group product when Gale and Information Plus merged in early 2000. Those of you familiar with the series as published by Information Plus will notice a few changes from the 2000 edition. Gale has adopted a new layout and style that we hope you will find easy to use. Other improvements include greatly expanded indexes in each book, and more descriptive tables of contents.

While some changes have been made to the design, the purpose of the Information Plus Reference Series remains the same. Each volume of the series presents the latest facts on a topic of pressing concern in modern American life. These topics include today's most controversial and most studied social issues: abortion, capital punishment, care for the elderly, crime, health care, the environment, immigration, minorities, social welfare, women, youth, and many more. Although written especially for the high school and undergraduate student, this series is an excellent resource for anyone in need of factual information on current affairs.

By presenting the facts, it is Gale's intention to provide its readers with everything they need to reach an informed opinion on current issues. To that end, there is a particular emphasis in this series on the presentation of scientific studies, surveys, and statistics. These data are generally presented in the form of tables, charts, and other graphics placed within the text of each book. Every graphic is directly referred to and carefully explained in the text. The source of each graphic is presented within the graphic itself. The data used in these graphics are drawn from the most reputable and reliable sources, in particular from the various branches of the U.S. government and from major independent polling organizations.

Every effort has been made to secure the most recent information available. The reader should bear in mind that many major studies take years to conduct, and that additional years often pass before the data from these studies are made available to the public. Therefore, in many cases the most recent information available in 2002 dated from 1999 or 2000. Older statistics are sometimes presented as well, if they are of particular interest and no more recent information exists.

Although statistics are a major focus of the Information Plus Reference Series, they are by no means its only content. Each book also presents the widely held positions and important ideas that shape how the book's subject is discussed in the United States. These positions are explained in detail and, where possible, in the words of their proponents. Some of the other material to be found in these books includes: historical background; descriptions of major events related to the subject; relevant laws and court cases; and examples of how these issues play out in American life. Some books also feature primary documents, or have pro and con debate sections giving the words and opinions of prominent Americans on both sides of a controversial topic. All material is presented in an even-handed and unbiased manner; the reader will never be encouraged to accept one view of an issue over another.

HOW TO USE THIS BOOK

The status of endangered species is an issue of concern both for many Americans and for people around the world. In particular, balancing biodiversity with economics has led to much controversy. This book looks at what has been done to protect endangered species in America and around the world, and examines the debate over what future actions are warranted.

Endangered Species: Must They Disappear? consists of eleven chapters and three appendices. Each chapter is devoted to a particular aspect of endangered species. For a summary of the information covered in each chapter, please see the synopses provided in the Table of Contents at the front of the book. Chapters generally begin with an overview of the basic facts and background information on the chapter's topic, then proceed to examine sub-topics of particular interest. For example, Chapter 2: Working Towards Species Conservation begins with an overview of the history of efforts to save endangered species from extinction. The process of listing species on the U.S. Endangered Species List, and the methods by which species on that list are actually protected, are examined in particular detail. Opposition to the Endangered Species Act is also discussed. The chapter then moves on to look at endangered species on federal lands, ecosystem conservation, international conservation efforts, and the role of zoos. Readers can find their way through a chapter by looking for the section and sub-section headings, which are clearly set off from the text. Or, they can refer to the book's extensive index if they already know what they are looking for.

Statistical Information

The tables and figures featured throughout *Endangered Species: Must They Disappear?* will be of particular use to the reader in learning about this issue. The tables and figures represent an extensive collection of the most recent and important statistics on endangered species, as well as related issues—for example, graphics in the book cover the number of endangered species and the reasons for their endangerment; the locations of National Parks; grizzly bear recovery zones; pesticide runoff threats; and medically useful plant species. The photographs illustrate some of the most threatened species on earth, including the Asian box turtle, the Texas horned lizard, and the red wolf. Gale believes that making this information available to the reader is the most important way in which we fulfill the goal of this book: to help readers understand the issues and controversies surrounding endangered species and reach their own conclusions about them.

Each table or figure has a unique identifier appearing above it, for ease of identification and reference. Titles for the tables and figures explain their purpose. At the end of each table or figure, the original source of the data is provided.

In order to help readers understand these often complicated statistics, all tables and figures are explained in the text. References in the text direct the reader to the relevant statistics. Furthermore, the contents of all tables and figures are fully indexed. Please see the opening section of the index at the back of this volume for a description of how to find tables and figures within it.

Appendices

In addition to the main body text and images, *Endangered Species: Must They Disappear?* has three appendices. The first is the Important Names and Addresses directory. Here the reader will find contact information for a number of government and private organizations that can provide further information on aspects of endangered species. The second appendix is the Resources section, which can also assist the reader in conducting his or her own research. In this section, the author and editors of *Endangered Species: Must They Disappear?* describe some of the sources that were most useful during the compilation of this book. The final appendix is the index. It has been greatly expanded from previous editions, and should make it even easier to find specific topics in this book.

ADVISORY BOARD CONTRIBUTIONS

The staff of Information Plus would like to extend their heartfelt appreciation to the Information Plus Advisory Board. This dedicated group of media professionals provides feedback on the series on an ongoing basis. Their comments allow the editorial staff who work on the project to continually make the series better and more user-friendly. Our top priorities are to produce the highest-quality and most useful books possible, and the Advisory Board's contributions to this process are invaluable.

The members of the Information Plus Advisory Board are:

- Kathleen R. Bonn, Librarian, Newbury Park High School, Newbury Park, California

- Madelyn Garner, Librarian, San Jacinto College—North Campus, Houston, Texas

- Anne Oxenrider, Media Specialist, Dundee High School, Dundee, Michigan

- Charles R. Rodgers, Director of Libraries, Pasco-Hernando Community College, Dade City, Florida

- James N. Zitzelsberger, Library Media Department Chairman, Oshkosh West High School, Oshkosh, Wisconsin

COMMENTS AND SUGGESTIONS

The editors of the Information Plus Reference Series welcome your feedback on *Endangered Species: Must They Disappear?* Please direct all correspondence to:

Editors
Information Plus Reference Series
27500 Drake Rd.
Farmington Hills, MI 48331-3535

ACKNOWLEDGMENTS

The editors wish to thank the copyright holders of material included in this volume and the permissions managers of many book and magazine publishing companies for assisting us in securing reproduction rights. We are also grateful to the staffs of the Detroit Public Library, the Library of Congress, the University of Detroit Mercy Library, Wayne State University Purdy/Kresge Library Complex, and the University of Michigan Libraries for making their resources available to us.

Following is a list of the copyright holders who have granted us permission to reproduce material in Information Plus: Endangered Species. *Every effort has been made to trace copyright, but if omissions have been made, please let us know.*

For more detailed source citations, please see the sources listed under each individual table and figure.

Animal Welfare Institute and Environmental Investigation Agency: Table 10.1

AP/Wide World Photos: Figure 3.14 (photograph, reproduced by permission), Figure 3.18 (photograph, reproduced by permission), Figure 5.8 (photograph, reproduced by permission), Figure 7.11 (photograph by Sasa Kralj, reproduced by permission), Figure 8.2 (photograph by Jack Smith, reproduced by permission), Figure 11.6 (photograph by Peter Lennihan, reproduced by permission)

Corbis: Figure 6.1 (photograph by David Northcott, reproduced by permission), Figure 6.9 (photograph by David Northcott, reproduced by permission), Figure 7.9 (photograph by Jeff Vanuga, reproduced by permission), Figure 10.1 (photograph by Galen Rowell, reproduced by permission)

Corbis/Brandon D. Cole: Figure 5.18 (photograph by Brandon D. Cole, reproduced by permission)

Endangered Species Coalition: Table 4.6

Environmental Investigation Agency: Figure 10.2 (photograph)

Federal Task Force on Amphibian Decline and Deformities: Table 6.1, Table 6.4

Field Mark Publications: Figure 7.5 (photograph by Robert J. Huffman, reproduced by permission), Figure 7.7 (photograph by Robert J. Huffman, reproduced by permission), Figure 7.8 (photograph by Robert J. Huffman, reproduced by permission), Figure 7.10 (photograph by Robert J. Huffman, reproduced by permission), Figure 8.4 (photograph by Robert J. Huffman, reproduced by permission), Figure 8.6 (photograph by Robert J. Huffman, reproduced by permission), Figure 10.3 (photograph by Robert J. Huffman, reproduced by permission), Figure 11.3 (photograph by Robert J. Huffman, reproduced by permission)

Greater Toledo Convention and Visitors Bureau: Figure 2.15 (photograph, reproduced by permission of the Toledo Zoo)

Interagency Grizzly Bear Committee: Figure 7.4

Intergovernmental Panel on Climate Change: Figure 3.3, Figure 3.4, Figure 3.5, Figure 3.15, Figure 3.16, Figure 3.17, Table 3.2

JLM Visuals: Figure 6.4 (photograph, reproduced by permission)

Michigan Sea Grant College Program, www.miseagrant.org: Figure 5.10 (photograph, reproduced by permission)

National Aeronautics and Space Administration: Figure 3.7, Figure 3.11, Figure 3.12, Figure 3.13

National Park Service: Figure 4.5 (photograph by W.S. Kelly), Figure 4.8 (photograph by M. Woodbridge Williams)

North Carolina Sea Grant College Program: Figure 5.3

H. Douglas Pratt: Figure 8.1 (photograph by H. Douglas Pratt, reproduced by permission)

TRAFFIC: Table 10.2

U.S. Department of Agriculture: Table 1.3, Figure 4.4, Figure 10.4, Figure 10.5

U.S. Department of Agriculture Forest Service: Figure 1.6, Figure 1.8, Figure 1.9, Table 1.4, Table 1.5, Table 1.6, Figure 2.9, Table 2.8, Figure 4.6

U.S. Department of Energy: Figure 3.2, Figure 3.6, Figure 5.7

U.S. Environmental Protection Agency: Figure 3.1, Figure 3.8, Figure 3.9, Figure 3.10, Table 3.1, Figure 5.1, Figure 5.2, Figure 5.6, Figure 5.13, Figure 5.14, Figure 5.15, Table 5.1

U.S. Fish and Wildlife Service: Figure 1.2, Figure 1.3 (photograph by John and Karen Hollingsworth), Figure 1.7, Table 1.1, Table 1.2, Figure 2.1, Figure 2.2, Figure 2.3, Figure 2.4 (photograph), Figure 2.5 (photograph), Figure 2.8, Figure 2.10, Figure 2.12, Figure 2.13, Figure 2.14, Table 2.1, Table 2.2, Table 2.3, Table 2.4, Table 2.5, Table 2.6, Table 2.7, Table 2.9, Table 2.10, Table 2.11, Table 2.12, Table 2.13, Figure 4.7, Figure 4.9, Table 4.1, Table 4.2, Table 4.5, Figure 5.16 (photograph, reproduced by permission), Table 5.2, Figure 6.5 (photograph by Glenn Langley), Figure 6.7 (photograph by Ross Haley ©), Figure 6.10, Table 6.2, Table 6.5, Figure 7.1 (photograph), Figure 7.2, Figure 7.3 (photograph), Figure 7.6 (photograph), Table 7.1, Table 7.2, Figure 8.3, Figure 8.5, Figure 8.7, Table 8.1, Table 8.2, Table 9.1, Figure 11.1, Figure 11.2, Figure 11.4, Figure 11.5, Table 11.1, Table 11.2, Table 11.3

U.S. General Accounting Office: Figure 2.6, Figure 2.7, Figure 2.11, Figure 5.19, Figure 5.20, Figure 5.21

U.S. Geological Survey: Figure 1.5, Figure 4.1, Figure 4.2, Figure 4.3, Table 4.3, Table 4.4, Figure 5.4, Figure 5.5, Figure 5.9, Figure 5.11, Figure 5.12, Figure 6.6

University of California, Berkeley, CA: Figure 6.2, Figure 6.3, Table 6.3

World Resources Institute: Figure 1.1, Figure 1.4

WWF/James Watt/Panda Photo: Figure 5.17 (photograph, reproduced by permission)

WWF/Michel Terrettaz: Figure 6.8 (photograph, reproduced by permission)

CHAPTER 1
EXTINCTION AND ENDANGERED SPECIES

Earth is a biosphere, a globe richly supplied with different types of living organisms, including animals, plants, fungi, protists, and bacteria. Different types of living organisms are known as different species. Living species co-exist in their environments, forming complex, interrelated communities. Because all species depend on others for nutrients, shelter, or other resources necessary for survival, the removal of even one species in a community can set off a chain reaction affecting many others. In recent decades, large numbers of species have disappeared, often as a result of the actions of human beings. The consequences of this loss of biological diversity, or biodiversity, are manyfold, and difficult to predict.

WHAT ARE ENDANGERED SPECIES?

A species is described as extinct when no living members remain. Scientists know from their study of fossils that dinosaurs, mammoths, and many thousands of other animals and plants that once lived on Earth no longer exist. These species have "died out," or gone extinct. Once a species is extinct, there is no way to bring it back.

Endangered species are those at risk of extinction through all or a significant portion of their natural habitats. Threatened species are those that are likely to become endangered in the foreseeable future. The U.S. Fish and Wildlife Service, an agency of the federal government, maintains a list of species that are endangered or threatened in the U.S. and abroad. Both endangered and threatened species are protected by laws aimed to save them from extinction. In many cases, recovery plans for endangered species have also been developed and implemented. These include measures designed to protect endangered and threatened species and to help their populations grow. Nevertheless, scientists estimate that we lose hundreds, or even thousands, of species each year.

MASS EXTINCTION

Over the billions of years since life began on Earth, countless species have formed, existed, and then gone extinct naturally. Scientists call the natural extinction of a few species per million years a background rate. When the extinction rate doubles for many different groups of plants and animals at the same time, this is described as a mass extinction. Mass extinctions have occurred infrequently in Earth's history and, in general, have been attributed to major cataclysmic geological or astronomical events. Five mass extinctions have occurred in the last 600 million years. These five episodes, known as the Big Five, occurred at the end of five geologic periods—the Ordovician (505–440 million years ago), Devonian (410–360 million years ago), Permian (286–245 million years ago), Triassic (245–208 million years ago), and Cretaceous (146–65 million years ago). After each mass extinction, the floral (plant) and faunal (animal) composition of the Earth changed drastically. The largest mass extinction on record occurred at the end of the Permian, when an estimated 90–95 percent of species went extinct. The Cretaceous extinction is perhaps the most familiar—it was at the end of the Cretaceous that the numerous species of dinosaurs went extinct. The Cretaceous extinction is hypothesized to have resulted from the collision of an asteroid with the earth.

The Sixth Mass Extinction?

According to many biologists, plant and animal species are now disappearing at a rate of one per day. This suggests that we are currently in the midst of another mass extinction. Unlike previous mass extinctions, however, the current extinction does not appear to be associated with a cataclysmic physical event. Rather, the heightened extinction rate has coincided with the success and spread of human beings. Researchers predict that as humans continue to alter natural ecosystems through destruction of natural habitats, pollution, introduction of non-native species, and

TABLE 1.1

Extinct species in Illinois, Indiana, Iowa, Michigan, Minnesota, Missouri, Ohio, and Wisconsin

These are some of the animals that were once part of the fauna in this region but are now extinct.

Mammals

Eastern Elk *(Cervus canadensis canadensis)*
Formerly found in: United States east of Great Plains
Extinct in 1880

Birds

Carolina parakeet *(Conuropsis carolinensis carolinensis)*
Formerly found in: Southeastern United States
Extinct about 1920
Heath Hen *(Tympanuchus cupido cupido)*
Formerly found in: Eastern United States
Extinct in 1932
Passenger Pigeon (*Ectopistes migratorius*)
Formerly found in: Central and eastern North America
Extinct in 1914

Fish

Blackfin cisco
(Coregonus nigripinnis)
Formerly found in: Lakes Huron, Michigan, Ontario, and Superior
Extinct in 1960s
Blue pike
(Stizostedion vitreum glacum)
Formerly found in: Lakes Erie and Ontario
Declared extinct in 1983
Deepwater cisco
(Coregonus johannae)
Formerly found in: Lakes Huron and Michigan
Extinct in 1960s
Harelip sucker
(Lagochila lacera)
Found in a few clear streams of the upper Mississippi Valley; Scioto River in Ohio; Tennesse River in Georgia; White River in Arkansas; Lake Erie drainage, Blanchard and Auglaize Rivers in northwestern Ohio
Not seen since 1900
Longjaw cisco
(Coregonus alpenae)
Formerly found in: Lakes Erie, Huron, and Michigan
Declared extinct in 1983
Shortnose cisco
(Coregonus reighardi)
Formerly found in: Lakes Huron, Michigan, and Ontario
No individuals collected since 1985

Clams

Leafshell
(Epioblasma flexuosa)
Formerly found in: Alabama, Illinois, Indiana, Kentucky, Ohio, Tennessee
Has not been found alive in over 75 years and since 1988 has been considered extinct
Round combshell
(Epioblasma personata)
Formerly found in: Illinois, Indiana, Kentucky, Ohio
Has not been found alive in over 75 years and since 1988 has been considered extinct
Sampson's pearlymussel (Wabash riffleshell)
Epioblasma sampsonii
Formerly found in: Illinois, Indiana, Kentucky
Declared extinct in 1984
Scioto pigtoe
(Pleurobema bournianum)
Formerly found in: Ohio
Tennessee riffleshell
(Epioblasma propinqua)
Formerly found in: Alabama, Illinois, Indiana, Kentucky, Ohio, Tennessee
Has not been found alive in over 75 years and since 1988 has been considered extinct

TABLE 1.1

Extinct species in Illinois, Indiana, Iowa, Michigan, Minnesota, Missouri, Ohio, and Wisconsin [CONTINUED]

These are some of the animals that were once part of the fauna in this region, but are now extinct.

Plants

Bigleaf scurfpea
(Orbexilum macrophyllum)
Formerly found in: Indiana and Kentucky
Thismia americana (no common name)
Found in Illinois
Last seen in 1916; declared extinct in 1995

SOURCE: "Extinct Species," in *U.S. Fish and Wildlife Service Region 3: Endangered Species,* U.S. Fish & Wildlife Service, Fort Snelling, MN, 2002. [Online] http://midwest.fws.gov/Endangered/lists/extinct.html [Accessed May 15, 2002]

ronmental issues, has suggested that, without effective intervention, more species of flora and fauna may disappear in one human lifetime than were lost in the mass extinction that wiped out the dinosaurs 65 million years ago.

The World Conservation Union (IUCN) reports that in the last 500 years, at least 816 species are known to have gone extinct as a result of human activity. The actual number is probably much higher. Table 1.1 lists some U.S. animal and plant species that are now extinct from the midwestern United States.

HOW MANY SPECIES ARE THREATENED OR ENDANGERED?

It is difficult to determine how many species of plants and animals are threatened or endangered in the world. Only a small fraction of the species in existence have even been identified and named, let alone studied in detail. Estimates of the total number of species on Earth range from 5 million to 100 million, with most estimates figuring around 10 million species worldwide. Of these, only some 1.75 million species have been named and described. Figure 1.1 shows the numbers of named and described species by major taxonomic group. Mammals, which are probably the best-studied group—and the one that includes humans—make up only 0.3 percent of all known organisms. Insects are a particularly rich group, with over 750,000 species identified.

Several organizations have devoted effort to examining the status of biological species across the globe. Since 1960 the World Conservation Union (IUCN), based in Gland, Switzerland, has compiled the *IUCN Red List of Threatened Species*. Their most recent update on the status of plants and animals was published in 2000. Worldwide, in 2000, 11,046 of the 18,000 species examined were listed by the IUCN as threatened—that is, as either critically endangered, endangered, or vulnerable. A total of 5,435 animal species were listed, including 1,130

global climate change, the extinction rate may eventually approach several hundred species per day. This would be a rate millions of times higher than normal background levels. The Worldwatch Institute, a think tank devoted to envi-

species of mammals, 1,183 birds, 296 reptiles, 146 amphibians, 742 fish, 555 insects, 408 crustaceans, 846 snails, and several species in other groups. In addition, 5,611 plant species were listed as threatened. Note that the majority of biological groups have yet to be thoroughly assessed by the IUCN. Birds and mammals are fairly well studied, and many of the threatened species in these groups probably have been identified. However, other vertebrate groups (such as amphibians, reptiles, and fish), invertebrate groups (insects, spiders, mollusks, worms, and others), and plants have not been examined nearly as exhaustively. Further study will likely result in many more threatened species being added to the *Red List*.

In 1996 The Nature Conservancy, a private conservation group, conducted what is considered the most comprehensive assessment of the state of American flora and fauna. It found that approximately one-third of U.S. species were rare or imperiled. This represented a larger percentage than most scientists had expected. Of the 20,481 species examined by The Nature Conservancy, about two-thirds were found to be secure, 1.3 percent were either extinct or possibly extinct, 6.5 percent were considered critically imperiled, 8.9 percent were imperiled, and 15 percent were vulnerable. The study also concluded that mammals and birds were doing relatively well compared with other groups. A large proportion of flowering plants were imperiled, as were large numbers of freshwater species such as mussels, crayfish, and fish. Destruction of natural habitat was identified as the main factor leading to species endangerment.

Table 1.2 lists the number of species identified as threatened or endangered by the U.S. Fish & Wildlife Service under the Endangered Species Act as of April 2002. Of the 1,816 species listed, 1,258 are found in the United States. Among these, 983 are endangered and 275 are threatened. More than half of the United States' endangered or threatened species are plant forms. Among animal species, the greatest numbers of endangered and threatened species occur among fish, birds, mammals, and reptiles. Most of the endangered plants are flowering plant species. However, it is important to remember that these are among the more examined biological groups. Figure 1.2 shows the number of listed U.S. species per calendar year from 1980 to 2001. From 1976 to 1989 endangered and threatened species were listed at an average rate of 34 species per year. Between 1990 and 2001 the average rate exceeded 68 species per year. There was a marked rise in the number of U.S. species listings between 1980 and 2001. In 2001 the number surpassed 1,200, up dramatically from the 281 listings in 1980.

Species Loss—Crisis or False Alarm?

As with many other environmental issues, which tend to pit conservation interests against big business and eco-

FIGURE 1.1

Relative number of species by major taxa

Insecta
751,000 described species

Plantae (Multicellular Plants)
248,428 described species

**Non-insect Arthropoda
(Mites, Spiders, Crustaceans etc.)**
123,151 described species

Mollusca (Mollusks)
50,000 described species

Fungi
46,983 described species

Protozoa
30,800 described species

Algae
26,900 described species

Pisces (Fish)
19,056 described species

Platyhelminthes (Flatworms)
12,200 described species

Nematoda (Roundworms)
12,000 described species

Annelida (Earthworms etc.)
12,000 described species

Aves (Birds)
9,040 described species

**Coelenterata
(Jellyfish, Corals, Comb Jellies)**
9,000 described species

Reptilia (Reptiles)
6,300 described species

**Echinodermata
(Starfish, etc.)**
6,100 described species

Porifera (Sponges)
5,000 described species

**Monera
(Bacteria, Blue-green Algae)**
4,760 described species

Amphibia (Amphibians)
4,184 described species

Mammalia (Mammals)
4,000 described species

SOURCE: "Relative Number of Species by Major Taxa," in *Biological Diversity*, World Resources Institute, Washington, DC, 2002 [Online] http://www.wri.org/biodiv/f01-key.html#number [accessed May 13, 2002]

nomic development, there is debate regarding the current threat to species diversity. Challenges to endangered species advocates take several forms. First, some challengers argue that the scale of biodiversity loss remains unproven. Even though huge amounts of wild habitat are disappearing due to human expansion, they say, claims about the scale of the current extinction are exaggerated. These objectors point to uncertainty regarding the total number of species, as well as the geographic distributions of species. Second, some challengers claim that disruptions caused by human activity are not enough to create the massive extinction being documented. They argue that only catastrophic geological or astronomical events can result in mass extinction. Third, some objectors contend that extinction is inevitable, and that the Earth has experienced mass extinctions before. These objectors conclude that the current biodiversity loss, while huge, is not disastrous.

Perhaps the most common argument of opponents of species protection is that "green" policies place the needs of humans second to those of wildlife. These critics object strenuously to the U.S. Endangered Species Act, which they claim protects wildlife without considering the economic costs to human beings. This issue played a role in the battle fought over habitat for the northern spotted owl. In 1990 declining populations caused the U.S. Fish and Wildlife Service to place the northern spotted owl (Figure

TABLE 1.2

Summary of listed species and recovery plans, April 30, 2002

Group	Endangered		Threatened		Total Species	U.S. Species with Recovery Plans[2]
	U.S.	Foreign	U.S.	Foreign		
Mammals	65	251	9	17	342	53
Birds	78	175	14	6	273	75
Reptiles	14	64	22	15	115	32
Amphibians	11	8	8	1	28	12
Fishes	71	11	44	0	126	95
Clams	62	2	8	0	72	56
Snails	21	1	11	0	33	27
Insects	35	4	9	0	48	29
Arachnids	12	0	0	0	12	5
Crustaceans	18	0	3	0	21	12
Animal SubTotal	387	516	128	39	1070	396
Flowering Plants	568	1	144	0	713	556
Conifers and Cycads	2	0	1	2	5	2
Ferns and Allies	24	0	2	0	26	26
Lichens	2	0	0	0	2	2
Plant SubTotal	596	1	147	2	746	586
Grand Total	**983**	**517**	**275**	**41**	**1816**[1]	**982**

Total U.S. Endangered – 983 (387 animals, 596 plants)
Total U.S. Threatened – 275 (128 animals, 147 plants)
Total U.S. Species – 1258 (515 animals[3], 743 plants)

[1]There are 1846 total listings (1283 U.S.). The following types of listings are combined as single counts in the table above: species listed both as threatened and endangered (dual status), and subunits of a single species listed as distinct population segments. Only the endangered population is tallied for dual status populations (except for the following: olive ridley sea turtle; for which only the threatened U.S. population is tallied). The dual status U.S. species that are tallied as endangered are: chinook salmon, gray wolf, green sea turtle, piping Plover, roseate tern, sockeye salmon, steelhead, Steller sea-lion. The dual status foreign species that are tallied as endangered are: argali, chimpanzee, leopard, saltwater crocodile. Distinct population segments tallied as one include: chinook salmon, chum salmon, coho salmon, steelhead. Entries that represent entire genera or families include: African viviparous toads, gibbons, lemurs, musk deer, Oahu tree snails, sifakas, uakari.

[2]There are 566 distinct approved recovery plans. Some recovery plans cover more than one species, and a few species have separate plans covering different parts of their ranges. Recovery plans are drawn up only for listed species that occur in the United States.

[3]9 animal species have dual status in the U.S.

SOURCE: "Summary of Listed Species: Species and Recovery Plans as of 4/30/2002," *Threatened and Endangered Species System (TESS)*, U.S. Fish and Wildlife Service, Washington, DC, 2002 [Onlne] http://ecos.fws.gov/tess/html/boxscore-apr-2002-print.html [accessed May 1, 2002]

1.3) on the list of threatened species. In 1992 Fish and Wildlife set aside 7 million acres of forestland in the Pacific Northwest—both private and public—as critical habitat for the species. As a result, logging was banned on federal lands within these areas. Loggers protested, fearing that many people would lose jobs if trees could not be harvested at will. Supporters of the ban, on the other hand, claimed that most logging jobs had already been lost, and that continued logging would preserve existing jobs only for a short time. A long battle involving politicians, environmentalists, loggers, and businessmen began. Eventually, a compromise was reached in which logging was limited to trees under a certain size, leaving the mature growth for owl habitat. By early 1993 almost all old-growth logging on federal lands had been stopped by court action.

Why Save Endangered Species?

The conservation of species is important for many reasons. Species have both aesthetic and recreational value, as the great popularity of zoos, wildlife safaris, recreational hiking and wildlife watching (bird watching, whale watching, etc.) indicate. Wildlife also has educational and scientific value. In addition, because all species depend on other species for resources, the impact of a single lost species on an entire ecosystem may be immense—in addition to being difficult to predict. Scientists have shown that habitats with greater biodiversity are more stable—that is, they are better able to adjust to and recover from disturbances. This is because different species may perform overlapping functions in a biologically diverse ecosystem. Habitats with less diversity are more vulnerable, because a disturbance affecting one species may cause the entire network of interactions to collapse. Furthermore, many species, particularly plants, have great economic value to human beings. Plants provide the genetic diversity used to breed new strains of agricultural crops, and many have been used to develop pharmaceutical products. Aside from the economic or utilitarian reasons for preserving species, however, many people think that humankind has a moral responsibility to maintain the Earth's biodiversity. When species are lost, they believe, the quality of all life is diminished.

ARE SOME SPECIES MORE IMPORTANT THAN OTHERS? Some species are particularly valued by scientists because they are the last remnants of once flourishing biological groups. Examples of these include the coelacanth,

FIGURE 1.2

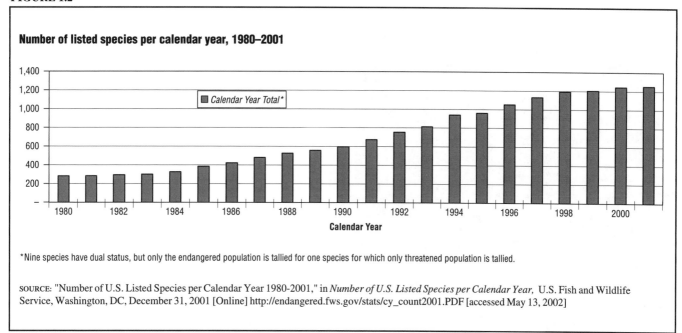

Number of listed species per calendar year, 1980–2001

*Nine species have dual status, but only the endangered population is tallied for one species for which only threatened population is tallied.

SOURCE: "Number of U.S. Listed Species per Calendar Year 1980-2001," in *Number of U.S. Listed Species per Calendar Year,* U.S. Fish and Wildlife Service, Washington, DC, December 31, 2001 [Online] http://endangered.fws.gov/stats/cy_count2001.PDF [accessed May 13, 2002]

one of the few species (along with lungfish) that help to document the transition from aquatic to terrestrial life in vertebrates, and the tuatara, a highly endangered reptile species found only on New Zealand. The extinction of species that have no closely-related species left on Earth represent particularly significant losses to the genetic diversity of the planet.

BIOLOGICAL INDICATOR SPECIES. The loss of so many species should also concern human beings because many are dying out due to pollution and environmental degradation, problems that can affect human health and well-being also. Species that are particularly relevant in reporting on the health of ecosystems are called biological indicator species. Environmental scientists rely on indicator species just as coal miners once relied on canaries to check air safety in underground tunnels, where dangerous gases frequently became concentrated enough to be poisonous. Miners carried a canary into the mineshaft, knowing that the air was safe to breathe as long as the canary lived. If the bird started to sicken, however, miners evacuated the tunnel. In the same way, the sudden deaths of large numbers of bald eagles and peregrine falcons warned people about the dangers of DDT, a powerful pesticide in wide use. The disappearance of fish from various rivers, lakes, and seas also alerted people to the presence of dangerous chemicals in those waters. During the final decades of the twentieth century, many scientists became seriously concerned about the sudden disappearance of many amphibians, particularly frogs, in many parts of the world. Most troubling was the fact that many species disappeared from national parks and protected wildlife refuges, areas that appeared relatively pristine and undisturbed. Amphibians are believed to be particularly sensitive to environmental disturbances such as pollution, because their skins are formed of living cells, and readily absorb substances from the environment. Their decline is a suggestion that all may not be well.

FACTORS THAT CONTRIBUTE TO SPECIES ENDANGERMENT

Experts believe that the increasing loss and decline of species cannot be attributed to natural processes, but results instead from the destructive effect of human activities. People hunt and collect wildlife. They destroy natural habitats by clearing trees and filling swamps for development. Aquatic habitats are altered or destroyed by the building of dams. Humans also poison habitats with polluting chemicals and industrial waste. Indeed, many believe that human activity is now causing change in climate patterns on a global scale.

Habitat Destruction

Habitat destruction is probably the single most important factor leading to the endangerment of species. It plays a role in the decline of 95 percent of federally listed threatened and endangered species, affecting nearly every type of habitat and all ecosystems.

With each passing day, humans require more space and resources. Figure 1.4 illustrates the increase in global human population over the millennia. The human population has been growing with particular rapidity in recent centuries, and passed the 6 billion mark in 1999. This puts tremendous pressure on other species, making it difficult for them to find the resources they need to survive and reproduce. Americans, because they consume more

FIGURE 1.3

The northern spotted owl inhabits old-growth forests in the Pacific Northwest, and was the subject of a lengthy battle pitting environmentalists against logging interests. *(U.S. Fish and Wildlife Service, Washington, DC)*

FIGURE 1.4

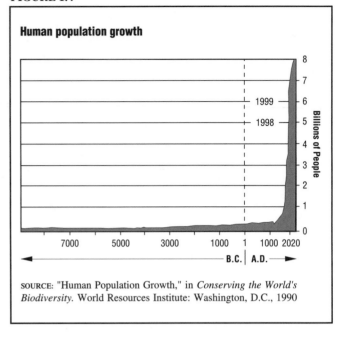

Human population growth

SOURCE: "Human Population Growth," in *Conserving the World's Biodiversity*. World Resources Institute: Washington, D.C., 1990

energy and other resources than populations in other industrialized countries or in the developing world, have an even greater impact on the environment.

Many types of human activity result in habitat destruction. Corporate farming is a leading cause, and has damaged forests, prairies, and wetland habitats in particular. Nearly 90 percent of wetland losses have resulted from drainage for agriculture. About 45 percent of the total land area in the U.S. is used for farming. Urban expansion results in the loss of wild habitat areas as well, and is a primary factor in the endangerment of many plant species in particular. Logging, particularly the practice of clear-cutting forests, destroys important habitat for numerous species. Clear-cutting or extensive logging can also lead to significant erosion, harming both soils and aquatic habitats, which become blocked with soil. Grazing by domestic livestock directly harms numerous plant

species, as well as animal species that have to compete with livestock for food or are unable to coexist with livestock. Mining activity results in habitat degradation due to pollution. The building of dams affects rivers and streams, causing changes in water flow and temperature. Finally, human recreational activity, particularly the use of off-road vehicles, results in the destruction of natural habitat.

Habitat Fragmentation

Human land-use patterns often result in the fragmentation of natural habitat areas that are available to other species. Studies have shown that habitat fragmentation is occurring in most habitat types. Habitat fragmentation can have significant effects on species. Human development isolates small populations, preventing dispersal from one habitat patch to another. Smaller populations may also be more likely to go extinct. In addition, because there are more "edges" when habitats are fragmented, there can be increased exposure to predators and increased vulnerability to disturbances associated with human activity.

Global Warming

The bulk of human energy requirements are obtained through the burning of fossil fuels. This results in the release of large amounts of carbon dioxide into the atmosphere. Increased levels of carbon dioxide create a "greenhouse effect," which results in warmer temperatures on Earth. A global temperature increase has been compellingly documented, and has already had important effects on ecosystems worldwide, although there is still debate as to what degree human activity has contributed. Global warming is predicted to accelerate quickly if measures are not adopted to address it.

The warming of the Earth would alter habitats drastically, with serious consequences for numerous species. Tundra and taiga, found in extremely cold areas such as Siberia and Northern Canada, are shrinking. Deserts are expanding. Forests and grasslands are beginning to shift towards more appropriate climate regimes. Animal and plant species that cannot shift their ranges quickly enough would die out. Some plants and animals that are found in precise, narrow bands of temperature and humidity, such as monarch butterflies or edelweiss, are likely to find their habitats wiped out altogether. In addition, sea levels rise as oceans warm and expand. Rising seas would cover coastal mangrove swamps, causing the loss of species such as the Bengal tiger. Global warming is already endangering some of the most diverse ecosystems on Earth, such as coral reefs and tropical cloud forests. The impact on endangered species, which are already in a fragile state, may be particularly great.

Pollution

Pollution is caused by the release of industrial and chemical wastes into the land, air, and water. It can damage habitats and kill or sicken animals and plants. Pollution comes from a wide variety of sources, including industrial plants, mining, automobiles, and agricultural products such as pesticides and fertilizers. Even animals that are not directly exposed to pollution can be affected, as the species that they rely on for food, shelter, or other purposes die out.

Hunting and Trade

Humans have hunted numerous animal species to extinction, and hunting continues to be a major threat to some species. In the United States, gray wolves were nearly wiped out because they were considered a threat to livestock. The Caribbean monk seal was viewed as a competitor for fish, and exterminated. Other animals are hunted for the value of their hides, tusks, or horns, including elephants and rhinoceroses. Many rare or exotic species, including parrots and other tropical birds, are taken from their natural habitats for the pet trade.

Introduction of Invasive Species

Invasive species are those that have been introduced from their native habitat into a new, non-native habitat. Some introductions are deliberate, but most are accidental. Invasive species harm native species by competing with them for food and other resources, or by preying on them or parasitizing them. By 2000 about 50,000 species were believed to have been introduced into the United States alone. There are many types of invasive species, some of which are listed in Table 1.3. Figure 1.5 illustrates the effect of some invasive species on the habitats they have colonized. While there are sometimes beneficial effects from invasive species, most of the effects are harmful. Some 35–46 percent of species listed by the U.S. Fish and Wildlife Service are endangered partly or entirely because of invasive species. Similarly, the *2000 IUCN Red List of Threatened Species* suggested that invasive species affect 350 species of threatened birds (30 percent) and 361 species of threatened plants (15 percent). In fact, the IUCN found that the majority of bird extinctions since 1800 were due to the effects of invasive species such as rats and snakes.

The zebra mussel is perhaps the best-known invasive species in the U.S. It was unintentionally introduced into the North American Great Lakes region from Europe in the mid-1980s. This non-native mollusk threatens native species by interfering with their feeding, growth, respiration, and reproduction.

Many human commensals (species that are used by and associated with humans, such as dogs, cats, and pigs) are often among the most destructive introduced species. Domestic cats brought to Australia by European settlers have run wild on that continent, feeding on untold numbers of rare native animals, most of which had not evolved to deal with so effective a predator.

Recognizing the threat posed by invasive species, President Bill Clinton signed Executive Order 13112 on Invasive Species in 1999. This order requires federal agencies to make every possible effort to control the spread of invasive species, and resulted in the formation of the Invasive Species Council, which drafted the National Invasive Species Management Plan in October 2000. The plan emphasizes prevention of introduction of alien species, early detection of invasions, rapid response to them, and coordination of national and international efforts in management and control of these species. In the year 2000 federal agencies spent $631.5 million dealing with damage caused by invasive species or attempting to control them.

SPECIES LOSS IN THE UNITED STATES

In the early 1990s the U.S. Forest Service conducted a major study of species loss in the United States, *Species Endangerment Patterns in the United States* (1994). Factors identified as adversely affecting U.S. species included habitat loss or alteration, human overuse, disease, predation, competition, natural causes, and inadequate resource-management laws (see Figure 1.6). Habitat loss was by far the most important factor. More than 95 percent of the 667 species examined in the study had suffered habitat loss or alteration. Interactions between organisms, such as disease, predation, and competition, adversely affected more than 50 percent of species. Human overuse—the harvest, collection, or commercial trade of species—was the third most important factor. Human overuse was the most common factor in the endangerment of mammal and reptile species. Table 1.4 lists the reasons

TABLE 1.3

Examples of invasive species

Terrestrial Plants

Downy brome (*Bromus tectorum*)
Garlic mustard (*Alliaria petiolata*)
Hogweed (*Heracleum mantegazzianum*)
Japanese honeysuckle (*Lonicera japonica*)
Japanese knotweed (*Polygonum cuspidatum*)
Kudzu (*Pueraria montana* var. *lobata*)
Leafy spurge (*Euphorbia esula*)
Mile-A-Minute Weed (*Polygonum perfoliatum*)
Multiflora rose (*Rosa multiflora*)
Musk thistle (*Carduus nutans*)
Russian olive (*Elaeagnus angustifolia*)
Saltcedar (*Tamarix* spp.)
Scotch broom (*Cytisus scoparius*)
Scotch thistle (*Onopordum acanthium*)
Spotted knapweed (*Centaurea maculosa*)
Tree-of-heaven (*Ailanthus altissima*)
Yellow star thistle (*Centaurea solstitialis*)

Terrestrial Animals

Africanized honeybee (*Apis mellifera scutellata*)
Asian long-horned beetle (*Anoplophora glabripennis*)
Asian tiger mosquito (*Aedes albopictus*)
Brown tree snake (*Boiga irregularis*)
Cane toad (*Bufo marinus*)
European gypsy moth (*Lymantria dispar*)
European starling (*Sturnus vulgaris*)
Glassy-winged sharpshooter (*Homalodisca coagulata*)
Hemlock Woolly adelgid (*Adelges tsugae*)
Red imported fire ant (*Solenopsis invicta*)
Wild Boar (*Sus scrofa*)

Aquatic & Wetlands Plants

Brazilian waterweed (*Egeria densa*)
Caulerpa, Mediterranean clone (*Caulerpa taxifolia*)
Common reed (*Phragmites australis*)
Eurasian water-milfoil (*Myriophyllum spicatum*)
Giant-reed (*Arundo donax*)
Giant salvinia (*Salvinia molesta*)
Hydrilla (*Hydrilla verticillata*)
Melaleuca (*Melaleuca quinquenervia*)
Purple loosestrife (*Lythrum salicaria*)
Water chestnut (*Trapa natans*)
Water hyacinth (*Eichhornia crassipes*)

Aquatic & Wetlands Animals

Alewife (*Alosa pseudoharengus*)
Asian swamp eel (*Monopterus albus*)
Bullfrog (*Rana catesbeiana*)
Eurasian ruffe (*Gymnocephalus cernuus*)
European green crab (*Carcinus maenas*)
Nutria (*Myocastor coypus*)
Round goby (*Neogobius melanostomus*)
Sea lamprey (*Petromyzon marinus*)
Veined rapa whelk (*Rapana venosa*)
Zebra mussel (*Dreissena polymorpha*)

Microbes

Fowlpox (*Avipoxvirus*)
West Nile virus (*Flavivirus*)

SOURCE: "Species Profiles," U.S. Department of Agriculture, National Agricultural Library, Beltsville, MD, December 14, 2001 [Online] http://www.invasivespecies.gov/profiles/main.shtml [accessed May 14, 2002]

FIGURE 1.5

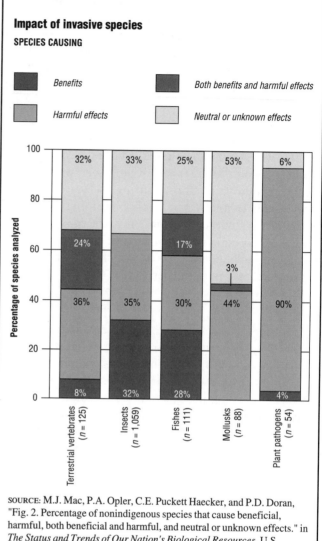

Impact of invasive species
SPECIES CAUSING

SOURCE: M.J. Mac, P.A. Opler, C.E. Puckett Haecker, and P.D. Doran, "Fig. 2. Percentage of nonindigenous species that cause beneficial, harmful, both beneficial and harmful, and neutral or unknown effects." in *The Status and Trends of Our Nation's Biological Resources*, U.S. Geological Survey, Reston, VA, 1998

cited for the endangerment of different groups of biological species and how frequently each reason was cited.

Regional Distribution of Listed Species

Endangered and threatened species are not evenly distributed across the United States. Instead, listed species tend to cluster in specific geographical areas. Regions where the number of threatened and endangered species is relatively high include southern Appalachia, Florida, the Southwest, California, and Hawaii. Hawaii harbors more threatened and endangered species than any other state, despite its small size. This is due largely to the fact that much of the plant and animal life there is endemic—that is, found nowhere else on Earth. Figure 1.7 shows the number of federally listed endangered and threatened species in each state in 2002. Table 1.5 shows the taxonomic composition of high-endangerment regions.

Different factors contribute to species endangerment in different parts of the country. Table 1.6 lists the most important contributing causes (those affecting more than 25 percent of the species) by region. Urban development is the most important factor in Florida, the eastern Gulf Coast, and central and southern California. Grazing is the primary factor in Colorado and the Arizona Basin. Endangerment in the East is frequently associated with intensive land-use activities, including road building, coastal area conversion, and construction. Catastrophic weather and human-caused mortality are significant along the Gulf Coast. In the West, rare-plant collecting, surface mining, oil and gas development, and water diversions are important factors. Recreational activities, specifically off-road driving, is critical in a number of Western regions.

Listed Species and Federal Lands

Endangered species are found on both federal and non-federal lands. A large majority of species listed as threatened or endangered occupy non-federal lands through the bulk of their range, as shown in Figure 1.8. Figure 1.9 shows the number of threatened and endangered species on federal lands by federal administering agency. The two agencies that account for the majority of federally owned lands are the U.S. Forest Service and the Bureau of Land Management. These lands support 24 percent and 17 percent of the country's endangered species, respectively. The number of threatened and endangered species that exist on Department of Defense land is disproportionately high—26 percent of listed species inhabit 3.4 percent of that federally administered land area. As all these agencies have functions other than species preservation, the protection of endangered species can present challenges.

FIGURE 1.6

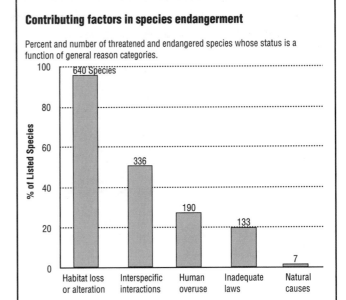

Contributing factors in species endangerment

Percent and number of threatened and endangered species whose status is a function of general reason categories.

SOURCE: Curtis H. Flather, Linda A. Joyce, and Carol A. Bloomgarden, "Contributing Factors in Species Endangerment," in *Species Endangerment Patterns in the United States,* U.S. Forest Service, Fort Collins, CO, 1994

TABLE 1.4

Number of threatened and endangered species, by reason contributing to endangerment

SPECIFIC REASONS HAD TO AFFECT ≥15% OF THE SPECIES FOR SPECIOSE TAXA (≥20 SPECIES LISTED), AND 25% OF THE SPECIES IN LESS SPECIOSE TAXA.

All T&E (667 spp.)
256 Agricultural Development
234 Exotic/Introduced Species
228 Rural/Resid./Indust. Areas
187 Grazing
176 Low Gene Pool
173 Predation
168 Veg. Composition Changes
165 Heavy Equipment
160 Competition
157 Forest Clearing
147 Highways/Railroads
138 Erosion
136 Recreational Areas
127 Channel Modification
124 Collecting
120 Forest Alteration
115 Water Diversion/Drawdown
114 Surface Mines

Plants (285 spp.)
110 Rural/Resid./Indust. Areas
104 Grazing
97 Heavy Equipment
90 Agricultural Development
84 Low Gene Pool
81 Highways/Railroads
76 Exotic/Introduced Species
69 Collecting
69 Recreational Areas
69 Veg. Composition Changes
65 Competition
62 Forest Clearing
56 Off-Road Vehicles
54 Surface Mines
53 Erosion
43 Forest Alteration

Fish (95 spp.)
49 Exotic/Introduced Species
49 Water Diversion/Drawdown
44 Channel Modification
42 Competition
43 Environ. Contaminants/Pollution
41 Agricultural Development
37 Sedimentation
36 Predation
34 Reservoirs
31 Erosion
26 Groundwater Drawdown
25 Passage Barriers
25 Water Temperature Fluctuation
23 Bank Modification/Devel.
22 Water Level Fluctuation
21 Hybridization
20 Low Gene Pool
19 Grazing
17 Flooding
17 Surface Mines

Birds (85 spp.)
52 Exotic/Introduced Species
49 Predation
47 Agricultural Development
45 Veg. Composition Changes
34 Forest Clearing
31 Grazing
31 Rural/Resid./Indust. Areas
30 Forest Alteration
28 Disease
25 Competition
24 Harassment/Indiscr. Killing
19 Adverse Weather
19 Low Gene Pool
18 Fire
18 Food Supply Reduction
18 Parasites
18 Wetland Filling
16 Pesticides
16 Recreational Areas
15 Shoreline Modif./Devel.
14 Channel Modification
14 Heavy Equipment
14 Highways/Railroads
14 Subsistence Hunting
13 Erosion

Mammals (68 spp.)
25 Rural/Resid./Indust. Areas
23 Agricultural Development
21 Forest Clearing
19 Predation
19 Recreational Areas
19 Veg, Composition Changes
17 Highways/Railroads
16 Forest Alteration
16 Heavy Equipment
15 Food Supply Reduction
14 Exotic/Introduced Species
14 Harassment/Indiscr. Killing
14 Low Gene Pool
14 Poaching
13 Competition
11 Incidental Capture/Killing
10 Commercial Exploitation
10 Grazing

Clams (42 spp.)
36 Channel Modification
34 Sedimentation
32 Environ. Contaminants/Pollution
24 Agricultural Development
24 Reservoirs
24 Water Level Fluctuations
23 Herbicides
23 Pesticides
23 Surface Mines
22 Passage Barriers
20 Erosion
19 Water Temperature Alteration
18 Inherent Reproductive Characteristics
17 Dissolved Oxygen Reduction
17 Exotic/Introduced Species
17 Low Gene Pool
13 Underground Mines
 9 Collecting
 8 Fertilizers
 7 Water Diversion/Drawdown

Reptiles (33 spp.)
16 Predation
14 Commercial Exploitation
12 Exotic/Introduced Species
12 Incidental Capture/Killing
11 Collecting
10 Rural/Resid./Indust. Areas
 9 Agricultural Development
 9 Environ. Contaminants/Pollution
 9 Forest Clearing
 9 Harassment/Indiscr. Killing
 9 Shoreline Modif./Devel.
 7 Channel Modification
 7 Erosion
 7 Highways/Railroads
 7 Poaching
 7 Recreational Areas
 6 Adverse Weather
 6 Grazing
 6 Inherent Reproductive Characteristics
 6 Off-Road Vehicles
 6 Subsistence Hunting
 5 Fire Suppression
 5 Forest Alteration
 5 Reservoirs
 5 Wetland Filling

Insects (22 spp.)
15 Rural/Resid./Indust. Areas
10 Veg. Composition Changes
 9 Grazing
 8 Agricultural Development
 8 Exotic/Introduced Species
 8 Heavy Equipment
 7 Highways/Railroads
 7 Low Gene Pool
 6 Fire Suppression
 6 Food Supply Reduction
 6 Recreational Areas
 5 Adverse Weather
 5 Collecting
 5 Surface Mines
 4 Fire
 4 Off-Road Vehicles
 4 Pesticides

Snails (13 spp.)
6 Collecting
6 Forest Alteration
6 Forest Clearing
5 Hiking/Camping
5 Low Gene Pool
4 Grazing
4 Highways/Railroads
4 Predation
4 Recreational Areas
4 Rock Climbing
4 Rural/Resid./Indust. Areas

Amphibians (11 spp.)
7 Agricultural Development
7 Rural/Resid./Industr. Areas
5 Highways/Railroads
5 Low Gene Pools
4 Grazing
3 Adverse Weather
3 Collecting
3 Food Supply Reduction
3 Forest Clearing
3 Groundwater Drawdown
3 Heavy Equipment
3 Inherent Reproductive Charact.
3 Predation
3 Veg. Composition Changes
3 Water Diversion/Drawdown

Crustaceans (10 spp.)
8 Environ. Contaminants/Pollution
5 Sedimentation
4 Agricultural Development
4 Collecting
4 Herbicides
4 Rural/Resid./Indust Areas
3 Flooding
3 Forest Clearing
3 Gas/Oil Development
3 Heavy Equipment
3 Highways/Railroads
3 Low Gene Pool
3 Predation
3 Spelunking
3 Surface Drainage
3 Water Diversion/Drawdown

Arachnids (3 spp.)
3 Environ, Contaminants/Pollution
3 Exotic/Introduced Species
3 Rural/Resid./Indust. Areas

Note: T&E = Threatened and Endangered species.

SOURCE: Curtis H. Flather, Linda A. Joyce, and Carol A. Bloomgarten, "Number of Threatened and Endangered Species, by Reason Contributing to Endangerment," in *Species Endangerment Patterns in the United States,* U.S. Forest Service, Fort Collins, CO, 1994.

FIGURE 1.7

Listed species range, by state/territory, May 14, 2002

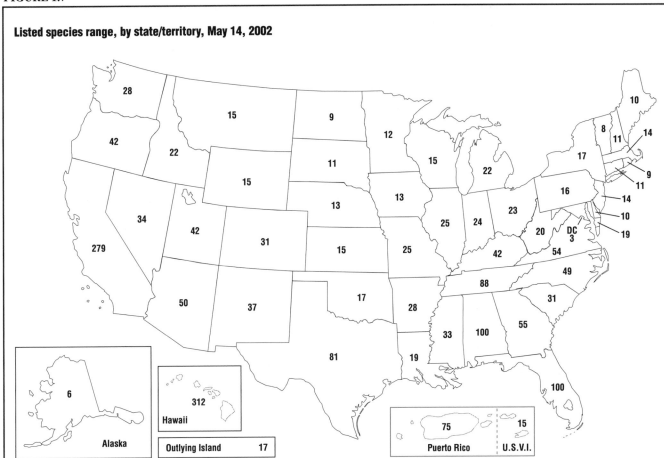

Omits "similarity of appearance" and experimental populations. Does not map whales and non-nesting sea turtles in state coastal waters.
Total U.S. Species is 1258. Numbers are not additive, a species often occurs in multiple states.

Note: The species counted include listed pinnipeds (seals, etc.) and anadromous fishes under the sole jurisdiction of the National Marine Fisheries Service that use land or fresh waters within the states and territories of the United States. Species are not broken up into listing entities as they are in the State List reports, however, if a species is not listed in a state it is not counted, although it may occur there in a non-protected population.

SOURCE: "Listed Species Range by State/Territory as of Tue May 14 23:30:02 MDT 2002," in *Species Information: Threatened and Endangered Animals and Plants,* U.S. Fish and Wildlife Service, Washington, DC, May 14, 2002 [Online] http://ecos.fws.gov/webpage/usmap.html?module=undefined&status= listed [accessed May 15, 2002]

TABLE 1.5

Taxonomic composition of high-endangerment regions

	Southern Appalachia	Peninsular Florida	Eastern Gulf Coast	Southern Desertic Basins, Plains, and Mountains	Arizona Basin	Colorado/ Green River Plateaus	Central Desertic Basins and Plateaus	Southern Nevada/ Sonoran Basin	Central/ Southern California	Northern California
Mammals	3	10	4	1	4	1		3	8	3
Birds	1	10	7	5	6	4	3	6	11	7
Fish	6	1	1	6	9	6	4	23	6	1
Reptiles		11	8					2	4	1
Amphibians								1	1	
Vertebrates	10	32	20	12	19	11	7	35	30	12
Clams	17									
Snails		1		2		1				
Insects		1						15		7
Crustaceans	1	1		1						1
Invertebrates	18	3		3		1		1	5	8
Animals	28	35	20	15	19	12	7	36	35	20
Plants	11	29	7	17	8	17	11	17	14	12
Total	39	64	27	32	27	29	18	53	49	32
Endemics[1]										
Total	2	17	2	15	5	7	4	20	16	13
Plant	1	10		10	2	7	4	7	11	7

[1]Endemics refers to species whose range is thought to be restricted to a single county.

SOURCE: Curtis H. Flather, Linda A. Joyce, and Carol A. Bloomgarten, "Taxonomic Composition of High-Endangerment Regions," in *Species Endangerment Patterns in the United States,* U.S. Forest Service, Fort Collins, CO, 1994.

TABLE 1.6

Number of threatened and endangered species, by region and reason contributing to endangerment

SPECIFIC REASONS HAD TO AFFECT ≥ 25% OF THE SPECIES FOUND IN EACH REGION.

Southern Appalachia (39 spp.)
29 Environ. Contaminants/ Pollution
26 Agricultural Development
25 Sedimentation
24 Channel Modification
24 Surface Mines
22 Reservoirs
20 Pesticides
18 Passage Barriers
18 Water Temperature Alteration
17 Herbicides
16 Dissolved Oxygen Reduction
16 Erosion
16 Exotic/Introduced Species
15 Inherent Reproductive Characteristics
15 Low Gene Pool
14 Forest Clearing
14 Water level Fluctuation
13 Collecting
13 Underground Mines

Peninsular Florida (64 spp.)
47 Rural/Resid./Indust. Areas
33 Forest Clearing
32 Agricultural Development
27 Fire Suppression.
19 Heavy Equipment
19 Veg. Composition Changes
18 Recreational Areas
17 Highways/Railroads
16 Competition

Eastern Gulf Coast (27 spp.)
11 Rural/Resid./Indust. Areas
11 Shoreline Modif./Devel.
10 Harassment/Indlscr. Killing
9 Recreational Areas
8 Adverse Weather
8 Commercial Exploitation
8 Erosion
8 Forest Alteration
8 Forest Clearing
8 Incidental Capture/Killing
8 Off-Road Vehicles
8 Predation
7 Agricultural Development
7 Channel Modification
7 Collecting
7 Environ. Contaminants/Pollution
7 Exotic/Introduced Species

Southern Desertic Basins, Plains, and Mountains (32 spp.)
13 Collecting
12 Recreational Areas
11 Grazing
11 Highways/Railroads
10 Commercial Exploitation
10 Heavy Equipment
10 Water Diversion/Draw-down
9 Competition
8 Exotic/Introduced Species

Arizona Basin (27 spp.)
15 Grazing
11 Erosion
10 Exotic/Introduced Species
10 Predation
10 Surface Mines
9 Heavy Equipment
8 Competition
8 Forest Alteration
8 Veg. Composition Changes
7 Agricultural Development
7 Flooding
7 Recreational Areas
7 Reservoirs

Colorado/Green River Plateaus (29 spp.)
12 Grazing
11 Collecting
10 Off-Road Vehicles
10 Surface Mines
8 Commercial Exploitation
8 Erosion
8 Gas/Oil Development
8 Water Diversion/Draw-down
7 Competition
7 Heavy Equipment

Central Desertic Basins and Plateaus (18 spp.)
9 Surface Mines
8 Gas/Oil Development
6 Water Diversion/Draw-down
5 Collecting
5 Grazing
5 Heavy Equipment
5 Recreational Areas
5 Transmission Lines/Towers

Southern Nevada/ Sonoran Basin (53 spp.)
36 Exotic/Introduced Species
32 Water Diversion/Draw-down
23 Grazing
22 Agricultural Development
21 Channel Modification
19 Competition
19 Groundwater Drawdown
19 Predation
19 Recreational Areas
18 Rural/Resid./Indust. Areas
17 Low Gene Pool
17 Off-Road Vehicles
17 Surface Mines
16 Heavy Equipment
16 Reservoirs
15 Veg. Composition Changes
14 Highways/Railroads

Central/Southern California (49 SPP.)
25 Rural/Resid./Indust. Areas
24 Agricultural Development
24 Exotic/Introduced Species
24 Grazing
23 Predation
18 Heavy Equipment
18 Off-Road Vehicles
16 Highways/Railroads
13 Gas/Oil Development
13 Surface Mines

Northern California (32 spp.)
18 Agricultural Development
18 Heavy Equipment
17 Rural/Resid./Indust. Areas
16 Grazing
15 Highways/Railroads
12 Off-Road Vehicles
11 Exotic/Introduced Species
10 Low Gene Pool
10 Recreational Areas
9 Adverse Weather
9 Food Supply Reduction
9 Veg. Composition Changes

SOURCE: Curtis H. Flather, Linda A. Joyce, and Carol A. Bloomgarten, "Number of Endangered and Threatened Species, by Region and Reason Contributing to Endangerment," in *Species Endangerment Patterns in the United States,* U.S. Forest Service, Fort Collins, CO, 1994.

FIGURE 1.8

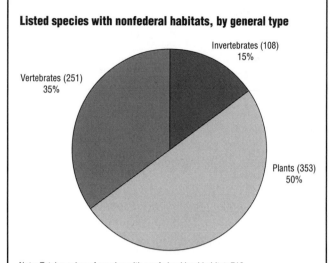

Listed species with nonfederal habitats, by general type

Invertebrates (108) 15%

Vertebrates (251) 35%

Plants (353) 50%

Note: Total number of species with nonfederal land habitat: 712

SOURCE: Curtis H. Flather, Linda A. Joyce, and Carol A. Bloomgarden, "Listed Species with Nonfederal Habitats, by General Type," *Species Endangerment Patterns in the United States*. U.S. Forest Service: Fort Collins, CO, 1994

FIGURE 1.9

Number of threatened and endangered species on federally administered land, by agency

Administered by Federal Agencies (in million of ha)	
BIA	21.7
BLM	108.9
DOD	9.7
FS	77.3
FWS	36.4
NPS	30.3

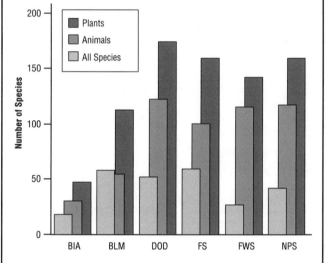

■ Plants
■ Animals
■ All Species

Number of Species

BIA BLM DOD FS FWS NPS

Note: BIA—Bureau of Indian Affairs, BLM—Bureau of Land Management, DOD—Department of Defense, FS—Forest Service, FWS—Fish and Wildlife Service, NPS—National Park Service

SOURCE: Curtis H. Flather, Linda A. Joyce, and Carol A. Bloomgarden, "Number of Threatened and Endangered Species on Federally Administered Land, by Agency," in *Species Endangerment Patterns in the United States*. U.S. Forest Service: Fort Collins, CO, 1994

CHAPTER 2
WORKING TOWARDS SPECIES CONSERVATION

Endangered species have different needs and require different intervention measures for protection and recovery. Many species of fish, for example, are threatened or endangered simply because they are being overfished. Halting or reducing fishing is sufficient for population recovery. For many other species, however, more active forms of intervention are necessary. The single most important issue for many threatened and endangered species is habitat. Setting aside protected reserves is essential to the continued survival of many endangered species. Sometimes, restoration of damaged or destroyed habitats is also necessary. For some species, captive breeding followed by reintroduction into wild habitats may help increase species numbers. In all cases, knowledge of the biology and natural history of endangered species is essential to acquiring a better understanding of species' needs, as well as to the development of measures that will aid in conservation.

HISTORY OF SPECIES PROTECTION

The idea of conserving nature has a long history. One of the oldest examples of conservation efforts dates from 242 B.C.E. ("before the common era"), when the Indian emperor Asoka created nature reserves in Asia. Marco Polo reported that the Asian ruler Kublai Khan (A.D. 1215–1294) helped conserve bird and mammal species valued for hunting by banning hunting during their reproductive periods. He further helped to increase their numbers by planting food and providing protected cover areas. In South America, during the reign of the Inca kings, many species of seabirds were protected.

By the mid-nineteenth century many governments had developed an interest in wildlife conservation and an awareness of the need to protect natural habitats. In 1861 painters of the Barbizon school established the first French nature reserve, which covered nearly 3,458 acres of forest at Fountainebleau. Three years later the Ameri-

can government set aside the Yosemite Valley in California as a National Reserve. (This became Yosemite National Park in 1890.) Wyoming's Yellowstone Park was created in 1872 to provide a leisure area for the public and became the first U.S. National Park.

Organizations and laws dedicated to the protection of species soon followed. In 1895 the first international meeting for the protection of birds was held in Paris, France. This resulted in new laws protecting species in several countries. In 1922 the International Council for the Protection of Birds was founded. The first international conference for the protection of nature was held in 1913, and the International Office followed in 1928. The World Conservation Union (IUCN) was founded in 1946. That same year the International Whaling Commission was established. In 1961 the private conservation organization, the World Wildlife Fund (WWF), was founded. The Chinese giant panda was selected as the WWF symbol, not only because of the animal's great popularity, but also to reaffirm the international character of nature conservation, and to emphasize the independence of wildlife conservation from political differences. The Convention on International Trade in Endangered Species (CITES), an international treaty established to regulate commerce in wildlife, was first ratified in 1975 in an attempt to block both the import and export of endangered species and to regulate international trade in threatened species.

There were also some significant U.S. government attempts in the mid-twentieth century to keep an eye on the status of endangered wildlife. Congress passed the Endangered Species Preservation Act in 1966. This established the listing of species as endangered and provided somewhat for protection of these species, though the species listed were only animal and only native to the U.S. Habit preservation (including land acquisition) was also part of this legislation. The Endangered Species Conservation Act of 1969 provided additional protection to species that might face the possibility of worldwide extinction, in the form of a prohibition on their import and sale within the U.S. Import of such species was prohibited, as was their sale within the U.S. Despite these advances, though, much more important legislation was yet to come.

THE ENDANGERED SPECIES ACT OF 1973— A LANDMARK PROTECTION

The Endangered Species Act (ESA) was passed by the U.S. Congress in 1973. It is generally considered one of the most far-reaching laws ever enacted by any nation for the preservation of wildlife. The passage of the Endangered Species Act resulted from alarm at the decline of numerous species worldwide, as well as from a recognition of the importance of preserving species diversity. The purpose of the Endangered Species Act is to identify species that are either endangered—at risk of extinction throughout all or a significant portion of their range—or threatened—likely to become endangered in the foreseeable future. With the exception of pest species, all animals and plants are eligible for listing under the Endangered Species Act. Listed species are protected without regard to either commercial or sport value. Listed species include not only the birds and mammals familiar to most people but also many species of invertebrates (like mollusks, crustaceans, and insects) and plants.

The Endangered Species Act is administered by the U.S. Department of the Interior through the U.S. Fish and Wildlife Service (FWS). This service is responsible for overseeing the protection and conservation of all forms of freshwater fish, wildlife, and plants found to be in jeopardy. The U.S. Department of Commerce, through the National Marine Fisheries Service (NMFS), has similar responsibility for marine species. The Fish and Wildlife Service has divided the United States into eight administrative regions. While endangered and threatened species are located throughout the country, certain regions harbor a disproportionate number of species—about one-third are located in the South, and about one-third are located in the West.

The Endangered Species List

After passage of the Endangered Species Act, the Fish and Wildlife Service was inundated with petitions for the listing of species—approximately 24,000 petitions were received in the first two years after passage. As of April 2002, in the United States alone, 387 animals and 596 plants were listed as endangered, and 128 animals and 147 plants were listed as threatened. (See Table 1.3 in Chapter 1.) Thousands of other species are being studied to see if they need to be added to the list.

The Listing Process

The process for listing a new species as endangered or threatened begins with a formal petition from a person or

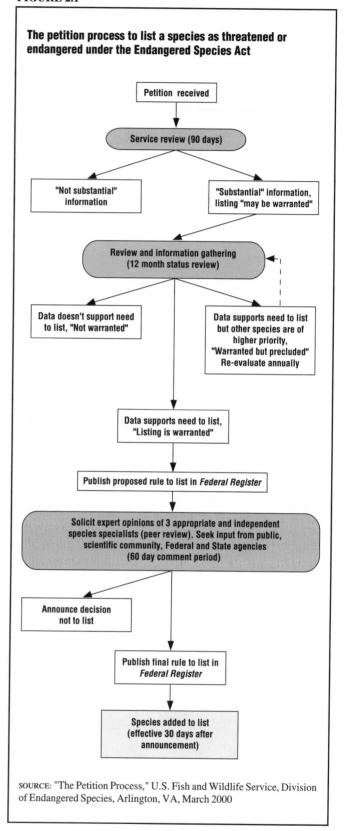

FIGURE 2.1

The petition process to list a species as threatened or endangered under the Endangered Species Act

SOURCE: "The Petition Process," U.S. Fish and Wildlife Service, Division of Endangered Species, Arlington, VA, March 2000

organization. (Figure 2.1 diagrams the petition process.) This petition is submitted to the FWS for terrestrial and freshwater species and to the NMFS for marine species. All petitions must be backed by published scientific data supporting the need for listing. Within 90 days, FWS or

FIGURE 2.2

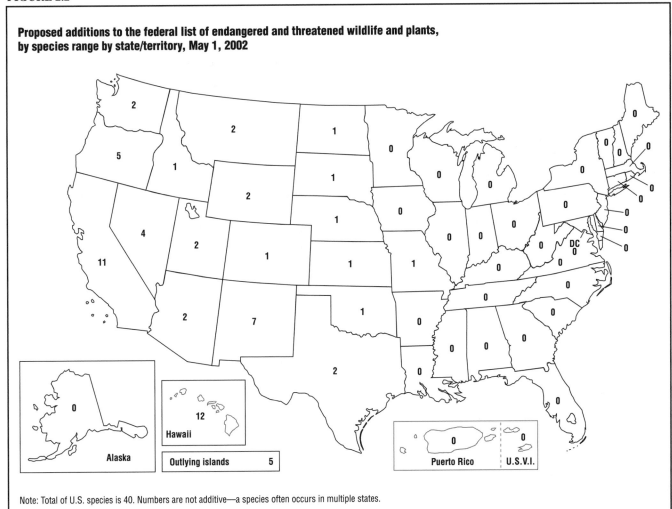

Proposed additions to the federal list of endangered and threatened wildlife and plants, by species range by state/territory, May 1, 2002

Note: Total of U.S. species is 40. Numbers are not additive—a species often occurs in multiple states.

SOURCE: "Proposed Species Range by State/Territory as of Wed May 1 23:30:21 MDT 2002," U.S. Fish and Wildlife Service, Division of Endangered Species, Arlington, VA, May 1, 2002 [Online] http://ecos.fws.gov/webpage/usmap.html?module=undefined&status=proposed [accessed May 1, 2002]

NMFS determines whether there is "substantial information" to suggest that a species may in fact require listing under the Endangered Species Act. Approximately 65 percent of petitions for species are found to have substantial information to warrant further study; 35 percent do not.

For petitions that present biological data suggesting that listing may be necessary, the FWS or NMFS then performs a status review to determine whether listing is warranted. This process must be completed within 12 months. In the past, the FWS/NMFS has found that over half the petitions warrant action. Once it has been determined that action on a species is warranted, that species becomes a candidate species. Candidate species may immediately join the list of proposed species. However, in some cases, it may be decided that other species have higher priority. If this is the case, the species is designated as "warranted but precluded" (immediate action is precluded by more urgent listing activity). Species that are listed as "warrant-

ed but precluded" are re-evaluated annually to confirm that listing continues to be warranted. These continue to be re-evaluated until they either join the list of proposed species or until their status has improved sufficiently that they are no longer warranted for listing.

A species is officially proposed for listing through the publication of this action in the *Federal Register*. At this point, the FWS asks three independent biological experts to verify that the petitioned species requires listing under either threatened or endangered status. After that is completed, input from the public, from other federal and state agencies, and from the scientific community is welcomed. This period of public comment lasts 60 days. Following the 60-day period, the final rule regarding listing of the species is published in the *Federal Register*, and listing is effective 30 days after publication.

Figure 2.2 shows the number of species proposed for listing under the Endangered Species Act by state, and

TABLE 2.1

Proposed species for listing as endangered or threatened, as of May 14, 2002

Status	Species Name
Mammals	
PE	Addax (*Addax nasomaculatus*)
PT	Bat, Mariana fruit (=Mariana flying fox) (*Pteropus mariannus mariannus*)
PE	Dugong (*Dugong dugon*)
PE	Fox, San Miguel Island (*Urocyon littoralis littoralis*)
PE	Fox, Santa Catalina Island (*Urocyon littoralis catalinae*)
PE	Fox, Santa Cruz Island (*Urocyon littoralis santacruzae*)
PE	Fox, Santa Rosa Island (*Urocyon littoralis santarosae*)
PE	Gazelle, dama (*Gazella dama*)
PE	Oryx, scimitar-horned (*Oryx dammah*)
PE	Rabbit, pygmy (*Brachylagus idahoensis*)
Birds	
PT	Plover, mountain (*Charadrius montanus*)
PE	White-eye, Rota bridled (*Zosterops conspicillata rotensis*)
Amphibians	
PT	Frog, Chiricahua leopard (*Rana chiricahuensis*)
PE	Frog, mountain yellow-legged (*Rana muscosa*)
Fishes	
PE	Chub, Cowhead Lake tui (*Gila bicolor vaccaceps*)
PT	Salmon, coho (*Oncorhynchus* (=*Salmo*) *kisutch*)
PT	Steelhead (*Oncorhynchus* (=*Salmo*) *mykiss*)
PT	Trout, coastal cutthroat (*Oncorhynchus clarki clarki*)
Snails	
PE	Cavesnail, Tumbling Creek (*Antrobia culveri*)
PE	Snail, Koster's tryonia (*Tryonia kosteri*)
PE	Snail, Pecos assiminea (*Assiminea pecos*)
PE	Springsnail, Roswell (*Pyrgulopsis roswellensis*)
Insects	
PE	Butterfly, Sacramento Mountains checkerspot (*Euphydryas anicia cloudcrofti*)
PE	Pomace fly, [unnamed] (*Drosophila aglaia*)
PE	Pomace fly, [unnamed] (*Drosophila differens*)
PE	Pomace fly, [unnamed] (*Drosophila hemipeza*)
PE	Pomace fly, [unnamed] (*Drosophila heteroneura*)
PE	Pomace fly, [unnamed] (*Drosophila montgomeryi*)
PE	Pomace fly, [unnamed] (*Drosophila mulli*)
PE	Pomace fly, [unnamed] (*Drosophila musaphila*)
PE	Pomace fly, [unnamed] (*Drosophila neoclavisetae*)
PE	Pomace fly, [unnamed] (*Drosophila obatai*)
PE	Pomace fly, [unnamed] (*Drosophila ochrobasis*)
PE	Pomace fly, [unnamed] (*Drosophila substenoptera*)
PE	Pomace fly, [unnamed] (*Drosophila tarphytrichia*)
PE	Skipper, Carson wandering (*Pseudocopaeodes eunus obscurus*)
Crustaceans	
PE	Amphipod, Noel's (*Gammarus desperatus*)
Flowering Plants	
PE	Ambrosia, San Diego (*Ambrosia pumila*)
PE	Meadowfoam, large-flowered wooly (*Limnanthes floccosa grandiflora*)
PE	Lomatium, Cook's (*Lomatium cookii*)
PE	*Nesogenes rotensis* (No common name)
PE	*Osmoxylon mariannense* (No common name)
PE	Polygonum, Scotts Valley (*Polygonum hickmanii*)
PE	*Tabernaemontana rotensis* (No common name)

Note: Proposed Species count is 44 (excludes proposed "similarity of appearance" and experimental populations)

PE = Proposed Endangered
PT = Proposed Threatened

SOURCE: "Proposed Species as of 5/14/2002," in *Species Information: Threatened and Endangered Animals and Plants,* U.S. Fish and Wildlife Service, Washington, DC, 2002 [Online] http://ecos.fws.gov/webpage/webpage_nonlisted.html?code=undefined&type=P&listings=1 [accessed May 14, 2002]

these species are listed in Table 2.1. There were a total of 40 proposed species in 2002. The FWS also keeps a list of candidate species (those for which there is scientific evidence warranting their proposal for listing, but which have yet to become proposed species). The FWS works with state wildlife agencies and other groups to help preserve and improve the status of candidate species, with the hope that populations may recover enough that species will not require listing. In 2002 there were 246 candidate species recognized by the FWS. Figure 2.3 shows the number of current candidate species per state.

After a species is listed, its condition and situation are reviewed at least every five years to decide whether it still requires government protection. Once the species is able to survive without government protection, it may be removed from the list. Conservation efforts for protected species include the preparation of a *Recovery Plan* by the FWS that details how the species will be protected and helped to thrive. In many cases, this includes the designation of critical habitat. Critical habitat includes areas of land, water, and air space that are used by threatened and endangered species for breeding, resting, and feeding. Critical habitat designation does not set up a refuge. It has no regulatory impact on private landowners, unless they wish to take actions on their land that involve federal funding or permits. Some examples of critical habitat designations for certain threatened and endangered species are provided in Table 2.2.

The Endangered Species Act gives the government and its agencies the power to do whatever is necessary to protect a threatened or endangered species. It is funded through the U.S. Department of the Interior. In 2002 the Fish and Wildlife Service budgeted approximately $9 million per year for listing of species, and $63.3 million per year for recovery programs for endangered wildlife.

The number of species being added to the federal threatened and endangered species list is likely to continue to grow. During the first two decades of implementation, an average of 34 new species per year received protection under the ESA; during the 1990s the average number of new listings rose to 68 per year. While vertebrate species dominated the list during the first years of the act, plants and invertebrate animals soon comprised a much greater proportion of listed species (see Table 1.3 in Chapter 1). These species are politically more difficult to defend than either mammals or birds, which are more appealing to most Americans because of the "warm and fuzzy" factor. These circumstances raise questions about the continued feasibility of a species-by-species preservation strategy, and the federal government struggles under intense legal and political pressures to decide which species to protect first.

For its supporters, the Endangered Species Act has proved to be one of the most effective conservation laws

FIGURE 2.3

Candidate species for the federal list of endangered and threatened wildlife and plants, by species range by state/territory, May 1, 2002

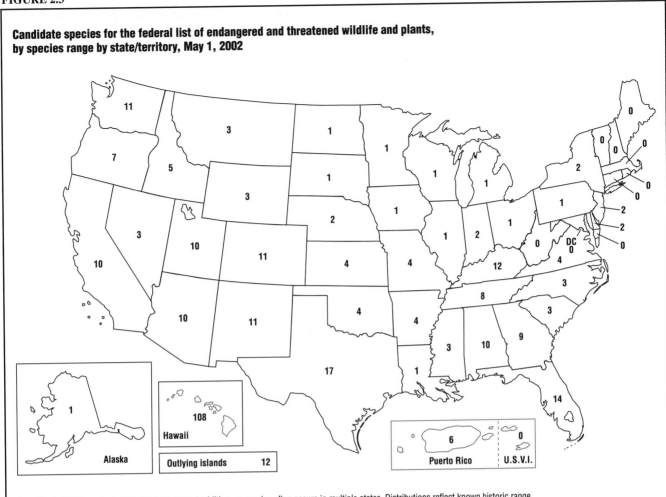

Note: Total of U.S. species is 246. Numbers are not additive—a species often occurs in multiple states. Distributions reflect known historic range.

SOURCE: "Proposed Species Range by State/Territory as of Wed May 1 23:30:21 MDT 2002," U.S. Fish and Wildlife Service, Division of Endangered Species, Arlington, VA, May 1, 2002 [Online] http://ecos.fws.gov/webpage/usmap.html?module=undefined&status=proposed [accessed May 1, 2002]

ever enacted. Many Americans believe that the Endangered Species Act has saved many species from extinction. An estimated 40 percent of species on the list are either stable or increasing in number. A number of species have improved sufficiently to have their listing status changed. In Table 2.3, those species whose status has been changed since listing under the Endangered Species Act are detailed. Many endangered species (E) have been reclassified as threatened (T), indicating that their status has improved since protection under the act. Other species have declined, however, and have shifted from threatened to endangered.

Extinct, Recovered, and Down-Listed Species

Species may be removed from the Endangered Species List for three reasons:

1) The species has become extinct.

2) The species has recovered to such an extent that it is no longer threatened or endangered.

3) The original information warranting listing has been shown to be incorrect, or new information suggests that species are not actually endangered or threatened.

As of 2002, 32 species that were once on the Endangered Species List had been removed from the list, or delisted. These species are listed in Table 2.4, along with the reason for being delisted. Of the species delisted, 7 were removed from the list because they became extinct, 13 species were delisted because they were considered recovered, and 12 species were delisted either because the original data was in error or because new information had been discovered. Reclassification has been proposed for another 14 species, shown in Table 2.5. This includes the proposed delisting of species such as the bald eagle due to recovery.

Habitat Conservation Plans

Endangered and threatened species live and roam wherever they find suitable habitat, without regard to whether the

Endangered Species

Working Towards Species Conservation **19**

TABLE 2.2

Listed species with critical habitat, April 23, 2002

Status	Species Name	Crit. Hab. in 50 CFR
Mammals		
E	Bat, Indiana (*Myotis sodalis*)	17.95(a)
E	Bat, Virginia big-eared (*Corynorhinus (=Plecotus) townsendii virginianus*)	17.95(a)
E	Kangaroo rat, Fresno (*Dipodomys nitratoides exilis*)	17.95(a)
E	Kangaroo rat, Morro Bay (*Dipodomys heermanni morroensis*)	17.95(a)
E	Manatee, West Indian (*Trichechus manatus*)	17.95(a)
E	Mouse, Alabama beach (*Peromyscus polionotus ammobates*)	17.95(a)
E	Mouse, Choctawhatchee beach (*Peromyscus polionotus allophrys*)	17.95(a)
E	Mouse, Perdido Key beach (*Peromyscus polionotus trissyllepsis*)	17.95(a)
E	Rice rat (lower FL Keys) (*Oryzomys palustris natator*)	17.95(a)
E	Seal, Hawaiian monk (*Monachus schauinslandi*)	226.201
E	Sea-lion, Steller (western pop.) (*Eumetopias jubatus*)	226.202
T	Sea-lion, Steller (eastern pop.) (*Eumetopias jubatus*)	226.202
E	Sheep, bighorn (Peninsular CA pop.) (*Ovis canadensis*)	17.95(a)
E	Squirrel, Mount Graham red (*Tamiasciurus hudsonicus grahamensis*)	17.95(a)
E	Vole, Amargosa (*Microtus californicus scirpensis*)	17.95(a)
E	Whale, right (*Balaena glacialis (incl. australis)*)	226.203
E	Wolf, gray (lower 48 States, except MN and where XN; Mexico) (*Canis lupus*)	17.95(a)
T	Wolf, gray (MN) (*Canis lupus*)	17.95(a)
Birds		
E	Blackbird, yellow-shouldered (*Agelaius xanthomus*)	17.95(b)
E	Condor, California (U.S.A. only) (*Gymnogyps californianus*)	17.95(b)
E	Crane, Mississippi sandhill (*Grus canadensis pulla*)	17.95(b)
E	Crane, whooping (except where XN) (*Grus americana*)	17.95(b)
T	Eider, spectacled (*Somateria fischeri*)	17.95(b)
T	Eider, Steller's (AK breeding pop.) (*Polysticta stelleri*)	17.95(b)
E	Elepaio, Oahu (*Chasiempis sandwichensis ibidus*)	17.95(b)
E	Flycatcher, southwestern willow (*Empidonax traillii extimus*)	17.95(b)
T	Gnatcatcher, coastal California (*Polioptila californica californica*)	17.95(b)
E	Kite, Everglade snail (FL pop.) (*Rostrhamus sociabilis plumbeus*)	17.95(b)
T	Murrelet, marbled (CA, OR, WA) (*Brachyramphus marmoratus marmoratus*)	17.95(b)
T	Owl, Mexican spotted (*Strix occidentalis lucida*)	17.95(b)
T	Owl, northern spotted (*Strix occidentalis caurina*)	17.95(b)
E	Palila (honeycreeper) (*Loxioides bailleui*)	17.95(b)
E	Plover, piping (Great Lakes watershed) (*Charadrius melodus*)	17.95(b)
T	Plover, piping (except Great Lakes watershed) (*Charadrius melodus*)	17.95(b)
T	Plover, western snowy (Pacific coastal pop.) (*Charadrius alexandrinus nivosus*)	17.95(b)
E	Pygmy-owl, cactus ferruginous (AZ pop.) (*Glaucidium brasilianum cactorum*)	17.95(b)
E	Sparrow, Cape Sable seaside (*Ammodramus maritimus mirabilis*)	17.95(b)
T	Towhee, Inyo California (*Pipilo crissalis eremophilus*)	17.95(b)
E	Vireo, least Bell's (*Vireo bellii pusillus*)	17.95(b)

TABLE 2.2

Listed species with critical habitat, April 23, 2002 [CONTINUED]

Status	Species Name	Crit. Hab. in 50 CFR
Reptiles		
E	Anole, Culebra Island giant (*Anolis roosevelti*)	17.95(c)
T	Boa, Mona (*Epicrates monensis monensis*)	17.95(c)
E	Crocodile, American (*Crocodylus acutus*)	17.95(c)
E	Gecko, Monito (*Sphaerodactylus micropithecus*)	17.95(c)
T	Iguana, Mona ground (*Cyclura stejnegeri*)	17.95(c)
T	Lizard, Coachella Valley fringe-toed (*Uma inornata*)	17.95(c)
E	Lizard, St. Croix ground (*Ameiva polops*)	17.95(c)
T	Rattlesnake, New Mexican ridge-nosed (*Crotalus willardi obscurus*)	17.95(c)
T	Sea turtle, green (except where endangered) (*Chelonia mydas*)	226.208
E	Sea turtle, hawksbill (*Eretmochelys imbricata*)	7.95(c), 226.209
E	Sea turtle, leatherback (*Dermochelys coriacea*)	7.95(c), 226.207
T	Snake, Concho water (*Nerodia paucimaculata*)	17.95(c)
T	Tortoise, desert (U.S.A., except in Sonoran Desert) (*Gopherus agassizii*)	17.95(c)
E	Turtle, Plymouth redbelly (*Pseudemys rubriventris bangsi*)	17.95(c)
T	Whipsnake (=striped racer), Alameda (*Masticophis lateralis euryxanthus*)	17.95(c)
Amphibians		
T	Coqui, golden (*Eleutherodactylus jasperi*)	17.95(d)
T	Frog, California red-legged (subspecies range clarified) (*Rana aurora draytonii*)	17.95(d)
T	Salamander, San Marcos (*Eurycea nana*)	17.95(d)
E	Toad, arroyo (=arroyo southwestern) (*Bufo californicus (=microscaphus*)	17.95(d)
E	Toad, Houston (*Bufo houstonensis*)	17.95(d)
Fishes		
T	Catfish, Yaqui (*Ictalurus pricei*)	17.95(e)
E	Cavefish, Alabama (*Speoplatyrhinus poulsoni*)	17.95(e)
E	Chub, bonytail (*Gila elegans*)	17.95(e)
E	Chub, Borax Lake (*Gila boraxobius*)	17.95(e)
E	Chub, humpback (*Gila cypha*)	17.95(e)
E	Chub, Owens tui (*Gila bicolor snyderi*)	17.95(e)
T	Chub, slender (*Erimystax cahni*)	17.95(e)
T	Chub, Sonora (*Gila ditaenia*)	17.95(e)
T	Chub, spotfin Entire (*Cyprinella monacha*)	17.95(e)
E	Chub, Virgin River (*Gila seminuda (=robusta)*)	17.95(e)
E	Chub, Yaqui (*Gila purpurea*)	17.95(e)
E	Dace, Ash Meadows speckled (*Rhinichthys osculus nevadensis*)	17.95(e)
T	Dace, desert (*Eremichthys acros*)	17.95(e)
T	Darter, amber (*Percina antesella*)	17.95(e)
E	Darter, fountain (*Etheostoma fonticola*)	17.95(e)
T	Darter, leopard (*Percina pantherina*)	17.95(e)
E	Darter, Maryland (*Etheostoma sellare*)	17.95(e)
T	Darter, Niangua (*Etheostoma nianguae*)	17.95(e)
T	Darter, slackwater (*Etheostoma boschungi*)	17.95(e)
E	Gambusia, San Marcos (*Gambusia georgei*)	17.95(e)
E	Goby, tidewater Entire (*Eucyclogobius newberryi*)	17.95(e)
E	Logperch, Conasauga (*Percina jenkinsi*)	17.95(e)
E	Madtom, smoky Entire (*Noturus baileyi*)	17.95(e)
T	Madtom, yellowfin (except where XN) (*Noturus flavipinnis*)	17.95(e)
T	Minnow, loach (*Tiaroga cobitis*)	17.95(e)
E	Minnow, Rio Grande silvery (*Hybognathus amarus*)	17.95(e)
E	Pikeminnow (=squawfish), Colorado (except Salt and Verde R. drainages, AZ) (*Ptychocheilus lucius*)	17.95(e)
E	Pupfish, Ash Meadows Amargosa (*Cyprinodon nevadensis mionectes*)	17.95(e)
E	Pupfish, desert (*Cyprinodon macularius*)	17.95(e)
E	Pupfish, Leon Springs (*Cyprinodon bovinus*)	17.95(e)
E	Salmon, chinook (winter Sacramento R.) (*Oncorhynchus (=Salmo) tshawytscha*)	226.204
T	Salmon, chinook (CA coastal) (*Oncorhynchus (=Salmo) tshawytscha*)	226.212

Status	Species Name	Crit. Hab. in 50 CFR
T	Salmon, chinook (CA Central Valley spring-run) (*Oncorhynchus* (=*Salmo*) *tshawytscha*)	226.212
T	Salmon, chinook (spring upper Columbia R.) (*Oncorhynchus* (=*Salmo*) *tshawytscha*)	226.212
T	Salmon, chinook (upper Willamette R.) (*Oncorhynchus* (=*Salmo*) *tshawytscha*)	226.212
T	Salmon, chinook (Puget Sound) (*Oncorhynchus* (=*Salmo*) *tshawytscha*)	226.212
T	Salmon, chinook (spring/summer Snake R.) (*Oncorhynchus* (=*Salmo*) *tshawytscha*)	226.205
T	Salmon, chinook (fall Snake R.) (*Oncorhynchus* (=*Salmo*) *tshawytscha*)	226.205
T	Salmon, chinook (lower Columbia R.) (*Oncorhynchus* (=*Salmo*) *tshawytscha*)	226.212
T	Salmon, chum (summer-run Hood Canal) (*Oncorhynchus* (=*Salmo*) *keta*)	226.212
T	Salmon, chum (Columbia R.) (*Oncorhynchus* (=*Salmo*) *keta*)	226.212
T	Salmon, coho (OR, CA pop.) (*Oncorhynchus* (=*Salmo*) *kisutch*)	226.212
E	Salmon, sockeye U.S.A. (Snake River, ID stock wherever found.) (*Oncorhynchus* (=*Salmo*) *nerka*)	226.205
T	Salmon, sockeye U.S.A. (Ozette Lake, WA) (*Oncorhynchus* (=*Salmo*) *nerka*)	226.212
T	Shiner, Arkansas River (Arkansas R. Basin) (*Notropis girardi*)	17.95(e)
T	Shiner, beautiful (*Cyprinella formosa*)	17.95(e)
E	Shiner, Cape Fear (*Notropis mekistocholas*)	17.95(e)
T	Shiner, Pecos bluntnose (*Notropis simus pecosensis*)	17.95(e)
T	Silverside, Waccamaw (*Menidia extensa*)	17.95(e)
T	Smelt, delta (*Hypomesus transpacificus*)	17.95(e)
T	Spikedace (*_eda fulgida*)	17.95(e)
T	Spinedace, Big Spring (*Lepidomeda mollispinis pratensis*)	17.95(e)
T	Spinedace, Little Colorado (*Lepidomeda vittata*)	17.95(e)
E	Spinedace, White River (*Lepidomeda albivallis*)	17.95(e)
E	Springfish, Hiko White River (*Crenichthys baileyi grandis*)	17.95(e)
T	Springfish, Railroad Valley (*Crenichthys nevadae*)	17.95(e)
E	Springfish, White River (*Crenichthys baileyi baileyi*)	17.95(e)
E	Steelhead (upper Columbia R. Basin) (*Oncorhynchus* (=*Salmo*) *mykiss*)	226.212
E	Steelhead (southern CA coast) (*Oncorhynchus* (=*Salmo*) *mykiss*)	226.212
T	Steelhead (upper Willamette R.) (*Oncorhynchus* (=*Salmo*) *mykiss*)	226.212
T	Steelhead (Central Valley CA) (*Oncorhynchus* (=*Salmo*) *mykiss*)	226.212
T	Steelhead (middle Columbia R.) (*Oncorhynchus* (=*Salmo*) *mykiss*)	226.212
T	Steelhead (lower Columbia R.) (*Oncorhynchus* (=*Salmo*) *mykiss*)	226.212
T	Steelhead (central CA coast) (*Oncorhynchus* (=*Salmo*) *mykiss*)	226.212
T	Steelhead (south central CA coast) (*Oncorhynchus* (=*Salmo*) *mykiss*)	226.212
T	Steelhead (Snake R. Basin) (*Oncorhynchus* (=*Salmo*) *mykiss*)	226.212
E	Sturgeon, white U.S.A. (ID, MT), Canada (B.C.), (Kootenai R. system) (*Acipenser transmontanus*)	17.95(e)
E	Sucker, June (*Chasmistes liorus*)	17.95(e)
E	Sucker, Modoc (*Catostomus microps*)	17.95(e)
E	Sucker, razorback (*Xyrauchen texanus*)	17.95(e)
T	Sucker, Warner (*Catostomus warnerensis*)	17.95(e)
T	Trout, Little Kern golden (*Oncorhynchus aguabonita whitei*)	17.95(e)
E	Woundfin (except Gila R. drainage, AZ, NM) (*Plagopterus argentissimus*)	17.95(e)

Status	Species Name	Crit. Hab. in 50 CFR
Snails		
E	Snail, Morro shoulderband (=Banded dune) (*Helminthoglypta walkeriana*)	17.95(j)
Insects		
T	Beetle, delta green ground (*Elaphrus viridis*)	17.95(i)
T	Beetle, valley elderberry longhorn (*Desmocerus californicus dimorphus*)	17.95(i)
T	Butterfly, bay checkerspot (*Euphydryas editha bayensis*)	17.95(i)
T	Butterfly, Oregon silverspot (*Speyeria zerene hippolyta*)	17.95(i)
E	Butterfly, Palos Verdes blue (*Glaucopsyche lygdamus palosverdesensis*)	17.95(i)
E	Grasshopper, Zayante band-winged (*Trimerotropis infantilis*)	17.95(i)
T	Naucorid, Ash Meadows (*Ambrysus amargosus*)	17.95(i)
Arachnids		
E	Spider, spruce-fir moss (*Microhexura montivaga*)	17.95(f)
Crustaceans		
E	Fairy shrimp, Riverside (*Streptocephalus woottoni*)	17.95(h)
E	Fairy shrimp, San Diego (*Branchinecta sandiegonensis*)	17.95(h)
E	Shrimp, Kentucky cave (*Palaemonias ganteri*)	17.95(h)
Flowering Plants		
E	Bladderpod, Zapata (*Lesquerella thamnophila*)	17.96(a)
T	Blazingstar, Ash Meadows (*Mentzelia leucophylla*)	17.96(a)
T	Centaury, spring-loving (*Centaurium namophilum*)	17.96(a)
E	Checkermallow, Wenatchee Mountains (*Sidalcea oregana* var. *calva*)	17.96(a)
E	Cinquefoil, Robbins' (*Potentilla robbinsiana*)	17.96(a)
E	Evening-primrose, Antioch Dunes (*Oenothera deltoides* ssp. *howellii*)	17.96(a)
E	Fiddleneck, large-flowered (*Amsinckia grandiflora*)	17.96(a)
T	Groundsel, San Francisco Peaks (*Senecio franciscanus*)	17.96(a)
T	Gumplant, Ash Meadows (*Grindelia fraxino-pratensis*)	17.96(a)
T	Heather, mountain golden (*Hudsonia montana*)	17.96(a)
T	Ivesia, Ash Meadows (*Ivesia kingii* var. *eremica*)	17.96(a)
E	Koki'o (*Kokia drynarioides*)	17.96(a)
T	Milk-vetch, Ash meadows (*Astragalus phoenix*)	17.96(a)
T	Milk-vetch, heliotrope (*Astragalus montii*)	17.96(a)
T	Milkweed, Welsh's (*Asclepias welshii*)	17.96(a)
E	Niterwort, Amargosa (*Nitrophila mohavensis*)	17.96(a)
E	*Gouania hillebrandii* (No common name)	17.96(a)
E	Panicgrass, Carter's (*Panicum fauriei* var. *carteri*)	17.96(a)
E	Pennyroyal, Todsen's (*Hedeoma todsenii*)	17.96(a)
T	Seagrass, Johnson's (*Halophila johnsonii*)	226.213
T	Sedge, Navajo (*Carex specuicola*)	17.96(a)
T	Sunray, Ash Meadows (*Enceliopsis nudicaulis* var. *corrugata*)	17.96(a)
E	Wallflower, Contra Costa (*Erysimum capitatum* var. *angustatum*)	17.96(a)
E	Water-umbel, Huachuca (*Lilaeopsis schaffneriana* var. *recurva*)	17.96(a)
E	Wild-buckwheat, clay-loving (*Eriogonum pelinophilum*)	17.96(a)
T	Wild-buckwheat, gypsum (*Eriogonum gypsophilum*)	17.96(a)
E	Wild-rice, Texas (*Zizania texana*)	17.96(a)
E	Wire-lettuce, Malheur (*Stephanomeria malheurensis*)	17.96(a)

SOURCE: "Listed Species with Critical Habitat as of 4/23/2002," *Threatened and Endangered Species System (TESS),* U.S. Fish and Wildlife Service, Division of Endangered Species, Arlington, VA, April 23, 2002 [Online] http://ecos.fws.gov/webpage/webpage_crithab.html?module=undefined&listings=0&nmfs=1 [accessed April 23, 2002]

TABLE 2.3

Reclassified threatened and endangered species as of May 15, 2002

Current Status	Species Name	Status Change
T	Argali (Kyrgyzstan, Mongolia, Tajikistan) (*Ovis ammon*)	06/23/1992: E->T
T	Birch, Virginia round-leaf (*Betula uber*)	11/16/1994: E->T
E	Butterfly, Schaus swallowtail (*Heraclides aristodemus ponceanus*)	08/31/1984: T->E
T	Cactus, Siler pincushion (*Pediocactus* (=*Echinocactus,*=*Utahia) sileri*)	12/27/1993: E->T
T	Caiman, Yacare (*Caiman yacare*)	05/04/2000: E->T
E	Cavefish, Alabama (*Speoplatyrhinus poulsoni*)	09/28/1988: T->E
E	Chimpanzee (in the wild) (*Pan troglodytes*)	03/12/1990: T->E
T	Chimpanzee (captive) (*Pan troglodytes*)	03/12/1990: E->T
E	Chimpanzee, pygmy (*Pan paniscus*)	03/12/1990: T->E
T	Crocodile, Nile (*Crocodylus niloticus*)	09/30/1988: E->T, 09/23/1993: E->T, 06/17/1987: E->T
T	Crocodile, saltwater (Australia) (*Crocodylus porosus*)	06/24/1996: E->T
T	Daisy, Maguire (*Erigeron maguirei*)	06/19/1996: E->T
T	Darter, snail (*Percina tanasi*)	07/05/1984: E->T
T	Eagle, bald (lower 48 States) (*Haliaeetus leucocephalus*)	07/12/1995: E->T
T	Four-o'clock, MacFarlane's (*Mirabilis macfarlanei*)	03/15/1996: E->T
T	Leopard (Gabon to Kenya & southward) (*Panthera pardus*)	01/28/1982: E->T
T	Monarch, Tinian (old world flycatcher)) (*Monarcha takatsukasae*)	04/06/1987: E->T
T	Pearlshell, Louisiana (*Margaritifera hembeli*)	09/24/1993: E->T
T	Pogonia, small whorled (*Isotria medeoloides*)	10/06/1994: E->T
T	Prairie dog, Utah (*Cynomys parvidens*)	05/29/1984: E->T
T	Salmon, chinook (fall Snake R.) (*Oncorhynchus (=Salmo) tshawytscha*)	11/02/1994: T->E
T	Salmon, chinook (spring/summer Snake R.) (*Oncorhynchus (=Salmo) tshawytscha*)	11/02/1994: T->E
E	Salmon, chinook (winter Sacramento R.) (*Oncorhynchus (=Salmo) tshawytscha*)	03/23/1994: T->E
E	Sea-lion, Steller (western pop.) (*Eumetopias jubatus*)	06/05/1997:T->E, 05/05/1997: T->E
T	Skullcap, large-flowered (*Scutellaria montana*)	01/14/2002: E->T
T	Trout, Apache (*Oncorhynchus apache*)	07/16/1975: E->T
T	Trout, greenback cutthroat (*Oncorhynchus clarki stomias*)	04/18/1978: E->T
T	Trout, Lahontan cutthroat (*Oncorhynchus clarki henshawi*)	07/16/1975: E->T
T	Trout, Paiute cutthroat (*Oncorhynchus clarki seleniris*)	07/16/1975: E->T
E	Wolf, gray (lower 48 States, except MN and where XN; Mexico) (*Canis lupus*)	03/09/1978: T->E

Note: E = Endangered
      T = Threatened

SOURCE: "Reclassified Threatened and Endangered Species as of 5/15/2002," in *Species Information: Threatened and Endangered Animals and Plants,* U.S. Fish and Wildlife Service, Washington, DC, 2002 [Online] http://ecos.fws.gov/webpage/webpage_reclass.html?module=undefined [accessed May 15, 2002]

land is federal or non-federal, or public or private. Many landowners fear being denied free use of their land because of laws protecting the endangered species that inhabit it. Recognizing this concern, Congress amended the ESA in 1982 to allow for the creation of Habitat Conservation Plans (HCPs) governing land use or development. HCPs are generally partnerships drawn up by people at the local level, working with FWS or NMFS officials. They frequently represent compromises between developers and environmentalists.

HCPs typically allow some individuals of a threatened or endangered species to be "taken" (harmed or killed) under a special authority called an incidental take permit, as long as land-use or development activity does not significantly reduce the species' chances of survival and recovery. Included in the agreement is a "no-surprise" policy that assures landowners or developers that the overall cost of protection measures will be limited to what has been agreed to under the HCP. HCPs often incorporate public participation, monitoring provisions, the establishment of clear biological goals, and adaptive management—that is, the development of flexible strategies that can be applied to alternative future scenarios. In recent years, HCPs have moved away from merely listing rules that developers must follow, instead emphasizing the development of measures that will obtain positive results for threatened and endangered species. Many HCPs include the preservation of significant areas of habitat for endangered species.

Although the HCP program was implemented in 1982, it was little used before 1992, with only 14 permits issued in that time period. However, by 2002, there were 380 plans in place. These HCPs affect over 200 listed plant and animal species on over 20 million acres of land. The FWS maintains a list of approved Habitat Conservation Plans with the locations of the sites as well as data on the listed and unlisted species involved. HCPs have become an important tool for wildlife conservation. Figure 2.4 and Figure 2.5 show an area along the Clinch River in Virginia before and after intervention. Protection of this habitat spared several species of endangered mussels and fish.

In 1997, after more than a decade of debate and negotiation, environmentalists and developers settled upon an HCP—the "Multispecies Conservation Plan"—for San Diego County. It is regarded by some experts as a possible national model. Under the HCP, certain undeveloped sections of land were permanently set aside as protected natural habitat, while other areas were opened to unrestricted development. Setting aside a connected (rather than fragmented) area of protected natural habitat is a crucial aspect of this HCP. The plan affects some 85 species of vulnerable plants and animals. The "Multispecies Conservation Plan" pleased environmentalists because of the creation of a large, permanent preserve for species protection. Developers were pleased that unrestricted development could proceed without costly legal challenges by environmentalists in defined areas.

In Washington County, Utah, an HCP was developed in 1996 to bridge differences between developers and conservationists concerned about the threatened desert tortoise. In 2001 an update on this HCP was published by the FWS. The FWS reported that a total of 1,500 acres of habitat were developed in Washington County after being cleared

TABLE 2.4

Delisted species report, May 15, 2002

Date Species First Listed	Date Delisted	Species Name	Reason Delisted
03/11/1967	06/04/1987	Alligator, American (*Alligator mississippiensis*)	Recovered
02/17/1984	02/06/1996	Bidens, cuneate (*Bidens cuneata*)	Taxonomic revision
04/28/1976	08/31/1984	Butterfly, Bahama swallowtail (*Heraclides andraemon bonhotei*)	Act amendment
10/26/1979	06/24/1999	Cactus, Lloyd's hedgehog (*Echinocereus lloydii*)	Taxonomic revision
11/07/1979	09/22/1993	Cactus, spineless hedgehog (*Echinocereus triglochidiatus* var. *inermis*)	Not a listable entity
03/11/1967	09/02/1983	Cisco, longjaw (*Coregonus alpenae*)	Extinct
06/02/1970	09/12/1985	Dove, Palau ground (*Gallicolumba canifrons*)	Recovered
03/11/1967	07/25/1978	Duck, Mexican (U.S.A. only) (*Anas "diazi"*)	Taxonomic revision
06/02/1970	08/25/1999	Falcon, American peregrine (*Falco peregrinus anatum*)	Recovered
06/02/1970	10/05/1994	Falcon, Arctic peregrine (*Falco peregrinus tundrius*)	Recovered
06/02/1970	09/12/1985	Flycatcher, Palau fantail (*Rhipidura lepida*)	Recovered
04/30/1980	12/04/1987	Gambusia, Amistad (*Gambusia amistadensis*)	Extinct
04/29/1986	06/18/1993	Globeberry, Tumamoc (*Tumamoca macdougalii*)	New information discovered
03/11/1967	03/20/2001	Goose, Aleutian Canada (*Branta canadensis leucopareia*)	Recovered
10/11/1979	11/27/1989	Hedgehog cactus, purple-spined (*Echinocereus engelmannii* var. *purpureus*)	Taxonomic revision
12/30/1974	03/09/1995	Kangaroo, eastern gray (*Macropus giganteus*)	Recovered
12/30/1974	03/09/1995	Kangaroo, red (*Macropus rufus*)	Recovered
12/30/1974	03/09/1995	Kangaroo, western gray (*Macropus fuliginosus*)	Recovered
04/26/1978	09/14/1989	Milk-vetch, Rydberg (*Astragalus perianus*)	Recovered
06/02/1970	09/12/1985	Owl, Palau (*Pyroglaux podargina*)	Recovered
06/14/1976	01/09/1984	Pearlymussel, Sampson's (*Epioblasma sampsoni*)	Extinct
06/02/1970	02/04/1985	Pelican, brown (U.S. Atlantic coast, FL, AL) (*Pelecanus occidentalis*)	Recovered
07/13/1982	09/22/1993	Pennyroyal, Mckittrick (*Hedeoma apiculatum*)	New information discovered
03/11/1967	09/02/1983	Pike, blue (*Stizostedion vitreum glaucum*)	Extinct
10/13/1970	01/15/1982	Pupfish, Tecopa (*Cyprinodon nevadensis calidae*)	Extinct
09/26/1986	02/28/2000	Shrew, Dismal Swamp southeastern (*Sorex longirostris fisheri*)	New information discovered
03/11/1967	12/12/1990	Sparrow, dusky seaside (*Ammodramus maritimus nigrescens*)	Extinct
06/04/1973	10/12/1983	Sparrow, Santa Barbara song (*Melospiza melodia graminea*)	Extinct
11/11/1977	11/22/1983	Treefrog, pine barrens (FL pop.) (*Hyla andersonii*)	New information discovered
09/13/1996	04/26/2000	Trout, coastal cutthroat (Umpqua R.) (*Oncorhynchus clarki clarki*)	Taxonomic revision
06/14/1976	02/29/1984	Turtle, Indian flap-shelled (*Lissemys punctata punctata*)	Erroneous data
06/02/1970	06/16/1994	Whale, gray (except where listed) (*Eschrichtius robustus*)	Recovered

SOURCE: "Delisted Species Report as of 5/15/2002," in *Species Information: Threatened and Endangered Animals and Plants,* U.S. Fish and Wildlife Service, Washington, DC, 2002 [Online] http://ecos.fws.gov/webpage/webpage_delisted.html?module=undefined&listings=0 [accessed May 15, 2002]

of tortoises—161 tortoises were legally "taken." The biological benefits of the HCP included the acquisition of a continuous area of habitat for desert tortoises administered by the Bureau of Land Management. This reserve was created through the exchange and purchase of land by the Bureau of Land Management. In addition, tortoises will be protected from other threats on the reserve. For example, grazing permits for reserve land have been retired, so cattle will no longer trample habitat and compete with tortoises for food. In addition, new restrictions were placed on the operation of off-road vehicles in the reserve, which damage habitats and sometimes hit tortoises. The development of a nature education center is in the works. There are still a number of contentious issues. For example, some members of the public have demanded that more recreational opportunities be made available on the reserve. Also, the Bureau of Land Management needs to purchase more land to complete the reserve, difficult on its limited budget.

Opposition to the Endangered Species Act

Opponents of the ESA believe the law violates private property rights and stifles economic growth by curbing development. They also charge that environmental protection often results in the loss of jobs and business profits.

One vocal critic of the ESA is Thomas Lambert. In *The Endangered Species Act: A Train Wreck Ahead* (Center for the Study of American Business, 1995), Lambert argues that private property will become increasingly restricted under the act. This is because more species are continually being added to the threatened and endangered list, while very few are removed from it. Lambert believes the best way to ensure that landowners are treated fairly is to require the federal government to compensate those whose property is devalued through ESA land-use restrictions. That way, he says, regulators will be forced to weigh the costs and benefits of recovering a species much more thoroughly and sensibly than they do now.

Is the Endangered Species Act Enough?

Other critics argue that the ESA is not enough. These critics charge that species are often listed for protection so late in the slide to extinction that their populations have already become perilously small. In addition, the listing process can be extremely slow. A number of species have become extinct while federal authorities deliberated about listing action. Even some supporters of the ESA believe that implementation of the act has been poor. In part, budget cuts are to blame. For example, in November 2000,

TABLE 2.5

Species proposed for status change or delisting, May 15, 2002

Status	Proposal Date	Species Name
AT	03/26/1998	Bat, Mariana fruit (=Mariana flying fox) (*Pteropus mariannus mariannus*)
AD	01/25/2002	Broadbill, Guam (*Myiagra freycineti*)
PXN	06/08/2001	Chub, spotfin Proposed experimental, non-essential population in the Tellico River (*Cyprinella monacha*)
AD	06/08/2001	Cinquefoil, Robbins' (*Potentilla robbinsiana*)
PXN	06/08/2001	Darter, duskytail Proposed experimental, non-essential population in the Tellico River (*Etheostoma percnurum*)
AD	07/06/1999	Eagle, bald (lower 48 States) (*Haliaeetus leucocephalus*)
AD	06/24/1999	Goby, tidewater Populations north of Orange County, CA (*Eucyclogobius newberryi*)
AT	08/05/1993	Hawk, Hawaiian (*Buteo solitarius*)
PXN	06/08/2001	Madtom, smoky Proposed experimental, non-essential population in the Tellico River (*Noturus baileyi*)
PXN	06/08/2001	Madtom, yellowfin Proposed experimental, non-essential population in the Tellico River (*Noturus flavipinnis*)
AD	01/25/2002	Mallard, Mariana (*Anas oustaleti*)
AT	09/22/1993	Poolfish, Pahrump (*Empetrichthys latos*)
PT(S/A)	01/09/2001	Trout, Dolly Varden (*Salvelinus malma*)
AT	07/13/2000	Wolf, gray U.S.A. (MI, MN, ND, SD, WI); captive wolves who were, or whose ancestors were, removed from the wild in this area. (*Canis lupus*)
AE	07/13/2000	Wolf, gray U.S.A. (portions of AZ, NM, TX), Mexico, except where listed as an experimental population, captive wolves who were, or whose ancestors were, removed from the wild in this area. (*Canis lupus*)
AT	07/13/2000	Wolf, gray U.S.A. (ME, NH, NY, VT); captive wolves who were, or whose ancestors were, removed from the wild in this area. (*Canis lupus*)
AT	07/13/2000	Wolf, gray U.S.A. (CO, ID, MT, OR, UT, WA, WY; portions of AZ and NM), except where listed as an experimental population captive wolves who were, or whose ancestors were, removed from the wild in this area. (*Canis lupus*)
AD	07/13/2000	Wolf, gray U.S.A. (proposed delisting of all other lower 48 states or portions of lower 48 states not otherwise included in the 4 distinct population segments). (*Canis lupus*)
AD	03/06/2001	Woolly-star, Hoover's (*Eriastrum hooveri*)

PEXPN, PXN - Proposed Experimental Population, Non-Essential
PSAT, PT(S/A) - Proposed Similarity of Appearance to a Threatened Taxon
AD - Proposed Delisting
AE - Proposed Reclassification to Endangered
AT - Proposed Reclassification to Threatened

SOURCE: "Speicies Proposed for Status Change or Delisting, as of 5/15/2002," in *Species Information: Threatened and Endangered Animals and Plants*, U.S. Fish and Wildlife Service, Washington, DC, 2002 [Online] http://ecos.fws.gov/webpage/webpage_proposed_dr.html?module=undefined [accessed May 15, 2002]

the Fish and Wildlife Service announced that it would be unable to list any new species in 2001 because its budget would be entirely used up complying with court orders requiring designation of critical habitat for some currently listed species. However, an agreement was reached with some of the plaintiffs allowing some portions of the budget to be used in listing a few species. At the moment, numerous species await listing action, while others await the development and implementation of recovery plans.

Other critics charge that the ESA has failed in its central mission to preserve biodiversity. They argue that more must be done both to enforce the law and to supplement it.

The Wilderness Society, an environmental advocacy organization, believes that the Endangered Species Act, even strengthened and fully funded, will not be sufficient to maintain biological diversity. It argues that conservation efforts must be ecosystem-based, and that the ESA must be complemented with a biodiversity program which deals with units larger than single species.

FEDERAL LANDS AND WILDLIFE PROTECTION

The History of U.S. Land Management

In the United States' first century as a nation, the federal government owned about 80 percent of the nation's land. Beginning in 1785 the government began to survey and sell its vast land holdings to new states, settlers, and railroad companies. By the end of the nineteenth century, the government had transferred most of its lands to private ownership. It also allowed private use of remaining federal lands. After several decades of rapid development and unrestricted use, much of the nation's lands and natural resources were significantly degraded. Responding to growing concerns, Congress slowly redefined the federal government's role in land management from temporary to permanent retention as well as active stewardship.

Half a century later, in the 1960s, increasing scientific and public concern about the declining condition of the country's natural resources led Congress to enact a number of laws to conserve both federal and nonfederal lands. These laws cover air, water, soil, plants, and animals. Most of the federal acreage with conservation restrictions is located in 13 western states, as shown in Figure 2.6. Figure 2.7 shows the percentage of land in each of these states restricted for conservation purposes. These numbers can change, depending on congressional decisions on the establishment of wilderness areas and national parks.

With increasing environmental legislation, the land management framework evolved into a complex collection of agencies, land units, and laws. Different agencies had different priorities, which were reflected in how they managed the resources under their care. The effects of these different missions are particularly evident in places where two agencies hold adjacent lands. For example, the National Park Service (Department of the Interior) oversees Yellowstone National Park, where timber harvesting is prohibited, whereas the U.S. Forest Service (Department of Agriculture) allows large areas to be clear-cut in Targhee National Forest in Idaho.

The National Park System

The National Park System began with the establishment of Yellowstone National Park in 1872. By 2002 there were 384 national parks, monuments, preserves, memorials, historic sites, recreational areas, seashores, and other units. These cover a total of 83.6 million acres. The National Park System has units in all U.S. states and territories

FIGURE 2.4

The Clinch River in southwestern Virginia is home to endangered fish and mussels, but belonged to private landowners. This made it a good candidate for a habitat conservation plan. *(U.S. Fish & Wildlife Service, Washington, DC)*

with the exception of Delaware and the District of Columbia, American Samoa, Guam, Puerto Rico, and the Virgin Islands. In addition to preserving habitats that range from arctic tundra to tropical rain forest, the system protects representatives of more than half of North America's plant species and a large proportion of animal species. The map in Figure 2.8 shows the location and ranges of National Parks in the United States. The National Park Service is also responsible for encouraging public enjoyment of its natural areas. Balancing these objectives shapes the debate over how best to manage the National Parks. There were over 424 million visitations to National Parks in 2001.

Working closely with the Fish and Wildlife Service, the National Park Service plays an important role in protecting and restoring threatened and endangered species. Three measures that the NPS takes to protect wildlife include:

1) Education of park visitors about species loss and the value of biodiversity.

2) Enforcement of laws related to protecting species under the Endangered Species Act.

3) Provision of a protected and undisturbed habitat for animals.

The National Parks have played a significant role in the return of several species, including red wolves and peregrine falcons. National Parks also contain designated critical habitat for numerous listed species. However, not all these are disclosed, in order to protect rare species from collectors, vandals, or curiosity seekers. In 2002 some 398 federally listed endangered species were found in National Parks. This represents nearly a third of all threatened and endangered U.S. species. Table 2.6 lists some of the types of endangered, threatened, proposed, and candidate species that are found within the National Park System. Some parks provide important habitat for disproportionately large numbers of endangered species. These are listed in Table 2.7. Several are in Hawaii and California, states that have large numbers of listed threatened and endangered species.

The National Forests

The National Forests encompass more land than the National Park Service, including over 232 million acres in 155 national forests and 20 national grasslands (Table 2.8). A map of the locations of U.S. National Forests is shown in Figure 2.9. In addition to forest and grassland areas, National Forest lands also include numerous lakes

FIGURE 2.5

Only a year after a habitat conservation plan was implemented for the Clinch River, the protected sections had already returned to a more natural state. *(U.S. Fish & Wildlife Service, Washington, DC)*

and ponds. Within the Forest Service, the Threatened, Endangered, and Sensitive Species Program focuses on wildlife conservation. A total of 421 listed endangered or threatened species are found on National Forest lands. The Forest Service has also designated over 2,900 species as sensitive, and has developed protective measures to help keep these species from becoming endangered. National Forest land is, in general, not conserved to the same degree as National Parks. For example, much logging occurs within these forests.

The National Wildlife Refuge System

The National Wildlife Refuge System is the only network of federal lands and waters managed principally for the protection of fish and wildlife. In 1999, the total acreage in the system was well over 93 million (Table 2.9). This includes 547 Wildlife Refuges; 38 Wetland Management Districts, which administer over 26,000 Waterfowl Protection Areas; and 50 Coordination Areas, which are jointly administered with a state wildlife agency. Figure 2.10 shows the distribution of units within the National Wildlife Refuge System. The first unit of what would later become the refuge system was the Peli-

can Island Bird Reservation in Florida, established in 1903 to protect the dwindling populations of wading birds in Florida. Today the 16 wildlife refuges in Alaska account for 83 percent of land in the refuge system. Yukon Delta, the largest of the Alaskan refuges, comprises 20 million acres. Approximately one-third of the total refuge acreage is wetland habitat, reflecting the importance of wetlands for wildlife survival.

Of the many species listed under the Endangered Species Act, a quarter have habitat on National Wildlife Refuges. Many other listed species use refuge lands on a temporary basis for breeding or migratory rest stops. A list of wildlife refuges established explicitly for endangered species appears, by state, along with the species of concern and the number of protected acres in Table 2.10. Figure 2.11 shows the types of listed species found on refuges by taxonomic group. Lists of endangered animals and plants found within the National Wildlife Refuge System appear in Table 2.11 and Table 2.12, respectively. Virtually every species of bird in North America has been recorded in the refuge system. The wide variety of wildlife found on refuges also includes over 220 mammals, 250 reptiles and amphibians, and 200 fish species.

FIGURE 2.6

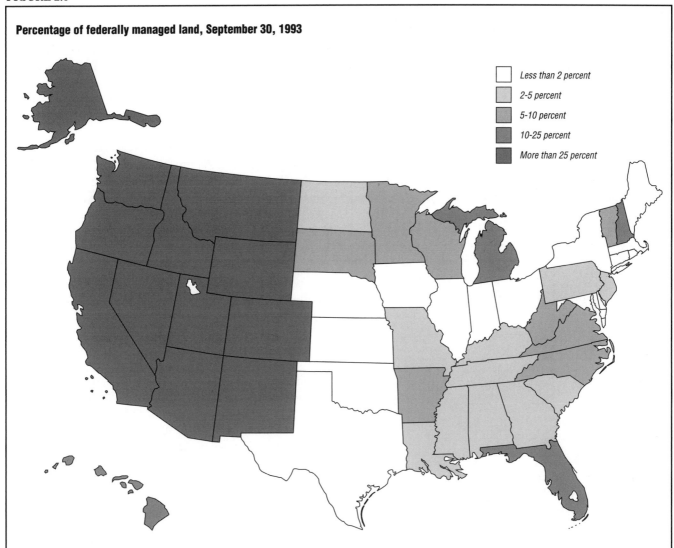

Percentage of federally managed land, September 30, 1993

Less than 2 percent

2-5 percent

5-10 percent

10-25 percent

More than 25 percent

Note: Map includes percentages of land managed by the four main federal agencies that manage land: the Department of Agriculture's Forest Service and the Department of the Interior's Bureau of Land Management, Fish and Wildlife Service, and National Park Service. These agencies manage about 95 percent of all Federal land.

SOURCE: "Percentage of Federal Land in Each State Managed by the Four Federal Agencies, September 30, 1993," *Federal Lands—Information on Land Owned and on Acreage with Conservation Restrictions,* U.S. General Accounting Office, Washington, DC, March 2, 1995

Funding limitations constrain efforts to manage wildlife refuges. The FWS reports that the refuge system's current annual funding is less than half the amount needed to meet established objectives. The 2002 budget for the system included $241.9 million for refuge operations and $77 million for refuge maintenance.

America's Wild Lands under Attack

Since the passage of the Wilderness Act in 1964, 630 areas have been designated wilderness. These cover a total of more than 103 million acres. Much of the designated land is located within the National Wildlife Refuge System under the management of the Fish and Wildlife Service. Table 2.13 shows the acreage of wilderness areas within the National Wildlife Refuges and National Fish Hatch-

eries Systems. Unlike National Parks, which are intended for use by large numbers of visitors, wilderness areas are intended to be pristine, with limited access and no amenities. True wilderness remains, for most humans, a place to visit only rarely. Nonetheless, the number of people using wilderness areas has increased steadily. Many visitors, as well as park managers, have wearied particularly of intrusions of civilization—in the form of cell phones, snowmobiles, and aircraft—into wilderness areas.

Many national parks and monuments are suffering as well, in part because of the high volume of visitors. More than five million people visit the Grand Canyon each year. On a busy day, 6,500 vehicles compete for 2,000 parking spaces. By 2001, Grand Canyon, Zion, and Yosemite National Parks required visitors to use mass transit.

FIGURE 2.7

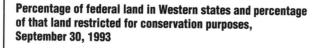

Percentage of federal land in Western states and percentage of that land restricted for conservation purposes, September 30, 1993

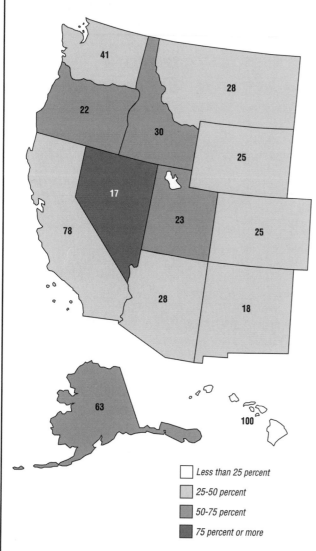

Less than 25 percent

25-50 percent

50-75 percent

75 percent or more

Note: Map includes percentages of land managed by the four main federal agencies that manage land: the Department of Agriculture's Forest Service and the Department of the Interior's Bureau of Land Management, Fish and Wildlife Service, and National Park Service. These agencies manage about 95 percent of all federal land. The shading of each state indicates the percentage of land in that state that is managed by the federal government. The number in each state represents the percentage of federal acreage in that state that has conservation restrictions placed on its use.

SOURCE: "Percentage of Four Agencies' Land in Western States and Percentage of That Land Restricted for Conservation Purposes, as of September 30, 1993," *Federal Lands—Information on Land Owned and on Acreage with Conservation Restrictions,* U. S. General Accounting Office, Washington, DC, March 2, 1995

In 1997 the Wilderness Society listed "America's 10 Most Endangered Wild Lands." These were identified based on their natural resources, national significance, and the immediate threats to their integrity. Most are wildlife reserves. Among the 10 were the Arctic National Wildlife Refuge (Alaska), Klamath Basin National Wildlife Refuge (Oregon/California), Snoqualmie Pass (Washington), Boundary Waters Canoe Area (Minnesota), and the Grand Staircase/Escalante National Monument (Utah). Also included were Owyhee Canyonlands (Idaho), Okefenokee National Wildlife Refuge (Georgia/Florida), Cabeza Prieta National Wildlife Refuge (Arizona), the Whitney Estate in New York, and California's Mojave Desert.

OIL DRILLING IN THE ARCTIC NATIONAL WILDLIFE REFUGE? The Arctic National Wildlife Refuge (ANWR) is the largest National Wildlife Refuge in the United States. It harbors a multitude of unique species, including caribou, musk oxen, polar bears, Arctic foxes, and snow geese. Because of the harsh climate, Arctic habitats are generally characterized by short food chains and extreme vulnerability to habitat disturbance. The majority of Arctic species already live "on the edge." Consequently, the decline of even a single species is likely to have dramatic effects on the entire community.

The protected status of the Arctic National Wildlife Refuge has been challenged by large oil companies and their political supporters. There has been interest in tapping the oil deposits in northern Alaska since the early 1900s, and the area was first explored for oil and gas resources in the 1940s and 1950s. It was also in the 1950s, however, that people became aware of the ecological value of these lands, and a compromise was reached in which the northeastern part of the state was set aside as a wildlife range (later refuge), while drilling began (and continues) in the northwestern part of the state. Figure 2.12 shows northern Alaskan refuge and oil drilling areas respectively. Production of oil and gas in the refuge area was also specifically prohibited at this time unless authorized by Congress.

Congress passed legislation to allow for drilling in 1995, but President Clinton vetoed this bill, saying, "I want to protect this biologically rich wilderness permanently." Environmentalists note that studies by the Fish and Wildlife Service have suggested that oil drilling in the refuge will result in harm to many Arctic species, by taking over their habitat, damaging habitats through pollution, interfering with their activities directly, or increasing opportunities for invasive species such as gulls and ravens through the availability of garbage as a food source.

The succeeding administration under George W. Bush has been much more supportive of drilling in the refuge. Attention is now focused particularly on the "1002 Area" within the refuge, which some environmentalists consider one of the most ecologically diverse and valuable. Among the species that would be particularly affected if drilling is permitted are polar bears, whose preferred sites for building dens are in the 1002 Area (see Figure 2.13) and caribou, which also use this area for calving—giving birth to their young (see Figure 2.14).

FIGURE 2.8

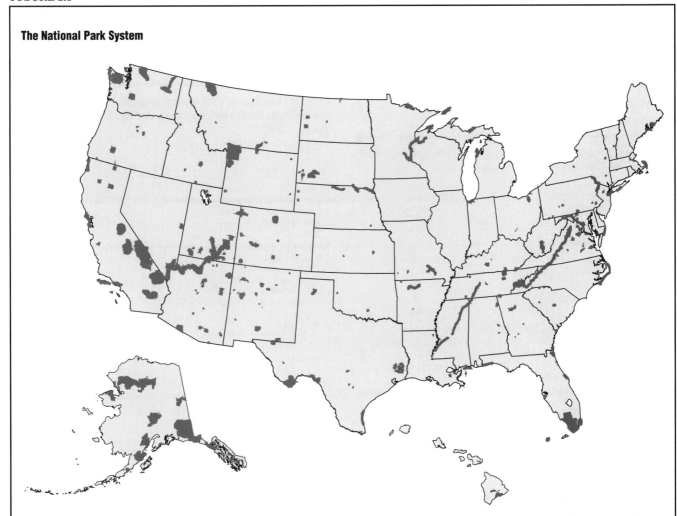

The National Park System

SOURCE: Loyal A. Mehrhoff and Peter A. Dratch, "The National Park System," in "Endangered Species and the National Park Service," in *Endangered Species Bulletin,* vol. XXVII, no. 1, U.S. Fish and Wildlife Service, Washington, DC, January/February 2002

However, since the terrorist attacks of September 11, 2001, drilling in ANWR has taken on another aspect—national security. Many politicians, particularly Republicans, argue that America cannot be truly secure until it reduces its dependence on foreign oil, much of which comes from unstable regions of the world such as the Mideast. One enthusiastic supporter of drilling in ANWR is Walter J. Hickel, former Secretary of the Interior and twice-governor of Alaska, as well as author of the recent book *Crisis in the Commons: The Alaska Solution* (ICS Press, Oakland, California, 2002). In the magazine *The American Enterprise* (June 2002), Hickel states, "Overdependence on foreign oil exposes us to energy blackmail and compromises our ability to protect our citizens and assist our friends in times of crisis. Our goal as Americans must be to produce as much energy as we can for ourselves." In the same issue, Hickel goes on to state his belief that "[t]he very small portion of the refuge with oil potential can be explored and drilled without damaging

the environment." Many supporters of drilling argue that recent advances in technology will allow oil drilling in ANWR without significant damage to its ecosystem.

In August 2001, the House of Representatives again passed a bill allowing for drilling within the refuge. However, the Senate rejected this proposal in April 2002 and the refuge continues to be protected. It is likely, though, that oil drilling within ANWR will remain a bone of contention among politicians and the American public.

ECOSYSTEM CONSERVATION—AN ALTERNATIVE APPROACH

In the 1990s there was growing concern that traditional methods of species protection, using a species-by-species approach, were ineffective. Many alternatives were proposed. One of the most popular was a method variously termed the "habitat," "ecosystem," or "community" approach. The Fish and Wildlife Service defines an ecosystem as a "geographic area including all the living organisms (people, plants, animals, and microorganisms), their physical surroundings (such as soil, water, and air), and the natural cycles that sustain them." Central to these approaches is a focus on conservation of large intact areas of habitat. It was hoped that by focusing on entire habi-tats, rather than individual species recovery, numerous species would be protected before they reached critically low population sizes.

TABLE 2.6

Endangered, threatened, proposed, and candidate species found in units of the National Park Service, June 1, 2001

Taxonomic group	Species
Plants	193
Invertebrates	43
Fish	40
Amphibians	4
Reptiles	19
Birds	53
Mammals	46
Total	**398**

SOURCE: Loyal A. Mehrhoff and Peter A. Dratch, "Table 1. Endangered, threatened, proposed, and candidate species found in units of the National Park Service," in "Endangered Species and the National Park Service," *Endangered Species Bulletin,* vol. XXVII, no. 1, U.S. Fish and Wildlife Service, Washington, DC, January/February 2002

TABLE 2.7

Areas in the National Park System with the largest numbers of endangered, threatened, proposed, and candidate species, June 1, 2001

National Park	Plants	Animals	Total
Haleakala National Park, Hawai' i	35	12	47
Hawaii Volcanoes National Park, Hawai' i	27	15	42
Channel Islands National Park, California	15	18	33
Golden Gate National Recreation Area, California	14	15	29
Santa Monica Mountains National Recreation Area, California	10	13	23
Kalaupapa National Historic Park, Hawai' i	15	7	22
Natchez Trace Parkway, Mississippi	8	12	20
Everglades National Park, Florida	7	12	19
Great Smoky Mountains National Park, Tennessee	4	12	16

SOURCE: Loyal A. Mehrhoff and Peter A. Dratch, "Table 2. Areas in the National Park System with the largest numbers of endangered, threatened, proposed, and candidate species," in "Endangered Species and the National Park Service," *Endangered Species Bulletin,* vol. XXVII, no. 1, U.S. Fish and Wildlife Service, Washington, DC, January/February 2002

TABLE 2.8

National and regional land areas of the National Forest System, by number of areas and acreage, September 30, 2001

Area kind	No. of units	Gross acreage	NFS acreage	Other acreage
National totals				
National Forests	155	225,463,786	187,760,642	37,703,144
Purchase Units	56	2,233,077	355,236	1,877,841
National Grasslands	20	4,264,663	3,838,685	425,978
Land Utilization Projects	6	1,876	1,876	0
Research and Experimental Areas	20	73,154	64,871	8,283
Other Areas	34	296,406	295,814	592
National Preserves	1	89,716	89,716	0
Total	292	232,422,678	192,406,840	40,015,838
Western regional totals (regions 1 through 6)				
National Forests	101	156,007,366	141,044,329	14,963,037
Purchase Units	17	162,011	10,734	151,277
National Grasslands	18	4,080,564	3,800,503	280,061
Land Utilization Projects	4	1,834	1,834	0
Research and Experimental Areas	6	60,598	60,598	0
Other Areas	28	109,023	108,431	592
National Preserves	1	89,716	89,716	0
Total	175	160,511,112	145,116,145	15,394,967
Eastern regional totals (regions 8 and 9)				
National Forests	52	45,101,285	24,729,289	20,371,996
Purchase Units	39	2,071,066	344,502	1,726,564
National Grasslands	2	184,099	38,182	145,917
Land Utilization Projects	2	42	42	0
Research and Experimental Areas	14	12,556	4,273	8,283
Other Areas	6	187,383	187,383	0
Total	115	47,556,431	25,303,671	22,252,760
Alaska region totals (region 10)				
National Forests	2	24,355,135	21,987,024	2,368,111
Total	2	24,355,135	21,987,024	2,368,111

SOURCE: "Table 1 -- National and Regional Areas Summary," U.S. Department of Agriculture Forest Service, Lands and Realty Management, Washington, DC [Online] http://www.fs.fed.us/land/staff/lar/LAR01/table1.htm [accessed May 15, 2002]

FIGURE 2.9

National Forest System

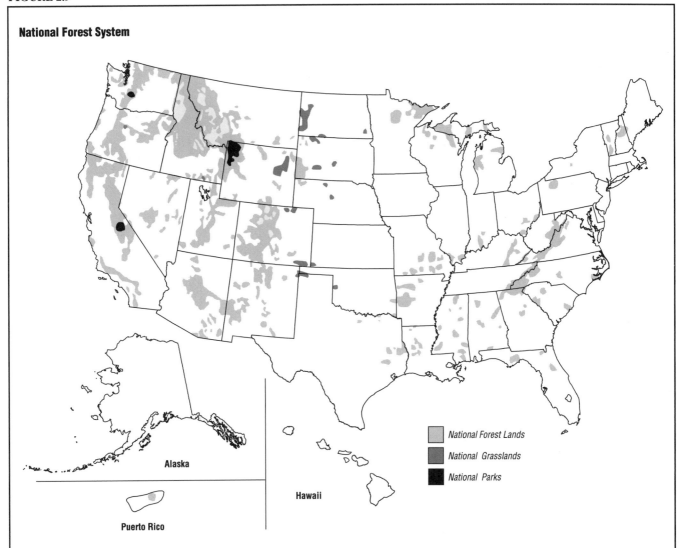

SOURCE: "The National Forests," U.S. Department of Agriculture Forest Service, Lands and Realty Management, Washington, DC [Online] http://www.fs.fed.us/land/staff/lar/nfsmap.htm [accessed May 15, 2002]

The National Biological Service (NBS) was created in 1993 by the Department of the Interior. This agency was responsible for gathering, analyzing, and disseminating biological information necessary for stewardship of the nation's resources. The NBS conducted the first large-scale study of ecosystems in the United States and found that many U.S. ecosystems are imperiled. In 1996 the NBS was integrated into the United States Geological Survey (USGS) as the Biological Resources Division (BRD).

In 1993 the White House Office on Environmental Policy established the Interagency Ecosystem Management Task Force to implement an ecosystem approach to environmental management. The task force included representatives from each of the four primary federal land-management agencies. A total of $700 million was appropriated to facilitate the implementations. The ambi-

TABLE 2.9

Summary of National Wildlife Refuge System land holdings, as of September 30, 1999

Reserved From Public Domain	Acquired by Other Federal Agency	Devise or Gift	Purchased	Agreement, Easement or Lease	Total
82,085,483.61	2,717,198.55	664,254.82	4,532,441.93	3,605,242.69	93,604,621.6

SOURCE: "National Wildlife Refuge System Acreage," in *Annual Report of Lands Under Control of the U.S. Fish and Wildlife Service, as of September 30, 1999,* U.S. Fish and Wildlife Service, Washington, DC, September 30, 1999 [Online] http://refugedata.fws.gov/databases/national.taf?_function=list&<@UserReferenceArgument>&_start=1 [accessed May 15, 2002]

FIGURE 2.10

National Wildlife Refuge System, 2000

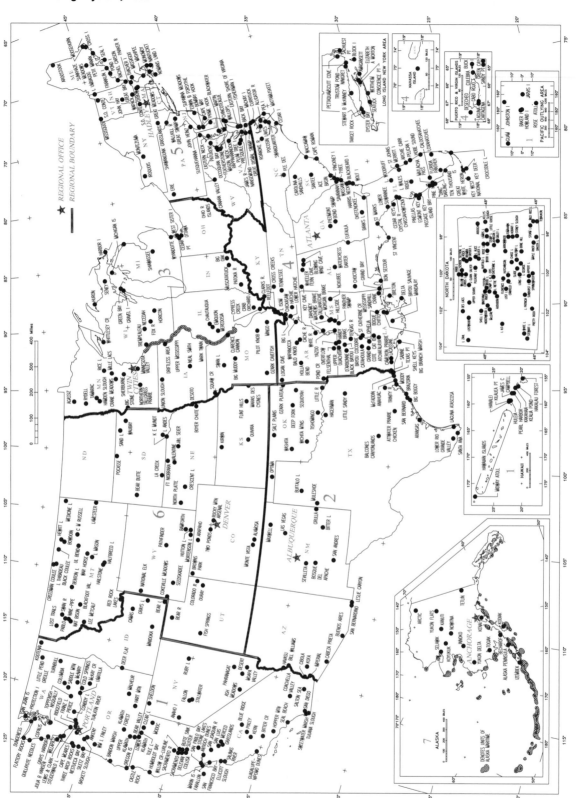

Note: Detroit River International Wildlife Rufuge was created on December 21, 2001, absorbing the area formerly known as the Wyandotte National Wildlife Refuge. The addition of Bayou Teche National Wildlife Refuge in St. Mary Parish, Louisiana brought the total number of Refuges to 538.

SOURCE: "National Wildlife Refuge System," in *National Wildlife Refuge System,* U.S. Fish and Wildlife Service, National Wildlife Refuge System, Washington, DC, 2002 [Online] http://refuges.fws.gov/refugeMapJan2000.pdf [accessed May 15, 2002]

TABLE 2.10

National Wildlife Refuges established for endangered species as of January 1998

State	Unit Name	Species of Concern	Unit Acreage as of (1/13/98)
Alabama	Blowing Wind Cave NWR	Indiana Bat, Gray Bat	264
	Fern Cave NWR	Indiana Bat, Gray Bat	199
	Key Cave NWR	Alabama Cavefish, Gray Bat	1,060
	Watercress Darter NWR	Watercress Darter	7
Arkansas	Logan Cave NWR	Cave Crayfish, Gray Bat, Indiana Bat, Ozark Cavefish	124
Arizona	Buenos Aires NWR	Masked Bobwhite Quail	116,585
	Leslie Canyon	Gila Topminnow, Yaqui Chub, Peregrine Falcon	2,765
	San Bernardino NWR	Gila Topminnow, Yaqui Chub, Yaqui Catfish, Beautiful Shiner, Huachuca Water Umbel	2,369
California	Antioch Dunes NWR	Lange's Metalmark Butterfly, Antioch Dunes Evening-primrose, Contra Costa Wallflower	55
	Bitter Creek NWR	California Condor	14,054
	Blue Ridge NWR	California Condor	897
	Castle Rock NWR	Aleutian Canada Goose	14
	Coachello Valley NWR	Coachella Valley Fringe-toed Lizard	3,592
	Don Edwards San Francisco Bay NWR	California Clapper Rail, California Least Tern, Salt Marsh Harvest Mouse	21,524
	Ellicott Slough NWR	Santa Cruz Long-toed Salamander	139
	Hopper Mountain NWR	California Condor	2,471
	Sacramento River NWR	Valley Elderberry Longhorn Beetle, Bald Eagle, Least Bell's Vireo	7,884
	San Diego NWR	San Diego Fairy Shrimp, San Diego Mesa Mint, Otay Mesa Mint, California Orcutt Grass, San Diego Button-celery	1,840
	San Joaquin River NWR	Aleutian Canada Goose	1,638
	Seal Beach NWR	Light-footed Clapper Rail, California Least Tern	911
	Sweetwater Marsh NWR	Light-footed Clapper Rail	316
	Tijuana Slough NWR	Light-footed Clapper Rail	1,023

State	Unit Name	Species of Concern	Unit Acreage as of (1/13/98)
Florida	Archie Carr NWR	Loggerhead Sea Turtle, Green Sea Turtle	29
	Crocodile Lake NWR	American Crocodile	6,686
	Crystal River NWR	West Indian Manatee	80
	Florida Panther NWR	Florida Panther	23,379
	Hobe Sound NWR	Loggerhead Sea Turtle, Green Sea Turtle	980
	Lake Wales Ridge NWR	Florida Scrub Jay, Snakeroot, Scrub Blazing Star, Carter's Mustard, Papery Whitlow-wort, Florida Bonamia, Scrub Lupine, Highlands Scrub Hypericum, Garett's Mint, Scrub Mint, Pygmy Gringe-tree, Wireweed, Florida Ziziphus, Scrub Plum, Eastern Indigo Snake, Bluetail Mole Skink, Sand Skink	659
	National Key Deer Refuge	Key Deer	8,542
	St. Johns NWR	Dusky Seaside Sparrow	6,255
Hawaii	Hakalau Forest NWR	Akepa, Akiapolaau, 'O'u, Hawaiian Hawk, Hawaiian Creeper	32,730
	Hanalei NWR	Hawaiian Stilt, Hawaiian Coot, Hawaiian Moorhen, Hawaiian Duck	917
	Huleia NWR	Hawaiian Stilt, Hawaiian Coot, Hawaiian Moorhen, Hawaiian Duck	241
	James C. Campbell NWR	Hawaiian Stilt, Hawaiian Coot, Hawaiian Moorhen, Hawaiian Duck	164
	Kakahaia NWR	Hawaiian Stilt, Hawaiian Coot	45
	Kealia Pond NWR	Hawaiian Stilt, Hawaiian Coot	691
	Pearl Harbor NWR	Hawaiian Stilt	61
Iowa	Driftless Area NWR	Iowa Pleistocene Snail	521
Massachusetts	Massasoit NWR	Plymouth Red-bellied Turtle	184
Michigan	Kirtland's Warbler WMA	Kirtland's Warbler	6,535
Mississippi	Mississippi Sandhill Crane NWR	Mississippi Sandhill Crane	19,713
Missouri	Ozark Cavefish NWR	Ozark Cavefish	42
	Pilot Knob NWR	Indiana Bat	90
Nebraska	Karl E. Mundt NWR	Bald Eagle	19

tious proposals included four pilot projects addressing conservation of old-growth forests of the Pacific Northwest, habitats in the Everglades and Florida Bay, the urban watershed of the Anacostia River in Maryland and the District of Columbia, and Alaska's Prince William Sound. However, due to budget cuts enacted by Congress in 1994, efforts on the projects were sidelined.

By the turn of the twenty-first century, however, progress had been made on a number of key ecosystem fronts:

• In the late 1990s the Clinton administration secured $1.2 billion for Everglades restoration and added 70,000 acres to the Everglades National Park.

• A budget appropriation of $250 million was designated for the preservation of the Headwaters Forest in Northern California, where 2,000-year-old redwoods stand. Additionally, $220 million was appropriated for the restoration of the California Bay-Delta ecosystem, including $30 million in water management funds for the Bay-Delta.

• Death Valley National Park, the largest National Park in the lower 48 states, was created.

• The Clinton administration successfully blocked congressional proposals to open the Arctic National

TABLE 2.10

National Wildlife Refuges established for endangered species as of January 1998 [CONTINUED]

State	Unit Name	Species of Concern	Unit Acreage as of (1/13/98)
Nevada	Ash Meadows NWR	Devil's Hole Pupfish, Warm Springs Pupfish, Ash Meadows Amargosa Pupfish, Ash Meadows Speckled Dace, Ash Meadows Naucorid, Ash Meadows Blazing Star, Amargosa Niterwort, Ash Meadows Milk-Vetch, Ash Meadows Sunray, Spring-loving Centaury, Ash Meadows Gumplant, Ash Meadows Invesia	13,268
	Moapa Valley NWR	Moapa Dace	32
Oklahoma	Ozark Plateau NWR	Ozark Big-eared Bat, Gray Bat	2,208
Oregon	Bear Valley NWR	Bald Eagle	4,200
	Julia Butler Hansen Refuge for Columbian White-tail Deer	Columbian White-tailed Deer	2,750
	Nestucca Bay NWR	Aleutian Canada Goose	457
South Dakota	Karl E. Mundt NWR	Bald Eagle	1,044
Texas	Attwater Prairie Chicken NWR	Attwater's Greater Prairie Chicken	8,007
	Balcones Canyonlands NWR	Black-capped Vireo, Golden-cheeked Warbler	14,144
Virgin Islands	Green Cay NWR	St. Croix Ground Lizard	14
	Sandy Point NWR	Leatherback Sea Turtle	327
Virginia	James River NWR	Bald Eagle	4,147
	Mason Neck NWR	Bald Eagle	2,276
Washington	Julia Butler Hansen Refuge for Columbian White-tail Deer	Columbian White-tailed Deer	2,777
Wyoming	Mortenson Lake	Wyoming Toad	1,776

SOURCE: "National Wildlife Refuges Established For Endangered Species," U.S. Fish and Wildlife Service, National Wildlife Refuge System, Washington, DC [Online] http://refuges.fws.gov/wildlife/endsprefuges.html [accessed May 14, 2002]

FIGURE 2.11

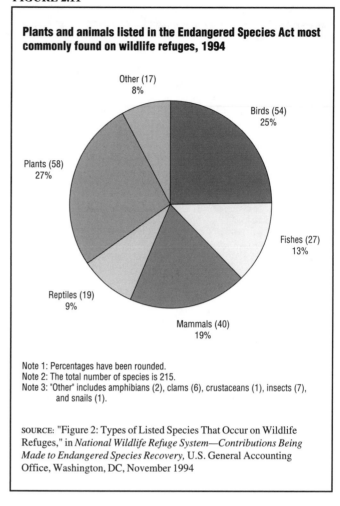

Plants and animals listed in the Endangered Species Act most commonly found on wildlife refuges, 1994

- Other (17) 8%
- Birds (54) 25%
- Fishes (27) 13%
- Mammals (40) 19%
- Reptiles (19) 9%
- Plants (58) 27%

Note 1: Percentages have been rounded.
Note 2: The total number of species is 215.
Note 3: "Other" includes amphibians (2), clams (6), crustaceans (1), insects (7), and snails (1).

SOURCE: "Figure 2: Types of Listed Species That Occur on Wildlife Refuges," in *National Wildlife Refuge System—Contributions Being Made to Endangered Species Recovery,* U.S. General Accounting Office, Washington, DC, November 1994

Wildlife Refuge, located in Alaska, to oil drilling. A second attempt to open the refuge to drilling was defeated by the Senate in 2002.

Adaptive Management

Adaptive management describes a conservation strategy that involves active, experimental manipulation of the environment in order to restore damaged ecosystems. It is being pursued in a variety of primarily aquatic habitats, including the Florida Everglades, San Francisco Bay, and the Great Barrier Reef in Australia. One of the oldest examples of adaptive management is an effort to restore Colorado River habitats by the Department of the Interior and the U.S. Bureau of Reclamation. These ecosystems were originally damaged by water control measures following the completion of the Glen Canyon Dam at the northern edge of the Grand Canyon in 1963. The dam was built to store water for

portions of Colorado, New Mexico, Utah, and Wyoming, and also to provide hydroelectric power. Water flow management has caused severe ecological damage to Colorado River habitats in Glen Canyon National Recreation Area and Grand Canyon National Park. This includes large-scale erosion, including the loss of sandy beaches, invasion by non-native species, and the extinction of four species of native fish. Another native species, the humpback chub, is currently in serious decline, partly because of the purposeful introduction of predatory rainbow trout. The humpback chub has been listed as endangered since 1967 and has declined by 75 percent in the last 10 years alone.

As adaptive management is dependent on experimentation and manipulation, it can sometimes lead to unintended and unfortunate consequences. For example, an early effort at restoring Colorado River habitats involved sending huge amounts of water down the river. This was expected to lift sand from the river bottom, and did. However, the sand was quickly lost again to fluctuating river flows. Attention is now turning to the Paria River, which supplies the Colorado River with sand. The Paria feeds into the Colorado downstream of the Glen Canyon Dam, and it is hoped that a large pulse of floodwater from the dam following natural mon-

TABLE 2.11

Threatened and endangered animal species found on the National Wildlife Refuge System

Amphibians
- Frog, California Red-legged
- Salamander, Cheat Mountain
- Salamander, Santa Cruz long-toed
- Toad, Arroyo
- Toad, Wyoming

Birds
- Akepa, Hawaii
- Akiapolaau
- Albatross, short-tailed
- Blackbird, yellow-shouldered
- Bobwhite, masked (quail)
- Broadbill, Guam
- Caracara, Audubon's crested
- Condor, California
- Coot, Hawaiian
- Crane, Mississippi sandhill
- Crane, whooping
- Creeper, Hawaii
- Crow, Mariana
- Curlew, Eskimo
- Duck, Hawaiian
- Duck, Laysan
- Eider, spectacled
- Eider, Stellar's
- Falcon, northern aplomado
- Finch, Laysan
- Finch, Nihoa
- Flycatcher, southwestern willow
- Gnatcatcher, coastal California
- Goose, Hawaiian (=nene)
- Hawk, Hawaiian
- Jay, Florida scrub
- Kingfisher, Guam Micronesian
- Kite, Everglade snail
- Millerbird, Nihoa
- Moorhen (=gallinule), Hawaiian common
- Moorhen, Mariana common
- Murrelet, marbled
- 'O'u (honeycreeper)
- Owl, northern spotted
- Pelican, brown
- Plover, piping
- Plover, western snowy (Pacific coastal)
- Prairie-chicken, Attwater's greater
- Pygmy-owl, cactus ferruginous
- Rail, California clapper
- Rail, light-footed clapper
- Rail, Yuma clapper

Birds (continued)
- Stilt, Hawaiian
- Stork, wood
- Swiftlet, Vanikoro
- Tern, California least
- Tern, least (interior)
- Tern, roseate
- Vireo, black-capped
- Vireo, least Bell's
- Warbler, Bachman's
- Warbler, golden-cheeked
- Warbler, Kirtland's
- White-eye, bridled
- Woodpecker, red-cockaded

Clams
- Clubshell
- Fanshell
- Mussel, ring pink (=golf stick pearly)
- Mussel, winged mapleleaf
- Pearlymussel, Higgin's eye
- Pearlymussel, orange-footed pimple back
- Pearlymussel, pink mucket
- Pigtoe, rough
- Pocketbook, Fat
- Riffleshell, northern

Crustaceans
- Cambarus aculabrum (crayfish with no common name)
- Fairy shrimp, Riverside
- Fairy shrimp, San Diego
- Tadpole shrimp, vernal pool

Fishes
- Catfish, Yaqui
- Cavefish, Alabama
- Cavefish, Ozark
- Chub, bonytail
- Chub, humpback
- Chub, Oregon
- Chub, Yaqui
- Dace, Ash Meadows speckled
- Dace, Moapa
- Darter, watercress
- Gambusia, Pecos
- Madtom, Neosho
- Madtom, Pygmy
- Minnow, Rio Grande Silvery
- Poolfish (=killifish), Pahrump

Fishes (continued)
- Pupfish, Ash Meadows amargosa
- Pupfish, Devils Hole
- Pupfish, Warm Springs
- Salmon, chinook
- Shiner, beautiful
- Shiner, Pecos bluntnose
- Shiner, Topeka
- Squawfish, Colorado
- Sturgeon, Gulf
- Sturgeon, pallid
- Sturgeon, shortnose
- Sturgeon, white, Kootenai River pop.
- Sucker, Lost River
- Sucker, razorback
- Sucker, short-nose
- Topminnow, Gila (incl. Yaqui)

Insects
- Beetle, American burying
- Beetle, Valley elderberry longhorn
- Butterfly, Karner blue
- Butterfly, Lange's metalmark
- Butterfly, Quino checkerspot
- Butterfly, Schaus swallowtail
- Butterfly, Smith's blue
- Dragonfly, Hine's emerald
- Naucorid, Ash Meadows

Mammals
- Bat, gray
- Bat, Hawaiian hoary
- Bat, Indiana
- Bat, lesser (=Sanborn's) long-nosed
- Bat, little Mariana fruit
- Bat, Mariana fruit
- Bat, Ozark big-eared
- Bear, grizzly
- Bear, Louisiana black
- Deer, Columbian white-tailed
- Deer, Key
- Ferret, Black-footed
- Fox, San Joaquin kit
- Jaguar
- Jaguarundi
- Manatee, West Indian (Florida)
- Mouse, Alabama beach
- Mouse, Key Largo cotton
- Mouse, salt marsh harvest
- Mouse, southeastern beach

Mammals (continued)
- Ocelot
- Panther, Florida
- Pronghorn, Sonoran
- Puma, eastern
- Rabbit, Lower Keys
- Rat, rice (=silver rice)
- Rat, Tipton kangaroo
- Sea-lion, Steller (=northern)
- Seal, Hawaiian monk
- Squirrel, Delmarva Peninsula fox
- Squirrel, Virginia northern flying
- Whale, blue
- Whale, bowhead
- Whale, finback
- Whale, gray
- Whale, humpback
- Whale, right
- Whale, sei
- Whale, sperm
- Wolf, gray
- Wolf, Mexican
- Wolf, red
- Woodrat, Key Largo

Reptiles
- Anole, Culebra Island giant
- Crocodile, American
- Lizard, blunt-nosed leopard
- Lizard, Coachella Valley fringe-toed
- Lizard, St. Croix ground
- Skink, blue-tailed mole
- Skink, sand
- Snake, Atlantic salt marsh
- Snake, eastern indigo
- Snake, giant garter
- Snake, northern copperbelly water
- Tortoise, desert
- Tortoise, gopher
- Turtle, green sea
- Turtle, hawksbill sea
- Turtle, Kemp's (=Atlantic) ridley sea
- Turtle, leatherback sea
- Turtle, loggerhead sea
- Turtle, Plymouth redbelly
- Turtle, ringed map (= sawback)

Snails
- Snail, Iowa Pleistocence
- Snail, Stock Island tree

SOURCE: "Threatened and Endangered Animal Species Found on the National Wildlife Refuge System," U.S. Fish and Wildlife Service, National Wildlife Refuge System, Washington, DC [Online] http://refuges.fws.gov/wildlife/EndSpAnimals.html [accessed May 14, 2002]

soon storms will carry sand to new beaches along the Colorado. Another plan being contemplated is the running of high fluctuating flows of water through the Grand Canyon for three months—it is hoped that this would reduce rainbow trout numbers by killing eggs. Native fish species tend to inhabit side channels, and are less likely to be affected. There are also plans in place to try to warm water released from the dam, which the Fish and Wildlife Service believes would aid endangered native fish species.

INTERNATIONAL EFFORTS

The United Nations Environment Programme (UNEP) was established to address diverse environmental issues on an international level. Many of its conventions have been extremely valuable in protecting global biodiversity and natural resources. UNEP has also helped to regulate pollution and the use of toxic chemicals.

Convention on Biological Diversity

The United Nations Convention on Biological Diversity was set up to conserve biodiversity and to promote the sustainable use of biodiversity. The Convention supports national efforts in the documentation and monitoring of biodiversity, the establishment of refuges and other protected areas, and the restoration of degraded ecosystems. It also supports goals related to the maintenance of

TABLE 2.12

Threatened and endangered plant species found on the National Wildlife Refuge System

- *Aconitum noveboracense* - Northern Wild Monkshood
- *Aeschynomene virginica* - Sensitive Joint-vetch
- *Agalinis acuta* - Sandplain Gerardia
- *Amaranthus brownii* - Brown's Pigweed
- *Amaranthus pumilus* - Seabeach Amaranth
- *Apios priceana* - Price's Potato-bean
- *Aristida chasae* - no common name
- *Asclepias meadii* - Mead's Milkweed
- *Asimina tetramera* - Four-petal Pawpaw
- *Asplenium scolopendrium* var. *americana* - American Hart's-tongue Fern
- *Astragalus phoenix* - Ash Meadows Milk-vetch
- *Boltonia decurrens* - Decurrent False Aster
- *Bonamia grandiflora* - Florida Bonamia
- *Centaurium namophilum* - Spring-loving Centaury
- *Cereus eriophorus* var. *fragrans* - Fragrant Prickly-apple
- *Cereus robinii* - Key tree-cactus
- *Chamaesyce garberi* (=*Euphorbia garberi*) Garber's Spurge
- *Chionanthus pygmaeus* - Pygmy Fringe-tree
- *Chorizante pungens* var *pungens* - Monterey Spineflower
- *Cirsium pitcheri* - Pitcher's Thistle
- *Clermontia pyrularia* - 'oha wai
- *Clitoria fragrans* - Pigeon Wings
- *Cordylanthus maritimus* ssp. *maritimus* - Salt Marsh Bird's-beak
- *Cordylanthus palmatus* - Palmate-bracted Bird's-beak
- *Coryphantha sneedii* var. *robustispina* - Pima Pineapple Cactus
- *Coryphantha sneedii* var. *sneedii* - Sneed Pincushion Cactus
- *Cyanea schipmanii* - haha
- *Dicerandra christmaii* - Garett's Mint
- *Echinocereus fendleri* var. *kuenzleri* - Kuenzler Hedgehog Cactus
- *Enceliopsis nudicaulis* var. *corrugata* - Ash Meadows Sunray
- *Eriogonum longifolium* var. *gnaphalifolium* - Scrub Buckwheat
- *Eryngium aristulatum* var. *parishii* - San Diego Button-celery
- *Erysimum capitatum* var. *angustatum* - Contra Costa Wallflower
- *Eugenia woodburyana* - no common name
- *Frankenia johnstonii* - Johnston's frankenia
- *Grindelia fraxino-pratensis* - Ash Meadows Gumplant
- *Harrisia portorricensis* - Higo Chumbo
- *Helonias bullata* - Swamp Pink
- *Howellia aquatilus* - Water Howellia

- *Hymenoxys aculis* var. *glabra* - Lakeside Daisy
- *Iris lacustris* - Dwarf Lake Iris
- *Ivesia kingii* var. *eremica* - Ash Meadows Ivesia
- *Lespedeza leptosyachya* - Prairie Bush-clover
- *Liatris ohlingerae* - Scrub Blazingstar
- *Lilaeopsis schaffneriana* var. *recurva* - Huachuca Water Umbel
- *Lomatium bradshawii* - Bradshaw's Desert-parsley
- *Manihot walkerae* - Walker's Manioc
- *Mariscus pennatiformis* ssp. *bryanii* - no common name
- *Mentzelia leucophylla* - Ash Meadows Blazing-star
- *Nitrophila mohavensis* - Amargosa Niterwort
- *Oenothera deltoides* - ssp. *howellii* - Antioch Dunes Evening-primose
- *Orcuttia californica* - California Orcutt Grass
- *Oxypolis canbyi*- Canby's Dropwort
- *Oxytropis campestris* var. *chartacea* - Fassett's locoweed
- *Paronychia chartacea* (=*Nyachia pulvinata*) - Papery whitlow-wort
- *Penstemon haydenii* - Blowout penstemon
- *Peperomia wheeleri*- Wheeler's Peperomia
- *Phyllostegia racemosa* - kiponapona
- *Platanthera leucophaea* - Eastern prairie fringed orchid
- *Platanthera praeclara* - Western Prairie Fringed Orchid
- *Pogogyne abramsii* - San Diego Mesa Mint
- *Pogogyne nudiuscula* - Otay Mesa Mint
- *Polygonella basiramia* (=*P. ciliata* var. *b.*) - Wireweed
- *Polystichum aleuticum* - Aleutian Shield-fern
- *Pritchardia remota* - Loulu
- *Prunus geniculata* - Scrub Plum
- *Sarracenia oreophila* - Green Pitcher-plant
- *Schiedea verticillata* - Whorled Schiedea
- *Schwalbea americana* - American Chaffseed
- *Sclerocactus glaucus* - Unita Basin Hookless Cactus
- *Sedum integrifolium leedyi* - Leedy's Roseroot
- *Serianthes nelsonii* - Hayun Lagu
- *Sesbania tomentosa* - 'ohai
- *Sidalcea nelsoniana* - Nelson's Checker-mallow
- *Stahlia monosperma* - Cobana Negra
- *Thymophylla tephroleuca* - Ashy Dogweed
- *Trifolium stoloniferum* - Running Buffalo Clover

SOURCE: "Threatened and Endangered Plant Species Found on the National Wildlife Refuge System," U.S. Fish and Wildlife Service, National Wildlife Refuge System, Washington, DC [Online] http://refuges.fws.gov/plants/EndSpPlants.html [accessed May 14, 2002]

traditional knowledge of sustainable resource use, the prevention of invasive species introductions, and the control of invasive species that are already present. Finally, it funds education programs promoting public awareness of the value of natural resources.

CITES

The Convention on International Trade in Endangered Species of Wild Fauna and Flora (CITES) is an international agreement administered under UNEP which regulates international trade in wildlife. CITES is perhaps the single most important international agreement relating to endangered species and has contributed critically to the protection of many threatened species. The international wildlife trade is estimated to involve hundreds of millions of specimens annually.

CITES was first drafted in 1963 at a meeting of the IUCN, and went into effect in 1975. As of 2002, CITES safeguards approximately 5,000 animal species and 25,000 plant species worldwide. These are listed in three separate

CITES appendices depending on degree of endangerment. Appendix I includes species that are in immediate danger of extinction. CITES generally prohibits international trade of these species. Appendix II lists species that are likely to become in danger of extinction without strict protection from international trade. Permits may be obtained for the trade of Appendix II species only if trade will not harm the survival prospects of the species in the wild. Appendix III lists species whose trade is regulated in one or more nations. Any member nation can list a species in Appendix III to request international cooperation in order to prevent unsustainable levels of international trade. Nations agree to abide by CITES rules voluntarily. Over 150 nations are currently party to the agreement.

Convention on Migratory Species of Wild Animals

The Convention on Migratory Species of Wild Animals (CMS) recognizes that certain migratory species cross national boundaries and require protection throughout their range. This convention aims to "conserve terrestrial, marine, and avian migratory species throughout their

TABLE 2.13

Wilderness areas in national wildlife refuges and national fish hatcheries, September 30, 1997

Wilderness Area: Service land designated by Congress to be managed as a unit of the National Wilderness Preservation System, in accordance with the terms of the Wilderness Act of 1964. All Service Wilderness Areas occur within National Wildlife Refuges, with the exception of the Mount Massive Wilderness Area which is located at the Leadville National Fish Hatchery.

State and unit	Wilderness name	Wilderness acres	Refuge acres	Public law Number	Public law Date
Alaska					
Alaska Maritime	Aleutian Islands	1,300,000.00	3,435,639.77	96-487	12-02-80
Alaska Maritime	Bering Sea	81,340.00	0	91-504	10-23-70
Alaska Maritime	Bogoslof	175	0	91-504	10-23-70
Alaska Maritime	Chamisso	455	0	93-632	01-03-75
Alaska Maritime	Forrester Island	2,832.00 0.00	0	91-504	10-23-70
Alaska Maritime	Hazy Island	32	0	91-504	10-23-70
Alaska Maritime	Semidi	250,000.00	0	96-487	12-02-80
Alaska Maritime	Simeonof	25,855.00	0	94-557	10-19-76
Alaska Maritime	St. Lazaria	65	0	91-504	10-23-70
Alaska Maritime	Tuxedni	5,566.00	0	91-504	10-23-70
Alaska Maritime	Unimak	910,000.00	0	96-487	12-02-80
Arctic	Mollie Beattie	8,000,000.00	19,575,711.36	96-487	12-02-80
Becharof	Becharof	400,000.00	1,200,017.75	96-487	12-02-80
Innoko	Innoko	1,240,000.00	3,850,000.19	96-487	12-02-80
Izembek	Izembek	300,000.00	303,094.00	96-487	12-02-80
Kenai	Kenai	1,350,000.00	1,906,214.22	96-487	12-02-80
Koyukuk	Koyukuk	400,000.00	3,550,000.01	96-487	12-02-80
Selawik	Selawik	240,000.00	2,150,002.01	96-487	12-02-80
Togiak	Togiak	2,270,000.00	4,097,431.02	96-487	12-02-80
Yukon Delta	Andreafsky	1,300,000.00	19,131,645.67	96-487	12-02-80
Yukon Delta	Nunivak	600,000.00	0	96-487	12-02-80
State Total		**18,676,320.00**	**59,199,916.00**		
Arizona					
Cabreza Prieta	Cabreza Prieta	803,418.00	860,041.32	101-628	11-28-90
Havasu	Havasu	14,606.00	30,279.82	101-628	11-28-90
Imperial	Imperial	9,220.00	17,809.76	101-628	11-28-90
Kofa	Kofa	516,200.00	666,480.00	101-628	11-28-90
State Total		**1,343,444.00**	**1,574,610.90**		
Arkansas					
Big Lake	Big Lake	2,143.80	11,036.10	94-557	10-19-76
State Total		**2,143.80**	**11,036.10**		
California					
Farallon	Farallon	141	211.00	93-550	12-26-74
Havasu	Havasu	3,195.00	7,235.34	103-433	10-31-94
Imperial	Imperial	5,836.00	7,958.19	103-433	10-31-94
State Total		**9,172.00**	**15,404.53**		
Colorado					
Leadville	Mount Massive	2,560.00	3,065.88	96-560	12-22-80
State Total		**2,560.00**	**3,065.88**		
Florida					
Cedar Keys	Cedar Keys		379 832.15	92-364	08-07-72
Chassahowitzka	Chassahowitzka	23,578.93	30,842.91	94-557	10-19-76
Great White Heron	Florida Keys	1,900.00	192,493.53	93-632	01-03-75
Island Bay	Island Bay	20.24	20.24	91-504	10-23-70
J.N. Ding Darling	J.N. Ding Darling	2,619.13	6,310.24	94-557	10-19-76
Key West	Florida Keys	2,019.00	208,308.17	93-632	01-03-75
Lake Woodruff	Lake Woodruff	1,066.00	21,559.02	94-557	10-19-76
National Key Deer	Florida Keys (1)	2,278.00	8,542.01	93-632	01-03-75
National Key Deer	Florida Keys (2)	0	0	97-211	06-30-82
Passage Key	Passage Key	36.37	63.87	91-504	10-23-70
Pelican Island	Pelican Island	5.5	4,763.61	91-504	10-23-70
St. Marks	St. Marks	17,350.00	66,536.05	93-632	01-03-75
State Total		**51,252.17**	**537,271.80**		
Georgia					
Blackbeard Island	Blackbeard Island	3,000.00	5,617.64	93-632	10-23-70
Okefenokee	Okefenokee	353,981.00	391,401.99	93-429	10-01-74
Wolf Island	Wolf Island	5,125.82	5,125.82	93-632	01-03-75
State Total		**362,106.82**	**402,145.45**		
Illinois					
Crab Orchard	Crab Orchard	4,050.00	43,661.74	94-557	10-19-76
State Total		**4,050.00**	**43,661.74**		

TABLE 2.13

Wilderness areas in national wildlife refuges and national fish hatcheries, September 30, 1997 [CONTINUED]

State and unit	Wilderness name	Wilderness acres	Refuge acres	Public law Number	Public law Date
Louisiana					
Breton	Breton	5,000.00	9,047.00	93-632	01-01-75
Lacassine	Lacassine	3,345.60	34,378.77	94-557	10-19-76
State Total		**8,345.60**	**43,425.77**		
Maine					
Moosehorn	Baring Unit	4,680.00	24,519.04	93-632	01-03-75
Moosehorn	Birch Islands Unit	6	0	91-504	10-23-70
Moosehorn	Edmunds Unit	2,706.00	0	91-504	10-23-70
State Total		**7,392.00**	**24,519.04**		
Massachusetts					
Monomoy	Monomoy	2,420.00	2,701.85	91-504	10-23-70
State Total		**2,420.00**	**2,701.85**		
Michigan					
Huron	Huron Islands	147.5	147.5	91-504	10-23-70
Michigan Islands	Michigan Islands	2	374.59	91-504	10-23-70
Seney	Seney	25,150.00	95,205.56	91-504	10-23-70
State Total		**25,309.50**	**95,727.65**		
Minnesota					
Agassiz	Agassiz	4,000.00	61,500.93	94-557	10-19-76
Tamarac	Tamarac	2,180.00	35,191.38	94-557	10-19-76
State Total		**6,180.00**	**96,692.31**		
Missouri					
Mingo	Mingo	7,730.00	21,745.64	94-557	10-19-76
State Total		**7,730.00**	**21,745.64**		
Montana					
Medicine Lake	Medicine Lake	11,366.00	31,484.01	94-557	10-19-76
Red Rock Lakes	Red Rock Lakes	32,350.00	45,597.71	94-557	10-19-76
UI Bend UI Bend (1)		20,819.00	56,049.56	94-557	10-19-76
UI Bend UI Bend (2)		0	0	98-140	10-31-83
State Total		**64,535.00**	**133,131.28**		
Nebraska					
Fort Niobrara	Fort Niobrara	4,635.00	19,132.53	94-557	10-19-76
State Total		**4,635.00**	**19,132.53**		
New Jersey					
Edwin B. Forsythe	Brigantine	6,681.00	43,079.95	93-632	01-03-75
Great Swamp	Great Swamp	3,660.00	7,415.14	90-532	09-28-68
State Total		**10,341.00**	**50,495.09**		
New Mexico					
Bitter Lake	Salt Creek	9,621.00	24,542.49	91-504	10-23-70
Bosque Del Apache	Chupadea Unit	5,289.00	57,191.10	93-632	01-03-75
Bosque Del Apache	Indian Well Unit	5,139.00	0	93-632	01-03-75
Bosque Del Apache	Little San Pascual Unit	19,859.00	0	93-632	01-03-75
State Total		**39,908.00**	**81,733.59**		
North Carolina					
Swanquarter	Swanquarter	8,784.93	16,411.11	94-557	10-19-76
State Total		**8,784.93**	**16,411.11**		
North Dakota					
Chase Lake	Chase Lake	4,155.00	4,384.65	93-632	01-03-75
Lostwood	Lostwood	5,577.00	26,903.99	96-632	01-03-75
State Total		**9,732.00**	**31,288.64**		
Ohio					
West Sister Island	West Sister Island	77 80.13		93-632	01-03-75
State Total		**77 80.13**			
Oklahoma					
Wichita Mountains	Charons Garden Unit	5,723.00	59,019.60	91-504	10-23-70
Wichita Mountains	North Mountain Unit	2,847.00	0	91-504	10-23-70
State Total		**8,570.00**	**59,019.60**		

TABLE 2.13

Wilderness areas in national wildlife refuges and national fish hatcheries, September 30, 1997 [CONTINUED]

State and unit	Wilderness name	Wilderness acres	Refuge acres	Public law Number	Public law Date
Oregon					
Oregon Islands	Oregon Islands (1)	21	963.35	91-504	10-23-70
Oregon Islands	Oregon Islands (2)	459	0	5-450	10-11-78
Three Arch Rocks	Three Arch Rocks	15	15	91-504	10-23-70
State Total		**495**	**978.35**		
South Carolina					
Cape Romain	Cape Romain	29,000.00	65,224.94	93-632	01-03-75
State Total		**29,000.00**	**65,224.94**		
Washington					
Copalis	Washington Islands	60.8	60.80	91-504	10-23-70
Flattery Rocks	Washington Islands	125	25.00	91-504	10-23-70
Quillayute Needles	Washington Islands	300.2	300.20	91-504	10-23-70
San Juan Islands	San Juan Islands	353	448.53	94-557	10-19-76
State Total		**839**	**934.53**		
Wisconsin					
Gravel Island	Wisconsin Islands	27	27.00	91-504	10-23-70
Green Bay	Wisconsin Islands	2	2.00	91-504	10-23-70
State Total		**29**	**29.00**		
Grand Total		**20,685,371.82**	**62,533,385.35**		

SOURCE: "Wilderness Areas in National Wildlife Refuges and National Fish Hatcheries," in *National Wildlife Refuge System,* U.S. Fish and Wildlife Service, Washington, DC, 2002 [Online] http://realty.fws.gov/table10.html [accessed May 4, 2002]

range." CMS went into effect in 1983. As of February 2002, 79 nations were involved in the agreement. These include countries in Africa, Central and South America, Asia, Europe, and Oceania. The United States and several other nations are not official parties in the agreement but nonetheless abide by its rules. In 2002 CMS rules covered 85 species, all of which are listed under CITES Appendix I and Appendix II. Some groups that have received particular attention include European bats, Mediterranean and Black Sea cetaceans, Baltic and North Sea cetaceans, Wadden Sea seals, African-Eurasian migratory water birds, and marine turtles. Some of the most endangered species offered protection under CMS include the Siberian crane, the white-tailed eagle, the hawksbill turtle, the Mediterranean monk seal, and the Dama gazelle.

Protected Areas

The IUCN's Commission on National Parks and Protected Areas (CNPPA) is the leading international body dedicated to the selection, establishment, and management of national parks and protected areas. It has helped set up many natural areas around the world for the protection of plant and animal species, and also maintains a database of protected areas. Protected areas often consist of a core zone where wildlife cannot legally be disturbed by human beings. Around the core are "buffer zones," transitional spaces that act as shields for the core zone. On the periphery are areas for managed human living. In 1998 there were 30,000 protected areas worldwide covering 13.2 million square kilometers of land, freshwater

habitat, and ocean. The terrestrial portion of the network, which is by far the largest, accounted for 11.7 million square kilometers—nearly 8 percent of the world's land area. A protected area is defined as "an area of land and/or sea especially dedicated to the protection and maintenance of biological diversity, and of natural and associated cultural resources, and managed through legal or other effective means."

Conservation biology theory advocates that protected areas should be as large as possible in order to increase biological diversity and to buffer refuges from outside pressures. The world's largest protected areas are Greenland National Park (Greenland), Ar-Rub'al-khali Wildlife Management Area (Saudi Arabia), Great Barrier Reef Marine Park (Australia), Qiang Tang Nature Reserve (China), Cape Churchill Wildlife Management Area (Canada), and the Northern Wildlife Management Zone (Saudi Arabia).

ZOOS

Although some animal lovers object to caging wild species and keeping them in unnatural enclosures, zoos play one absolutely critical role—fostering interest in animal species, biodiversity, and conservation (Figure 2.15). The majority of zoo animals are not collected from the wild but bred in captivity. For example, among U.S. zoos, 90 percent of mammals and 74 percent of birds added to zoo collections since 1985 were born in captivity. Zoos have also contributed significantly to the survival of some highly endangered species through captive breeding efforts.

Captive Breeding

Many captive breeding efforts take place at zoos. Captive breeding has increased the number of many endangered species, and in several cases, saved them from certain extinction. Captive breeding has helped increase population sizes of species such as the California condor and the black-footed ferret. Both these species have thrived in captive breeding efforts, making reintroductions into wild habitat possible. Captive breeding offers the greatest hope for survival of additional species as well, including the highly endangered Florida panther. Although some species are notoriously difficult to breed in captivity, including the giant panda, many species have been bred in captivity, including over 3,000 species of vertebrates—some 19 percent of mammal species and 10 percent of bird species. A small selection of the many ongoing captive breeding efforts and the institutions leading the efforts include: the giant panda (San Diego Zoo), Guam rail (Lincoln Park Zoological Gardens), white rhinoceros (Fort Worth Zoological Park), Mexican gray wolf (Arizona-Sonora Desert Museum), wattled crane (Franklin Park Zoo), and the Chinese alligator (Bronx Zoo). Species Survival Plans for captive breeding programs are organized by the American Zoo and Aquarium Association (AZA).

Captive breeding is not without its critics, however. These critics charge that it is costly, and that funds used to support captive breeding programs would be better used

FIGURE 2.12

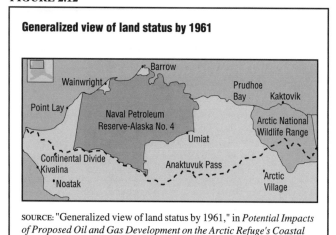

Generalized view of land status by 1961

SOURCE: "Generalized view of land status by 1961," in *Potential Impacts of Proposed Oil and Gas Development on the Arctic Refuge's Coastal Plain: Historical Overview and Issues of Concern,* U.S. Fish and Wildlife Service, Fairbanks, AK, January 17, 2001

FIGURE 2.13

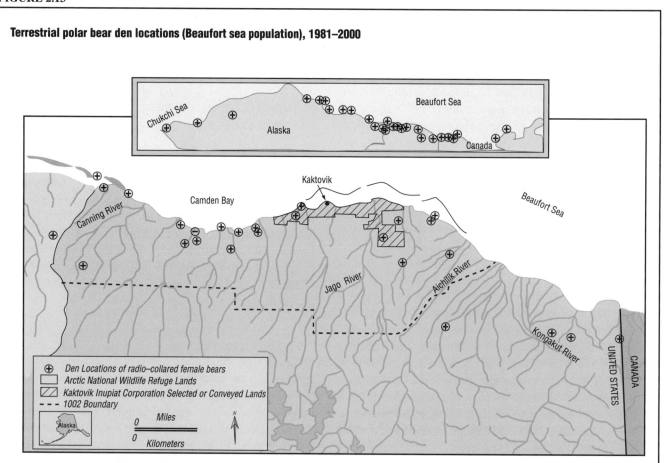

Terrestrial polar bear den locations (Beaufort sea population), 1981–2000

SOURCE: "Terrestrial Polar Bear Den Locations (Beaufort Sea Population) 1981–2000," in *Potential Impacts of Proposed Oil and Gas Development on the Arctic Refuge's Coastal Plain: Historical Overview and Issues of Concern,* U.S. Fish and Wildlife Service, Fairbanks, AK, Januray 17, 2001 [Online] http://arctic.fws.gov/issues1.html [Accessed June 5, 2002]

FIGURE 2.14

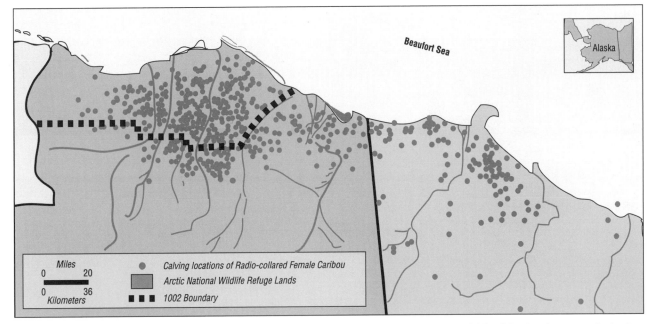

Calving locations of radio-collared female caribou during 1983–99

SOURCE: "Calving locations of radio-collared female caribou during 1983–99," in *Potential Impacts of Proposed Oil and Gas Development on the Arctic Refuge's Coastal Plain: Historical Overview and Issues of Concern*, U.S. Fish and Wildlife Service, Fairbanks, AK, January 17, 2001

to conserve natural habitats. Critics also charge that captive breeding is able to focus only on a few charismatic species, and that it often gives the false impression that the battle against extinction is being won.

A New Role For Zoos

At one time, zoos kept animals tightly caged and in conditions that were unnatural and unhealthy. Today, however, many zoos have been redesigned to house animals in areas more similar to their natural habitats. For many people, a zoo is the only place to see wildlife, including endangered species. Many zoos have developed public education programs tying zoo exhibits to natural ecology. Some zoos have also evolved from being "menageries" for the pleasure of humans to living museums and ecological conservation centers for species.

Zoos and aquariums also constitute an extraordinary base of data for field conservation operations. The aim is to apply expertise on animal health, nutrition, handling, and reproduction to the needs of animals in the wild. The Bronx Zoo in New York is pioneering new efforts to extend its expertise into field study. With habitats for large animals becoming increasingly degraded, Bronx Zoo veterinarians are closely monitoring animal health in the field. Zoo resources are also being directed towards con-

FIGURE 2.15

The Hippoquarium at the Toledo Zoo in Ohio. Zoos foster interest in biodiversity and conservation. Many zoos now also play an active role in the captive breeding of endangered species. *(Greater Toledo Convention and Visitors Bureau)*

servation. Bronx-based conservationists are working with national governments, local politicians, and international aid agencies to develop measures to preserve habitat and protect wildlife. One particular goal is to transfer technology and expertise to developing countries so that they can develop their own conservation efforts.

CHAPTER 3
GLOBAL CLIMATE CHANGE

Although large changes in climate are a natural part of Earth history, there is little doubt that human activities have caused observed patterns of global warming in the twentieth and twenty-first centuries. Global climate change has large implications for both humans and wildlife. Many threatened and endangered species, which already lead a precarious existence, are likely to suffer further declines. Global warming also threatens populations of species that were once relatively secure, and is likely to result in the endangerment of more species in the future.

CLIMATE CHANGE IN EARTH HISTORY

Over hundreds of millions of years geological and astronomical forces have changed Earth's environment from hot to cold, wet to dry, and back again. Studies have shown that the climate has fluctuated between long periods of cold lasting 50,000 to 80,000 years and shorter periods of warmth lasting about 10,000 years. The Earth is in the midst of one of those warm periods now. These climate cycles are caused by tiny irregularities (known as Milankovitch Cycles) in the Earth's orbit around the sun. The climate of the past 10,000 years, during which human civilization developed, is a mere blip in a much larger history of climate change. However, human influences on the climate are significant, and effects are already being seen on species worldwide.

GLOBAL WARMING—THE RESULT OF HUMAN ACTIVITY

The Greenhouse Effect

Earth's climate is a delicate balance of energy input, chemical and biological processes, and physical phenomena. The Earth's atmosphere plays a critical role in planetary surface temperature. Some gases, such as carbon dioxide (CO_2) and methane (CH_4), absorb and maintain heat in the same way that glass traps heat in a greenhouse.

These greenhouse gases in Earth's atmosphere allow temperatures to build up, keeping the planet warm and habitable to the life forms that have evolved here. This phenomenon is called the greenhouse effect. Figure 3.1 shows how the greenhouse effect causes elevation of surface temperatures on Earth.

The "natural greenhouse effect" creates a climate in which life can exist. It maintains the mean temperature of Earth's surface at about 33 degrees warmer than if natural greenhouse gases were not present. Without this process, Earth would be frigid and uninhabitable. However, an

FIGURE 3.1

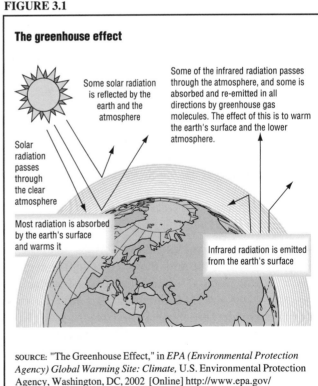

The greenhouse effect

Some solar radiation is reflected by the earth and the atmosphere

Some of the infrared radiation passes through the atmosphere, and some is absorbed and re-emitted in all directions by greenhouse gas molecules. The effect of this is to warm the earth's surface and the lower atmosphere.

Solar radiation passes through the clear atmosphere

Most radiation is absorbed by the earth's surface and warms it

Infrared radiation is emitted from the earth's surface

SOURCE: "The Greenhouse Effect," in *EPA (Environmental Protection Agency) Global Warming Site: Climate*, U.S. Environmental Protection Agency, Washington, DC, 2002 [Online] http://www.epa.gov/globalwarming/climate/index.html [accessed May 16, 2002]

FIGURE 3.2

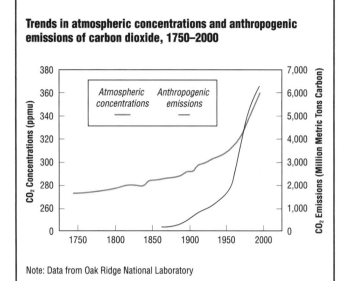

Trends in atmospheric concentrations and anthropogenic emissions of carbon dioxide, 1750–2000

Note: Data from Oak Ridge National Laboratory

SOURCE: "Figure 1: Trends in Atmospheric Concentrations and Anthropogenic Emissions of Carbon Dioxide, 1750–2000" in *Greenhouse Gases, Global Climate Change, and Energy,* U.S. Department of Energy, Energy Information Administration, National Energy Information Center, Washington, DC, 2002. [Online] http://www.eia.doe.gov/oiaf/1605/ggccebro/chapter1.html [accessed May 16, 2002]

"enhanced greenhouse effect," sometimes called the "anthropogenic effect," refers to the increase in Earth's surface temperature due to human activity.

A Revolutionary Idea

Earth's atmosphere was compared to a glass vessel in 1827 by the French mathematician Jean-Baptiste Fourier. In the 1850s British physicist John Tyndall measured the heat-trapping properties of various components of the atmosphere. By the 1890s scientists had concluded that the great increase in combustion in the Industrial Revolution had the potential to change the atmosphere's load of carbon dioxide. In 1896 the Swedish chemist Svante Arrhenius made the revolutionary suggestion that the rapid increase in coal use during the Industrial Revolution could increase carbon dioxide concentrations and cause a gradual rise in temperatures. For almost six decades, his theory stirred little interest.

Then in 1957 studies at the Scripps Institute of Oceanography in California showed that, in fact, half the carbon dioxide released by industry remained permanently trapped in the atmosphere. Atmospheric concentrations of carbon dioxide were shown to have reached their highest level in 160,000 years. Figure 3.2 shows carbon dioxide emissions levels over time and the associated rise in atmospheric levels of carbon dioxide.

More recent studies have provided further evidence that levels of greenhouse gasses are increasing. Two other naturally-occurring greenhouse gases besides carbon dioxide show increased atmospheric concentrations due to human activity:

- Methane (CH_4). Its atmospheric concentration is now about 150 times higher than in the pre-industrial era. Some estimates indicate that methane's concentration in the atmosphere could double again during the next 100 years.

- Nitrous oxide (N_2O). This gas comes from fertilizers used in agriculture, combustion of fossil fuels and solid waste, and industrial processes. Scientists estimate that there is 16 percent more nitrous oxide in the atmosphere presently than there was in 1750.

Manmade greenhouse gases, particularly fluorinated compounds, have particularly high Global Warming Potentials (GWPs). They include:

- Chlorofluorocarbons (CFCs). The Montreal Protocol on Substances That Deplete the Ozone Layer phased out, with a few exceptions, the use of these popular aerosols, refrigerants, and solvents.

- Hydrochlorofluorocarbons (HCFCs). Designed as substitutes for the ozone-depleting CFCs, they have about one-fifth the stratospheric ozone depletion potential of CFCs and most of the same uses.

- Hydrofluorocarbons (HFCs). These low-cost and often energy-efficient compounds are used in insulation, air conditioning, refrigeration, fire suppression, and medical metered dose inhalers.

Most man-made gases are present in the atmosphere now at concentrations about 25 percent greater than 150 years ago. Figure 3.3 shows documented increases in the levels of a number of greenhouse gases. The data are derived from studies of ice cores obtained from Antarctica and Greenland. Ice gradually accumulates over millennia in these places, trapping tiny air bubbles that yield information on the atmospheric conditions of the time. Some of the ice cores examined required drilling to depths of thousands of feet.

Earth's Increasing Temperature

As of the year 2002, experts are almost certain that human-induced climate change is occurring due to increased levels of greenhouse gases. The Intergovernmental Panel on Climate Change (IPCC), sponsored jointly by the United Nations Environmental Programme (UNEP) and the World Meteorological Organization, was formed to study climate change and to advise policymakers worldwide. Evidence that global temperatures have been increasing come from sources as diverse as fossils, corals, ancient ice, and growth rings in trees. Figure 3.4, from an IPCC report published in 2001, shows global surface temperatures as measured by thermometers in the

FIGURE 3.3

Concentrations of carbon dioxide, methane, and nitrous oxide, years 1000–2000, and sulphate aerosols, 1600–2000

(a) Global atmospheric concentrations of three well mixed greenhouse gases

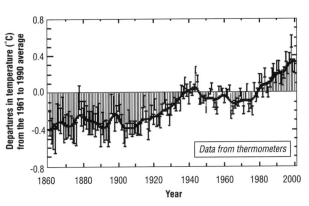

(b) Sulphate aerosols deposited in Greenland ice

SOURCE: "Figure 2: Long records of past changes in atmospheric composition provide the context for the influence of anthropogenic emissions," in *Summary for Policymakers: A Report of Working Group I of the Intergovernmental Panel on Climate Change*, Intergovernmental Panel on Climate Change, Geneva, Switzerland, 2001

FIGURE 3.4

Global variations of the Earth's surface temperature, 1860–2000

Note: The Earth's surface temperature is shown year by year (gray bars) and approximately decade by decade (black line, a filtered annual curve suppressing fluctuations below near decadal time-scales). There are uncertainties in the annual data (thin black whisker bars represent the 95% confidence range) due to data gaps, random instrumental errors and uncertainties, uncertainties in bias corrections in the ocean surface temperature data and also in adjustments for urbanisation over the land. Over both the last 140 years and 100 years, the best estimate is that the global average surface temperature has increased by 0.6 ± 0.2°C.

SOURCE: Adapted from "Figure 1: Variations of the Earth's surface temperature over the last 140 years and the last millennium," in *Summary for Policymakers: A Report of Working Group I of the Intergovernmental Panel on Climate Change*, Intergovernmental Panel on Climate Change, Geneva, Switzerland, 2001

mented in the twentieth century. These data are derived from tree rings, corals, ice cores, and historical temperature records. Climate models suggest that the Earth will warm another two to six degrees between 2000 and 2100. If this happens, it will be the warmest Earth has been for millions of years.

Greenhouse Gases

In addition to carbon dioxide, many other gases contribute to global warming. Figure 3.6 shows U.S. greenhouse gas emission by type of gas in the year 2000.

CARBON DIOXIDE. Carbon dioxide, a naturally occurring component of Earth's atmosphere, is generally considered the major cause of global warming. Carbon is an essential component of all living organisms. The carbon cycle, which shows the movement of carbon from organic to inorganic forms, is shown in Figure 3.7. Plants perform the essential function of taking carbon dioxide from the atmosphere and converting it to organic matter, a form that can be used by other living species.

The Energy Information Administration of the U.S. Department of Energy reported in 2000 that carbon dioxide accounted for approximately 81 percent of greenhouse gas emissions in the United States. The burning of fossil fuels by industry and motor vehicles is, by far, the leading

last 140 years. The bars show annual measured temperatures, while the black line shows how temperatures have changed decade by decade. The error bars indicate the range of uncertainty due to gaps in the data or random instrumental errors. A marked rise of approximately one degree has occurred during the 140-year time course. Figure 3.5 shows surface temperatures in the last thousand years. There are extremely striking increases docu-

FIGURE 3.5

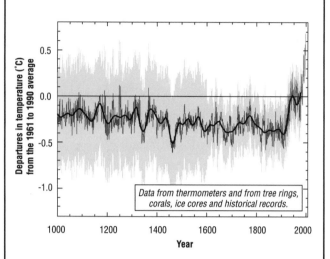

Northern hemisphere variations of the Earth's surface temperature, 1000–2000

Data from thermometers and from tree rings, corals, ice cores and historical records.

Note: The year by year (dark gray curve) and 50 year average (black curve) variations of the average surface temperature of the Northern Hemisphere for the past 1000 years have been reconstructed from "proxy" data calibrated against thermometer data (see list of the main proxy data in the diagram). The 95% confidence range in the annual data is represented by the light gray region. These uncertainties increase in more distant times and are always much larger than in the instrumental record due to the use of relatively sparse proxy data. Nevertheless the rate and duration of warming of the 20th century has been much greater than in any of the previous nine centuries. Similarly, it is likely that the 1990s have been the warmest decade and 1998 the warmest year of the millennium.

SOURCE: Adapted from "Figure 1: Variations of the Earth's surface temperature over the last 140 years and the last millennium," in *Summary for Policymakers: A Report of Working Group I of the Intergovernmental Panel on Climate Change,* Intergovernmental Panel on Climate Change, Geneva, Switzerland, 2001

FIGURE 3.6

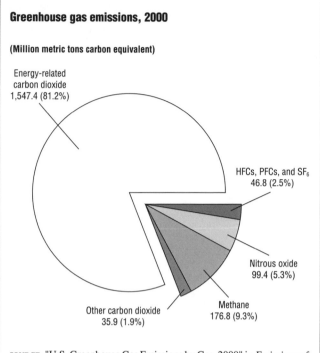

Greenhouse gas emissions, 2000

(Million metric tons carbon equivalent)

Energy-related carbon dioxide 1,547.4 (81.2%)

HFCs, PFCs, and SF$_6$ 46.8 (2.5%)

Nitrous oxide 99.4 (5.3%)

Methane 176.8 (9.3%)

Other carbon dioxide 35.9 (1.9%)

SOURCE: "U.S. Greenhouse Gas Emissions by Gas, 2000" in *Emissions of Greenhouse Gases in the United States 2000*, U.S. Department of Energy, Energy Information Administration, Washington, DC, 2000

source of carbon dioxide in the atmosphere, accounting for 99 percent of carbon dioxide emissions. (See Table 3.1 and Figure 3.8.) In 1998 fossil fuel combustion totaled almost 1.5 million metric tons of carbon equivalents (MMTCE), up from 1.3 MMTCE in 1990. As populations and economies expand, they use ever-greater amounts of fossil fuels. Consequently, most carbon dioxide emission comes from the developed world. Contributions from the developing world are expected to increase as these countries industrialize. (See Figure 3.9.) The United States, despite having only 5 percent of the world's population, accounts for 25 percent of the world's energy use, making it the most carbon-intensive country on Earth. Figure 3.10 documents the sources of energy in the United States—the bulk is derived from fossil fuels.

METHANE. Methane is second only to carbon dioxide in its effect on global warming. While there is less methane than carbon dioxide in the atmosphere, scientists estimate that it is as much as 21 times more effective at trapping heat in the atmosphere. Since the 1800s, the amount of methane in the atmosphere has

more than doubled. Scientists attribute this rise to human sources, including landfills, natural gas systems, agricultural activities, coal mining, and wastewater treatment. According to the Environmental Protection Agency (EPA), in 1998, methane emissions totaled almost 181 MMTCE, up from almost 178 MMTCE in 1990.

NITROUS OXIDE. Nitrous oxide is a greenhouse gas with natural biological sources as well as human sources. Although nitrous oxide makes up a much smaller portion of greenhouse gases than carbon dioxide, it is as much as 310 times more powerful than carbon dioxide at trapping heat.

CHLOROFLUOROCARBONS. Chlorofluorocarbons (CFCs), an important class of modern industrial chemicals, caused some of the anthropogenic greenhouse effect and global warming experienced during the 1980s. CFCs are also responsible for depletion of the ozone layer in the stratosphere, which has resulted in increased levels of damaging ultraviolet radiation on Earth. The United States is the leading producer of CFCs. Beginning in the 1970s the United States and some other nations banned the use of CFCs in aerosol sprays. In 1987 leaders of many world nations met in Montreal, Canada, and agreed to cut CFC output by 50 percent by the year 2000. In 1989, 82 nations signed the Helsinki Declaration, pledging to completely phase out five CFCs.

FIGURE 3.7

The carbon cycle

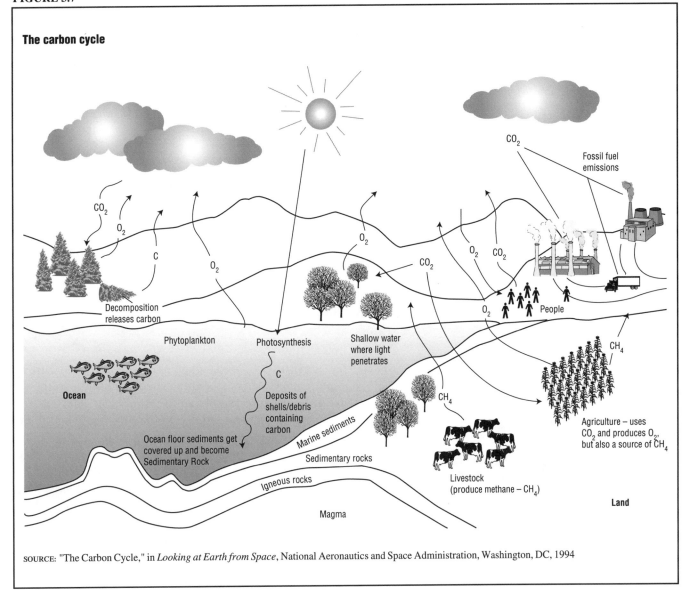

SOURCE: "The Carbon Cycle," in *Looking at Earth from Space*, National Aeronautics and Space Administration, Washington, DC, 1994

Forests and Oceans as Carbon Sinks

Because plants naturally take in carbon dioxide from the atmosphere for photosynthesis, large forests act as sinks, or repositories, for carbon. There has been some debate about whether forests are capable of soaking up the excess carbon dioxide emitted through human activity. Some scientists have also argued that the increasing levels of carbon dioxide in the atmosphere might be better tolerated if not for the additional complicating factor of global deforestation. (See Figure 3.11.)

Oceans may also have a profound effect on climate change, both because of their tremendous heat storage capability and because they affect levels of atmospheric gases. The ocean is by far the largest reservoir of carbon in the carbon cycle. It holds approximately 50 times more carbon than the atmosphere and 20 times more than the terrestrial reservoir. Ocean currents also transport stored heat, causing heating and cooling in different parts of the world. It is still unclear, however, what effects oceans may have on global warming.

Other Factors Affecting Global Climate

VOLCANOES. Volcanic activity, such as the 1991 eruption of Mount Pinatubo in the Philippines, can temporarily offset global warming trends. Volcanoes spew vast quantities of particles and gases into the atmosphere. Sulfur dioxide, a frequent product of eruptions, combines with water to form tiny super-cooled sulfuric acid droplets. These create a long-lasting global haze that reflects sunlight, reducing the amount of heat absorbed and cooling the planet. (See Figure 3.12.) The effects of the Mount Pinatubo cloud—the largest volcanic cloud of the twentieth century—was felt for years. It not only blocked a significant portion of the imping-ing sunlight, but also affected wind and weather

TABLE 3.1

Sources of carbon dioxide emissions and sinks, 1990–99

Source or sink	1990	1995	1996	1997	1998	1999
Fossil fuel combustion	4,835.7	5,121.3	5,303.0	5,374.9	5,386.8	5,453.1
Cement manufacture	33.3	36.8	37.1	38.3	39.2	39.9
Natural gas flaring	17.6	23.1	24.0	25.7	25.1	26.0
Lime manufacture	11.2	12.8	13.5	13.7	13.9	13.4
Waste combustion	5.1	13.6	13.0	12.0	10.8	11.7
Limestone and dolomite use	5.1	7.0	7.3	8.3	8.1	8.3
Soda ash manufacture and consumption	4.1	4.3	4.3	4.4	4.3	4.2
Carbon dioxide consumption	0.8	1.0	1.1	1.3	1.4	1.6
Land-use change and forestry (sink)[a]	(1,059.9)	(1,019.1)	(1,021.6)	(981.9)	(983.3)	(990.4)
International bunker fuels[b]	114.0	101.0	102.2	109.8	112.8	107.3
Total emissions	**4,913.0**	**5,219.8**	**5,403.2**	**5,478.7**	**5,489.7**	**5,558.1**
Net emissions						
(Sources and sinks)	3,853.0	4,200.8	4,381.6	4,496.8	4,506.4	4,567.8

[a] Sinks are only included in net emissions total, and are based on projected activity data.
[b] Emissions from International Bunker Fuels are not included in totals.
Note: Totals may not sum due to independent rounding.
Note: Parentheses indicate negative values (or sequestration).

SOURCE: "Table ES-12: U.S. Sources of CO₂ Emissions and Sinks (Tg CO₂ Eq.)," in *EPA Global Warming Site:National Emissions*, U.S. Environmental Protection Agency, Washington, DC, 2002 [Online] http://www.epa.gov/globalwarming/emissions/national/co2.html [accessed April 26, 2002]

FIGURE 3.8

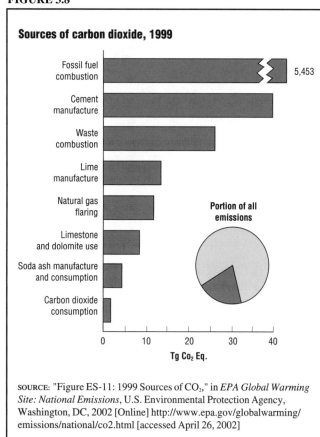

Sources of carbon dioxide, 1999

SOURCE: "Figure ES-11: 1999 Sources of CO₂," in *EPA Global Warming Site: National Emissions*, U.S. Environmental Protection Agency, Washington, DC, 2002 [Online] http://www.epa.gov/globalwarming/emissions/national/co2.html [accessed April 26, 2002]

CLOUDS. Clouds also contribute to global climate patterns. Clouds can either reflect sunlight, cooling the Earth, or cause the planet to retain heat. These differing effects depend largely on the brightness and thickness of the clouds in question. Marine stratocumulus clouds, which occur at low altitudes over the ocean, are known to reflect solar energy, resulting in a cooling of the Earth. (See Figure 3.13.) Other clouds, however, such as the cirrus clouds that occur at high altitudes, actually enhance global warming effects. A 2000 study at NASA's Goddard Institute for Space Studies reported that global warming results in the formation of thinner clouds that are less capable of reflecting sunlight.

SOLAR CYCLES. Finally, the sun is not a completely steady source of energy. It has seasons, storms, and characteristic patterns of activity. Sunspots and flares appear in cycles of roughly 11 years, and may well play a role in climate change on Earth. The sun is now approaching a stormy period in its 11-year cycle, promising a wealth of new data that will increase understanding of these phenomena.

EFFECTS OF A WARMING CLIMATE

In 1990 the Intergovernmental Panel on Climate Change noted several early signs of climate change in the Earth's colder habitats. The average warm-season temperature in Alaska had increased three degrees in 50 years. Glaciers had receded and thinned by 30 feet in 40 years. There was significantly less sea ice in the Bering Sea than in the 1950s. Permafrost had thawed, causing landslides, erosion, and local floods. Ice cellars in northern villages

patterns. Cooler summers and warmer winters, as well as an overall cooling effect, were observed for several years. Similarly, the explosion of the El Chichon volcano in Mexico in 1982 depressed global temperatures for about four years.

FIGURE 3.9

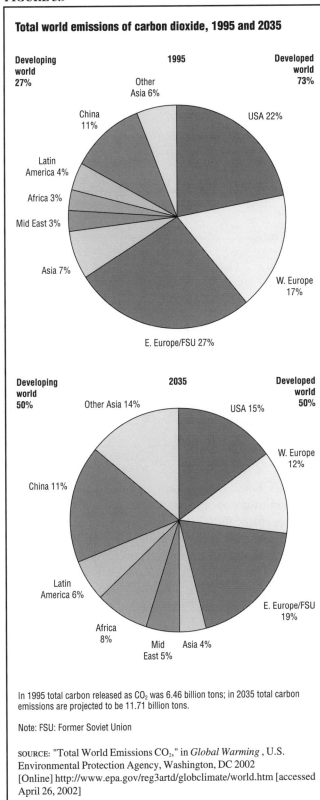

Total world emissions of carbon dioxide, 1995 and 2035

Developing world 27% **1995** **Developed world 73%**

Other Asia 6%
China 11%
USA 22%
Latin America 4%
Africa 3%
Mid East 3%
Asia 7%
W. Europe 17%
E. Europe/FSU 27%

Developing world 50% **2035** **Developed world 50%**

Other Asia 14%
USA 15%
W. Europe 12%
China 11%
E. Europe/FSU 19%
Latin America 6%
Africa 8%
Mid East 5%
Asia 4%

In 1995 total carbon released as CO_2 was 6.46 billion tons; in 2035 total carbon emissions are projected to be 11.71 billion tons.

Note: FSU: Former Soviet Union

SOURCE: "Total World Emissions CO_2," in *Global Warming*, U.S. Environmental Protection Agency, Washington, DC 2002 [Online] http://www.epa.gov/reg3artd/globclimate/world.htm [accessed April 26, 2002]

FIGURE 3.10

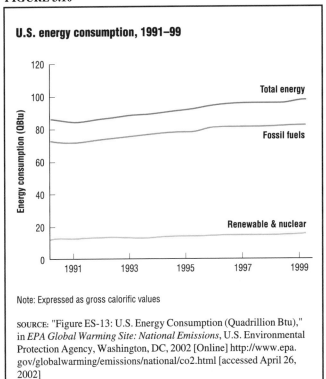

U.S. energy consumption, 1991–99

Total energy
Fossil fuels
Renewable & nuclear

Note: Expressed as gross calorific values

SOURCE: "Figure ES-13: U.S. Energy Consumption (Quadrillion Btu)," in *EPA Global Warming Site: National Emissions*, U.S. Environmental Protection Agency, Washington, DC, 2002 [Online] http://www.epa.gov/globalwarming/emissions/national/co2.html [accessed April 26, 2002]

• Heat waves and unusually warm weather have been reported at numerous locales, and has resulted in increased levels of human heat-related illness and death.

• Sea level rise, resulting from the expansion of warmer sea water and the melting of glaciers, is estimated at 4 to 10 inches over the course of the twentieth century. Sea level rise has resulted in land inundation, coastal flooding, and erosion.

• The number of incidents of heavy snowstorms and rainfall has increased.

• The number of droughts has increased.

• Mountain glaciers have continued to shrink, disappearing from lower latitudes.

• Diseases formerly confined to tropical regions, including several mosquito-borne diseases, have increased their range to higher altitudes and latitudes.

• Spring arrives earlier in many places.

• Numerous biological species have shifted their ranges to occupy higher latitudes and higher elevations.

In March 2002, in what is perhaps the most dramatic event resulting from global warming to date, the giant Larsen B ice shelf collapsed off the coast of Antarctica (Figure 3.14). Ice shelves are thick blocks of ice that are continuations of the ice sheets that cover the continent. The Larsen B shelf was larger than the state of Rhode

thawed, becoming useless. More precipitation fell as rain than snow, and snow melted faster, causing more running and standing water.

Since then, further evidence of global warming effects have been frequent and diverse:

FIGURE 3.11

The effect of forests on carbon dioxide concentrations

As plants and trees grow, photosynthesis — involving the interaction of sunlight, chlorophyll in green leaves, carbon dioxide (CO_2) and water (H_2O) — results in a net removal of CO_2 from the air and the release of oxygen (O_2) as a by-product. Also, moisture is released to the air through evapotranspiration.

When forests die and decay, or are burned, the biomass is oxidized and CO_2 is returned to the air.

SOURCE: "Figure 2a" and "Figure 2b," in *Biosphere*, *NASA Facts*, National Aeronautics and Space Administration, Goddard Space Flight Center, Greenbelt, MD, April 1998

FIGURE 3.12

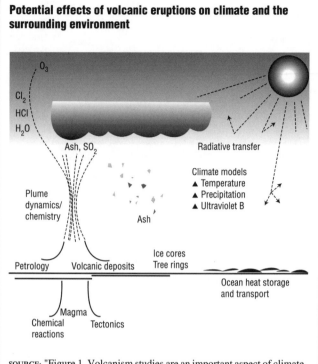

Potential effects of volcanic eruptions on climate and the surrounding environment

SOURCE: "Figure 1. Volcanism studies are an important aspect of climate research," in *Volcanoes and Global Climate Change*, *NASA Facts*, National Aeronautics and Space Administration, Goddard Space Flight Center, Greenbelt, MD, May 1998

Island and likely had existed since the end of the last ice age 12,000 years ago.

Global temperatures are predicted to continue to rise, as shown in Figure 3.15. Some of the major effects of global climate change, and the likelihood of their occurrence, were listed by the IPCC in 2001 (see Table 3.2). Many of these predictions have drastic consequences for humans as well as for wildlife.

Global Warming and Human Health

Higher temperatures alone are killing some people, particularly young and old people in urban areas. Over 250 died during a heat wave across the eastern United States in 1999. Many such deaths occur directly from heat-induced strokes and heart attacks. Air quality also deteriorates as temperatures rise. Hot, stagnant air contributes to the formation of atmospheric ozone, the main component of smog. Poor air quality also aggravates asthma and other respiratory diseases. Higher temperatures and increased rainfall could create ideal conditions for the spread of a host of infectious diseases by insects, including mosquito-borne malaria, dengue fever, and encephalitis. Some tropical diseases have already spread beyond their old ranges, affecting people at higher altitudes and latitudes. For example, dengue fever, once restricted to altitudes below 3,300 feet, was reported at altitudes above 4,000 feet in Central America in 1999, at 5,600 feet in Mexico in 1998, and at 7,200 feet in the Andes Mountains of Columbia in 1998. Similarly, malaria was detected at high altitudes in Indonesia in 1997. Expansion of malarial ranges have also been reported in parts of Africa.

Sea Levels and Precipitation Patterns

The National Climatic Data Center reports that sea levels rose by as much as 10 inches in the twentieth century. The Climate Institute in Washington, D.C., forecasts a further rise of 8 inches by 2030 and 26 inches by 2100 if current trends continue. These would be caused by the expansion of seawater as it is warmed, as well as by melting glaciers and ice caps. Predicted future sea level changes from a 2001 IPCC report are shown in Figure 3.16.

Rising sea levels would narrow or destroy beaches, flood wetland areas, and either submerge or require costly fortification of shoreline property. Numerous coastal cities worldwide would be flooded. Rising waters would also intrude on inland rivers, destroying freshwater habi-

FIGURE 3.13

Clouds and their effect on global temperature

The shortwave rays from the sun are scattered in a cloud. Many of the rays return to space. The resulting "cloud albedo forcing," taken by itself, tends to cause a cooling of the Earth.

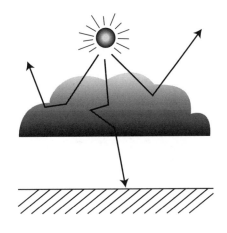

Longwave rays emitted by the Earth are absorbed and reemitted by a cloud, with some rays going to space and some going to the surface. Wavy arrows indicate longwave rays (distinguished from straight arrows, which indicate shortwave rays, as in the previous figure), and thicker arrows indicate more energy. The resulting "cloud greenhouse forcing," taken by itself, tends to cause a warming of the Earth.

SOURCE: "Figure 1" and "Figure 2," in *Clouds and the Energy Cycle. NASA Facts*, National Aeronautics and Space Administration, Goddard Space Flight Center, Greenbelt, MD, May 1998

tats, threatening human water supplies, and increasing the salt content of groundwater.

A warmer climate is also likely to shift the rain belt of the middle latitudes toward the poles, affecting rainfall patterns around the world. Wetter, more violent weather is projected for some regions. The opposite problem—too little water—could worsen in arid areas such as the Middle East and parts of Africa. Frequent droughts could plague North America and Asia as well. Some experts have suggested that "global warming" is a mild term for an era marked by heat waves that make certain regions virtually uninhabitable.

Decreasing Biological Diversity

Global biodiversity is also predicted to suffer from planetary warming. Certain ecosystems will shrink or be lost entirely, including cold-temperature habitats such as tundra, and specialized habitats such as coral reefs and coastal mangrove swamps. Other species expected to be heavily affected include those that require habitat within narrow bands of temperature and humidity, such as the monarch butterfly or the edelweiss flower.

Many ecosystems are expected to shift geographically toward more appropriate climate regimes. However, some species may be unable to migrate rapidly enough to cope with climate change at the projected rates. Species expected to be most successful, in fact, include opportunistic varieties such as weeds and pests. The EPA warned in 1988, "If

FIGURE 3.14

Satellite photo of the Larsen B ice shelf retreating to the rock cliffs. *(AP/Wide World Photos)*

FIGURE 3.15

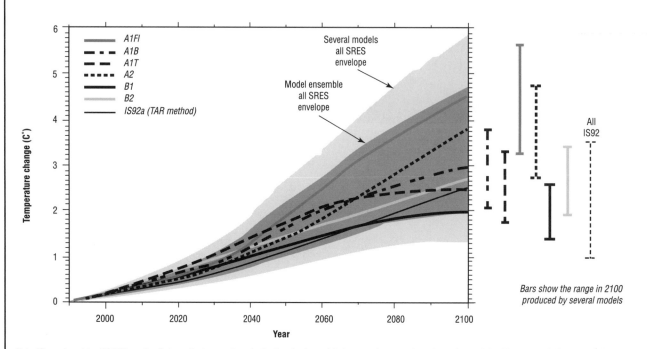

Global temperature change projections, 2000–2100

Note: "Several models all SRES envelope" shows the temperature rise for the simple model when tuned to a number of complex models with a range of climate sensitivities. All SRES envelopes refer to the full range of 35 SRES scenarios. Note that the warming rise from these emissions would continue well beyond 2100. Also note that this range does not allow for uncertainty relating to ice dynamical changes in the West Antarctic ice sheet, nor does it account for uncertainties in projecting non-sulphate aerosols and greenhouse gas concentrations. The models used here come from the Intergovernmental Panel on Climate Changes *Special Report on Emission Scenarios* (SRES). They are:

A1. The A1 storyline and scenario family describes a future world of very rapid economic growth, global population that peaks in mid-century and declines thereafter, and the rapid introduction of new and more efficient technologies. Major underlying themes are convergence among regions, capacity building and increased cultural and social interactions, with a substantial reduction in regional differences in per capita income. The A1 scenario family develops into three groups that describe alternative directions of technological change in the energy system. The three A1 groups are distinguished by their technological emphasis: fossil intensive (A1FI), non-fossil energy sources (A1T), or a balance across all sources (A1B) (where balanced is defined as not relying too heavily on one particular energy source, on the assumption that similar improvement rates apply to all energy supply and end use technologies).

A2. The A2 storyline and scenario family describes a very heterogeneous world. The underlying theme is self-reliance and preservation of local identities. Fertility patterns across regions converge very slowly, which results in continuously increasing population. Economic development is primarily regionally oriented and per capita economic growth and technological change more fragmented and slower than other storylines.

B1. The B1 storyline and scenario family describes a convergent world with the same global population, that peaks in midcentury and declines thereafter, as in the A1 storyline, but with rapid change in economic structures toward a service and information economy, with reductions in material intensity and the introduction of clean and resource-efficient technologies. The emphasis is on global solutions to economic, social and environmental sustainability, including improved equity, but without additional climate initiatives.

B2. The B2 storyline and scenario family describes a world in which the emphasis is on local solutions to economic, social and environmental sustainability. It is a world with continuously increasing global population, at a rate lower than A2, intermediate levels of economic development, and less rapid and more diverse technological change than in the B1 and A1 storylines. While the scenario is also oriented towards environmental protection and social equity, it focuses on local and regional levels.

An illustrative scenario was chosen for each of the six scenario groups A1B, A1FI, A1T, A2, B1 and B2. All should be considered equally sound.

The SRES scenarios do not include additional climate initiatives, which means that no scenarios are included that explicitly assume implementation of the United Nations Framework Convention on Climate Change or the emissions targets of the Kyoto Protocol.

SOURCE: Adapted from "Figure 5: The global climate of the 21st century will depend on natural changes and the response of the climate system to human activities," in *Summary for Policymakers: A Report of Working Group I of the Intergovernmental Panel on Climate Change,* Intergovernmental Panel on Climate Change, Geneva, Switzerland, 2001

current trends continue, it is likely that climate may change too quickly for many natural systems to adapt."

Effects of global warming on wildlife are already apparent worldwide. Figure 3.17 shows geographical locations that were the focus of studies that support the existence of climate change, as compiled by the IPCC in 2001. Many of these demonstrate an effect on either animal or plant life.

SPECIES RANGE SHIFTS. The ranges of most species depend, among other things, on temperature and climate. A number of plant and animal species have already shifted their geographic ranges in response to warming pat-

TABLE 3.2

Examples of impacts resulting from projected changes in extreme climate events

Projected Changes during the 21st Century in Extreme Climate Phenomena and their Likelihood[a]	Representative Examples of Projected Impacts[b] *(all high confidence of occurrence in some areas)*
Simple Extremes	
Higher maximum temperatures; more hot days and heat waves over nearly all land areas (*very likely*[a])	• Increased incidence of death and serious illness in older age groups and urban poor • Increased heat stress in livestock and wildlife • Shift in tourist destinations • Increased risk of damage to a number of crops • Increased electric cooling demand and reduced energy supply reliability
Higher (increasing) minimum temperatures; fewer cold days, frost days, and cold waves over nearly all land areas (*very likely*[a])	• Decreased cold-related human morbidity and mortality • Decreased risk of damage to a number of crops, and increased risk to others • Extended range and activity of some pest and disease vectors • Reduced heating energy demand
More intense precipitation events (*very likely*[a] over many areas)	• Increased flood, landslide, avalanche, and mudslide damage • Increased soil erosion • Increased flood runoff could increase recharge of some floodplain aquifers • Increased pressure on government and private flood insurance systems and disaster relief
Complex Extremes	
Increased summer drying over most mid-latitude continental interiors and associated risk of drought (*likely*[a])	• Decreased crop yields • Increased damage to building foundations caused by ground shrinkage • Decreased water resource quantity and quality • Increased risk of forest fire
Increase in tropical cyclone peak wind intensities, mean and peak precipitation intensities (*likely*[a] over some areas)[c]	• Increased risks to human life, risk of infectious disease epidemics, and many other risks • Increased coastal erosion and damage to coastal buildings and infrastructure • Increased damage to coastal ecosystems such as coral reefs and mangroves
Intensified droughts and floods associated with El Niño events in many different regions (*likely*[a]) (see also under droughts and intense precipitation events)	• Decreased agricultural and rangeland productivity in drought- and flood-prone regions • Decreased hydro-power potential in drought-prone regions
Increased Asian summer monsoon precipitation variability (*likely*[a])	• Increased flood and drought magnitude and damages in temperate and tropical Asia
Increased intensity of mid-latitude storms (little agreement between current models)	• Increased risks to human life and health • Increased property and infrastructure losses • Increased damage to coastal ecosystems

[a]Likelihood refers to judgmental estimates of confidence: *very likely* (90-99% chance); *likely* (66-90% chance).
[b]These impacts can be lessened by appropriate response measures.
[c]Changes in regional distribution of tropical cyclones are possible but have not been established.

SOURCE: "Table SPM-1. Examples of impacts resulting from projected changes in extreme climate events," in *Summary for Policymakers: Climate Change 2001: Impacts, Adaptation, and Vulnerability,* Intergovernmental Panel on Climate Change, Geneva, Switzerland, 2001

terns. Range shifts have been reported in alpine plants, butterflies, birds, invertebrates, and mosquitoes.

A 1999 study by Dr. Camille Parmesan and colleagues showed that among surveyed European butterfly species, 63 percent had shifted their ranges northward. Moreover, these species had shifted northward by a distance corresponding to temperature rises on the European continent. Dr. Parmesan also showed that one California species, Edith's checkerspot butterfly, has been disappearing from the southern parts of its range, as well as from lower-elevation habitats. Similarly, a 1999 study of bird species in the United Kingdom revealed that ranges have shifted north by an average of 12 miles. In the Olympic Mountains in the state of Washington, biologists reported in 1994 that sub-alpine forests have shifted to higher elevations previously characterized by alpine meadows. In

Monterey Bay, California, a 1995 study showed that invertebrate species such as snails and starfish have shifted north as well. In Germany, a study of mollusk species showed that 20 percent of species had shifted their ranges. Range shifts of mosquitoes are supported by the occurrence of mosquito-borne diseases such as dengue fever at more northern latitudes and at higher altitudes.

DISAPPEARING SPECIES. Some species will be unable to shift their ranges in response to global warming. There may be physical barriers that are difficult or impossible to cross—mountains, perhaps, or oceans or other bodies of water. The species they depend on for food or other resources may not have shifted their ranges. Or, species may encounter new competitors or predators as they try to move into new habitats. These species are likely to decline with global warming.

FIGURE 3.16

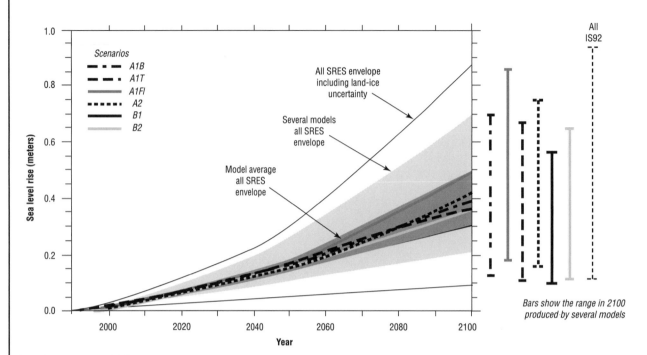

Global sea level rise projections, 2000–2100

Note: "Several models all SRES envelope" shows the sea level rise for the simple model when tuned to a number of complex models with a range of climate sensitivities. All SRES envelopes refer to the full range of 35 SRES scenarios. The "model average all SRES envelope" shows the average from these models for the range of scenarios. Note that the sea level rise from these emissions would continue well beyond 2100. Also note that this range does not allow for uncertainty relating to ice dynamical changes in the West Antarctic ice sheet, nor does it account for uncertainties in projecting non-sulphate aerosols and greenhouse gas concentrations. The models used here come from the Intergovernmental Panel on Climate Changes *Special Report on Emission Scenarios* (SRES). They are:

A1. The A1 storyline and scenario family describes a future world of very rapid economic growth, global population that peaks in mid-century and declines thereafter, and the rapid introduction of new and more efficient technologies. Major underlying themes are convergence among regions, capacity building and increased cultural and social interactions, with a substantial reduction in regional differences in per capita income. The A1 scenario family develops into three groups that describe alternative directions of technological change in the energy system. The three A1 groups are distinguished by their technological emphasis: fossil intensive (A1FI), non-fossil energy sources (A1T), or a balance across all sources (A1B) (where balanced is defined as not relying too heavily on one particular energy source, on the assumption that similar improvement rates apply to all energy supply and end use technologies).

A2. The A2 storyline and scenario family describes a very heterogeneous world. The underlying theme is self-reliance and preservation of local identities. Fertility patterns across regions converge very slowly, which results in continuously increasing population. Economic development is primarily regionally oriented and per capita economic growth and technological change more fragmented and slower than other storylines.

B1. The B1 storyline and scenario family describes a convergent world with the same global population, that peaks in midcentury and declines thereafter, as in the A1 storyline, but with rapid change in economic structures toward a service and information economy, with reductions in material intensity and the introduction of clean and resource-efficient technologies. The emphasis is on global solutions to economic, social and environmental sustainability, including improved equity, but without additional climate initiatives.

B2. The B2 storyline and scenario family describes a world in which the emphasis is on local solutions to economic, social and environmental sustainability. It is a world with continuously increasing global population, at a rate lower than A2, intermediate levels of economic development, and less rapid and more diverse technological change than in the B1 and A1 storylines. While the scenario is also oriented towards environmental protection and social equity, it focuses on local and regional levels.

An illustrative scenario was chosen for each of the six scenario groups A1B, A1FI, A1T, A2, B1 and B2. All should be considered equally sound.

The SRES scenarios do not include additional climate initiatives, which means that no scenarios are included that explicitly assume implementation of the United Nations Framework Convention on Climate Change or the emissions targets of the Kyoto Protocol.

SOURCE: Adapted from "Figure 5: The global climate of the 21st century will depend on natural changes and the response of the climate system to human activities," in *Summary for Policymakers: A Report of Working Group I of the Intergovernmental Panel on Climate Change*, Intergovernmental Panel on Climate Change, Geneva, Switzerland, 2001

Population declines have recently been reported in a number of habitats and species. Mangrove forests have been inundated by water due to rising sea levels and are dying. Arctic species are particularly vulnerable. An Arctic bird species, the black guillemot, is declining because of reductions in the amount of floating sea ice—ice formed by frozen saltwater. This has resulted in decreased food availability for guillemots as well as a reduction in the number of available nesting sites. Caribou in the Canadian Arctic have decreased in population size from 24,000 individuals in 1961 to just over 1,000 individuals in 1997. Caribou decline is likely due to loss of food resources.

FIGURE 3.17

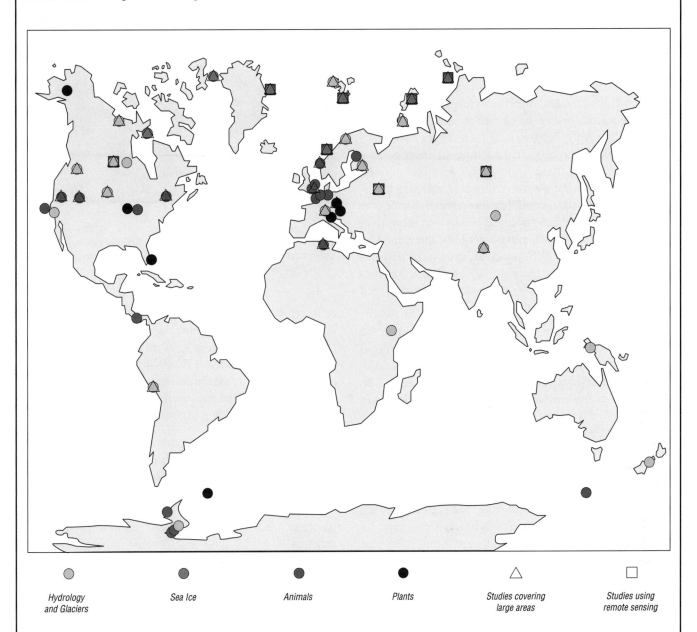

Studies documenting climate change

⬤	⬤	⬤	⬤	△	☐
Hydrology and Glaciers	*Sea Ice*	*Animals*	*Plants*	*Studies covering large areas*	*Studies using remote sensing*

Note: Hydrology, glacial retreat, and sea-ice data represent decadal to century trends. Terrestrial and marine ecosystem data represent trends of at least 2 decades. Remote-sensing studies cover large areas. Data are for single or multiple impacts that are consistent with known mechanisms of physical/biological system responses to observed regional temperature-related changes. For reported impacts spanning large areas, a representative location on the map was selected.

SOURCE: "Figure SPM-1: Locations at which systematic long-term studies meet stringent criteria documenting recent temperature-related regional climate change impacts on physicial and biological systems." in *Summary for Policymakers: Climate Change 2001: Impacts, Adaptation, and Vulnerability,* Intergovernmental Panel on Climate Change, Geneva, Switzerland, 2001

Adelie penguin populations have declined dramatically in Antarctica, probably because of a reduction in sea ice availability, which provides penguin habitat in addition to being essential to their primary food source, krill. In the Monteverde cloud forest of Costa Rica, where a unique, moist habitat is created by large amounts of water mist, an elevational rise in the cloud bank has resulted in the extinction of some 20 frog species as of 1999. Declines in lizard

populations have also been documented, as well as altitudinal shifts by populations of birds and bats.

An issue of particular concern is the loss of plant species due to global warming. Plants are often less able to shift their ranges than are animals, which are mobile. As plants form the basis of many ecosystems, the loss of plant species would impact numerous animal species as well. Several factors may limit the ability of trees to shift their ranges. First, seed dispersal by wind or by bird species may not be fast enough to keep pace with climate change. In addition, trees are long-lived species with long maturation times, and it takes some time before forests become fully established in new areas. In terms of altitudinal shifts, soils at high altitudes tend to be poorer than at lower altitudes. Consequently, species may not be able to colonize higher elevations.

In the United States, the Forest Service believes that Eastern hemlock, yellow birch, beech, and sugar maple forests will gradually have to shift their ranges northward by 300 to 600 miles if projected warming trends become a reality. Several of these ecosystems are likely to be severely limited by the warming, however, and may largely die out, along with the wildlife they shelter. Studies by World Wildlife Fund International report that more than half the world's parks and reserves could be threatened by climate change. Some U.S. parks believed to be particularly vulnerable include the Florida Everglades, Yellowstone National Park, the Great Smoky Mountains, and Redwood National Park in California.

In 2002 extensive forest damage was reported on the Kenai Peninsula near Anchorage, Alaska. Over 38 million dead spruce trees, some of them over a hundred years old, had to be cleared from 4 million acres of forest habitat. The cause of this environmental catastrophe was an explosion in the number of spruce bark beetles. Spruce bark beetles have always preyed on spruce trees in the Kenai Peninsula, but have been reproducing much more quickly because of warmer temperatures. This represents the worst insect decimation of forests ever reported in North America.

CORAL BLEACHING. Coral reefs (see Figure 3.18) are among the ecosystems most immediately threatened by global warming. Coral reef habitats are found in coastal marine waters in tropical areas, and are among the richest and most diverse of marine ecosystems. In fact, one-quarter of all marine species are found in coral reefs. The corals that form the basis of this ecosystem normally have a close relationship with species of algae. This relationship benefits both members—the algae receive shelter and protection within the calcium carbonate skeletons of corals, and the corals receive nutrients from the algae. Coral bleaching occurs when the corals eject the algae with which they normally live. This process is called bleaching because the corals lose their normally bright colors and take on a stark, white appearance. Coral bleaching has been shown to result from unusually warm oceanic water temperatures. Coral may recover after a bleaching episode when temperatures cool down again and the algae return. However, if the ejected algae die during a bleaching episode, the corals are doomed as well.

Widespread coral bleaching was reported beginning in the 1990s. In the spring of 2002 coral bleaching affected numerous coral reef ecosystems, including the Great Barri-

FIGURE 3.18

Coral reefs are among the most diverse ecosystems in the world. They are also immediately threatened by global warming, which has caused unprecedented episodes of coral bleaching in recent years. *(AP/Wide World Photos)*

er Reef off the coast of Australia, the largest coral reef in the world. This is the second major bleaching event in four years, and it is believed to be extending throughout tropical Pacific coral reef systems. Professor Ove Hoegh-Guldberg, a leading authority on corals and coral bleaching, predicts that if warming trends continue, all coral will be extinct—and the diverse coral reef ecosystems lost—by 2030.

TURTLES. Turtles and some other reptile species, including lizards and crocodilians, are characterized by an unusual sex determination system called temperature-dependent sex determination. This differs from the chromosomal system familiar in humans and other mammals, where two X chromosomes (XX) result in production of females and an X and a Y chromosome (XY) lead to males. In species with temperature-dependent sex determination, the sex of an individual depends on the temperature at which egg development occurs.

Global climate change has resulted in skewed sex ratios in several turtle species. Generally, warmer temperatures favor the production of females. Among loggerhead turtles in Florida, for example, females made up 87 to 99.9 percent of the hatchling population in 1992, depending on the precise nesting site used. This is apparently due to warmer sand temperatures on beaches. Among Mississippi painted turtles, almost 100 percent of hatchlings were female in 1994. Continued production of large numbers of females and few or no males could have drastic implications for many turtle populations.

INTERNATIONAL EFFORTS AND GLOBAL WARMING

In order to slow or halt global warming, many industrialized countries are committed to stabilizing or reducing carbon dioxide emissions. The first Bush Administration (1989–1992) opposed precise deadlines for carbon dioxide limits, arguing that the extent of the problem was too uncertain to justify painful economic measures. When President Bill Clinton took office in 1993, he joined the European community in calling for overall emissions to be stabilized at 1990 levels by the year 2000. However, this goal was not met. The administration of George W. Bush has shown little desire to address the problem of global climate change. Oil interests in particular have vigorously opposed emissions standards, fearing that these will decrease demand for oil. Many environmentalists believe that fighting global warming will require advances in energy efficiency. Others have promoted a gradual shift from fossil-fuel burning to renewable energy, an idea most industrialized countries have been slow to embrace.

The Kyoto Protocol

The aim of the United Nations Framework Convention on Climate Change is to stabilize global atmospheric greenhouse gases at levels "that would prevent dangerous anthropogenic interference with the climate system." In December 1997 delegates from 166 countries met in Kyoto, Japan, to formulate a plan for reducing greenhouse gas emissions as the first step towards this goal. The task was more complicated and difficult than envisioned in 1995, when parties to the 1992 Rio climate change treaty decided that stronger action was necessary. The "simple" matter of deciding on a reduction target and creating a timetable for reductions broadened into contentious debate on several fronts.

First, some developed nations, including the United States, argued that both industrialized and developing countries should be required to reduce greenhouse gas emissions. Developing countries, however, argued that because industrialized nations had caused most of the global warming, and were still emitting the bulk of global greenhouse gases, industrialized nations should bear most of the economic burden of the cleanup. It was ultimately decided that the Kyoto Protocol would address only emissions reductions for developed countries. Second, there was debate over whether development of carbon sinks—such as through the building of tree farms—could offset emissions targets. Many countries wanted sinks to be excluded, in part because their role in global warming has not been well studied and remains uncertain. However, the United States insisted on this clause, which it argued would allow businesses low-cost means for complying with treaty requirements. Finally, the United States successfully battled to allow for emissions trading among nations. This permits businesses or countries to purchase less expensive emissions permits from foreign countries, rather than cutting emissions.

In the end, the Kyoto Protocol called for industrialized nations to reduce emissions from 1990 levels by an average

of 5 percent by 2008–2012. It was signed by over 170 nations, including the United States, which committed to legally binding emissions reductions of 7 percent below 1990 levels. European Union nations were required to reduce emission by 8 percent, Japan by 6 percent. However, ratification by 55 nations, jointly responsible for 55 percent of 1990 emissions, was required for the treaty to enter into force.

The United States has made no move towards ratifying the Kyoto Protocol. In fact, President Bush confirmed in March 2001 that the United States would withdraw from the Kyoto Protocol. Bush said that he believed the emissions reductions would be too costly. Christine Todd Whitman, Bush's appointed head of the Environmental Protection Agency, said, "We have no interest in implementing that treaty." The United States was responsible for 25 percent of global emissions in 1990, and it was widely believed that the treaty could not enter into force without U.S. ratification. Despite the withdrawal of the United States from the treaty, however, other countries, including the European Union, Japan, Canada, and Russia, have gone ahead with a modified version of the protocol. The Kyoto Protocol is one of several international treaties enjoying broad international support in which the United States has not participated. President Bush has since proposed alternative strategies for dealing with global warming based on tax incentives and volunteer emissions reductions by industry. These plans have been widely attacked as vague and unenforceable.

In June 2002 the administration's *U.S. Climate Action Report 2002* conceded first, that global warming exists and is largely the result of human activity, and second, that global warming will cause substantial and far-reaching effects in the United States. The Bush Administration has voiced support for adapting to these changes rather than adopting serious measures to reduce greenhouse gas emissions. Soon after the release of the report, President Bush, when asked if he planned any new initiatives to combat global warming, responded, "No, I've laid out that very comprehensive initiative. I read the report put out by the bureaucracy. I do not support the Kyoto treaty. The Kyoto treaty would severely damage the United States economy, and I don't accept that. I accept the alternative we put out, that we can grow our economy and, at the same time, through technologies, improve our environment."

U.S. Public Opinion

A November 1997 *New York Times* poll found that Americans were more willing than the government to take steps to counter the threat of global warming. When asked if they would be willing to invest in new appliances and insulation to cut household emissions of greenhouse gases, 47 percent said they would, 21 percent indicated they would not, 10 percent said "it depends," and 4 percent said they already were doing so. Sixty-five percent of those polled said they wanted to take steps immediately to cut greenhouse gas emissions. Only 15 percent preferred to wait until many other countries took steps. When asked whether they thought recent weather had been "normal" or "stranger than normal," 67 percent thought it had been "stranger than normal," 31 percent thought it had been "normal," and 1 percent had no opinion.

A November 1997 Gallup Poll suggested that despite their concern about global climate change, Americans were unlikely to support strict measures regarding greenhouse gas emissions. Sixty-nine percent of respondents did not think global warming would be a threat in their own lifetimes, but 65 percent believed it would be a problem in their children's lifetimes. Even so, 48 percent said they were unwilling to reduce global warming if costs for energy went up. (However, 44 percent said they were willing to pay higher energy costs.) An even greater percentage—54 percent—said they would be unwilling to take steps to reduce global warming if unemployment would rise as a result.

Gallup conducted another survey on environmental attitudes in April 2001, coincident with the annual celebration of "Earth Day." Regarding global warming, most Americans surveyed said that they believe global warming's effects will be visible in their lifetimes. One-third of those surveyed said they worry about global warming "a great deal." In fact, a quarter of Americans believe that "immediate and drastic" action must be taken to help preserve environmental resources. A majority, 57 percent, also said that environmental concerns should take precedence over economic considerations when these clash, as they often do. Americans also disagree with several choices made by the Bush Administration, in general favoring environmentally friendly choices on issues such as regulating industrial emissions, drilling in the Arctic National Wildlife Refuge, and participating in the Kyoto Protocol on global warming.

CHAPTER 4
ENDANGERED PLANTS AND ECOSYSTEMS

Well over half the threatened and endangered species listed with the U.S. Fish and Wildlife Service are plants. There are a total of 713 threatened and endangered flowering plants (712 U.S. species, 1 foreign species), 5 threatened and endangered conifers and cycads (3 U.S. species, 2 foreign species), 26 listed ferns and allied species (all U.S.), and 2 listed lichen species (both U.S.). Listed U.S. species are shown in Table 4.1 and Table 4.2. Table 4.1 lists flowering plants. Table 4.2 lists endangered conifers, ferns, and lichens. Because the status of most plant species has not been studied in detail, many more plants are probably in danger of extinction than appear on these lists.

There are many factors leading to the endangerment of plant species. Numerous plants are the victims of habitat loss due to land and agricultural development. Others have declined due to pollution or habitat damage, or as a result of competition with invasive species. Still others have succumbed to introduced plant diseases. Finally, collectors or dealers often illegally seek rare, showy, or unusual plants, and have depleted populations through over-collection.

The preservation of plant species is important for many reasons. Not only are plants of aesthetic value, they are crucial components of every ecosystem on earth. Plants also serve several functions directly beneficial to humans. First, they provide genetic variation essential to the breeding of new crop varieties—native plants provide genes that allow for adaptation to local environments, as well as resistance to pests, disease, or drought. Second, plants are the source of numerous human medicines.

PLANTS IN DECLINE

The *1997 IUCN Red List of Threatened Plants* from the World Conservation Union represents the first global assessment of plants, and was the result of over 20 years of study by botanists, conservation organizations, botanical gardens, and museums around the world. It revealed that 12.5 percent—one of every eight—of the world's plant species are in danger of extinction. In the United States, the figure is even higher, with 29 percent of the nation's 16,000 plant species threatened. Other findings included:

- Of the estimated 270,000 known species of vascular plants (ferns, conifers, and flowering plants, but not mosses, lichens, and algae), 33,798 species are in danger of extinction.

- Of the plant species at risk, 91 percent are found only in a single nation. These species are particularly vulnerable, having only limited options for recovery.

- Many plant species known to have medicinal value are at risk of disappearing. For example, 75 percent of species in the yew family, a source of cancer-fighting compounds, are threatened. Twelve percent of the willow family, from which aspirin is derived, are threatened.

- About 33 percent of the dipterocarps, a tree group that includes valuable timber species in Asia, are threatened.

- The loss of each species causes a loss of genetic material that could be used to produce stronger, healthier crops for human and animal consumption.

- Close relatives to many familiar plants are at risk of extinction, including 14 percent of the rose family and 32 percent of lilies and irises.

- Numerous species whose value has not yet been studied are at risk.

According to the *1997 IUCN Red List of Threatened Plants*, the primary reasons for plant endangerment are habitat loss and introduction of invasive species. The ten areas with the greatest percentage of threatened flora are St. Helena (41.2 percent), Mauritius (39.2 percent), Seychelles (31.2 percent), the United States (29 percent),

Status	Species Name
Flowering Plants	
E	Sand-verbena, large-fruited (*Abronia macrocarpa*)
E	*Abutilon eremitopetalum* (No common name)
E	Ko'oloa'ula (*Abutilon menziesii*)
E	*Abutilon sandwicense* (No common name)
E	Liliwai (*Acaena exigua*)
T	Thornmint, San Diego (*Acanthomintha ilicifolia*)
E	Thornmint, San Mateo (*Acanthomintha obovata* ssp. *duttonii*)
E	*Achyranthes mutica* (No common name)
E	Chaff-flower, round-leaved (*Achyranthes splendens* var. *rotundata*)
T	Monkshood, northern wild (*Aconitum noveboracense*)
T	Joint-vetch, sensitive (*Aeschynomene virginica*)
E	Gerardia, sandplain (*Agalinis acuta*)
E	Agave, Arizona (*Agave arizonica*)
E	Mahoe (*Alectryon macrococcus*)
E	Onion, Munz's (*Allium munzii*)
E	Alopecurus, Sonoma (*Alopecurus aequalis* var. *sonomensis*)
E	Kuawawaenohu (*Alsinidendron lychnoides*)
E	*Alsinidendron obovatum* (No common name)
E	*Alsinidendron trinerve* (No common name)
E	*Alsinidendron viscosum* (No common name)
E	*Amaranthus brownii* (No common name)
T	Amaranth, seabeach (*Amaranthus pumilus*)
E	Ambrosia, south Texas (*Ambrosia cheiranthifolia*)
E	Lead-plant, Crenulate (*Amorpha crenulata*)
T	Amphianthus, little (*Amphianthus pusillus*)
E	Fiddleneck, large-flowered (*Amsinckia grandiflora*)
E	Blue-star, Kearney's (*Amsonia kearneyana*)
E	Cactus, Tobusch fishhook (*Ancistrocactus tobuschii*)
T	Potato-bean, Price's (*Apios priceana*)
E	Rock-cress, Hoffmann's (*Arabis hoffmannii*)
E	Rock-cress, McDonald's (*Arabis mcdonaldiana*)
E	Rock-cress, Braun's (*Arabis perstellata*)
E	Rock-cress, shale barren (*Arabis serotina*)
E	Bear-poppy, dwarf (*Arctomecon humilis*)
E	Manzanita, Santa Rosa Island (*Arctostaphylos confertiflora*)
E	Manzanita, Del Mar (*Arctostaphylos glandulosa* ssp. *crassifolia*)
E	Manzanita, Presidio (*Arctostaphylos hookeri* var. *ravenii*)
T	Manzanita, Morro (*Arctostaphylos morroensis*)
T	Manzanita, Ione (*Arctostaphylos myrtifolia*)
T	Manzanita, pallid (*Arctostaphylos pallida*)
E	Sandwort, Cumberland (*Arenaria cumberlandensis*)
E	Sandwort, Marsh (*Arenaria paludicola*)
T	Sandwort, Bear Valley (*Arenaria ursina*)
E	Poppy, Sacramento prickly (*Argemone pleiacantha* ssp. *pinnatisecta*)
E	Silversword, Mauna Loa (=Ka'u) (*Argyroxiphium kauense*)
T	'Ahinahina (*Argyroxiphium sandwicense* ssp. *macrocephalum*)
E	'Ahinahina (*Argyroxiphium sandwicense* ssp. *sandwicense*)
E	*Aristida chaseae* (No common name)
E	Pelos del diablo (*Aristida portoricensis*)
T	Milkweed, Mead's (*Asclepias meadii*)
T	Milkweed, Welsh's (*Asclepias welshii*)
E	Pawpaw, four-petal (*Asimina tetramera*)
E	Milk-vetch, Cushenbury (*Astragalus albens*)
E	Milk-vetch, Shivwitz (*Astragalus ampullarioides*)
E	Milk-vetch, Applegate's (*Astragalus applegatei*)
E	Ground-plum, Guthrie's (=Pyne's) (*Astragalus bibullatus*)
E	Milk-vetch, Braunton's (*Astragalus brauntonii*)
E	Milk-vetch, Clara Hunt's (*Astragalus clarianus*)
E	Milk-vetch, Sentry (*Astragalus cremnophylax* var. *cremnophylax*)
T	Milk-vetch, Deseret (*Astragalus desereticus*)
E	Milk-vetch, Holmgren (*Astragalus holmgreniorum*)
E	Milk-vetch, Mancos (*Astragalus humillimus*)
E	Milk-vetch, Lane Mountain (*Astragalus jaegerianus*)
E	Milk-vetch, Coachella Valley (*Astragalus lentiginosus* var. *coachellae*)
T	Milk-vetch, Fish Slough (*Astragalus lentiginosus* var. *piscinensis*)
T	Milk-vetch, Peirson's (*Astragalus magdalenae* var. *peirsonii*)
T	Milk-vetch, heliotrope (*Astragalus montii*)
E	Milk-vetch, Osterhout (*Astragalus osterhoutii*)
T	Milk-vetch, Ash meadows (*Astragalus phoenix*)
E	Milk-vetch, Ventura Marsh (*Astragalus pycnostachyus* var. *lanosissimus*)
E	Milk-vetch, Jesup's (*Astragalus robbinsii* var. *jesupi*)
E	Milk-vetch, coastal dunes (*Astragalus tener* var. *titi*)
E	Milk-vetch, triple-ribbed (*Astragalus tricarinatus*)
E	Cactus, star (*Astrophytum asterias*)
E	Crownscale, San Jacinto Valley (*Atriplex coronata* var. *notatior*)
E	*Auerodendron pauciflorum* (No common name)
E	Ayenia, Texas (*Ayenia limitaris*)
T	Baccharis, Encinitas (*Baccharis vanessae*)
E	Palo de ramon (*Banara vanderbiltii*)
E	Rattleweed, hairy (*Baptisia arachnifera*)
E	Barberry, Truckee (*Berberis* (=*Mahonia*) *sonnei*)
E	Barberry, Nevin's (*Berberis nevinii*)
E	Barberry, island (*Berberis pinnata* ssp. *insularis*)
T	Birch, Virginia round-leaf (*Betula uber*)
E	Ko'oko'olau (*Bidens micrantha* ssp. *kalealaha*)
E	Ko'oko'olau (*Bidens wiebkei*)
E	Sunshine, Sonoma (*Blennosperma bakeri*)
T	Aster, decurrent false (*Boltonia decurrens*)
E	Bonamia, Florida (*Bonamia grandiflora*)
E	*Bonamia menziesii* (No common name)
E	Olulu (*Brighamia insignis*)
E	Pua 'ala (*Brighamia rockii*)
T	Brodiaea, thread-leaved (*Brodiaea filifolia*)
T	Brodiaea, Chinese Camp (*Brodiaea pallida*)
E	Boxwood, Vahl's (*Buxus vahlii*)
E	Uhiuhi (*Caesalpinia kavaiense*)
E	Capa rosa (*Callicarpa ampla*)
E	Poppy-mallow, Texas (*Callirhoe scabriuscula*)
T	Mariposa lily, Tiburon (*Calochortus tiburonensis*)
E	*Calyptranthes thomasiana* (No common name)
T	Pussypaws, Mariposa (*Calyptridium pulchellum*)
T	Manaca, palma de (*Calyptronoma rivalis*)
E	Morning-glory, Stebbins' (*Calystegia stebbinsii*)
T	Evening-primrose, San Benito (*Camissonia benitensis*)
E	Bellflower, Brooksville (*Campanula robinsiae*)
E	'Awikiwiki (*Canavalia molokaiensis*)
E	Bittercress, small-anthered (*Cardamine micranthera*)
E	Sedge, white (*Carex albida*)
E	Sedge, golden (*Carex lutea*)
T	Sedge, Navajo (*Carex specuicola*)
E	Paintbrush, Tiburon (*Castilleja affinis* ssp. *neglecta*)
T	Owl's-clover, fleshy (*Castilleja campestris* ssp. *succulenta*)
E	Paintbrush, ash-grey (*Castilleja cinerea*)
E	Indian paintbrush, San Clemente Island (*Castilleja grisea*)
T	Paintbrush, golden (*Castilleja levisecta*)
E	Paintbrush, soft-leaved (*Castilleja mollis*)
E	*Catesbaea melanocarpa* (No common name)
E	Jewelflower, California (*Caulanthus californicus*)
E	Ceanothus, coyote (*Ceanothus ferrisae*)
T	Ceanothus, Vail Lake (*Ceanothus ophiochilus*)
E	Ceanothus, Pine Hill (*Ceanothus roderickii*)
E	Kamanomano (*Cenchrus agrimonioides*)
T	Centaury, spring-loving (*Centaurium namophilum*)
E	Awiwi (*Centaurium sebaeoides*)
E	Mountain-mahogany, Catalina Island (*Cercocarpus traskiae*)
E	Prickly-apple, fragrant (*Cereus eriophorus* var. *fragrans*)
E	*Chamaecrista glandulosa* var. *mirabilis* (No common name)
E	'Akoko (*Chamaesyce celastroides* var. *kaenana*)
E	Spurge, deltoid (*Chamaesyce deltoidea* ssp. *deltoidea*)
E	'Akoko (*Chamaesyce deppeana*)
T	Spurge, Garber's (*Chamaesyce garberi*)
E	*Chamaesyce halemanui* (No common name)
E	'Akoko (*Chamaesyce herbstii*)
T	Spurge, Hoover's (*Chamaesyce hooveri*)
E	'Akoko (*Chamaesyce kuwaleana*)
E	'Akoko (*Chamaesyce rockii*)
E	'Akoko, Ewa Plains (*Chamaesyce skottsbergii* var. *kalaeloana*)
E	Fringe-tree, pygmy (*Chionanthus pygmaeus*)
T	Amole, purple (*Chlorogalum purpureum*)

Status	Species Name
E	Spineflower, Howell's (*Chorizanthe howellii*)
E	Spineflower, Orcutt's (*Chorizanthe orcuttiana*)
E	Spineflower, Ben Lomond (*Chorizanthe pungens* var. *hartwegiana*)
T	Spineflower, Monterey (*Chorizanthe pungens* var. *pungens*)
E	Spineflower, Robust (incl. Scotts Valley) (*Chorizanthe robusta* (incl. vars. *robusta* and *hartwegii*))
E	Spineflower, Sonoma (*Chorizanthe valida*)
E	Aster, Florida golden (*Chrysopsis floridana*)
E	Thistle, fountain (*Cirsium fontinale* var. *fontinale*)
E	Thistle, Chorro Creek bog (*Cirsium fontinale* var. *obispoense*)
E	Thistle, Suisun (*Cirsium hydrophilum* var. *hydrophilum*)
E	Thistle, La Graciosa (*Cirsium loncholepis*)
T	Thistle, Pitcher's (*Cirsium pitcheri*)
T	Thistle, Sacramento Mountains (*Cirsium vinaceum*)
E	Clarkia, Presidio (*Clarkia franciscana*)
E	Clarkia, Vine Hill (*Clarkia imbricata*)
E	Clarkia, Pismo (*Clarkia speciosa* ssp. *immaculata*)
T	Clarkia, Springville (*Clarkia springvillensis*)
E	Leather flower, Morefield's (*Clematis morefieldii*)
E	Leather flower, Alabama (*Clematis socialis*)
E	'Oha wai (*Clermontia drepanomorpha*)
E	'Oha wai (*Clermontia lindseyana*)
E	'Oha wai (*Clermontia oblongifolia* ssp. *brevipes*)
E	'Oha wai (*Clermontia oblongifolia* ssp. *mauiensis*)
E	'Oha wai (*Clermontia peleana*)
E	'Oha wai (*Clermontia pyrularia*)
E	'Oha wai (*Clermontia samuelii*)
T	Pigeon wings (*Clitoria fragrans*)
E	Kauila (*Colubrina oppositifolia*)
E	Rosemary, short-leaved (*Conradina brevifolia*)
E	Rosemary, Etonia (*Conradina etonia*)
E	Rosemary, Apalachicola (*Conradina glabra*)
T	Rosemary, Cumberland (*Conradina verticillata*)
E	*Cordia bellonis* (No common name)
E	Bird's-beak, salt marsh (*Cordylanthus maritimus* ssp. *maritimus*)
E	Bird's-beak, soft (*Cordylanthus mollis* ssp. *mollis*)
E	Bird's beak, palmate-bracted (*Cordylanthus palmatus*)
E	Bird's-beak, Pennell's (*Cordylanthus tenuis* ssp. *capillaris*)
E	Palo de nigua (*Cornutia obovata*)
E	Cactus, Nellie cory (*Coryphantha minima*)
T	Cory cactus, bunched (*Coryphantha ramillosa*)
T	Cactus, Cochise pincushion (*Coryphantha robbinsorum*)
E	Cactus, Pima pineapple (*Coryphantha scheeri* var. *robustispina*)
T	Cactus, Lee pincushion (*Coryphantha sneedii* var. *leei*)
E	Cactus, Sneed pincushion (*Coryphantha sneedii* var. *sneedii*)
E	*Cranichis ricartii* (No common name)
E	Higuero de sierra (*Crescentia portoricensis*)
E	Harebells, Avon Park (*Crotalaria avonensis*)
E	Cat's-eye, Terlingua Creek (*Cryptantha crassipes*)
E	Gourd, Okeechobee (*Cucurbita okeechobeensis* ssp. *okeechobeensis*)
E	Haha (*Cyanea acuminata*)
E	Haha (*Cyanea asarifolia*)
E	Haha (*Cyanea copelandii* ssp. *copelandii*)
E	Haha (*Cyanea copelandii* ssp. *haleakalaensis*)
E	Haha (*Cyanea dunbarii*)
E	Haha (*Cyanea glabra*)
E	Haha (*Cyanea grimesiana* ssp. *grimesiana*)
E	Haha (*Cyanea grimesiana* ssp. *obatae*)
E	Haha (*Cyanea hamatiflora carlsonii*)
E	Haha (*Cyanea hamatiflora* ssp. *hamatiflora*)
E	Haha (*Cyanea humboldtiana*)
E	Haha (*Cyanea koolauensis*)
E	Haha (*Cyanea lobata*)
E	Haha (*Cyanea longiflora*)
E	Haha (*Cyanea macrostegia* ssp. *gibsonii*)
E	Haha (*Cyanea mannii*)
E	Haha (*Cyanea mceldowneyi*)
E	Haha (*Cyanea pinnatifida*)
E	Haha (*Cyanea platyphylla*)
E	Haha (*Cyanea procera*)

Status	Species Name
T	Haha (*Cyanea recta*)
E	Haha (*Cyanea remyi*)
E	*Cyanea (=Rollandia) crispa* (No common name)
E	Haha (*Cyanea shipmannii*)
E	Haha (*Cyanea stictophylla*)
E	Haha (*Cyanea st-johnii*)
E	Haha (*Cyanea superba*)
E	Haha (*Cyanea truncata*)
E	Haha (*Cyanea undulata*)
T	Cycladenia, Jones (*Cycladenia jonesii (=humilis)*)
E	Pu'uka'a (*Cyperus trachysanthos*)
E	Ha'iwale (*Cyrtandra crenata*)
E	Mapele (*Cyrtandra cyaneoides*)
E	Ha'iwale (*Cyrtandra dentata*)
E	Ha'iwale (*Cyrtandra giffardii*)
T	Ha'iwale (*Cyrtandra limahuliensis*)
E	Ha'iwale (*Cyrtandra munroi*)
E	Ha'iwale (*Cyrtandra polyantha*)
E	Ha'iwale (*Cyrtandra subumbellata*)
E	Ha'iwale (*Cyrtandra tintinnabula*)
E	Ha'iwale (*Cyrtandra viridiflora*)
E	Prairie-clover, leafy (*Dalea foliosa*)
E	*Daphnopsis hellerana* (No common name)
E	Pawpaw, beautiful (*Deeringothamnus pulchellus*)
E	Pawpaw, Rugel's (*Deeringothamnus rugelii*)
T	Tarplant, Otay (*Deinandra (=Hemizonia) conjugens*)
E	*Delissea rhytidosperma* (No common name)
E	Oha (*Delissea rivularis*)
E	Oha (*Delissea subcordata*)
E	*Delissea undulata* (No common name)
E	Larkspur, Baker's (*Delphinium bakeri*)
E	Larkspur, yellow (*Delphinium luteum*)
E	Larkspur, San Clemente Island (*Delphinium variegatum* ssp. *kinkiense*)
E	Mint, Garrett's (*Dicerandra christmanii*)
E	Mint, longspurred (*Dicerandra cornutissima*)
E	Mint, scrub (*Dicerandra frutescens*)
E	Mint, Lakela's (*Dicerandra immaculata*)
E	Spineflower, slender-horned *Dodecahema leptoceras*
E	Na'ena'e (*Dubautia herbstobatae*)
E	Na'ena'e (*Dubautia latifolia*)
E	Na'ena'e (*Dubautia pauciflorula*)
E	Na'ena'e (*Dubautia plantaginea* ssp. *humilis*)
T	Dudleya, Conejo (*Dudleya abramsii* ssp. *parva*)
T	Dudleya, marcescent (*Dudleya cymosa* ssp. *marcescens*)
T	Dudleyea, Santa Monica Mountains (*Dudleya cymosa* ssp. *ovatifolia*)
T	Dudleya, Santa Cruz Island (*Dudleya nesiotica*)
E	Dudleya, Santa Clara Valley (*Dudleya setchellii*)
T	Liveforever, Laguna Beach (*Dudleya stolonifera*)
E	Liveforever, Santa Barbara Island (*Dudleya traskiae*)
T	Dudleya, Verity's (*Dudleya verityi*)
E	Coneflower, smooth (*Echinacea laevigata*)
E	Coneflower, Tennessee purple (*Echinacea tennesseensis*)
E	Cactus, Nichol's Turk's head (*Echinocactus horizonthalonius* var. *nicholii*)
T	Cactus, Chisos Mountain hedgehog (*Echinocereus chisoensis* var. *chisoensis*)
E	Cactus, Kuenzler hedgehog (*Echinocereus fendleri* var. *kuenzleri*)
E	Cactus, black lace (*Echinocereus reichenbachii* var. *albertii*)
E	Cactus, Arizona hedgehog (*Echinocereus triglochidiatus* var. *arizonicus*)
E	Pitaya, Davis' green (*Echinocereus viridiflorus* var. *davisii*)
T	Cactus, Lloyd's Mariposa (*Echinomastus mariposensis*)
T	Sunray, Ash Meadows (*Enceliopsis nudicaulis* var. *corrugata*)
E	Love grass, Fosberg's (*Eragrostis fosbergii*)
E	Mallow, Kern (*Eremalche kernensis*)
E	Woolly-star, Santa Ana River (*Eriastrum densifolium* ssp. *sanctorum*)
T	Woolly-star, Hoover's (*Eriastrum hooveri*)
E	Daisy, Willamette (*Erigeron decumbens* var. *decumbens*)
T	Daisy, Maguire (*Erigeron maguirei*)
T	Daisy, Parish's (*Erigeron parishii*)
T	Fleabane, Zuni (*Erigeron rhizomatus*)
E	Mountain balm, Indian Knob (*Eriodictyon altissimum*)

TABLE 4.1

Flowering plant species listed as endangered or threatened, May 15, 2002 [CONTINUED]

Status	Species Name
E	Yerba santa, Lompoc (*Eriodictyon capitatum*)
E	Buckwheat, Ione (incl. Irish Hill) (*Eriogonum apricum (incl.* var. *prostratum)*)
T	Wild-buckwheat, gypsum (*Eriogonum gypsophilum*)
T	Wild-buckwheat, southern mountain (*Eriogonum kennedyi* var. *austromontanum*)
T	Buckwheat, scrub (*Eriogonum longifolium* var. *gnaphalifolium*)
E	Buckwheat, cushenbury (*Eriogonum ovalifolium* var. *vineum*)
E	Buckwheat, steamboat (*Eriogonum ovalifolium* var. *williamsiae*)
E	Wild-buckwheat, clay-loving (*Eriogonum pelinophilum*)
E	Sunflower, San Mateo woolly (*Eriophyllum latilobum*)
E	Button-celery, San Diego (*Eryngium aristulatum* var. *parishii*)
E	Thistle, Loch Lomond coyote (*Eryngium constancei*)
E	Snakeroot (*Eryngium cuneifolium*)
E	Wallflower, Contra Costa (*Erysimum capitatum* var. *angustatum*)
E	Wallflower, Menzies' (*Erysimum menziesii*)
E	Wallflower, Ben Lomond (*Erysimum teretifolium*)
E	Lily, Minnesota dwarf trout (*Erythronium propullans*)
E	Uvillo (*Eugenia haematocarpa*)
E	Nioi (*Eugenia koolauensis*)
E	*Eugenia woodburyana* (No common name)
E	'Akoko (*Euphorbia haeleeleana*)
T	Spurge, telephus (*Euphorbia telephioides*)
T	Mustard, Penland alpine fen (*Eutrema penlandii*)
E	Heau (*Exocarpos luteolus*)
E	Mehamehame (*Flueggea neowawraea*)
E	Frankenia, Johnston's (*Frankenia johnstonii*)
E	Flannelbush, Pine Hill (*Fremontodendron californicum* ssp. *decumbens*)
E	Flannelbush, Mexican (*Fremontodendron mexicanum*)
E	Fritillary, Gentner's (*Fritillaria gentneri*)
E	*Gahnia lanaiensis* (No common name)
E	Milkpea, Small's (*Galactia smallii*)
E	Bedstraw, island (*Galium buxifolium*)
E	Bedstraw, El Dorado (*Galium californicum* ssp. *sierrae*)
E	Gardenia (=Na'u), Hawaiian (*Gardenia brighamii*)
E	Nanu (*Gardenia mannii*)
T	Butterfly plant, Colorado (*Gaura neomexicana* var. *coloradensis*)
T	*Geocarpon minimum* (No common name)
E	Geranium, Hawaiian red-flowered (*Geranium arboreum*)
E	Nohoanu (*Geranium multiflorum*)
T	Gesneria pauciflora (No common name)
E	Avens, spreading (*Geum radiatum*)
E	Gilia, Monterey (*Gilia tenuiflora* ssp. *arenaria*)
E	Gilia, Hoffmann's slender-flowered (*Gilia tenuiflora* ssp. *hoffmannii*)
E	Goetzea, beautiful (*Goetzea elegans*)
E	*Gouania hillebrandii* (No common name)
E	*Gouania meyenii* (No common name)
E	*Gouania vitifolia* (No common name)
T	Gumplant, Ash Meadows (*Grindelia fraxino-pratensis*)
E	Stickseed, showy (*Hackelia venusta*)
T	Seagrass, Johnson's (*Halophila johnsonii*)
E	Honohono (*Haplostachys haplostachya*)
E	Beauty, Harper's (*Harperocallis flava*)
T	Higo, chumbo (*Harrisia portoricensis*)
E	Pennyroyal, Todsen's (*Hedeoma todsenii*)
E	Awiwi (*Hedyotis cookiana*)
E	Kio'ele (*Hedyotis coriacea*)
E	*Hedyotis degeneri* (No common name)
E	Pilo (*Hedyotis mannii*)
E	*Hedyotis parvula* (No common name)
E	Bluet, Roan Mountain (*Hedyotis purpurea* var. *montana*)
E	Kopa (*Hedyotis schlechtendahliana* var. *remyi*)
E	Hedyotis, Na Pali beach (*Hedyotis st.-johnii*)
T	Sneezeweed, Virginia (*Helenium virginicum*)
T	Rush-rose, island (*Helianthemum greenei*)
T	Sunflower, Eggert's (*Helianthus eggertii*)
T	Sunflower, Pecos (=puzzle, =paradox) (*Helianthus paradoxus*)
E	Sunflower, Schweinitz's (*Helianthus schweinitzii*)
T	Pink, swamp (*Helonias bullata*)
E	Tarplant, Gaviota (*Hemizonia increscens* ssp. *villosa*)

Status	Species Name
T	Dwarf-flax, Marin (*Hesperolinon congestum*)
E	*Hesperomannia arborescens* (No common name)
E	*Hesperomannia arbuscula* (No common name)
E	*Hesperomannia lydgatei* (No common name)
T	Heartleaf, dwarf-flowered (*Hexastylis naniflora*)
E	Kauai hau kuahiwi (*Hibiscadelphus distans*)
E	Hau kuahiwi (*Hibiscadelphus giffardianus*)
E	Hau kuahiwi (*Hibiscadelphus hualalaiensis*)
E	Hau kuahiwi (*Hibiscadelphus woodii*)
E	Koki'o ke'oke'o (*Hibiscus arnottianus* ssp. *immaculatus*)
E	Ma'o hau hele, (=native yellow hibiscus) (*Hibiscus brackenridgei*)
E	Hibiscus, Clay's (*Hibiscus clayi*)
E	Koki'o ke'oke'o (*Hibiscus waimeae* ssp. *hannerae*)
E	Rush-pea, slender (*Hoffmannseggia tenella*)
T	Tarplant, Santa Cruz (*Holocarpha macradenia*)
T	Howellia, water (*Howellia aquatilis*)
T	Heather, mountain golden (*Hudsonia montana*)
T	Daisy, lakeside (*Hymenoxys herbacea*)
E	Dawn-flower, Texas prairie (*Hymenoxys texana*)
T	Hypericum, highlands scrub (*Hypericum cumulicola*)
E	Holly, Cook's (*Ilex cookii*)
E	*Ilex sintenisii* (No common name)
E	Mallow, Peter's Mountain (*Iliamna corei*)
E	Ipomopsis, Holy Ghost (*Ipomopsis sancti-spiritus*)
T	Iris, dwarf lake (*Iris lacustris*)
E	Ischaemum, Hilo (*Ischaemum byrone*)
E	Aupaka (*Isodendrion hosakae*)
E	Aupaka (*Isodendrion laurifolium*)
E	Aupaka (*Isodendrion longifolium*)
E	Kula wahine noho (*Isodendrion pyrifolium*)
T	Pogonia, small whorled (*Isotria medeoloides*)
T	Ivesia, Ash Meadows (*Ivesia kingii* var. *eremica*)
E	Jacquemontia, beach (*Jacquemontia reclinata*)
E	Walnut, West Indian or nogal (*Juglans jamaicensis*)
E	Water-willow, Cooley's (*Justicia cooleyi*)
E	Kohe malama malama o kanaloa (*Kanaloa kahoolawensis*)
E	Koki'o, Cooke's (*Kokia cookei*)
E	Koki'o (*Kokia drynarioides*)
E	Koki'o (*Kokia kauaiensis*)
E	Kamakahala (*Labordia cyrtandrae*)
E	Kamakahala (*Labordia lydgatei*)
E	Kamakahala (*Labordia tinifolia* var. *lanaiensis*)
E	Kamakahala (*Labordia tinifolia* var. *wahiawaensis*)
E	Kamakahala (*Labordia triflora*)
E	Goldfields, Burke's (*Lasthenia burkei*)
E	Goldfields, Contra Costa (*Lasthenia conjugens*)
E	Layia, beach (*Layia carnosa*)
E	*Lepanthes eltoroensis* (No common name)
E	'Anaunau (*Lepidium arbuscula*)
E	Ridge-cress, Barneby (*Lepidium barnebyanum*)
E	*Leptocereus grantianus* (No common name)
T	Bush-clover, prairie (*Lespedeza leptostachya*)
T	Bladderpod, Dudley Bluffs (*Lesquerella congesta*)
E	Bladderpod, Missouri (*Lesquerella filiformis*)
E	Bladderpod, San Bernardino Mountains (*Lesquerella kingii* ssp. *bernardina*)
T	Bladderpod, lyrate (*Lesquerella lyrata*)
E	Bladderpod, white (*Lesquerella pallida*)
E	Bladderpod, Spring Creek (*Lesquerella perforata*)
E	Bladderpod, Zapata (*Lesquerella thamnophila*)
E	Bladderpod, kodachrome (*Lesquerella tumulosa*)
E	Lessingia, San Francisco (*Lessingia germanorum* (=*L.g.* var. *germanorum*))
T	Blazingstar, Heller's (*Liatris helleri*)
E	Blazingstar, scrub (*Liatris ohlingerae*)
E	Water-umbel, Huachuca (*Lilaeopsis schaffneriana* var. *recurva*)
E	Lily, Western (*Lilium occidentale*)
E	Lily, Pitkin Marsh (*Lilium pardalinum* ssp. *pitkinense*)
E	Meadowfoam, Butte County (*Limnanthes floccosa* ssp. *californica*)
E	Meadowfoam, Sebastopol (*Limnanthes vinculans*)

Status	Species Name
E	Pondberry (*Lindera melissifolia*)
E	Nehe (*Lipochaeta fauriei*)
E	Nehe (*Lipochaeta kamolensis*)
E	Nehe (*Lipochaeta lobata* var. *leptophylla*)
E	Nehe (*Lipochaeta micrantha*)
E	Nehe (*Lipochaeta tenuifolia*)
E	*Lipochaeta venosa* (No common name)
E	Nehe (*Lipochaeta waimeaensis*)
E	Woodland-star, San Clemente Island (*Lithophragma maximum*)
E	*Lobelia gaudichaudii* ssp. *koolauensis* (No common name)
E	*Lobelia monostachya* (No common name)
E	*Lobelia niihauensis* (No common name)
E	*Lobelia oahuensis* (No common name)
E	Desert-parsley, Bradshaw's (*Lomatium bradshawii*)
E	Broom, San Clemente Island (*Lotus dendroideus* ssp. *traskiae*)
E	Lupine, scrub (*Lupinus aridorum*)
E	Lupine, Nipomo Mesa (*Lupinus nipomensis*)
T	Lupine, Kincaid's (*Lupinus sulphureus* (=*oreganus*) ssp. *kincaidii* (=var. *kincaidii*))
E	Lupine, clover (*Lupinus tidestromii*)
E	*Lyonia truncata* var. *proctorii* (No common name)
E	Loosestrife, rough-leaved (*Lysimachia asperulaefolia*)
E	*Lysimachia filifolia* (No common name)
E	*Lysimachia lydgatei* (No common name)
E	*Lysimachia maxima* (No common name)
T	Birds-in-a-nest, white (*Macbridea alba*)
E	Bush-mallow, San Clemente Island (*Malacothamnus clementinus*)
E	Bush-mallow, Santa Cruz Island (*Malacothamnus fasciculatus* var. *nesioticus*)
E	Malacothrix, Santa Cruz Island (*Malacothrix indecora*)
E	Malacothrix, island (*Malacothrix squalida*)
E	Manioc, Walker's (*Manihot walkerae*)
E	*Mariscus fauriei* (No common name)
E	*Mariscus pennatiformis* (No common name)
T	Button, Mohr's Barbara (*Marshallia mohrii*)
E	Alani (*Melicope adscendens*)
E	Alani (*Melicope balloui*)
E	Alani (*Melicope haupuensis*)
E	Alani (*Melicope knudsenii*)
E	Alani (*Melicope lydgatei*)
E	Alani (*Melicope mucronulata*)
E	Alani (*Melicope munroi*)
E	Alani (*Melicope ovalis*)
E	Alani (*Melicope pallida*)
E	Alani (*Melicope quadrangularis*)
E	Alani (*Melicope reflexa*)
E	Alani (*Melicope saint-johnii*)
E	Alani (*Melicope zahlbruckneri*)
T	Blazingstar, Ash Meadows (*Mentzelia leucophylla*)
E	Monkey-flower, Michigan (*Mimulus glabratus* var. *michiganensis*)
T	Four-o'clock, MacFarlane's (*Mirabilis macfarlanei*)
E	*Mitracarpus maxwelliae* (No common name)
E	*Mitracarpus polycladus* (No common name)
E	Monardella, willowy (*Monardella linoides* ssp. *viminea*)
E	Wooly-threads, San Joaquin (*Monolopia* (=*Lembertia*) *congdonii*)
E	*Munroidendron racemosum* (No common name)
E	*Myrcia paganii* (No common name)
E	Kolea (*Myrsine juddii*)
T	Kolea (*Myrsine linearifolia*)
T	Navarretia, spreading (*Navarretia fossalis*)
E	Navarretia, few-flowered (*Navarretia leucocephala* ssp. *pauciflora* (=*N. pauciflora*))
E	Navarretia, many-flowered (*Navarretia leucocephala* ssp. *plieantha*)
T	Grass, Colusa (*Neostapfia colusana*)
E	*Neraudia angulata* (No common name)
E	*Neraudia ovata* (No common name)
E	*Neraudia sericea* (No common name)
E	Niterwort, Amargosa (*Nitrophila mohavensis*)
E	Beargrass, Britton's (*Nolina brittoniana*)
E	'Aiea (*Nothocestrum breviflorum*)

Status	Species Name
E	'Aiea (*Nothocestrum peltatum*)
E	Kulu'i (*Nototrichium humile*)
E	Holei (*Ochrosia kilaueaensis*)
E	Evening-primrose, Eureka Valley (*Oenothera avita* ssp. *eurekensis*)
E	Evening-primrose, Antioch Dunes (*Oenothera deltoides* ssp. *howellii*)
E	Cactus, Bakersfield (*Opuntia treleasei*)
E	Orcutt grass, California (*Orcuttia californica*)
T	Orcutt grass, San Joaquin (*Orcuttia inaequalis*)
E	Orcutt grass, hairy (*Orcuttia pilosa*)
T	Orcutt grass, slender (*Orcuttia tenuis*)
E	Orcutt grass, Sacramento (*Orcuttia viscida*)
E	Palo de rosa (*Ottoschulzia rhodoxylon*)
E	Dropwort, Canby's (*Oxypolis canbyi*)
E	Oxytheca, cushenbury (*Oxytheca parishii* var. *goodmaniana*)
T	Locoweed, Fassett's (*Oxytropis campestris* var. *chartacea*)
E	Panicgrass, Carter's (*Panicum fauriei* var. *carteri*)
E	Lau 'ehu (*Panicum niihauense*)
T	Whitlow-wort, papery (*Paronychia chartacea*)
E	Stonecrop, Lake County (*Parvisedum leiocarpum*)
E	Lousewort, Furbish (*Pedicularis furbishiae*)
E	Cactus, Brady pincushion (*Pediocactus bradyi*)
E	Cactus, San Rafael (*Pediocactus despainii*)
T	Cactus, Siler pincushion (*Pediocactus* (=*Echinocactus*,=*Utahia*) *sileri*)
E	Cactus, Knowlton (*Pediocactus knowltonii*)
E	Cactus, Peebles Navajo (*Pediocactus peeblesianus peeblesianus*)
T	Cactus, Winkler (*Pediocactus winkleri*)
E	Penstemon, blowout (*Penstemon haydenii*)
E	Beardtongue, Penland (*Penstemon penlandii*)
E	Pentachaeta, white-rayed (*Pentachaeta bellidiflora*)
E	Pentachaeta, Lyon's (*Pentachaeta lyonii*)
E	Peperomia, Wheeler's (*Peperomia wheeleri*)
T	Makou (*Peucedanum sandwicense*)
E	Phacelia, clay (*Phacelia argillacea*)
E	Phacelia, North Park (*Phacelia formosula*)
E	Phacelia, island (*Phacelia insularis* ssp. *insularis*)
E	Phlox, Yreka (*Phlox hirsuta*)
E	Phlox, Texas trailing (*Phlox nivalis* ssp. *texensis*)
E	*Phyllostegia glabra* var. *lanaiensis* (No common name)
E	*Phyllostegia hirsuta* (No common name)
E	*Phyllostegia kaalaensis* (No common name)
E	*Phyllostegia knudsenii* (No common name)
E	*Phyllostegia mannii* (No common name)
E	*Phyllostegia mollis* (No common name)
E	*Phyllostegia parviflora* (No common name)
E	Kiponapona (*Phyllostegia racemosa*)
E	*Phyllostegia velutina* (No common name)
E	*Phyllostegia waimeae* (No common name)
E	*Phyllostegia warshaueri* (No common name)
E	*Phyllostegia wawrana* (No common name)
T	Twinpod, Dudley Bluffs (*Physaria obcordata*)
E	Cactus, Key tree (*Pilosocereus robinii*)
T	Butterwort, Godfrey's (*Pinguicula ionantha*)
E	Piperia, Yadon's (*Piperia yadonii*)
E	Aster, Ruth's golden (*Pityopsis ruthii*)
E	Popcornflower, rough (*Plagiobothrys hirtus*)
E	Allocarya, Calistoga (*Plagiobothrys strictus*)
E	Kuahiwi laukahi (*Plantago hawaiensis*)
E	Kuahiwi laukahi (*Plantago princeps*)
E	*Platanthera holochila* (No common name)
T	Orchid, eastern prairie fringed (*Platanthera leucophaea*)
T	Orchid, western prairie fringed (*Platanthera praeclara*)
E	Chupacallos (*Pleodendron macranthum*)
E	Hala pepe (*Pleomele hawaiiensis*)
E	Bluegrass, San Bernardino (*Poa atropurpurea*)
E	Bluegrass, Mann's (*Poa mannii*)
E	Bluegrass, Napa (*Poa napensis*)
E	Bluegrass, Hawaiian (*Poa sandvicensis*)
E	*Poa siphonoglossa* (No common name)
E	Mesa-mint, San Diego (*Pogogyne abramsii*)
E	Mesa-mint, Otay (*Pogogyne nudiuscula*)

Status	Species Name
E	Polygala, Lewton's (*Polygala lewtonii*)
E	Polygala, tiny (*Polygala smallii*)
E	Wireweed (*Polygonella basiramia*)
E	Sandlace (*Polygonella myriophylla*)
E	Po'e (*Portulaca sclerocarpa*)
E	Pondweed, Little Aguja Creek (*Potamogeton clystocarpus*)
E	Potentilla, Hickman's (*Potentilla hickmanii*)
E	Cinquefoil, Robbins' (*Potentilla robbinsiana*)
T	Primrose, Maguire (*Primula maguirei*)
E	Lo'ulu (*Pritchardia affinis*)
E	Wahane (*Pritchardia aylmer-robinsonii*)
E	Lo'ulu (*Pritchardia kaalae*)
E	Lo'ulu (*Pritchardia munroi*)
E	Lo'ulu (*Pritchardia napaliensis*)
E	Lo'ulu (*Pritchardia remota*)
E	Lo'ulu (*Pritchardia schattaueri*)
E	Lo'ulu (*Pritchardia viscosa*)
E	Plum, scrub (*Prunus geniculata*)
E	Sunburst, Hartweg's golden (*Pseudobahia bahiifolia*)
T	Sunburst, San Joaquin adobe (*Pseudobahia peirsonii*)
E	Kaulu (*Pteralyxia kauaiensis*)
E	Harperella (*Ptilimnium nodosum*)
E	Cliff-rose, Arizona (*Purshia (=Cowania) subintegra*)
T	Oak, Hinckley (*Quercus hinckleyi*)
E	Buttercup, autumn (*Ranunculus aestivalis (=acriformis)*)
E	*Remya kauaiensis* (No common name)
E	Remya, Maui (*Remya mauiensis*)
E	*Remya montgomeryi* (No common name)
E	Rhododendron, Chapman (*Rhododendron chapmanii*)
E	Sumac, Michaux's (*Rhus michauxii*)
T	Beaked-rush, Knieskern's (*Rhynchospora knieskernii*)
T	Gooseberry, Miccosukee (*Ribes echinellum*)
E	Watercress, Gambel's (*Rorippa gambellii*)
E	Arrowhead, bunched (*Sagittaria fasciculata*)
T	Water-plantain, Kral's (*Sagittaria secundifolia*)
E	*Sanicula mariversa* (No common name)
E	*Sanicula purpurea* (No common name)
E	Sandalwood, Lanai (='iliahi) (*Santalum freycinetianum* var. *lanaiense*)
E	Pitcher-plant, green (*Sarracenia oreophila*)
E	Pitcher-plant, Alabama canebrake (*Sarracenia rubra alabamensis*)
E	Pitcher-plant, mountain sweet (*Sarracenia rubra* ssp. *jonesii*)
E	Naupaka, dwarf (*Scaevola coriacea*)
E	Schiedea, Diamond Head (*Schiedea adamantis*)
E	Ma'oli'oli (*Schiedea apokremnos*)
E	*Schiedea haleakalensis* (No common name)
E	*Schiedea helleri* (No common name)
E	*Schiedea hookeri* (No common name)
E	*Schiedea kaalae* (No common name)
E	*Schiedea kauaiensis* (No common name)
E	Ma'oli'oli (*Schiedea kealiae*)
E	*Schiedea lydgatei* (No common name)
E	*Schiedea membranacea* (No common name)
E	*Schiedea nuttallii* (No common name)
E	*Schiedea sarmentosa* (No common name)
E	*Schiedea spergulina* var. *leiopoda* (No common name)
T	*Schiedea spergulina* var. *spergulina* (No common name)
E	Laulihilihi (*Schiedea stellarioides*)
E	*Schiedea verticillata* (No common name)
T	Reed-mustard, clay (*Schoenocrambe argillacea*)
E	Reed-mustard, Barneby (*Schoenocrambe barnebyi*)
E	Reed-mustard, shrubby (*Schoenocrambe suffrutescens*)
T	*Schoepfia arenaria* (No common name)
E	Chaffseed, American (*Schwalbea americana*)
E	Bulrush, Northeastern (*Scirpus ancistrochaetus*)
T	Cactus, Uinta Basin hookless (*Sclerocactus glaucus*)
T	Cactus, Mesa Verde (*Sclerocactus mesae-verdae*)
E	Cactus, Wright fishhook (*Sclerocactus wrightiae*)
T	Skullcap, Florida (*Scutellaria floridana*)
T	Skullcap, large-flowered (*Scutellaria montana*)
T	Roseroot, Leedy's (*Sedum integrifolium* ssp. *leedyi*)

Status	Species Name
T	Groundsel, San Francisco Peaks (*Senecio franciscanus*)
T	Butterweed, Layne's (*Senecio layneae*)
E	Iagu, Hayun (=(Guam), Tronkon guafi (Rota)) (*Serianthes nelsonii*)
E	Ohai (*Sesbania tomentosa*)
E	Rockcress, Santa Cruz Island (*Sibara filifolia*)
E	'Anunu (*Sicyos alba*)
E	Checker-mallow, Keck's (*Sidalcea keckii*)
T	Checker-mallow, Nelson's (*Sidalcea nelsoniana*)
E	Checker-mallow, Kenwood Marsh (*Sidalcea oregana* ssp. *valida*)
E	Checkermallow, Wenatchee Mountains (*Sidalcea oregana* var. *calva*)
E	Checker-mallow, pedate (*Sidalcea pedata*)
E	*Silene alexandri* (No common name)
T	*Silene hawaiiensis* (No common name)
E	*Silene lanceolata* (No common name)
E	*Silene perlmanii* (No common name)
E	Campion, fringed (*Silene polypetala*)
T	Catchfly, Spalding's (*Silene spaldingii*)
E	Irisette, white (*Sisyrinchium dichotomum*)
E	Erubia (*Solanum drymophilum*)
E	Popolo ku mai (*Solanum incompletum*)
E	'Aiakeakua, popolo (*Solanum sandwicense*)
T	Goldenrod, white-haired (*Solidago albopilosa*)
E	Goldenrod, Houghton's (*Solidago houghtonii*)
E	Goldenrod, Short's (*Solidago shortii*)
T	Goldenrod, Blue Ridge (*Solidago spithamaea*)
E	*Spermolepis hawaiiensis* (No common name)
E	Pinkroot, gentian (*Spigelia gentianoides*)
T	Spiraea, Virginia (*Spiraea virginiana*)
E	Ladies'-tresses, Canelo Hills (*Spiranthes delitescens*)
T	Ladies'-tresses, Ute (*Spiranthes diluvialis*)
E	Ladies'-tresses, Navasota (*Spiranthes parksii*)
E	Cobana negra (*Stahlia monosperma*)
E	*Stenogyne angustifolia* var. *angustifolia* (No common name)
E	*Stenogyne bifida* (No common name)
E	*Stenogyne campanulata* (No common name)
E	*Stenogyne kanehoana* (No common name)
E	Wire-lettuce, Malheur (*Stephanomeria malheurensis*)
E	Jewelflower, Metcalf Canyon (*Streptanthus albidus* ssp. *albidus*)
E	Jewelflower, Tiburon (*Streptanthus niger*)
E	Palo de jazmin (*Styrax portoricensis*)
E	Snowbells, Texas (*Styrax texanus*)
E	Seablite, California (*Suaeda californica*)
E	Grass, Eureka Dune (*Swallenia alexandrae*)
E	Taraxacum, California (*Taraxacum californicum*)
E	Palo colorado (*Ternstroemia luquillensis*)
E	*Ternstroemia subsessilis* (No common name)
E	*Tetramolopium arenarium* (No common name)
E	Pamakani (*Tetramolopium capillare*)
E	*Tetramolopium filiforme* (No common name)
E	*Tetramolopium lepidotum* ssp. *lepidotum* (No common name)
E	*Tetramolopium remyi* (No common name)
T	*Tetramolopium rockii* (No common name)
E	'Ohe'ohe (*Tetraplasandra gymnocarpa*)
E	Meadowrue, Cooley's (*Thalictrum cooleyi*)
T	Thelypody, Howell's spectacular (*Thelypodium howellii spectabilis*)
E	Mustard, slender-petaled (*Thelypodium stenopetalum*)
E	Penny-cress, Kneeland Prairie (*Thlaspi californicum*)
E	Dogweed, ashy (*Thymophylla tephroleuca*)
E	Fringepod, Santa Cruz Island (*Thysanocarpus conchuliferus*)
T	Townsendia, Last Chance (*Townsendia aprica*)
E	*Trematolobelia singularis* (No common name)
E	Bariaco (*Trichilia triacantha*)
T	Bluecurls, Hidden Lake (*Trichostema austromontanum* ssp. *compactum*)
E	Clover, showy Indian (*Trifolium amoenum*)
E	Clover, running buffalo (*Trifolium stoloniferum*)
E	Clover, Monterey (*Trifolium trichocalyx*)
E	Trillium, persistent (*Trillium persistens*)
E	Trillium, relict (*Trillium reliquum*)
E	Tuctoria, Greene's (*Tuctoria greenei*)
E	Grass, Solano (*Tuctoria mucronata*)

TABLE 4.1

Flowering plant species listed as endangered or threatened, May 15, 2002 [CONTINUED]

Status	Species Name
E	Opuhe (*Urera kaalae*)
T	Vervain, Red Hills (*Verbena californica*)
T	Crownbeard, big-leaved (*Verbesina dissita*)
E	*Vernonia proctorii* (No common name)
E	Vetch, Hawaiian (*Vicia menziesii*)
E	*Vigna o-wahuensis* (No common name)
E	Pamakani (*Viola chamissoniana* ssp. *chamissoniana*)
E	*Viola helenae* (No common name)
E	Nani wai'ale'ale (*Viola kauaiensis* var. *wahiawaensis*)
E	*Viola lanaiensis* (No common name)
E	*Viola oahuensis* (No common name)
E	Warea, wide-leaf (*Warea amplexifolia*)
E	Mustard, Carter's (*Warea carteri*)
E	Iliau, dwarf (*Wilkesia hobdyi*)
E	*Xylosma crenatum* (No common name)
E	Grass, Tennessee yellow-eyed (*Xyris tennesseensis*)
T	Yellowhead, desert (*Yermo xanthocephalus*)
E	A'e (*Zanthoxylum dipetalum* var. *tomentosum*)
E	A'e (*Zanthoxylum hawaiiense*)
E	Prickly-ash, St. Thomas (*Zanthoxylum thomasianum*)
E	Wild-rice, Texas (*Zizania texana*)
E	Ziziphus, Florida (*Ziziphus celata*)

Notes: E = endangered
T = threatened

SOURCE: "U.S. Listed Flowering Plant Species Report by Taxonomic Group as of 5/15/2002," U.S. Fish & Wildlife Service, Threatened and Endangered Species System, Washington, DC, May 15, 2002 [Online] http://ecos.fws.gov/webpage/webpage_vip_listed.html?module=undefined&code=F&listings=0 [accessed May 15, 2002]

TABLE 4.2

Nonflowering plant species listed as endangered or threatened, May 15, 2002

Status	Species Name
Conifers and Cycads	
E	Cypress, Santa Cruz (*Cupressus abramsiana*)
T	Cypress, Gowen (*Cupressus goveniana* ssp. *goveniana*)
E	Torreya, Florida (*Torreya taxifolia*)
Ferns and Allies	
E	Fern, pendant kihi (*Adenophorus periens*)
E	*Adiantum vivesii* (No common name)
E	*Asplenium fragile* var. *insulare* (No common name)
T	Fern, American hart's-tongue (*Asplenium scolopendrium* var) *americanum*
E	Pauoa (*Ctenitis squamigera*)
E	Fern, Elfin tree (*Cyathea dryopteroides*)
E	Diellia, asplenium-leaved (*Diellia erecta*)
E	*Diellia falcata* (No common name)
E	*Diellia pallida* (No common name)
E	*Diellia unisora* (No common name)
E	*Diplazium molokaiense* (No common name)
E	*Elaphoglossum serpens* (No common name)
E	Wawae'iole (*Huperzia mannii*)
E	Quillwort, Louisiana (*Isoetes louisianensis*)
E	Quillwort, black spored (*Isoetes melanospora*)
E	Quillwort, mat-forming (*Isoetes tegetiformans*)
E	Wawae'iole (*Lycopodium* (=*Phlegmariurus*) *nutans*)
E	Ihi'ihi (*Marsilea villosa*)
E	Fern, Aleutian shield (*Polystichum aleuticum*)
E	*Polystichum calderonense* (No common name)
E	*Pteris lidgatei* (No common name)
E	*Tectaria estremerana* (No common name)
E	*Thelypteris inabonensis* (No common name)
T	Fern, Alabama streak-sorus (*Thelypteris pilosa* var. *alabamensis*)
E	*Thelypteris verecunda* (No common name)
E	*Thelypteris yaucoensis* (No common name)
Lichens	
E	Cladonia, Florida perforate (*Cladonia perforata*)
E	Lichen, rock gnome (*Gymnoderma lineare*)

SOURCE: "U.S. Listed Nonflowering Plant Species Report by Taxonomic Group as of 5/15/2002," U.S. Fish & Wildlife Service, Threatened and Endangered Species System, Washington, DC, May 15, 2002 [Online] http://ecos.fws.gov/webpage/webpage_vip_listed.html?module=undefined&code=N&listings=0 [accessed May 15, 2002]

Jamaica (22.5 percent), Turkey (21.7 percent), Spain (19.5 percent), French Polynesia (19.5 percent), Pitcairn (18.4 percent), and Reunion (18.1 percent). Islands are disproportionately represented in the top ten.

However, the *1997 IUCN Red List of Threatened Plants* contains regional biases—assessments of flora in North America, Australia, and Southern Africa were more comprehensive than those for other regions. It is likely that significantly greater numbers of threatened plant species will be found in Asia, the Caribbean, South America, and the rest of Africa when these areas are fully studied.

Information from the *1997 IUCN Red List of Threatened Plants* is being incorporated into new versions of IUCN publications. The *2000 IUCN Red List of Threatened Species* lists 5,611 species of threatened plants. However, only about 4 percent of plant species have been studied in sufficient detail to assess their status, and the actual number of threatened species is likely to be very much higher. The majority of IUCN-listed plants in 2000 are trees, a group that is generally well-studied. The conifers—cone-bearing evergreen species such as pines, spruce, and fir—represent the only plant group that has been thoroughly examined. Among conifers, 140 species, or 16 percent of the total, are threatened. About 91 percent of IUCN-listed plants are threatened, partly because of habitat loss. The greatest number of threatened species are found in Central and South America, Central and West Africa, and Southeast Asia. Countries with the largest number of listed plants include Malaysia (681 species), Indonesia (384 species), Brazil (338 species), and Sri Lanka (280 species). Many of the threatened species from these countries represent tropical timber trees. The IUCN is continuing to update their information on plants. Ongoing studies, for example, suggest that approximately 59 percent of the 10,000 tree species examined are in danger of extinction.

THE AMERICAN LANDSCAPE

Although North America has less plant diversity than the tropics, it is nonetheless amazingly rich. The diverse environmental conditions found on the continent allow representatives of most of the world's major plant groups to flourish in one region or another. For example, North America is home to more than 211 flowering plant

FIGURE 4.1

Distribution of critically endangered, endangered, and threatened ecosystem types

A

Aquatic (15)
10%

Forested wetlands (16)
10%

Grasslands,
savannas,
barrens (35)
22%

Shrublands
(10) 6%

Forests (45)
30%

Other wetlands (35)
22%

B

Grasslands,
savannas,
barrens (22)
55%

Shrublands (10)
24%

Forests (7)
17%

Forested wetlands (1)
2%

Aquatic (1)
2%

(A) Distribution of critically endangered, endangered, and threatened ecosystem types in six general categories. To include general wetland-loss statistics, which are usually organized by state, a number was added in the wetland category for each state with declines of more than 70%. The greatest number of reported declines is among forest and wetland habitats and communities. (B) For ecosystems that have declined by more than 98% (i.e., critically endangered), the greatest losses are among grassland, savanna, and barrens communities.

SOURCE: Reed F. Noss, Edward T. LaRoe III, and J. Michael Scott, "Figure 1," in *Endangered Ecosystems of the United States: A Preliminary Assessment of Loss and Degradation*, U.S. Geological Survey, Reston, VA, 1995 [Online] http://biology.usgs.gov/pubs/ecosys.htm [accessed May 15, 2002]

FIGURE 4.2

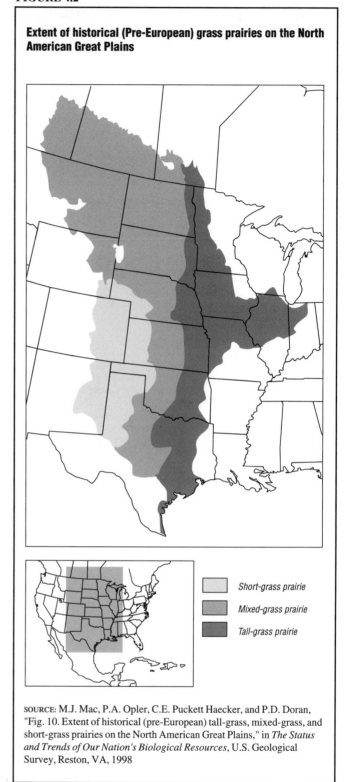

Extent of historical (Pre-European) grass prairies on the North American Great Plains

Short-grass prairie

Mixed-grass prairie

Tall-grass prairie

SOURCE: M.J. Mac, P.A. Opler, C.E. Puckett Haecker, and P.D. Doran, "Fig. 10. Extent of historical (pre-European) tall-grass, mixed-grass, and short-grass prairies on the North American Great Plains," in *The Status and Trends of Our Nation's Biological Resources*, U.S. Geological Survey, Reston, VA, 1998

families alone. The richest assemblages of flowering plants are found in Florida and Texas.

Botanists have divided North America into a series of ecosystems based on the underlying vegetation. Northern coniferous forests make up 28 percent of the North American continent; grasslands, 21–25 percent; arctic ecosystems, 19 percent; eastern deciduous forests, 11 percent; coastal plain ecosystems, 3 percent; desert ecosystems, 5 percent; western mountain coniferous forests, 7 percent; tidal wetlands, 1 percent; Mediter-

ranean scrublands and woodlands, 1 percent; and beach vegetation, less than 1 percent.

Endangered U.S. Ecosystems

In 1995 the first full review of the health of the American landscape, "Endangered Ecosystems of the United States—A Preliminary Assessment of Loss and Degradation," was released by the National Biological Service (NBS), an Interior Department research organization created in 1993. Although individual species had been studied previously, the health of the larger ecosystems had never before been considered. The study was based on surveys of state databases and the scientific literature. The report concluded that vast stretches of natural habitat, totaling nearly half the area of the 48 contiguous states, had declined to the point of endangerment. Ecosystems suffered in two ways. Quantitative losses were measured by a decline in the area of an ecosystem. Qualitative losses involved degradation in the structure, function, or composition of an ecosystem.

Of the ecosystems that had declined by over 70 percent, 58 percent were terrestrial, 32 percent were wetland areas, and 10 percent were aquatic. Forests, grasslands, barrens, and savannas dominated the list. (See Figure 4.1.) American ecosystems identified by the NBS as suffering the greatest overall decline include tall-grass prairies and oak savannas of the Midwest, deciduous forests of the East, and longleaf pine forests of the southern coastal plains. The midwestern prairies have been all but destroyed through conversion to agriculture—the original extent of these prairies is shown in Figure 4.2. As ecosystems shrink, the species that live in them become imperiled as well. The longleaf pine ecosystem of the southern coastal plain, for instance, is currently home to 27 species on the Endangered Species List and another 99 species that have been proposed for listing.

The full NBS list of the most endangered ecosystems of the United States appears in Table 4.3. Thirty-two American ecosystems had declined by more than 98 percent and were classified as "critically endangered." Fifty-eight had declined by 85 to 98 percent and were classified as "endangered." Thirty-eight others declined by 70 to 84 percent and were listed as "threatened."

Endangered ecosystems were found in all major regions of the United States except Alaska (Figure 4.3). The greatest losses occurred in the Northeast, the South, and the Midwest, as well as in California. A list of some Californian plant communities, most of which are unique to the state, and percentage reductions in these community types appear in Table 4.4. Native grasslands, needlegrass steppes, and alkali sink scrubs are among the communities that have declined most precipitously in California.

Hawaiian Plants

Because of its isolation from continental land masses, many of the species found in Hawaii exist nowhere else in the world. An estimated 90 percent of Hawaiian plant species are in fact endemic. Because of large-scale deforestation and habitat destruction on the Hawaiian islands, Hawaii is home to more endangered plants than any other state in the nation, with 289 listed species in 2002. Hawai-

FIGURE 4.3

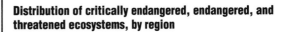

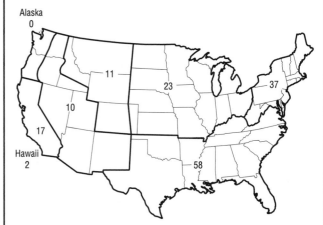

Distribution of critically endangered, endangered, and threatened ecosystems, by region

Distribution of critically endangered, endangered, and threatened ecosystem types by geographic region. Each region received a point when types overlapped regions. Regions with fewer types are not necessarily in better condition because numbers reflect sampling and reporting biases in the literature and in heritage programs.

SOURCE: Reed F. Noss, Edward T. LaRoe III, and J. Michael Scott, "Figure 2," in *Endangered Ecosystems of the United States: A Preliminary Assessment of Loss and Degradation*, U.S. Geological Survey, Reston, VA, 1995 [Online] http://biology.usgs.gov/pubs/ecosys.htm [accessed May 15, 2002]

ian plants have suffered from the introduction of invasive predators such as cows, pigs, and insects, as well as the loss of critical pollinators with the decline of numerous species of native birds and insects. Over 10 percent of Hawaiian plant species have gone extinct in the last few hundred years, and nearly 30 percent are currently believed to be imperiled.

In April 2002, the Fish and Wildlife Service proposed critical habitat for native plant species on the islands of Maui and Kahoolawe. The proposal includes 15 habitat areas covering approximately 128,000 acres. Protection of these areas would benefit at least 61 threatened and endangered species by preserving current habitat, as well as allowing for natural range expansion and the reintroduction of endangered species into portions of their historic ranges. The areas proposed for critical habitat include Hawaii state lands (45 percent), federal lands (17 percent), and privately owned land (37 percent). Only activity on federal lands is legally affected by critical habitat designation. Critical habitat has also been proposed on the islands of Kauai, Niihau, and Lanai, and the Fish and Wildlife Service expects to publish proposals for Molokai, Oahu, and the northwestern Hawaiian islands later in 2002.

Profiles of Endangered North American Plants

ENDANGERED CACTI. Over 30 cactus species are currently listed with the U.S. Fish and Wildlife Service as either threatened or endangered. Most of these species are

TABLE 4.3

Critically endangered, endangered, and threatened ecosystems

Decline refers to destruction, conversion to other land uses, or significant degradation of ecological structure, function, or composition since European settlement. Estimates are from quantitative studies and qualitative assessments.

Critically endangered (>98% decline) ecosystems

Old-growth and other virgin stands in the eastern deciduous forest biome.

Spruce-fir (*Picea rubens-Abies fraseri*) forest in the southern Appalachians.

Red pine (*Pinus resinosaa*) and white pine (*Pinus strobus*) forests (mature and old-growth) in Michigan

Longleaf pine (*Pinus palustris*) forests and savannas in the southeastern coastal plain.

Slash pine (*Pinus elliottii*) rockland habitat in South Florida.

Loblolly pine-shortleaf pine (*Pinus taeda-Pinus echinata*) hardwood forests in the West Gulf Coastal Plain.

Arundinaria gigantea canebrakes in the Southeast.

Tallgrass prairie east of the Missouri River and on mesic sites across range.

Bluegrass savanna-woodland and prairies in Kentucky.

Black Belt prairies in Alabama and Mississippi and in the Jackson Prairie in Mississippi.

Ungrazed dry prairie in Florida.

Oak (*Quercus* spp.) savanna in the Midwest.

Wet and mesic coastal prairies in Louisiana.

Lakeplain wet prairie in Michigan.

Sedge (*Carex* spp. and others) meadows in Wisconsin.

Hempstead Plains grasslands on Long Island, New York.

Lake sand beaches in Vermont.

Serpentine barrens, maritime heathland, and pitch pine (*Pinus rigida*)-heath barrens in New York.

Prairies (all types) and oak savannas in the Willamette Valley and in the foothills of the Coast Range, Oregon.

Palouse prairie (Idaho, Oregon, and Washington and in similar communities in Montana).

Native grasslands (all types) in California.

Alkali sink scrub in southern California.

Coastal strand in southern California.

Ungrazed sagebrush steppe in the Intermountain West.

Basin big sagebrush (*Artenisia tridentata*) in the Snake River Plain of Idaho.

Atlantic white-cedar (*Chamaecyparis thyoides*) stands in the Great Dismal Swamp of Virginia and in North Carolina and possibly across the entire range.

Streams in the Mississippi Alluvial Plain.

Endangered (85-98% decline)

Old-growth and other virgin forests in regions and in states other than in those already listed, except in Alaska.

Mesic limestone forest and barrier island beaches in Maryland.

Coastal plain Atlantic white-cedar swamp, maritime oak-holly (*Quercus* spp.-*Ilex* spp.) forest, maritime redcedar (*Juniperus virginiana*) forest, marl fen, marl pond shore, and oak openings in New York.

Coastal heathland in southern New England and on Long Island.

Pine-oak-heath sandplain woods and lake sand beach in Vermont.

Floodplain forests in New Hampshire.

Red spruce (*Picea rubens*) forests in the central Appalachians (West Virginia).

Upland hardwoods in the Coastal Plain of Tennessee.

Lowland forest in southeastern Missouri.

High-quality oak-hickory (*Quercus* spp.-*Carya* spp.) forest on the Cumberland Plateau and on the Highland Rim of Tennessee.

Limestone redcedar (*Juniperus virginianus*) glades in Tennessee.

Wet longleaf pine savanna and eastern upland longleaf pine forest in Louisiana.

Calcareous prairie, Fleming glade, shortleaf pine/oak-hickory forest, mixed hardwood-loblolly pine forest, eastern xeric sandhill woodland, and stream terrace sandy woodland/savanna in Louisiana.

Slash pine (*Pinus elliottii*) forests in southwestern Florida.

Red pine and white pine forest in Minnesota.

Coastal redwood (*Sequoia semper virens*) forests in California.

Old-growth ponderosa pine (*Pinus ponderosa*) forests in the northern Rocky Mountains, Intermountain West, and eastside Cascades Mountains.

Riparian forests in California, Arizona, and New Mexico.

Coastal sage scrub (especially maritime) and coastal mixed chaparral in southern California.

Dry forest on main islands of Hawaii.

All types of native habitats in the lower delta of the Rio Grande River, Texas.

Tallgrass prairie (all types combined).

Native shrub and grassland steppe in Oregon and in Washington.

Low elevation grasslands in Montana.

Gulf Coast pitcher plant (*Sarracenia* spp.) bogs.

Pocosins (evergreen shrub bogs) and ultramafic soligenous wetlands in Virginia.

Mountain bogs (southern Appalachian bogs and swamp forest-bog complex) in Tennessee and in North Carolina.

Upland wetlands on the Highland Rim of Tennessee.

Saline wetlands in eastern Nebraska.

Wetlands (all types combined) in south-central California, Illinois, Indiana, Iowa, Missouri, Nebraska, and Ohio.

Marshes in the Carson-Truckee area of western Nevada.

Low-elevation wetlands in Idaho.

Woody hardwood draws, glacial pothole ponds, and peatlands in Montana.

Vernal pools in the Central Valley and in southern California.

Marshes in the Coos Bay area of Oregon.

Freshwater marsh and coastal salt marsh in Southern California.

Seasonal wetlands of the San Francisco Bay, California.

Large streams and rivers in all major regions.

Aquatic mussel (Unionidae) beds in Tennessee.

Submersed aquatic vegetation in the Chesapeake Bay, in Maryland, and in Virginia.

Mangrove swamps and salt marsh along the Indian River lagoon, Florida.

Seagrass meadows in Galveston Bay, Texas.

Threatened (70-84% decline)

Nationwide riparian forests (other than in already listed regions), including southern bottomland hardwood forests.

Xeric habitats (scrub, scrubby flatwoods, sandhills) on the Lake Wales Ridge, Florida.

Tropical hardwood hammocks on the central Florida keys.

Northern hardwood forest, aspen (*Populus* spp.) parkland, and jack pine (*Pinus banksiana*) forests in Minnesota.

Saline prairie, western upland longleaf pine forest, live oak-pine-magnolia (*Quercus virginiana-Pinus* spp.-*Magnolia* spp.) forest, western xeric sandhill woodland, slash pine-pond baldcypress-hardwood (*Pinus elliottii-Taxodium ascendens*) forest, wet and mesic spruce-pine (*P. glabra*)-hardwood flatwoods, wet mixed hardwood-loblolly pine (*Pinus taeda*) flatwoods, and flatwoods ponds in Louisiana.

Alvar grassland, calcareous pavement barrens, dwarf pine ridges, mountain spruce-fir forest, inland Atlantic whitecedar swamp, freshwater tidal swamp, inland salt marsh, patterned peatland, perched bog, pitch pine-blueberry (*Pinus rigida-Vaccinium* spp.) peat swamp, coastal plain poor fens, rich graminoid fen, rich sloping fen, and riverside ice meadow in New York.

Maritime-like forests in the Clearwater Basin of Idaho.

Woodland and chaparral on Santa Catalina Inland.

Southern tamarack (*Lark laricina*) swamp in Michigan.

Wetlands (all kinds) in Arkansas, Connecticut, Kentucky, and Maryland.

Marshes in the Puget Sound region, Washington.

Cienegas (marshes) in Arizona.

Coastal wetlands in California.

SOURCE: Reed F. Noss, Edward T. LaRoe III, and J. Michael Scott, "Appendix B," in *Endangered Ecosystems of the United States: A Preliminary Assessment of Loss and Degradation*, U.S. Geological Survey, Reston, VA, 1995 [Online] http://biology.usgs.gov/pubs/ecosys.htm [accessed May 15, 2002]

found in arid habitats in the Southwest, particularly Texas, New Mexico, Arizona, and Utah. In addition to habitat loss and degradation, a prime reason for the endangerment of cactus species in general is over-collection by enthusiasts.

The star cactus is a spineless species found in Texas and parts of Mexico, and was listed as endangered across its entire range in 1993. In Texas, it is found only along a single creek system in Starr County. The star cactus is several inches in diameter and only a few inches tall. The flowers have large yellow petals that form a deep bowl. Endangerment of this species resulted partly from over-collection in the wild by cactus enthusiasts, who greatly prize it. The star cactus has also suffered from habitat loss due to urban and agricultural development. The San Antonio Botanical Garden has attempted to aid conservation efforts by developing methods for propagating this species from seed.

The bunched cory cactus was first listed as threatened in 1979. It is a small species, reaching heights of up to four inches. The bunched cory cactus has rounded, single stems and occupies ledges and flats on limestone outcrops. Populations occur in Big Bend National Park in Texas, as well as on some private ranches—a total of approximately 25 different sites are known. Despite strict regulations against collection and monitoring in park sites, cactus poachers nonetheless continue to collect the plant illegally.

SHOWY STICKSEED. Showy stickseed is one of the most recent plants to be added to the Endangered Species List. It was officially listed in February 2002 as endangered throughout its habitat—a single site in the Wenatchee National Forest in Chelan County in the state of Washington. Showy stickseed was once observed at a second site in Chelan County but is now believed to be extinct there. Approximately 1,000 showy stickseed plants existed in the early 1980s, but only 500 plants were found in a 2001 survey. Critical habitat was not designated for showy stickseed by the Fish and Wildlife Service because it was believed to be imprudent to reveal the location of the sole population for fear of illegal collection.

Showy stickseed is an herb 8 to 16 inches tall. When in bloom, it has large, white flowers. Endangerment is believed to have resulted from competition with invasive species such as weeds, woody shrubs, and trees. Showy stickseed requires large amounts of sunlight, which has become increasingly blocked by the larger invasive species. A long history of fire suppression has also contributed to the shading problem. The other major factor contributing to endangerment of this species is collection from the wild. Now that the species is listed under the Endangered Species Act, collection is considered a federal crime. The Fish and Wildlife Service is cooperating with the Wenatchee National Forest and the Washington Department of Transportation to help improve habitat areas for the showy stickseed. This includes thinning of invasive tree species and control of

TABLE 4.4

Human-caused reductions in westside California plant communities and formations

Community/formation	Vegetation reduced (percent)
Native grasslands	99
Needlegrass steppe	99.9
Southern San Joaquin Valley alkali sink scrub	99
Southern California coastal sage-scrub	70–90
Vernal pools	91
Wetlands	91
Riparian woodlands	89
Coast redwood forest	85

SOURCE: M.J. Mac, P.A. Opler, C.E. Puckett Haecker, and P.D. Doran,"Table 1. Human-caused reductions in westside California plant communities and formations (after Noss and Peters, 1995)," in *The Status and Trends of Our Nation's Biological Resources,* U.S. Geological Survey, Reston,VA, 1998

weeds. In addition, experimental propagation of the stickseed is being pursued.

DESERT YELLOWHEAD. In March 2002, the desert yellowhead was listed as threatened in its only known habitat, 50 acres of federal land in Wyoming. There were about 12,000 plants found in a survey conducted in 2001. The desert yellowhead is related to sunflowers, and has 25 to 80 flowers crowded atop each 12-inch stem. The species was first discovered in 1990. The desert yellowhead is threatened due to human activity. Portions of its current habitat are being considered for oil and gas drilling. The Fish and Wildlife Service is working with the Bureau of Land Management, which manages desert yellowhead habitat, on a conservation plan.

ROBBINS' CINQUEFOIL. The Robbins' cinquefoil was officially listed as endangered in 1980. This plant species is related to roses, and is found in the alpine zone of the White Mountain National Forest in New Hampshire. It is a small species that bears a yellow flower. At the time of listing, there were approximately 3,700 plants surveyed. After concerted conservation efforts involving the Fish and Wildlife Service, the U.S. Forest Service, and the Appalachian Mountain Club, the population of the Robbins' cinquefoil increased to over 14,000 plants in 2001. In June 2001, the species was proposed for delisting. Critical actions that helped the population recover included a rerouting of the Appalachian Trail around the critical habitat areas of the species, as well as the building of an enclosure to protect the population from disturbance. In addition, two populations of Robbins' cinquefoil were introduced in new National Forest habitats.

ENDANGERED FORESTS

Forests perform a wide variety of social and ecological functions. They provide homes and sustenance for forest dwellers, protect and enrich soils, affect local and regional climate through the evaporation and storage of water, and help stabilize the global climate by processing carbon dioxide.

Forests are broadly classified by latitude as either tropical, temperate, or boreal. Tropical forests, or rainforests, are predominantly evergreen and occur close to the equator, in areas with plentiful rain and little temperature variation year-round. There are tropical forests in Central and South America, Africa, South and Southeast Asia, and Australia. Tropical forests are characterized by the greatest diversity of biological species. For example, as many as 100 distinct tree species may inhabit a square kilometer. Vegetation is often so dense in tropical forests that very little light penetrates to the ground. Temperate forests are found in areas with distinct warm and cold seasons, including North America, northern Asia, and western and central Europe. Many temperate forests are made up of deciduous trees, species that shed their leaves during winter. Plant diversity is not as great in temperate forests as in rainforests. There are perhaps three or four tree species per square kilometer. Boreal forests, also known as taiga, are found at high latitudes in extremely cold climates where the growing season is short. Precipitation generally falls as snow rather than rain. Boreal forest flora includes evergreen trees and lichen ground cover. Boreal forests are present in Siberia, Scandinavia, Alaska, and Canada.

Deforestation

Deforestation refers to the destruction of forests through the removal of trees, most often by clear-cutting or burning. It results in habitat loss for countless species of plants as well as animals. Deforestation is occurring globally, but is proceeding at a particularly alarming rate in the world's tropical rainforests, which comprise the most diverse ecosystems in the world. Deforestation is one of the most pressing environmental issues today.

In addition to destruction of habitat for numerous plant and animal species, the loss of forests has other effects as well. For example, forests play a crucial role in the global cycling of carbon—vegetation stores two trillion tons of carbon worldwide, roughly triple the amount stored in the atmosphere. When forest trees are cleared, the carbon they contain is oxidized and released to the air, adding to the carbon dioxide in the atmosphere. The burning of the Amazon rainforests and other forests thus has a two-fold effect—the release of large amounts of carbon dioxide into the atmosphere and the loss of the trees that help absorb carbon dioxide.

Furthermore, deforestation also results in forest fragmentation, which is itself detrimental for several reasons. First, forest fragmentation creates more "edge" habitats and destroys habitat for deep-forest creatures. Second, fragmentation isolates plant and animal populations, making them more vulnerable to local extinction. Third, some non-native species thrive in edge habitats, and are able to invade and displace native species in a fragmented habitat. In North America, for example, songbirds like the wood thrush and the promontory warbler are declining due to increasing numbers of blue jays and parasitic brown-headed cowbirds, both of which flourish at forest edges. Finally, most trees are more susceptible to weather at forest edges.

Rainforests

Tropical forests are the world's most biologically rich habitats. These storehouses of biological diversity cover less than 1 percent of the earth, but are home to 50 to 90 percent of the world's species. Many rainforest species have yet to be discovered and described by humans. In May 2002 for example, ornithologists announced the discovery of a new species of parrot, described as possessing green feathers, a hooked neck like a vulture, and a bald orange head. If new discoveries are being made even among well-studied groups such as birds, one can only imagine the untold number of insects or plants that remain to be studied.

Tropical forests are also the most critically endangered of habitats and are shrinking faster than ever—about 42 million acres a year are lost, or 80 acres each minute. The primary threats to rainforests are logging and clearing for farms and ranches. Satellite photographs show that as much as 10 percent of the Amazon rainforest has been destroyed, mainly through "slash and burn" clearing for agricultural use. Conservative estimates suggest rates of decline as high as 6.5 percent per year for rainforests in the Côte d'Ivoire in Africa, and an average of 0.6 percent per year for all tropical forests. At this pace, all rainforests will be cleared within 177 years. Given the growth in human population and economic activity in developing countries, the rate of deforestation is more likely to increase than to stabilize. Losses have been greatest so far in West Africa, Brazil, Central America, Mexico, Southeast Asia, and Madagascar.

The major underlying causes of tropical deforestation are underdevelopment, unemployment, and poverty among the growing populations of tropical countries. Unrestricted by enforceable regulations, farmers clear forests to create meager cropland that is often useless three years after its conversion—this is because tropical forest soils are poor, because almost all available nutrients are locked up in the trees and other biomatter. Logging and the conversion of forestland to unsustainable, short-term agricultural use have resulted in the destruction of habitats, declining fisheries, erosion, and flooding. Forest loss also disrupts regional weather patterns and contributes to global climate change. Finally, it eliminates plant and animal species that may serve important medical, industrial, and agricultural purposes. However, argu-

FIGURE 4.4

Common forest types on non-federal land, 1992

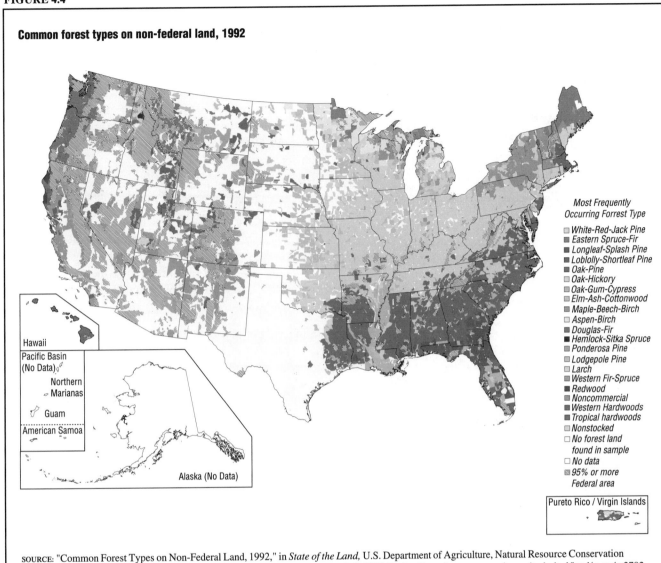

Most Frequently
Occurring Forrest Type

- White-Red-Jack Pine
- Eastern Spruce-Fir
- Longleaf-Splash Pine
- Loblolly-Shortleaf Pine
- Oak-Pine
- Oak-Hickory
- Oak-Gum-Cypress
- Elm-Ash-Cottonwood
- Maple-Beech-Birch
- Aspen-Birch
- Douglas-Fir
- Hemlock-Sitka Spruce
- Ponderosa Pine
- Lodgepole Pine
- Larch
- Western Fir-Spruce
- Redwood
- Noncommercial
- Western Hardwoods
- Tropical hardwoods
- Nonstocked
- No forest land found in sample
- No data
- 95% or more Federal area

Pureto Rico / Virgin Islands

Hawaii
Pacific Basin (No Data)
Northern Marianas
Guam
American Samoa
Alaska (No Data)

SOURCE: "Common Forest Types on Non-Federal Land, 1992," in *State of the Land,* U.S. Department of Agriculture, Natural Resource Conservation Service, Resource Assessment and Strategic Plannning Division, Washington, DC, 2002 [Online] http://www.nrcs.usda.gov/technical/land/meta/m2792. html [accessed July 23, 2002].

ments for protective measures that might not pay off for many decades are often of little interest to farmers with families to feed. Developing countries frequently voice resentment over what they see as the hypocrisy of industrialized nations, which invariably engaged in similarly destructive practices to build their own economies.

Conservation of tropical forests presents a considerable challenge. The creation of "protected areas" alone has often proven ineffectual, mostly because the people who exploit forests are given no other options for meeting their economic needs. Many conservationists have started to focus on the promotion of sustainable development within rainforests. Agroforestry describes an agricultural strategy that involves the maintenance of diversity within developed tropical forest areas. This includes planting many different types of crops in patches that are mixed in

among grazing lands and intact forest. Agroforestry often focuses on crops that produce goods for an indefinite period of time, including citrus fruits, bananas, cacao, coffee, and rubber. Agroforestry can help to maintain soil quality as well as tropical biodiversity, allowing for a sustained productivity that makes it unnecessary to clear more and more areas of forest. In addition, rainforest conservationists have promoted the harvest of sustainable rainforest products, rather than unsustainable products such as timber. Sustainable harvests include those of medicines, food, and rubber. Finally, a recent trend is certification of tropical timber. It is estimated that as much as 70 percent of tropical timber available for sale in the United States represents "stolen timber" obtained through illegal logging. The Forest Stewardship Council, based in Oaxaca, Mexico, runs a program that certifies timber obtained from sustainably managed forests. Large wood suppliers,

FIGURE 4.5

Coast redwood trees in Redwood National Park, California. Redwoods are found only on the west coast of North America and are the tallest trees on earth. *(National Park Service)*

such as Home Depot in 1999, opted to give preference to certified wood by 2002 following extensive picketing by protesters at several stores.

North American Forests

North America harbors a diverse variety of forest types, which are shown on the map in Figure 4.4. Some of these forests are highly imperiled. The greatest threat to North American forests is deforestation. Many forests are being depleted by clear cutting, a method of logging in which all the trees in an area are cut. Serious damage to the "old growth" forests of the Pacific Northwest, for example, is apparent from National Aeronautics and Space Administration (NASA) satellite photos. These "old growth" forests harbor many unique species, including several that are threatened or endangered. An alternative to clear-cutting is selective management, in which only some trees are removed from an area. Even selective management practices, however, frequently deplete

forests more quickly than they are able to recover. The lumber industry continues to battle with environmentalists and the U.S. Forest Service over the right to log National Forest lands, including the unique redwood forests of the West Coast (Figure 4.5).

The U.S. Forest Service, which manages National Forest lands for the U.S. Department of Agriculture, identified several other major threats to forests in its most recent (1999) summary of forest ecosystem health. These include:

- Forest fires. The long-term suppression of forest fires over the years has resulted in buildup of fuel, making large-scale, catastrophic fires likely. During the summer of 2002, for example, such wildfires raged out of control across the American West, destroying homes, displacing residents, and threatening the Giant Sequoia National Monument. Overcrowded forests also have increased vulnerability to pest species and tree diseases.

- Invasion of non-native pest species. Exotic species can be highly detrimental to trees. Examples of harmful invasive species include the Asian long-horned beetle, which feeds on hardwood species; the hemlock woolly adelgid; the pink hibiscus mealybug, which affects tropical and subtropical forests in the southern United States; and the gypsy moth, which threatens hardwood forests in the eastern United States.

- Plant diseases. Plant disease is responsible for the decline of many species. Butternut canker has brought about the endangerment of the butternut, which was designated a "species of federal concern" by the Fish and Wildlife Service. Some measures to protect the butternut include the development of conditions that will help enable recovery and the breeding of resistant strains of trees.

- Air pollution. Air pollution is particularly harmful to trees when it leads to acid rain or ground-level ozone. Acid rain depletes nutrients from the soil and can also damage foliage directly. Acid rain is particularly problematic in the Great Lakes region, the Northeast, and mid-Atlantic forests. Ozone pollution occurs at high levels in the Southwest and the eastern United States, and has also been a factor in the decline of some trees in California, including the Ponderosa and Jeffrey pines. In these species, ozone can cause pine needles to drop. Figure 4.6 shows the results of ozone damage monitoring in some midwestern and northeastern U.S. states.

TONGASS NATIONAL FOREST. During the first millennium A.D., an expanse of ancient forest flourished along the entire western coast of the United States and Canada. Today, a portion of this habitat, a 500-mile expanse along the southeastern coast of Alaska, has been preserved as Tongass National Forest. Tongass National Forest repre-

FIGURE 4.6

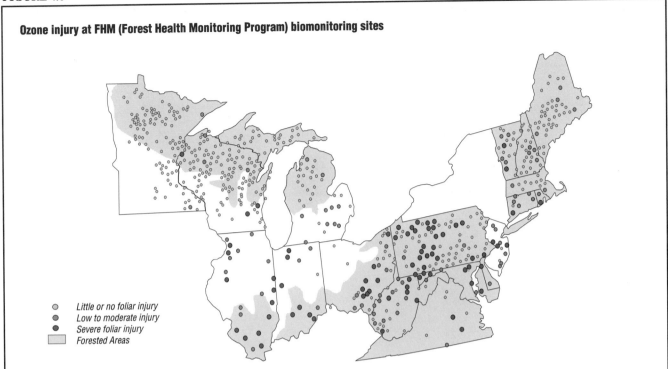

Ozone injury at FHM (Forest Health Monitoring Program) biomonitoring sites

○ Little or no foliar injury
◐ Low to moderate injury
● Severe foliar injury
▨ Forested Areas

SOURCE: "Figure 1. FMH Ozone Map: Ozone Injury At FHM Biomonitoring Sites," in *America's Forests: Health Update,* U.S. Department of Agriculture, U.S. Forest Service, Washington, DC, 1999 [Online] http://www.fs.fed.us/foresthealth/fh_update/update99/issues5.html [accessed April 28, 2002]

sents an unblemished stretch of trees and other wildlife that has existed as a completely intact ecosystem for over a thousand years. It includes 17 million acres of pristine woodland and has never experienced an extinction in modern times. The Tongass preserve comprises 26 percent of the world's temperate rainforest and is the largest on earth.

In the mid-twentieth century, however, the federal government began to negotiate with logging companies to open small portions of the ancient forest for clear-cutting. This has generated ongoing debate in Congress. In the 1990s loggers appealed to the government to open more access roads to facilitate logging, whereas environmentalists fought to preserve the area from human tampering altogether. In May 2000 the National Forest Service drafted a proposal urging renewed protection of roadless areas. However, a decision was postponed until 2004 in order to allow time for a formal review of the situation.

WETLANDS

Wetlands are transitional areas between land and water bodies where water periodically floods the land or saturates the soil. The term wetland includes environments such as marshes, swamps, bogs, and estuaries. Wetlands may be covered in shallow water most of the year or be wet only seasonally. Plants and animals found in wetlands are uniquely adapted to these conditions.

Wetlands in the United States are highly diverse because of regional differences in climate, geology, soils, and vegetation. There are approximately 105.5 million acres of wetlands in the country. The majority of this is freshwater wetland (95 percent, or 100.5 million acres). The rest is tidal, or saltwater, wetland and is found along the coasts. Wetlands are found in nearly all states—there are arctic tundra wetlands in Alaska, peat bogs in the Appalachians, and riparian (riverbank) wetlands in the arid west. Table 4.5 lists some of the different types of wetlands and their acreage in the 48 contiguous United States, as well as how acreage has changed in the last decades.

As of 2002, well over half the original North American wetlands have vanished. A few states have lost nearly all their original wetlands. With the recognition of the importance of wetlands and the institution of protective measures, the pace of wetland loss has slowed in recent decades. About 58,500 wetland acres were lost each year between 1986 and 1997, with forested wetlands suffering the most damage. Although this represents an 80 percent drop from the previous decade, wetland loss is still significant (see Figure 4.7). Wetlands provide critical habitats for fish and wildlife. They also purify polluted water and check the destructive power of floods and storms. Finally, wetlands provide recreational opportunities such as fishing, hunting, photography, and wildlife observation.

TABLE 4.5

Change in wetland area for selected wetland and deepwater categories, 1986–1997

The coefficient of variation (CV) for each entry (expressed as a percentage) is given in parentheses.

Wetland/Deepwater Category	Area in thousands of acres			
	Estimated area, 1986	Estimated area, 1997	Change, 1986–97	Change (in percent)
Marine Intertidal	133.1 (19.6)	130.9 (19.9)	−2.2 (88.5)	−1.7
Estuarine Intertidal Non-vegetated[1]	580.4 (10.7)	580.1 (10.6)	-0.3 (*)	−0.1
Estuarine Intertidal Vegetated[2]	4,623.1 (4.0)	4,615.2 (4.0)	-7.9 (75.1)	−0.2
All Intertidal Wetlands	5,336.6 (3.8)	5,326.2 (3.8)	−10.4 (73.0)	−0.2
Freshwater Non-vegetated[3]	5,251.0 (4.1)	5,914.3 (3.9)	663.3 (13.4)	12.6
Freshwater Vegetated[4]	95,548.1 (3.0)	94,251.2 (3.0)	−1,296.9 (17.1)	−1.4
Freshwater Emergent	26,383.3 (8.1)	25,157.1 (8.4)	−1,226.2 (18.2)	−4.6
Freshwater Forested	51,929.6 (2.8)	50,728.5 (2.8)	- 1,201.1 (23.8)	−2.3
Freshwater Shrub	17,235.2 (4.2)	18,365.6 (4.1)	1,130.4 (25.7)	6.6
All Freshwater Wetlands	100,799.1 (2.9)	100,165.5 (2.9)	- 633.6 (36.5)	−0.6
All Wetlands	106,135.7 (2.8)	105,491.7 (2.8)	−644.0 (36.0)	0.6
Deepwater Habitats				
Lacustrine[5]	14,608.9 (10.6)	14,725.3 (10.5)	116.4 (*)	0.8
Riverine	6,291.1 (9.6)	6,255.9 (9.4)	−35.2 (*)	−0.6
Estuarine Subtidal	17,637.6 (2.2)	17,663.9 (2.2)	26.3 (95.6)	0.1
All Deepwater Habitats	38,537.6 (4.4)	38,645.1 (4.4)	107.5 (*)	0.3
All Wetlands and Deepwater Habitats[1,2]	144,673.3 (2.4)	144,136.8 (2.4)	−536.5 (30.7)	−0.4

*Statistically unreliable
[1] Includes the categories: Estuarine Intertidal Aquatic Bed and Estuarine Intertidal Unconsolidated Shore.
[2] Includes the categories: Estuarine Intertidal Emergent and Estuarine Intertidal Shrub.
[3] Includes the categories: Paustrine Aquatic Bed, Palustrine Unconsolidated Bottom and Palustrine Unconsolidated Shore.
[4] Includes the categories: Palustrine Emergent, Palustrine Forested and Palustrine Shrub.
[5] Does not include the Great Lakes.

SOURCE: Thomas E. Dahl, "Table 2. Change in wetland area for selected wetland and deepwater categories, 1986 to 1997," in *Status and Trends of Wetlands in the Conterminous United States 1986 to 1997*, U.S. Fish and Wildlife Service, Washington, DC, 2000

Endangered Bog Plants

Bogs are non-tidal wetland ecosystems that form where poor drainage and low oxygen levels combine with a low mineral content to retard the decay of organic material. Over time, peat, partially decayed organic substances, begins to solidify, forming layers over the surface of ponds. Migrating birds and amphibians, including some salamanders, are among the animals most commonly found in bog habitats. Bog flora includes coarse, grasslike plants called sedges and unusual carnivorous plants such as sundew and pitcher plants. Carnivorous plants capture and digest small insects in order to obtain nutrients unavailable in their unique environments, most often minerals such as nitrogen and phosphorus. The leaves of the sundew are covered with hundreds of tiny "tentacles" that are used to trap insects. The sundew traps an average of five insects per month. Pitcher plants maintain a pool of acidic fluid at the bottom of their "pitchers." Hairs on the inside of the pitchers point downward, preventing insects from exiting once they enter. Insects are attracted to the pitchers by the enticing red color inside.

Bog plants are threatened primarily by encroaching urbanization. Boggy wetlands are either drained or filled for use as dumping grounds. In addition, the suppression of naturally occurring fires discourages the formation of bog ecosystems. One bog species, the funnel-shaped green pitcher plant, first appeared on the Endangered Species List in 1979. Found in Alabama, North Carolina, and Georgia, it has declined largely due to collection by humans, who find these insect-eating plants both interesting and exotic. The collection of carnivorous plant species has also disrupted bog ecosystems by allowing mosquitoes and flies to proliferate.

The Florida Everglades

The Everglades covers approximately 5,000 square miles of southern Florida. It includes a wide diversity of both temperate and tropical habitat types, including saw-grass prairies, mangrove swamps, pine forests, cypress forests, marshes, and estuaries, and represents one of the wildest and most inaccessible areas in the United States. The area was formed by centuries of water flow from Lake Okeechobee in south-central Florida to Florida Bay, and is often described as a shallow "river of grass." The highest land in the Everglades is a mere seven feet above sea level. Everglades National Park is the largest remaining subtropical wilderness in the United States, and is home to endangered species such as the American crocodile, Florida panther, wood stork, and West Indian manatee. The Everglades became a National Park in 1947, and has also been designated an International Biosphere Reserve, a World Heritage Site, and a Wetland of International Importance.

Everglades habitats are now threatened by many factors. First, water control through an extensive system of canals and levees has brought both droughts and floods to Everglades lands. Much of the Everglades' water has traditionally been diverted for irrigation or to supply metropolitan areas. In fact, the portion of the Everglades inundated by water has been reduced drastically over the twentieth century, destroying numerous habitat areas. Occasional releases of large amounts of water, on the other hand, flood habitats, harming species such as alligators, whose nests may be washed away. Pollution is a second factor in Everglades deterioration. Harmful pollutants now found in the Everglades include fertilizers and pesticides from agricultural runoff, as well as mercury. Fertilizers encourage the rampant growth of vegetation that chokes wetlands, while pesticides and mercury poison species. One plant species that is affected is Garber's spurge, a beach herb that thrives in sandy peripheral soil. With its decline, parts of the Everglades have been more prone to soil erosion. Invasive species have also altered Everglades habitats. Alien species such as Brazilian pepper and Australian pine have reduced native plant populations. Finally, fire suppression related to human encroachment has caused habitat alteration. Park officials now adhere to a prescribed burn schedule, setting fires in three- to ten-year intervals as necessary.

Multiple efforts were made in the 1990s and early 2000s to help restore the Everglades. Florida's Everglades Forever Act, passed in 1994, attempted to limit agricultural runoff as well as set water quality standards. The Comprehensive Everglades Restoration Plan, passed by Congress in 2000, is a 38-year project drawn up by the U.S. Army Corps of Engineers. It aims to restore natural water flow patterns in the Everglades and to redirect water to the marshes. In December 2000, President Bill Clinton signed the Water Resources Development Act of 2000, which committed over $4 billion to Everglades restoration.

FIGURE 4.7

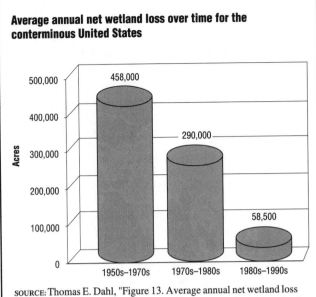

Average annual net wetland loss over time for the conterminous United States

SOURCE: Thomas E. Dahl, "Figure 13. Average annual net wetland loss over time for the conterminous United States," in *Status and Trends of Wetlands in the Conterminous United States 1986 to 1997,* U.S. Fish and Wildlife Service, Washington, DC, 2000

Tidal Wetlands—The Mangroves

Mangrove forests (Figure 4.8) are among the most biodiverse wetland ecosystems on earth. They are found in tropical coastal waters, often near river mouths. The tree species found in mangrove forests possess special roots that allow them to survive in brackish water. Mangrove forests harbor numerous unique species worldwide, such as crab-eating monkeys, fishing cats, and diverse species of birds and fish. They also provide food and wood for local communities, stabilize coastlines, and provide barriers from the sea during storms. Mangrove forests once lined three-quarters of the world's tropical coasts. Now, according to the World Resources Institute, an environmental advocacy group, less than half these forests remain. Indonesia, a country of more than 13,000 islands, possesses the most mangrove forestland of any country. Brazil and Australia also have extensive mangrove habitats.

Mangroves are disappearing in part because they have traditionally been regarded as sinister, malarial wastelands. In Florida, for example, mangroves were flooded every year to control mosquito populations. Mangrove forests have also been sold to logging companies for paper pulp, pest-proof timber, and chipboard for coastal development. Many mangrove forests have also been replaced with saltwater ponds for commercial shrimp-farming. The shrimp industry is perhaps the most immediate threat to mangrove forests today.

During the Vietnam War, herbicides were dumped on an estimated 124,000 hectares of mangrove forests in

FIGURE 4.8

A mangrove swamp in Florida. Mangroves are coastal wetlands home to a variety of unique organisms. *(National Park Service)*

South Vietnam. These areas remain, for the most part, entirely barren—a true wasteland.

PLANT CONSERVATION

Protection under the Endangered Species Act

The Endangered Species Act of 1973 protects listed plants from deliberate destruction or vandalism. Plants also receive protection under the consultation requirements of the act—that is, all federal agencies must consult with the Fish and Wildlife Service (FWS) to determine how best to conserve species as well as to ensure that no issued permits will jeopardize listed species or harm their habitats.

However, many conservationists believe that plants receive less protection than animals under the ESA. First, the ESA only protects plants that are found on federal lands. It imposes no restrictions on private landowners whose property is home to endangered plants. Critics also complain that the FWS has been slow to list plant species. Hundreds of plant species first proposed for listing in 1976 are still awaiting action. Critics also charge that damage to plant habitats is not addressed with the same seriousness as for animal species. The FWS only rarely designates critical habitat for plant species, and only rarely acquires national wildlife refuges to protect plants.

Finally, of all FWS funds spent on threatened and endangered species, about half goes to a handful of listed animal species. Plants typically receive less than 3 percent of the total, and about 15 percent of plant species—twice the proportion of animals—receive no funding at all.

In June 2000, in an effort to bolster conservation efforts for plants, the Fish and Wildlife Service announced an agreement with the Center for Plant Conservation (CPC), a national association of botanical gardens and arboreta. The two groups will cooperate in developing conservation measures to help save North American plant species, particularly those listed as threatened or endangered. Central to the effort will be the creation of educational programs aimed at informing the public about the importance of plant species for aesthetic, economic, biological, and medical reasons. The CPC will also aid in developing recovery plans for listed species.

Focus on Ecosystems, Not Species

Many environmentalists are now calling for the protection of entire ecosystems, which they believe will be more effective in preserving biodiversity than focusing on individual endangered species. Ecosystem approaches consider entire communities of species as well as their interactions with the physical environment, and aim to develop integrated plans involving wildlife, physical resources, and sustainable use. The Fish and Wildlife Service has divided the country into a series of 53 ecosystem units based on the location of watershed areas (Figure 4.9). Each unit is associated with a team that develops a comprehensive strategy for conservation. Central to ecosystem conservation strategies is the preservation of large, intact areas of habitat.

Ecosystem approaches sometimes attempt to consider human economic and social concerns as well. This is the case for several Habitat Conservation Plans developed in recent years. In Southern California developers and environmentalists had long battled over hundreds of thousands of biologically rich acres lying between Los Angeles and Mexico that were home to uncounted species of plants and animals. Developers wanted to build there, while federal regulators wanted to protect the habitat for wildlife. Haggling over small parcels of land had already cost significant time and money and resulted in frustration on both sides. A compromise resolution permitted developers to develop some large parcels of land while setting aside other large, intact regions as conservation areas. A similar agreement between developers and environmentalists was reached in the Texas Hill Country. The Balcones Canyonlands Conservation Plan set aside 111,428 acres for ecosystem enhancement, while allowing uncontested development of many thousands of acres of land in the central Texas corridor.

Wildcrafting

Wildcrafting describes the harvest of forest resources for profit or recreation without damaging habitat. Wildcrafting has enjoyed a resurgence since the government and courts curtailed logging on public land in the early 1990s. The industry brings in hundreds of millions of dollars annually.

In 1995 American exports of commercial moss and lichen alone amounted to $14 million, according to U.S. Forest Service scientists. Mushrooms—matsutakes, chanterelles, and morels—also bring good prices. Burls, hard woody growths on trees, which become unusually attractive when sanded and polished, can be used for furniture, cabinets, and trims. Ferns and shrubs for floral arrangements, Christmas greens, and more than 100 medicinal herbs are also collected.

The U.S. Forest Service, which issues permits to wildcrafters on public lands, is still examining how much wildcrafters can harvest without causing damage. Some rangers and environmentalists worry that forest products may be over-harvested, causing habitat damage, or that trampling will damage the forest floor.

Plant-Derived Medications

Numerous plant species have medicinal uses—in fact, the global market in plant-derived medications is worth $40 billion annually. Unfortunately, less than 1 percent of plant species have been evaluated for potential medical use. With as many as 50 plant species disappearing daily, botanists calculate that the planet's diversity could be reduced by 10 percent by the year 2015. Extinction will deprive future generations of potentially powerful medications. The rapid destruction of tropical rainforests is particularly alarming, as 60 percent of higher plant species occupy those ecosystems.

Between 25 and 40 percent of all prescription drugs in the United States contain active ingredients derived from plants. For example, *Cinchona ledgeriana* is the source of quinine, the oldest malaria medicine. The Madagascar periwinkle, found in a country that has lost 80 percent of its vegetation, provides two potent compounds used in the treatment of cancer. Vinblastine is used to treat Hodgkin's disease, and vincristine is used to treat leukemia. Sales of these two drugs exceed $180 million a year. Wild yam is the source of diosgenin (a key ingredient in some oral contraceptives), steroids, and muscle relaxants used in anesthesia. Morphine, a powerful pain medication, comes from the opium poppy. Scopolamine, a drug used for motion sickness, is derived from a plant called *Hyocyamus niger*. Taxol, a drug used to treat ovarian cancer, comes from the Pacific yew. Table 4.6 lists some other medications derived from plant species.

Numerous plants are also found on the non-prescription medicinal herb market. In the United States, some 175 North American species alone are available on the non-prescription market. U.S. sales of medicinal herbs totaled $3 billion in 1998 and are growing at the rate of 20 percent per year. Examples of medicinal herbs include mullein, which is said to relieve asthma, and ginseng, which is claimed to boost vitality.

The use of medicinal plants is even greater in non-industrial societies, where large segments of the population rely on traditional medicine. Traditional healers in South Asia use nearly 2,000 plant species. Over 5,000 species are used by traditional healers in China. Over 1,300 species are used by healers in Amazonia. Furthermore, nearly 100 commercial drugs derived from plants were originally discovered by traditional healers.

Medicinal plants are declining in many areas as a result of habitat degradation and non-sustainable use. The African cherry, which is used by traditional healers in Cameroon, has declined due to overexploitation. Much of the African cherry harvested is exported to Western Europe, where the plant is used to treat prostate disease. In North America, medically valuable species such as the Pacific yew, a "trash" evergreen found in old-growth forests of the Pacific Northwest, have been cleared to make way for tree species profitable to the timber industry. The cessation of logging in the Pacific Northwest—in

FIGURE 4.9

Ecosystem boundaries

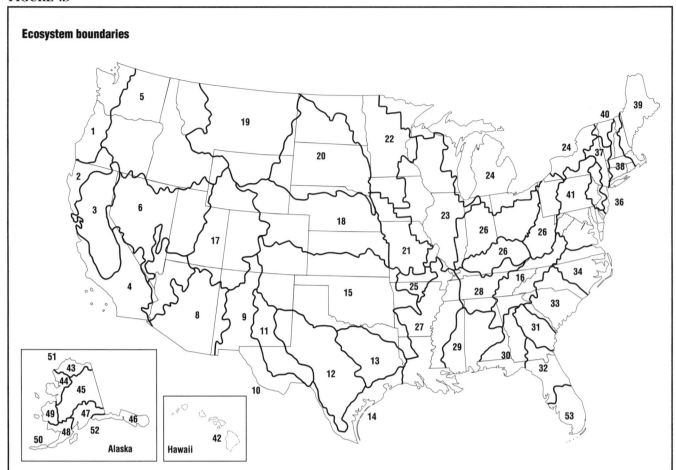

Unit #	Unit Name	Unit #	Unit Name
1	North Pacific Coast	27	Lower Mississippi River
2	Klamath/Central Pacific Coast	28	Tennessee/Cumberland River
3	Central Valley of California/San	29	Central Gulf Watersheds
	Francisco Bay	30	Florida Panhandle Watersheds
4	Southern California	31	Altamaha Watershed
5	Columbia Basin	32	Peninsular Florida
6	Interior Basin	33	Savannah/Santee/Pee Dee Rivers
7	Lower Colorado River	34	Roanoke/Tar/Neuse/Cape Fear Rivers
8	Gila/Salt/Verde River	35	Caribbean
9	Middle and Upper Rio Grande	36	Deleware River/Delmarva Coastal Area
10	Lower Rio Grande	37	Hudson River/New York Bight
11	Pecos River	38	Connecticut River/Long Island Sound
12	Edwards Plateau	39	Gulf of Maine Rivers
13	East Texas	40	Lake Champlain
14	Texas Gulf Coast	41	Chesapeake Bay/Susquehanna River
15	Arkansas/Red Rivers	42	Pacific Islands
16	Southern Appalachians	43	Arctic Alaska
17	Upper Colorado River	44	Northwest Alaska
18	Platte/Kansas Rivers	45	Interior Alaska
19	Upper Missouri, Yellowstone and Upper	46	Southeast Alaska
	Columbia River	47	South Central Alaska
20	Missouri Main Stem	48	Bristol Bay/Kodiak
21	Lower Missouri River	49	Yukon - Kuskokwim Delta
22	Mississippi Headwaters/Tallgrass Prarie	50	Bering Sea/Aleutian Islands
23	Upper Mississippi River/Tallgrass Prarie	51	Beaufort/Chukchi Seas
24	Great Lakes	52	North Pacific/Gulf of Alaska
25	Ozark Watersheds	53	South Florida
26	Ohio River Valley		

SOURCE: "Ecosystem Units" in *U.S. Fish and Wildlife Service Ecosystem Boundaries,* U.S. Fish and Wildlife Service, Division of Information Resources Management, Washington, DC, 2002 [Online] http://ecosystems.fws.gov [accessed May 8, 2002]

TABLE 4.6

Selected examples of medically useful plant species

Species	Drug & use
CANCER	
Madagascar periwinkle	vincristine & vinblastine: childhood (lymphocyctic) leukemia & Hodgkin's disease
Pacific yew	taxol: ovarian, breast
HIV/AIDS	
Cameroon vine	michellamine B
tree in Malaysia	calanolides
tree in Samoa	prostatin
bush in Australia	conocurvone
mulberry trees	Butyl-DNJ (analogue of natural compound)
HEART/CIRCULATORY	
foxglove	digitalis: regulates contractions
ergot (fungus of wheat)	atenolol & metoprolol: blocks adrenaline (especially in coronary disease)
Strophanthus gratus &	cardiac glycoside, G-strophanthin, K-
Strophanthus kombe	strophanthin: treatment of acute heart failure hypotension during surgery
snake venom	captopril & enalapril — reduces blood pressure
fungal metabolite	lovastatin — used to reduce cholesterol levels by blocking its biosynthesis
INFECTIOUS	
molds	avermectins: worm killers
molds	penicillin
sewer microbes	cephalosporin; developed into cefaclor, ceftriaxone, & cefoxitin — produces antibiotics
IMMUNOSUPPRESSANTS (used in organ transplants)	
molds	cyclosporin
molds	FK506
PARKINSON'S DISEASE	
Atropa acuminata, Atropa belladonna	hyosyamine: treatment of Parkinson's disease, epilepsy, and gastric ulcers
TRANQUILIZERS	
Indian snake root	reserpine: muscle relaxant, antianxiety; developed alprazolam
ANTI-INFLAMMATORY	
ergot (fungus on wheat)	anti-histimines Terphenadine (HI): used to treat allergies & motion sickness; ranitidine & cimetidine (H2) used to treat gastric ulcers

SOURCE: Endangered Species Coalition, Washington, DC, 1993

order to protect northern spotted owl habitat as required by the Endangered Species Act—has protected the Pacific yew as well.

In 1990 the National Institute for Biodiversity in Costa Rica entered into a landmark deal with Merck, a pharmaceutical company, in which the institute would provide rights to drug exploration, while Merck would fund tropical forest conservation and research. Tropical forests have produced at least 47 major pharmaceutical drugs, and scientists estimate that several hundred more plants with medicinal properties have yet to be discovered. This agreement became a model for other such arrangements. However, no deals were attempted in the United States until 1996, when the idea caught the attention of U.S. conservationists. That year Dr. James Tiedje, director of the National Science Foundation's Center for Microbial Ecology at Michigan State University, reported that a single gram of temperate forest soil could harbor as many as 10,000 species of bacteria. By 2000 a group of drug manufacturers had agreed to support a 270-acre pharmaceutical preserve in upstate New York, the first preserve outside the tropics set aside specifically for chemical prospecting. Scientists already have discovered a mold that produces a substance called cyclosporin, which is used to prevent the rejection of transplanted organs.

CHAPTER 5
AQUATIC SPECIES AND THEIR ENVIRONMENTS

Approximately 1.4 pentillion tons (1,400,000,000, 000,000,000) of water cover the surface of the Earth—466 billion tons for each of the 6 billion people on the planet. Amazing as it may seem, much of this water has been affected by human activity. Numerous aquatic species are in decline for a variety of reasons, including degraded water quality, development or alteration of aquatic habitats, and overhunting or overfishing.

THREATS TO AQUATIC SPECIES

Water Pollution—Many, Many Causes

Humans burn fuels, produce wastes, and use large amounts of fertilizers, pesticides, and other chemicals. These by-products of industrialization end up in the environment, and are often harmful to living organisms. The condition of water-dwelling animals is in fact often a good measure of the condition of the environment; their demise suggests that something may be wrong in their habitat and with the world. Figure 5.1 illustrates the overall condition of U.S. watersheds based on data collected by the U.S. Environmental Protection Agency (EPA). Large portions of the country suffer from serious water quality problems.

PESTICIDES. Pesticides are chemicals used to kill insects that feed on crops and vegetation. The first documented use of pesticides was by the ancient Greeks. Pliny the Elder (23–79 A.D.) reported using common compounds such as arsenic, sulfur, caustic soda, and olive oil to protect crops. The Chinese later used similar substances to retard infestation by insects and fungi. In the 1800s Europeans used heavy metal salts such as copper sulfate and iron sulfate as weed killers.

The invention of DDT (dichloro-diphenyl-trichloro-ethane) in 1939 marked a revolution in the war against pests. DDT was effective, relatively cheap, and apparently safe for people—certainly a miracle chemical. Its discov-

erer, Paul Muller, received a Nobel Prize for its discovery. DDT promised a world with unprecedented crop yields. In the United States, pesticide use in agriculture nearly tripled after 1965, as farmers began to use DDT and other pesticides, herbicides, and fungicides intensively and began to accept these chemicals as essential to agriculture.

For many years, it was thought that if pesticides were properly used, the risk of harm to humans and wildlife was slight. As the boom in pesticide use continued, however, it eventually became apparent that pesticides were not safe after all. The fundamental reason that pesticides are dangerous is that they are poisons purposely designed to kill living organisms. Part of the problem is biomagnification—a predator that eats other organisms with pesticides in their bodies ends up concentrating all those pesticides in its own tissues. Eventually, the concentration of pesticides causes serious problems. DDT was eventually shown to have harmed numerous bird species, particularly those high in the food chain, such as bald eagles and peregrine falcons. DDT caused the production of eggs with shells so thin they could not protect the developing chick. The populations of countless bird species plummeted.

As the dangers of pesticides became more apparent in the 1960s and 1970s, some of the most dangerous pesticides, like DDT, were banned in the United States. However, the use of other chemical pesticides increased until the 1980s. Use levels have generally held steady since then. Farmers continue to apply about one pound of pesticide per year for every person on Earth. The majority of pesticide use—75 percent—occurs in industrialized countries. Unfortunately, the primary reason that pesticide use has leveled off in recent decades is not concern regarding its safety, but declines in its effectiveness. This is due to the fact that pest species quickly evolve resistance to pesticides. Worldwide, the number of resistant pests continues to climb. Unfortunately, increased resistance has only created a demand for more, and more powerful, chemicals.

FIGURE 5.1

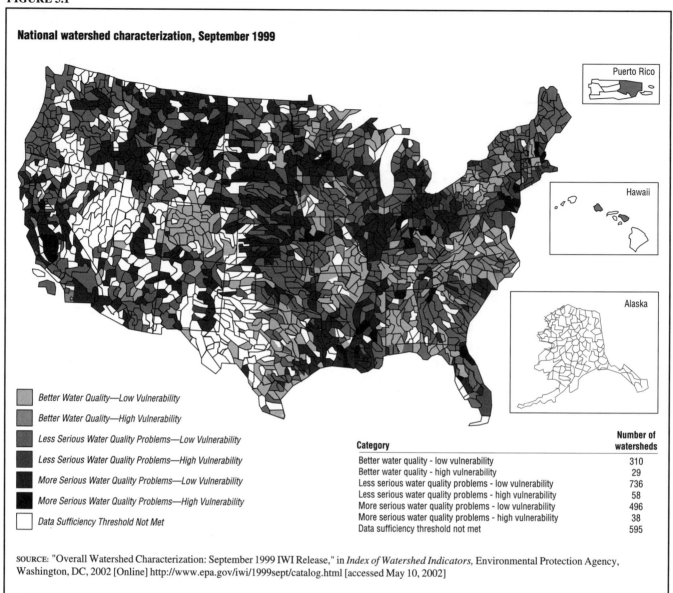

National watershed characterization, September 1999

Better Water Quality—Low Vulnerability

Better Water Quality—High Vulnerability

Less Serious Water Quality Problems—Low Vulnerability

Less Serious Water Quality Problems—High Vulnerability

More Serious Water Quality Problems—Low Vulnerability

More Serious Water Quality Problems—High Vulnerability

Data Sufficiency Threshold Not Met

Category	Number of watersheds
Better water quality - low vulnerability	310
Better water quality - high vulnerability	29
Less serious water quality problems - low vulnerability	736
Less serious water quality problems - high vulnerability	58
More serious water quality problems - low vulnerability	496
More serious water quality problems - high vulnerability	38
Data sufficiency threshold not met	595

SOURCE: "Overall Watershed Characterization: September 1999 IWI Release," in *Index of Watershed Indicators,* Environmental Protection Agency, Washington, DC, 2002 [Online] http://www.epa.gov/iwi/1999sept/catalog.html [accessed May 10, 2002]

Pesticides degrade numerous aquatic ecosystems after seeping into the ground as runoff from watering or rain. The U.S. Fish and Wildlife Service reports that pesticides harm about 20 percent of the country's threatened and endangered animal and plant species. Figure 5.2 shows the potential for pesticide seepage into groundwater in the United States. The pesticide seepage potential for Mississippi, Arkansas, Tennessee, New York, Massachusetts, Maine, much of the Midwest, and the Central Valley of California is particularly high.

FERTILIZERS. For decades, farmers have tried to increase the productivity of their land by using ever-increasing amounts of fertilizers. Fertilizers are biological products or chemicals applied to crops to increase their growth. Fertilizers may seep into water and collect in lakes, streams, and groundwater. While fertilizers are not poisonous by nature, large quantities of fertilizers can cause serious health problems in aquatic animals. Fertilizers also encourage the growth of aquatic plant life, disrupting food webs and biological communities. Aquatic plants and algae may grow so rapidly that they block off sunshine or deplete habitats of nutrients essential to other species.

OIL SPILLS AND RUNOFF. Oil spills represent periodic and devastating accidents to aquatic life. Oil spilled into the ocean floats on the water surface, cutting off oxygen to the sea life below and killing mammals, birds, fish, and other animals. The dangers presented by oil spills have grown worse over the years. In 1945 the largest tanker held 16,500 tons of oil. Now, super tankers the length of several football fields regularly carry more than 550,000 tons.

In 1989 the tanker *Exxon Valdez* ran aground on the pristine Alaskan coastline, spilling 11 million gallons of oil into the bay and killing millions of animals. In 1994 a federal jury assessed $5 billion in punitive damages and

FIGURE 5.2

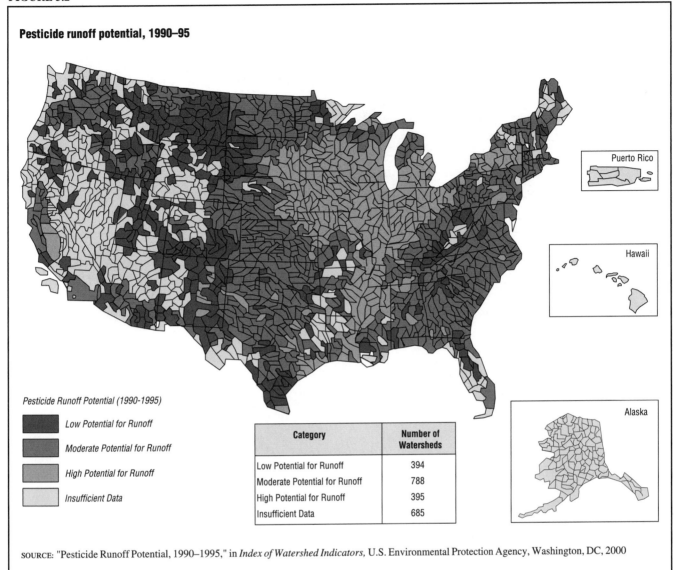

Pesticide runoff potential, 1990–95

Pesticide Runoff Potential (1990-1995)

- Low Potential for Runoff
- Moderate Potential for Runoff
- High Potential for Runoff
- Insufficient Data

Category	Number of Watersheds
Low Potential for Runoff	394
Moderate Potential for Runoff	788
High Potential for Runoff	395
Insufficient Data	685

Puerto Rico

Hawaii

Alaska

SOURCE: "Pesticide Runoff Potential, 1990–1995," in *Index of Watershed Indicators,* U.S. Environmental Protection Agency, Washington, DC, 2000

$3.5 billion in criminal fines and cleanup costs against Exxon. The *Valdez* spill led to additional safety requirements for tankers, including double hulls. Larger oil spills than the *Valdez* have occurred both before and since, but the incident alerted many people to the damage that can be done to marine habitats. Many species impacted by the spill, particularly seabird species, have yet to recover more than a decade later.

In January 2001 the tanker *Jessica* released 150,000 gallons of fuel near the Galapagos Islands, a biologically rich area harboring numerous unique species including Darwin's famous finches, marine iguanas, and a tropical penguin population. There was widespread relief when winds blew the oil slick seaward rather than towards the islands. Sea bird and sea lion deaths numbered in the dozens, and it was believed that a true catastrophe had been avoided. Ongoing studies of the Galapagos' unique marine iguanas, however, revealed in June 2002 that

numerous iguanas likely died due to oil-related injuries after the spill. In particular, 60 percent of the marine iguanas on Santa Fe Island died in 2001, despite the fact that oil contamination was relatively low, with only about one quart of oil per yard of shoreline. Similar deaths were not found on another, separate island where there was no contamination. Scientists believe that the deaths occurred when oil contamination killed the iguanas' gut bacteria, making them unable to digest seaweed and causing them to starve. Marine iguanas have no natural predators and generally die either of starvation or old age.

The U.S. National Research Council warns that, even without large catastrophic oil spills, many marine habitats are regularly exposed to oil pollution. Harbors and aquatic habitats near developed areas are in particular jeopardy. The U.S. National Research Council estimates that approximately 8.4 billion gallons of oil enter marine waters each year from street runoff, industrial liquid

FIGURE 5.3

Ocean debris: where it comes from and what it affects

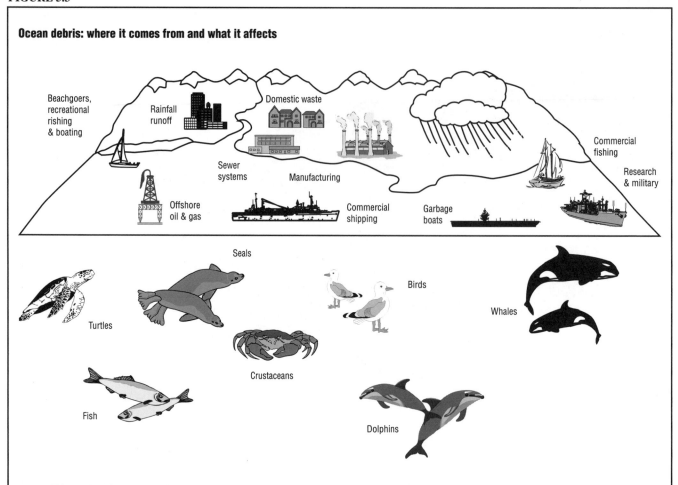

Beachgoers, recreational rishing & boating

Rainfall runoff

Domestic waste

Sewer systems

Manufacturing

Offshore oil & gas

Commercial shipping

Garbage boats

Commercial fishing

Research & military

Seals

Turtles

Birds

Whales

Crustaceans

Dolphins

Fish

SOURCE: "Ocean Debris: Where It Comes From and What It Affects," in *Sea of Debris: A Summary of the Third International Conference on Marine Debris,* North Carolina Sea Grant College Program, Raleighn, NC, n.d.

wastes, and intentional discharge from ships flushing their oil tanks. As little as one part of oil per million parts of water can be detrimental to the reproduction and growth of fish, crustaceans, and plankton.

OCEAN DUMPING AND DEBRIS. Ocean debris comes from many sources (see Figure 5.3) and affects diverse marine species. Waterborne litter entangles wildlife, masquerades as a food source, smothers beach and bottom-dwelling plants, provides a means for small organisms to invade non-native areas, and contributes to toxic water pollution. Records of interactions between ocean debris and wildlife date back to the first half of the twentieth century. Northern fur seals entangled in debris were spotted as early as the 1930s. In the 1960s, various seabirds were found to have plastic in their stomachs. By the early twenty-first century, a total of 255 species were documented to have become entangled in marine debris or to have ingested it.

Some scientists once thought it was safe to dump garbage into the oceans, believing the oceans were large enough to absorb sludge without harmful effects. Other sci-

entists argued dumping would eventually lead to the pollution of the oceans. Metropolitan centers such as New York City once loaded their sludge and debris onto barges, took the vessels out to sea, and dumped the refuse, in a practice called ocean dumping. Problems with ocean dumping were not fully recognized until floating plastic particles were found throughout the Atlantic and Pacific Oceans.

The perils of ocean dumping and debris struck home both literally and figuratively in the summer of 1988, when ocean washup, including sewage, garbage, and biohazards from medical waste, forced an unprecedented 803 beach closures along the Atlantic seaboard. In some cases authorities were alerted to beach washups when children turned up hypodermic needles in the sand. Aquatic species also faced serious dangers from these materials, including absorbing or ingesting hazardous waste substances, and ingesting needles, forceps, and other dangerous solid debris. In 1994 hundreds of dead dolphins washed up on Mediterranean beaches, killed by a virus linked to water pollution. Scientists pointed to this event as an indication of what may happen to other marine animals (and humans) if pollution continues.

At the urging of the Environmental Protection Agency (EPA), the dumping of potentially infectious medical waste into ocean waters from public vessels was prohibited in 1988. In 1992 the federal government banned ocean dumping. In 1995 the EPA stepped up efforts to educate people about the dangers of polluting coastal waters through improper disposal of trash on land, sewer overflows to rivers and streams, and dumping by ships and other vessels. The EPA further warned that marine debris poses not only a serious threat to wildlife, but remains in the environment for many years (Table 5.1).

MERCURY AND OTHER TOXIC POLLUTANTS. Mercury poisoning is a problem in many lakes and oceans. Mercury can cause brain damage and other serious health problems in both wild species and in humans. During the 1990s scientists began to report widespread mercury contamination in fish, including those inhabiting remote lakes that were assumed pristine. As a result, many states now warn people against eating certain types of fish. The EPA, in its *National Water Quality Inventory*, reported that in 1996 mercury was the cause of 1,675 fish and wildlife consumption advisories, by far the greatest number of advisories in the United States. Figure 5.4 shows states that had one or more fish consumption advisories for mercury by 1995. Scientists believe that the main source of mercury pollution is rainwater that carries mercury from coal-burning power plants, incinerators that burn garbage, and smelters that make metals. Because mercury becomes concentrated in organic tissues (Figure 5.5), like DDT, even small concentrations of mercury in the water can be harmful to health.

Other toxic pollutants are also monitored regularly for fish and wildlife consumption advisories, including calcium, copper, and lead. The U.S. Clean Water Act mandated that states establish clear emissions limits for industrial facilities. Under the National Pollutant Discharge Elimination System (NPDES), the EPA is authorized to set limits if states fail to do so, as well as to authorize permits for polluting industries. Figure 5.6 shows some U.S. trouble spots, where emissions from all industries combined exceed the limits set by the state or by the EPA in 1999. In 92 locales industrial emissions exceed limits; 54 of those locations are experiencing emissions more than 20 percent over the permitted limit. The largest concentration of severe polluters occurs in the mid-Atlantic states, New England, and the Southeast.

Dams

Some 100,000 dams regulate America's rivers and creeks. Of the major rivers in the lower 48 states (those more than 600 miles in length), only the Yellowstone River still flows freely. In fact, University of Alabama ecologist Arthur Benke notes that it is difficult to find any river in the U.S. that hasn't been dammed or channeled.

TABLE 5.1

How long does marine debris stay in the environment?

Cardboard box	2 weeks
Paper towels	2-4 weeks
Newspaper	6 weeks
Cotton glove	1-5 months
Apple core	2 months
Waxed milk carton	3 months
Cotton rope	3-14 months
Photodegredable 6-pack ring	6 months
Biodegradable diaper	1 year
Wool glove	1 year
Plywood	1-3 years
Painted wooden stick	13 years
Foam cup	50 years
Tin can	50 years
Styrofoam buoy	80 years
Aluminum Can	200 years
Plastic 6-pack ring	400 years
Disposable diapers	450 years
Plastic bottles	450 years
Microfilament fishing line	600 years
Glass bottles/jars	Undetermined

SOURCE: Adapted from "Marine Debris Timeline," U.S. Environmental Protection Agency, Gulf of Mexico Program, Stennis Space Center, MS, 2000 [Online] http://www.gmpo.gov/edresources/debris_1.html

Dams epitomized progress, American ingenuity, and humankind's mastery of nature. In North America, more than 200 major dams were completed each year between 1962 and 1968. Dams were promoted for their role in water storage, energy generation, flood control, irrigation, and recreation. Worldwide, dams now collectively store 15 percent of Earth's annual renewable water supply. Figure 5.7 shows the primary uses of U.S. dams.

The very success of the dam-building endeavor accounted, in part, for its decline. By 1980 nearly all the nation's best-suited sites—and many dubious ones—had been dammed. Three other factors, however, also contributed to the decline in dam construction: public resistance to the enormous costs, a growing belief that dams were unnecessary "pork-barrel" projects being used by politicians to boost their own popularity, and a developing awareness of the profound environmental degradation caused by dams. In 1986 Congress passed a law requiring the U.S. Bureau of Reclamation to balance issues of power generation and environmental protection when it licenses dams.

WHERE HAVE ALL THE RIVERS GONE? Dams have affected rivers, the lands abutting them, the water bodies they join, and aquatic wildlife throughout. Water flow is reduced or stopped altogether downstream of dams, altering aquatic habitats and drying wetlands. Some rivers, including the large Colorado River, no longer reach the sea at all, except in years of unusually high precipitation. Keeping enough water in rivers is especially difficult in the arid West.

Numerous species of salmon are in decline, at least partly due to the effects of dams. In the Pacific Northwest

FIGURE 5.4

Fish consumption advisories for mercury, by state, 1995

One or more advisories

No advisories

0   400   800 MILES

0   400   800 MILES

SOURCE: David P. Krabbenhoft and David A. Rickert, "Figure 1: States with at least one fish consumption advisory for mercury," in *Mercury Contamination of Aquatic Ecosystems*, U.S. Geological Survey, Reston, VA, 1995. Data from USEPA Fish Consumption Data Base

in particular, most experts estimate that native salmon will be gone in 25 years. Salmon have an unusual life cycle that involves a migration from freshwater habitats to oceans and back. Hatching and the juvenile period occur in rivers, followed by a long downstream migration to the ocean, where individuals mature. Adult salmon eventually make an arduous, upstream return to freshwater habitats, where they spawn (lay their eggs, burying them in gravel nests) and then die. Dams are associated with high salmon mortality during both downstream and upstream migrations.

There are ongoing debates regarding dam management throughout the Pacific Northwest. In April 2002, for exam-

ple, the National Wildlife Federation (NWF), in association with several fisheries groups, initiated a lawsuit against the Grant County Public Utility District (PUD) in eastern Washington state, over the management of two dams on the Columbia River. The NWF is charging that dam mismanagement is responsible for the continued decline of chinook and steelhead salmon, both of which are protected under the Endangered Species Act. Some 32 percent of juvenile salmon migrating downstream towards the ocean are killed at the dam. Many adult salmon are also dying as they swim upstream to spawning grounds. Fishermen are particularly outraged at the collapse of salmon runs, since they have been required to limit their catch in the hope of population recovery. There are a total of eight dams on the Columbia River, all of which must be surmounted successfully for salmon to complete their migrations.

TEARING DOWN DAMS? In November 1997, for the first time in U.S. history, the Federal Energy Regulatory Commission ordered the Edwards Dam removed from the Kennebec River in Augusta, Maine, to restore habitats for sea-run fish. The dam's owner, Edwards Manufacturing, appealed the decision, but the federal government prevailed. The 160-year old dam produced 1 percent of Maine's electricity. Normal river conditions were achieved at the site within days of water release. Environmentalists viewed the removal of the dam as a boon to both aquatic species and the terrestrial species that feed on them.

Conservation and fisheries interests have also argued for the removal of four dams on the Snake River in the Pacific Northwest, to allow salmon runs to recover. The issue was extremely contentious, with over 8,700 people attending public hearings on the debate and over 230,000 written comments submitted. The Army Corps of Engineers announced in February 2002 that the dams would not be removed, citing the fact that they produce $324 million in electricity and water with operating costs of only $36.5 million. The Corps will, however, budget $390 million over the next ten years to improve salmon survival, including trucking juvenile salmon around the dams. This decision represented the culmination of nearly ten years of debate regarding the Snake River dams.

FOREIGN INTEREST IN DAMS. As the era of big dams faded in North America, construction increased in Asia, fueled by growing demand for electricity and irrigation water. China now accounts for more than one-fourth of the big dams under construction, and China, Japan, South Korea, and India together account for more than half.

The proposed Three Gorges Dam on the Yangtze River in China (Figure 5.8) will, if it is completed, be the largest dam in the world. It will be 6,600 feet—over a mile—wide and over 600 feet high. The creation of a water reservoir upstream of the dam will flood 13 cities and countless villages, and displace well over a million people. In addition, the dam will disrupt water flow and increase water pollution, threatening unique species such as the Yangtze River dolphin, one of only five freshwater dolphin species in the world. The Yangtze River dolphin was placed on the Endangered Species List in 1989 and is at extreme risk of extinction, with only 150 individuals remaining. Other species likely to be threatened or wiped out altogether include the Chinese sturgeon, the Chinese tiger, the Chinese alligator, the Siberian crane, the giant panda, and countless species of fish, freshwater invertebrates, and plants. Several U.S. agencies provided much technical assistance in planning the Three Gorges Dam. However, U.S. government involvement ceased due to a challenge

FIGURE 5.5

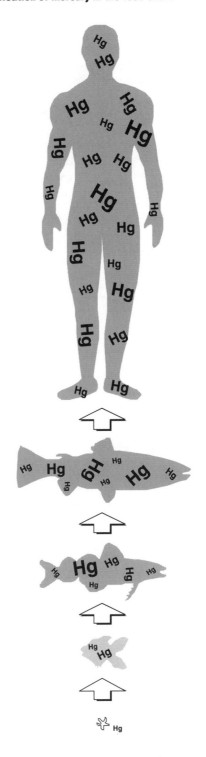

Biomagnification of mercury in the food chain

Note: Even at very low input rates to aquatic ecosystems that are remote from point sources, biomagnification effects can result in mercury levels of toxicological concern.

SOURCE: David P. Krabbenhoft and David A. Rickert, "Figure 4: Mercury (Hg) biomagnifies from the bottom to the top of the food chain," in *Mercury Contamination of Aquatic Ecosystems*, U.S. Geological Survey, Reston, VA, 1995

FIGURE 5.6

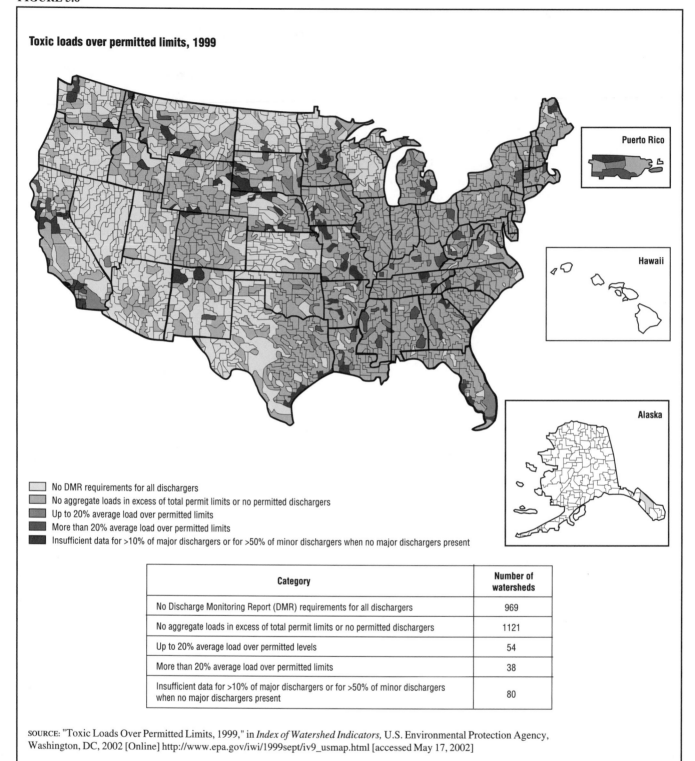

Toxic loads over permitted limits, 1999

Puerto Rico

Hawaii

Alaska

No DMR requirements for all dischargers

No aggregate loads in excess of total permit limits or no permitted dischargers

Up to 20% average load over permitted limits

More than 20% average load over permitted limits

Insufficient data for >10% of major dischargers or for >50% of minor dischargers when no major dischargers present

Category	Number of watersheds
No Discharge Monitoring Report (DMR) requirements for all dischargers	969
No aggregate loads in excess of total permit limits or no permitted dischargers	1121
Up to 20% average load over permitted levels	54
More than 20% average load over permitted limits	38
Insufficient data for >10% of major dischargers or for >50% of minor dischargers when no major dischargers present	80

SOURCE: "Toxic Loads Over Permitted Limits, 1999," in *Index of Watershed Indicators,* U.S. Environmental Protection Agency, Washington, DC, 2002 [Online] http://www.epa.gov/iwi/1999sept/iv9_usmap.html [accessed May 17, 2002]

under the Endangered Species Act, which prohibits government activity detrimental to listed species. Nonetheless, the dam is scheduled to be completed in 2009.

Water Diversion—The Aral Sea

The Aral Sea is bounded by Uzbekistan and Kazakhstan, and was once the fourth largest lake in the world. However, over the past 30 years, the lake has lost 60 percent of its water and shrunk to half its original area. This is due to the long practice of diverting water from the Amu-Darya and the Syr-Darya, two rivers that feed the lake, for irrigation and agriculture. With water loss, the lake has also increased in salinity—from 10 percent salt content to 23 percent salt content in 1999. Aral Sea habitats have been utterly destroyed. The Aral Sea was once a thriving fishery, with a total catch of 26,000 tons in 1957. Thousands of fishermen were once employed at the sea, and commercial species included carp, pike-perch, and roach. Commercial fishing in the Aral had ceased entirely by 1982.

The destruction of the Aral Sea has had numerous other consequences as well. Exposure of the lakebed has resulted in dust storms and air pollution, which affect much of the human population living around the Aral Sea. In the last 15 years, liver disease, kidney disease and chronic bronchitis have increased thirty-fold, and incidence of arthritic disease has increased by a factor of sixty. The loss of the lake has also affected regional climate patterns, so that summers are now hotter and drier and winters are longer and colder. Agriculture in the region has also been severely impaired, both by the shortening of the growing season and the degradation of soil, which is prone to high salinity and erosion.

Overfishing—Too Many Boats, Not Enough Fish

Worldwide, humans obtain 16 percent of their animal protein from fish. As the human population explodes, the fishing industry has tried to keep up with demand. Up to a certain point, fishermen are able to catch more fish without

FIGURE 5.7

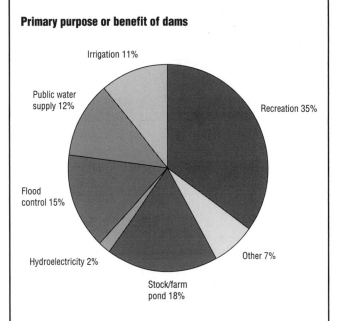

Primary purpose or benefit of dams

Irrigation 11%
Public water supply 12%
Recreation 35%
Flood control 15%
Hydroelectricity 2%
Other 7%
Stock/farm pond 18%

SOURCE: "Primary Purpose or Benefit of U.S. Dams," in *U.S. Department of Energy, Hydropower Program: Hydropower Facts Page*, U.S. Department of Energy, Washington, DC, 2002 [Online] http://hydropower.inel.gov/facts/benefit.htm [accessed May 17, 2002]. Data from U.S. Army Corps of Engineers, National Inventory of Dams

FIGURE 5.8

The Three Gorges Dam, currently in construction on the Yangtze River in China, will be the largest dam in the world when it is completed. This dam will likely result in the extinction of numerous unique species, including the Yangtze River dolphin. *(AP/Wide World Photos)*

FIGURE 5.9

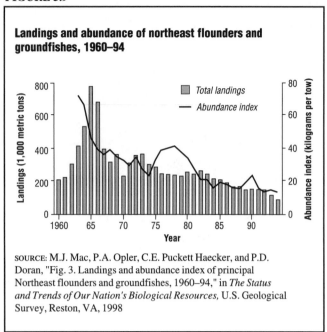

Landings and abundance of northeast flounders and groundfishes, 1960–94

SOURCE: M.J. Mac, P.A. Opler, C.E. Puckett Haecker, and P.D. Doran, "Fig. 3. Landings and abundance index of principal Northeast flounders and groundfishes, 1960–94," in *The Status and Trends of Our Nation's Biological Resources,* U.S. Geological Survey, Reston, VA, 1998

damaging the ecological balance. This is known as the maximum sustainable yield. Catches beyond the maximum sustainable yield represent overfishing. Overfishing removes fish faster than they can reproduce and causes serious population declines. Furthermore, once fishermen deplete all the large fish of a species, they often begin to target smaller, younger individuals. Targeting young fish undermines future breeding populations and guarantees a smaller biological return in future years. Swordfish have been seriously depleted in this way. In the early 1900s, the average weight of a swordfish when caught was around 300 pounds. By 1960, it was 266 pounds, and at the close of the twentieth century it was 90 pounds.

Technological advances have enabled numerous marine fisheries to be depleted in a short amount of time. In addition, the eight regional councils that regulate commercial fishing, all of which are dominated by the fishing industry, have been either unable or unwilling to set limits for themselves. As a result, most fishing areas are free-for-alls.

The U.S. government attempted to eliminate overfishing in U.S. coastal waters by passing the Magnuson Act in 1976. The Magnuson Act expanded the coastal economic zone claimed by the United States from 3 miles offshore to 200 miles offshore, preventing foreign fishing fleets from exploiting these waters. However, with foreign fleets gone, American fishermen built up their own fleets, buying large, well-equipped vessels with low-interest loans from the federal government. For several years U.S. fishermen reported record catches. Then these declined. Government officials now report that most of the major commercial fishing areas in the United States are in trouble. According to the National Marine Fisheries Service

(NMFS), about 40 percent of the nation's saltwater species have been overfished. In 1998 Canada was obliged to shut down two commercial fisheries in the North Atlantic. In New England the fishing industry is dying—numerous fishermen have lost their boats and have become unemployed. Figure 5.9 shows population declines in Northeast flounders and groundfishes.

INTERNATIONAL OVERFISHING. World fish catches increased from 21 million tons in 1950 to 93 million tons in 1996, and have since leveled off at around 90 million tons. Most experts believe that the catch will not rise any further. In 1994 the United Nations voiced the need to create a comprehensive multinational accord to conserve endangered fish species. The most daunting challenge, noted conference chairman Satya Nandan, would be to convince rival fishing nations that conservation measures should be applied to coastal waters as well as the high seas. In 1997, the Food and Agriculture Organization of the United Nations (FAO) reported that 11 of the world's 15 most important fishing areas and 60 percent of the major fish species were in decline.

FROM DRIFT NETS TO LONGLINES. Drift nets are the world's largest fishing nets, reaching lengths of up to 30 miles. Conservationists refer to them as "walls of death" because they indiscriminately catch and kill marine species. Over 100 species—including whales, sea turtles, dolphins, seabirds, sharks, salmon, and numerous other fish species—have been killed in drift nets. Drift nets were eventually banned because of their destructiveness to wildlife.

After the banning of drift nets, many fishermen turned to longlines. Longlines are fishing lines with a single main line attached to many shorter lines that terminate in baited hooks. They are used to catch wide-ranging oceanic species such as tuna, swordfish, and sharks, as well as bottom dwellers such as cod and halibut. A single boat can trail thousands of hooks from lines stretching 20 to 80 miles.

Longline fishing kills fewer marine mammals than drift nets but captures more surface-feeding sea birds, particularly the rare albatrosses. Longline fishing has in fact resulted in the decline of numerous albatross species, many of which are now listed as endangered. Australian scientists estimate that longline fishing kills more than 40,000 albatrosses each year. Longline fishing has also caused rapid declines in some fish species. Longlining is an old practice, but modern technology has vastly increased its efficiency and ecological impact. Experts report that the longline fleet is growing and now numbers several thousand vessels.

FISH DECLINES AND DEEP-SEA HARVESTING. As catches of shallow water fishes decline, trawlers have increasingly been used to scour the deep seas for new varieties of fish, such as the nine-inch long royal red shrimp, rattails, skates, squid, red crabs, orange roughy, oreos, hoki, blue ling, southern blue whiting, and spiny dogfish. Although limited commercial deep-sea fishing has occurred for decades, new technologies are making it considerably more practical and efficient. As stocks of better-known fish shrink and international quotas tighten, experts say deep ocean waters will increasingly be targeted as a source of seafood.

Unwelcome Guests—Aquatic Invasive Species

Invasive or non-native species are those that have been introduced to a new habitat. They frequently damage native species either by preying on them or competing with them. Once invasive species become established, they are virtually impossible to eliminate. According to the U.S. Fish and Wildlife Service, at least 2,300 species of non-native animals and 4,000 non-native plant species are now established in the United States. In 1996 the Nature Conservancy reported that 42 percent of the threatened or endangered species listed with the Fish and Wildlife Service have declined partly due to the effect of invasive species. For 18 percent of those listed plants or animals, invasive species are the primary threat to survival.

The primary source of aquatic invasive species has traditionally been ship ballast water, which is picked up in one location and released in another. In San Francisco Bay alone, it is estimated that a new invasive species becomes established every 14 weeks through this route. Invasive species may also become established through transfer from recreational boating vessels, intentional release of non-native species in an attempt to establish new populations for fishing, dumping of live bait, release of aquarium species, and accidental escapes from research facilities. The Nonindigenous Aquatic Nuisance Prevention and Control Act of 1990 and the National Invasive Species Act of 1996 are intended to help prevent unintentional introductions of aquatic nuisance species. In 2002 the Fish and Wildlife Service introduced several campaigns to educate people on how to avoid transportation of aquatic nuisance species such as the zebra mussel, the round goby, and the sea lamprey.

The zebra mussel (Figure 5.10) is an invasive species that both degrades aquatic resources and threatens native species, particularly native freshwater mussels. Zebra mussels first appeared in the United States in 1988 and since that time have spread throughout the Great Lakes. By 1999 zebra mussels were found throughout the eastern United States. (See Figure 5.11.) This pest species reproduces rapidly and threatens aquatic habitats by clogging water passages and starving out native species. U.S. freshwater mussel species are in fact disappearing at an alarming rate. Figure 5.12 shows the decline in the number of pearly mussel species in the Mississippi River.

FIGURE 5.10

The invasive zebra mussel, here shown anchored in large numbers to another bivalve. Zebra mussels were introduced to U.S. waters in 1988 and have since caused significant damage to waterworks. They have also contributed to the decline of numerous native freshwater mussel species. *(Michigan Sea Grant Society)*

In the state of Georgia, invasive Asian eels have increased in number in many habitats. These species were brought over from Southeast Asia or Australia, where they are considered delicacies. The three-foot-long, flesh-eating eel preys on species such as largemouth bass and crawfish in and around the Chattahoochee River. The eels have gills but can also breathe air—this enables them to worm their way across dry ground to get from one body of water to another. Asian eels have few predators in their new habitat, and humans have found no effective way to control them. In March 2000 an Asian eel was reported near Florida's Everglades National Park, confirming fears that the eel would spread beyond Georgia.

Striking at the Base of the Food Chain— Depletion of Phytoplankton

Phytoplankton are microscopic photosynthesizing species that form the basis of nearly all marine food chains (Figure 5.13). In many parts of the world, phytoplankton seems to be declining. The most severe damage appears to be in the waters off Antarctica, where phytoplankton resources are severely depleted. The depletion of phytoplankton has implications all the way up the food chain, affecting the zooplankton that consume them, as well as larger species such as penguins, seals, and whales. Scientists believe that phytoplankton declines result from the thinning of the atmospheric ozone layer (caused by industrial pollutants such as chlorofluorocarbons, or CFCs), which allows increasing amounts of ultraviolet radiation to penetrate the Earth's surface. Ultraviolet radiation decreases the ability of phytoplankton to photosynthesize and also damages genetic material.

FIGURE 5.11

Zebra mussel distribution 1988 and 1999

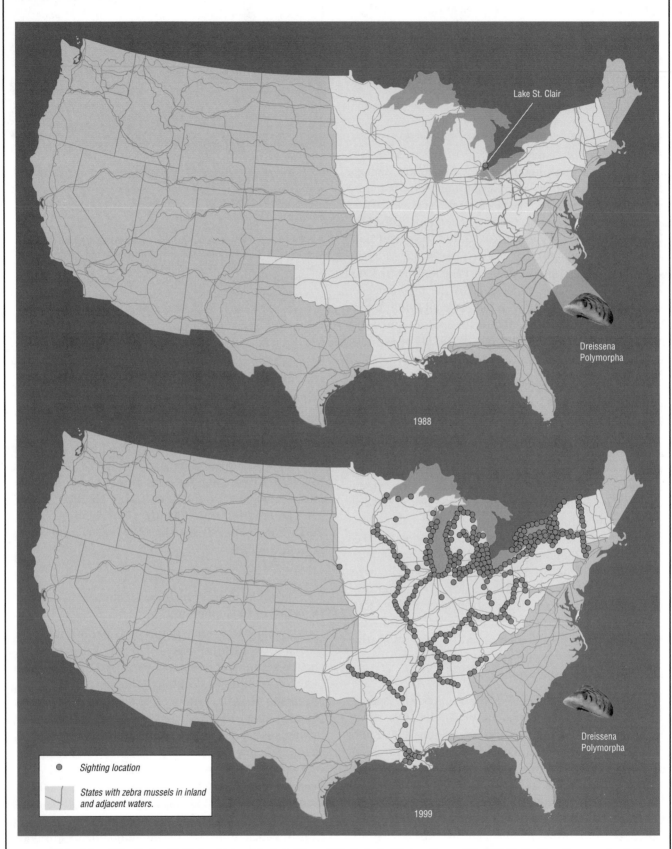

SOURCE: "Zebra Mussel Distribution," in *National Atlas of the United States,* U.S. Geological Survey, Reston, VA, 2000 [Online] http://www.nationalatlas. gov/zmussels1.html [accessed on April 30, 2002]

FIGURE 5.12

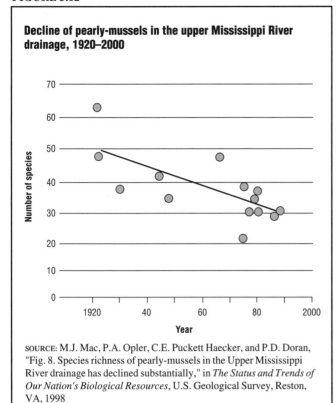

Decline of pearly-mussels in the upper Mississippi River drainage, 1920–2000

SOURCE: M.J. Mac, P.A. Opler, C.E. Puckett Haecker, and P.D. Doran, "Fig. 8. Species richness of pearly-mussels in the Upper Mississippi River drainage has declined substantially," in *The Status and Trends of Our Nation's Biological Resources*, U.S. Geological Survey, Reston, VA, 1998

IMPERILED AQUATIC SPECIES

Numerous aquatic species are endangered in the United States. In fact, Figure 5.14 shows that all the biological groups with the greatest proportion of endangered species—freshwater mussels, crayfishes, amphibians, and freshwater fishes—are aquatic. The U.S. also possesses some of the most diverse freshwater fauna in the world, including 29 percent of the world's freshwater mussels, 61 percent of crayfish, 17 percent of freshwater snails, and 10 percent of freshwater fish. Figure 5.15 shows the number of biological species at risk by watershed. Areas of the southeastern United States have particularly high levels of endangerment.

There are a total of 126 listed fish species—82 of these are endangered (71 U.S. and 11 foreign) and 44 are threatened (all U.S.). Table 5.2 shows the listed fish species found in the United States. There are also 72 threatened and endangered clams and other bivalves (70 U.S. and 2 foreign), 33 threatened and endangered snails (32 U.S. and 1 foreign), and 21 threatened and endangered crustaceans (all U.S.). Figure 4.4 in chapter four lists the threatened and endangered U.S. bivalve, snail, and crustacean species.

Freshwater Mussels

The United States has the greatest diversity of freshwater mussels in the world. Figure 5.16 shows a species

FIGURE 5.13

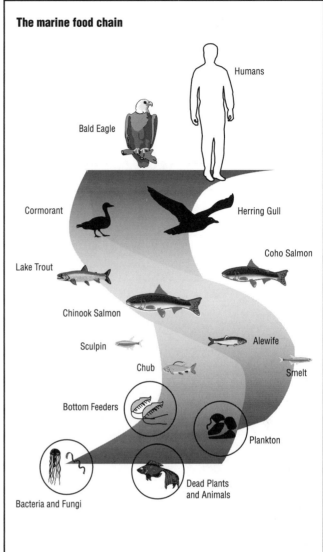

The marine food chain

SOURCE: "The Marine Food Chain," in *National Water Quality Inventory—1996 Report to Congress*, U.S. Environmental Protection Agency, Washington, DC, 1998

of pearly mussel. Unfortunately, many freshwater mussels are in decline. In 2002, of the 297 native mussel species in the United States, 12 percent were believed extinct and 23 percent were listed as threatened or endangered. Furthermore, numerous additional mussel species are being considered for listing. The Nature Conservancy and the American Fisheries Society estimate that about 70 percent of freshwater mussels will require protection. The decline of freshwater mussels, which began in the 1800s, has resulted largely from habitat disturbance, especially water pollution and the modification of aquatic habitats by dams. Dams have single-handedly caused the loss of 30 to 60 percent of native mussels in U.S. rivers. The invasive zebra mussel has also harmed native freshwater mussel species by competing with them for food and other resources.

FIGURE 5.14

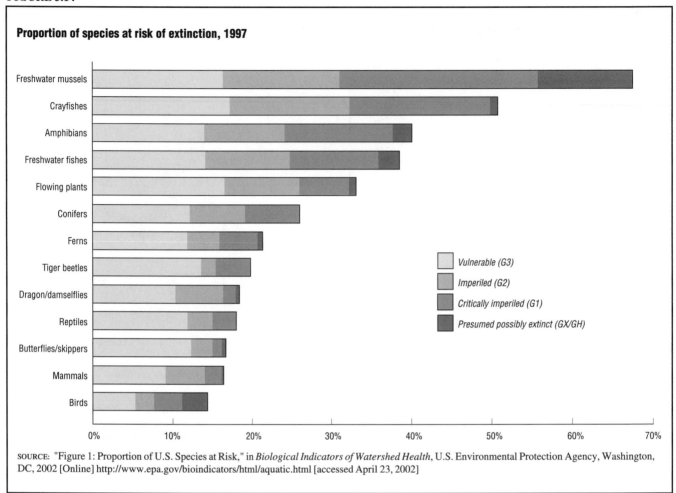

Proportion of species at risk of extinction, 1997

Legend:
- Vulnerable (G3)
- Imperiled (G2)
- Critically imperiled (G1)
- Presumed possibly extinct (GX/GH)

Categories (top to bottom): Freshwater mussels, Crayfishes, Amphibians, Freshwater fishes, Flowing plants, Conifers, Ferns, Tiger beetles, Dragon/damselflies, Reptiles, Butterflies/skippers, Mammals, Birds

X-axis: 0% 10% 20% 30% 40% 50% 60% 70%

SOURCE: "Figure 1: Proportion of U.S. Species at Risk," in *Biological Indicators of Watershed Health*, U.S. Environmental Protection Agency, Washington, DC, 2002 [Online] http://www.epa.gov/bioindicators/html/aquatic.html [accessed April 23, 2002]

The decline of freshwater mussels, scientists fear, is a sign of serious problems in freshwater ecosystems. Mussels perform many essential functions in these ecosystems, providing food for many species and improving water quality by filtering particles and excess nutrients. Other freshwater mollusks, particularly snails, may also be declining. Conservation efforts for freshwater mussels include the captive breeding and reintroduction of some species, as well as measures to restore damaged habitats.

Fish

Fish occur in nearly all permanent water environments, from deep oceans to remote alpine lakes and desert springs. They are the most diverse vertebrate group—scientists have officially catalogued nearly 24,000 fish species, about as many as all other vertebrates combined. Less than 10 percent of these species have been assessed for their conservation status.

The World Conservation Union (IUCN) listed 742 species of fish as threatened in its *2000 Red List of Threatened Species*. However, the IUCN reports that many more, perhaps as many as a third of all fish species, are likely to be listed once surveys are complete. The IUCN also reported that at least 60 percent of threatened freshwater fish species are in decline because of habitat alteration, whereas 34 percent face pressure from introduced species. The U.S. Fish and Wildlife Service listed a total of 82 endangered and 44 threatened fish species in 2002.

CICHLIDS. The cichlids are a large family of fish that evolved over a period of 750,000 years in African rift lakes including Lake Malawi, Lake Tanganyika, and Lake Victoria. Lake Malawi probably has more fish species than any other lake in the world, with over 1,000 identified—95 percent of these are cichlids. Many cichlid fishes, however, are now facing extinction. British colonialists introduced the Nile perch into Lake Victoria in 1954 because it is significantly larger (up to 300 pounds) than native fish species and can more easily be caught with nets. The aggressive Nile perch have since eaten about half the native cichlid species in Lake Victoria to extinction. With the loss of cichlid species, which feed on algae and insects, algae has grown out of control, damaging all lake habitats. Insects have also flourished.

SALMON. In recent decades, many salmon species, particularly those that inhabit the Columbia and Snake Rivers in the Pacific Northwest, have declined. Salmon

FIGURE 5.15

Number of species at risk by watershed

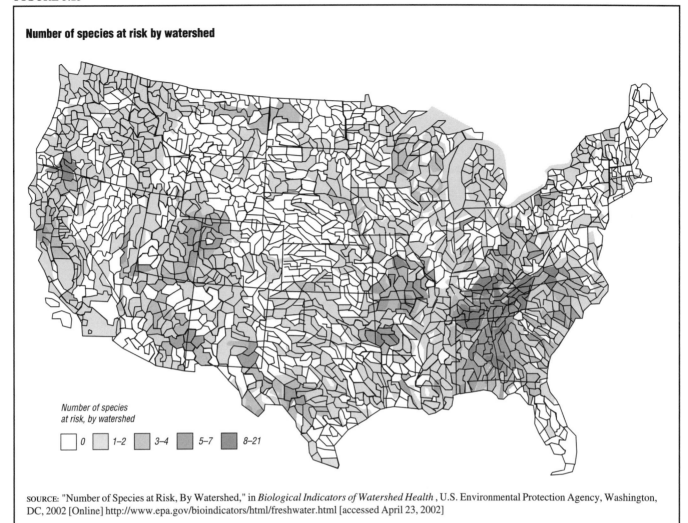

Number of species at risk, by watershed

☐ 0   ☐ 1–2   ☐ 3–4   ☐ 5–7   ☐ 8–21

SOURCE: "Number of Species at Risk, By Watershed," in *Biological Indicators of Watershed Health*, U.S. Environmental Protection Agency, Washington, DC, 2002 [Online] http://www.epa.gov/bioindicators/html/freshwater.html [accessed April 23, 2002]

are of significant economic and social importance for the commercial food harvest as well as for sport fishing. Salmon are also important to Pacific Northwest Native American tribes for economic as well as cultural and religious reasons. Species in danger of extinction include the coho, sockeye, chinook, and steelhead. Two major causes of salmon endangerment are overfishing and dams.

During the 1800s annual salmon runs were estimated to include some 10 to 16 million individuals. At present, total salmon runs have declined to an estimated 2.5 million annually. Declines prior to 1930 resulted largely from overfishing. Since then, however, the major causes of salmon declines have been dam construction in the Columbia River Basin and water pollution, including nitrogen saturation below dam spillways. In 1992, the National Marine Fisheries Service began to designate critical habitat for salmon species and to develop recovery plans. In 1994 the Pacific Fisheries Management Council issued strict regulations limiting salmon catches. Soon after that, the government announced that Pacific salmon were nearly extinct and began to list species for

protection under the Endangered Species Act. Listed species now include the chum salmon (threatened in Oregon and Washington, 1999), the coho salmon (threatened, California and Oregon, 1995–1996), the sockeye salmon (endangered in Idaho, 1992, and threatened in Washington, 1999), the chinook salmon (threatened or endangered in California, Oregon, Washington, and Idaho, 1990–1999), and the Atlantic salmon (endangered, Maine, 2000). Listing came after nearly 10 years of study, and marked the first time vast urban areas saw land and water use restricted under the Endangered Species Act. Controversy over dam management continues in the Pacific Northwest.

THE KLAMATH BASIN—AN ONGOING CONFLICT. The Klamath Basin in southern Oregon and northern California is the site of a heated battle pitting farmers against a coalition of fishermen and environmentalists who wish to protect three listed species, the coho salmon, shortnose sucker fish, and Lost River sucker fish. Opponents are battling over water, which has been in particularly short supply due to recent droughts in the Pacific Northwest.

TABLE 5.2

Animal species on the federal list of endangered and threatened wildlife, by taxonomic group, 2002

Status	Species name
Mammals	
E	Bat, gray (*Myotis grisescens*)
E	Bat, Hawaiian hoary (*Lasiurus cinereus semotus*)
E	Bat, Indiana (*Myotis sodalis*)
E	Bat, lesser long-nosed (*Leptonycteris curasoae yerbabuenae*)
E	Bat, little Mariana fruit (*Pteropus tokudae*)
E	Bat, Mariana fruit (=Mariana flying fox) (*Pteropus mariannus mariannus*)
E	Bat, Mexican long-nosed (*Leptonycteris nivalis*)
E	Bat, Ozark big-eared (*Corynorhinus (=Plecotus) townsendii ingens*)
E	Bat, Virginia big-eared (*Corynorhinus (=Plecotus) townsendii virginianus*)
T(S/A)	Bear, American black (*Ursus americanus*)
XN,T	Bear, grizzly (*Ursus arctos horribilis*)
T	Bear, Louisiana black (*Ursus americanus luteolus*)
E	Caribou, woodland (*Rangifer tarandus caribou*)
E	Deer, Columbian white-tailed (*Odocoileus virginianus leucurus*)
E	Deer, key (*Odocoileus virginianus clavium*)
E,XN	Ferret, black-footed (*Mustela nigripes*)
E	Fox, San Joaquin kit (*Vulpes macrotis mutica*)
E	Jaguar (*Panthera onca*)
E	Jaguarundi, Gulf Coast (*Herpailurus (=Felis) yagouaroundi cacomitli*)
E	Jaguarundi, Sinaloan (*Herpailurus (=Felis) yagouaroundi tolteca*)
E	Kangaroo rat, Fresno (*Dipodomys nitratoides exilis*)
E	Kangaroo rat, giant (*Dipodomys ingens*)
E	Kangaroo rat, Morro Bay (*Dipodomys heermanni morroensis*)
E	Kangaroo rat, San Bernardino Merriam's (*Dipodomys merriami parvus*)
E	Kangaroo rat, Stephens' (*Dipodomys stephensi (incl. D. cascus)*)
E	Kangaroo rat, Tipton (*Dipodomys nitratoides nitratoides*)
T	Lynx, Canada (*Lynx canadensis*)
E	Manatee, West Indian (*Trichechus manatus*)
E	Mountain beaver, Point Arena (*Aplodontia rufa nigra*)
E	Mouse, Alabama beach (*Peromyscus polionotus ammobates*)
E	Mouse, Anastasia Island beach (*Peromyscus polionotus phasma*)
E	Mouse, Choctawhatchee beach (*Peromyscus polionotus allophrys*)
E	Mouse, Key Largo cotton (*Peromyscus gossypinus allapaticola*)
E	Mouse, Pacific pocket (*Perognathus longimembris pacificus*)
E	Mouse, Perdido Key beach (*Peromyscus polionotus trissyllepsis*)
T	Mouse, Preble's meadow jumping (*Zapus hudsonius preblei*)
E	Mouse, salt marsh harvest (*Reithrodontomys raviventris*)
T	Mouse, southeastern beach (*Peromyscus polionotus niveiventris*)
E	Mouse, St. Andrew beach (*Peromyscus polionotus peninsularis*)
E	Ocelot (*Leopardus (=Felis) pardalis*)
XN,T	Otter, southern sea (*Enhydra lutris nereis*)
E	Panther, Florida (*Puma (=Felis) concolor coryi*)
T	Prairie dog, Utah (*Cynomys parvidens*)
E	Pronghorn, Sonoran (*Antilocapra americana sonoriensis*)
E	Puma (=cougar), eastern (*Puma (=Felis) concolor couguar*)
T(S/A)	Puma (=mountain lion) (*Puma (=Felis) concolor (all subsp. except coryi)*)
E	Rabbit, Lower Keys marsh (*Sylvilagus palustris hefneri*)
EmE	Rabbit, pygmy (*Brachylagus idahoensis*)
E	Rabbit, riparian brush (*Sylvilagus bachmani riparius*)
E	Rice rat (*Oryzomys palustris natator*)
E	Seal, Caribbean monk (*Monachus tropicalis*)
T	Seal, Guadalupe fur (*Arctocephalus townsendi*)
E	Seal, Hawaiian monk (*Monachus schauinslandi*)
E,T	Sea-lion, Steller (*Eumetopias jubatus*)
E	Sheep, bighorn (*Ovis canadensis*)
E	Sheep, bighorn (*Ovis canadensis californiana*)
E	Shrew, Buena Vista Lake ornate (*Sorex ornatus relictus*)
E	Squirrel, Carolina northern flying (*Glaucomys sabrinus coloratus*)
E,XN	Squirrel, Delmarva Peninsula fox (*Sciurus niger cinereus*)
E	Squirrel, Mount Graham red (*Tamiasciurus hudsonicus grahamensis*)
T	Squirrel, northern Idaho ground (*Spermophilus brunneus brunneus*)
E	Squirrel, Virginia northern flying (*Glaucomys sabrinus fuscus*)
E	Vole, Amargosa (*Microtus californicus scirpensis*)
E	Vole, Florida salt marsh (*Microtus pennsylvanicus dukecampbelli*)
E	Vole, Hualapai Mexican (*Microtus mexicanus hualpaiensis*)
E	Whale, blue (*Balaenoptera musculus*)
E	Whale, bowhead (*Balaena mysticetus*)
E	Whale, finback (*Balaenoptera physalus*)

Status	Species name
E	Whale, humpback (*Megaptera novaeangliae*)
E	Whale, right (*Balaena glacialis (incl. australis)*)
E	Whale, Sei (*Balaenoptera borealis*) E Whale, sperm (*Physeter catodon (=macrocephalus)*)
E,XN,T	Wolf, gray (*Canis lupus*)
E,XN	Wolf, red (*Canis rufus*)
E	Woodrat, Key Largo (*Neotoma floridana smalli*)
E	Woodrat, riparian (=San Joaquin Valley) (*Neotoma fuscipes riparia*)
Birds	
E	Akepa, Hawaii (honeycreeper) (*Loxops coccineus coccineus*)
E	Akepa, Maui (honeycreeper) (*Loxops coccineus ochraceus*)
E	Akialoa, Kauai (honeycreeper) (*Hemignathus procerus*)
E	Akiapola'au (honeycreeper) (*Hemignathus munroi*)
E	Albatross, short-tailed (*Phoebastria (=Diomedea) albatrus*)
E	Blackbird, yellow-shouldered (*Agelaius xanthomus*)
E	Bobwhite, masked (quail) (*Colinus virginianus ridgwayi*)
E	Broadbill, Guam (*Myiagra freycineti*)
E	Cahow (*Pterodroma cahow*)
T	Caracara, Audubon's crested (*Polyborus plancus audubonii*)
E,XN	Condor, California (*Gymnogyps californianus*)
E	Coot, Hawaiian (*Fulica americana alai*)
E	Crane, Mississippi sandhill (*Grus canadensis pulla*)
E,XN	Crane, whooping (*Grus americana*)
E	Creeper, Hawaii (*Oreomystis mana*)
E	Creeper, Molokai (*Paroreomyza flammea*)
E	Creeper, Oahu (*Paroreomyza maculata*)
E	Crow, Hawaiian (*Corvus hawaiiensis*)
E	Crow, Mariana (*Corvus kubaryi*)
E	Crow, white-necked (*Corvus leucognaphalus*)
E	Curlew, Eskimo (*Numenius borealis*)
E	Duck, Hawaiian (*Anas wyvilliana*)
E	Duck, Laysan (*Anas laysanensis*)
T	Eagle, bald (*Haliaeetus leucocephalus*)
T	Eider, spectacled (*Somateria fischeri*)
T	Eider, Steller's (*Polysticta stelleri*)
E	Elepaio, Oahu (*Chasiempis sandwichensis ibidus*)
E	Falcon, northern aplomado (*Falco femoralis septentrionalis*)
E	Finch, Laysan (honeycreeper) (*Telespyza cantans*)
E	Finch, Nihoa (honeycreeper) (*Telespyza ultima*)
E	Flycatcher, southwestern willow (*Empidonax traillii extimus*)
T	Gnatcatcher, coastal California (*Polioptila californica californica*)
E	Goose, Hawaiian (*Branta (=Nesochen) sandvicensis*)
E	Hawk, Hawaiian (*Buteo solitarius*)
E	Hawk, Puerto Rican broad-winged (*Buteo platypterus brunnescens*)
E	Hawk, Puerto Rican sharp-shinned (*Accipiter striatus venator*)
E	Honeycreeper, crested (*Palmeria dolei*)
T	Jay, Florida scrub (*Aphelocoma coerulescens*)
E	Kingfisher, Guam Micronesian (*Halcyon cinnamomina cinnamomina*)
E	Kite, Everglade snail (*Rostrhamus sociabilis plumbeus*)
E	Mallard, Mariana (*Anas oustaleti*)
E	Megapode, Micronesian (*Megapodius laperouse*)
E	Millerbird, Nihoa (old world warbler) (*Acrocephalus familiaris kingi*)
T	Monarch, Tinian (old world flycatcher) (*Monarcha takatsukasae*)
E	Moorhen, Hawaiian common (*Gallinula chloropus sandvicensis*)
E	Moorhen, Mariana common (*Gallinula chloropus guami*)
T	Murrelet, marbled (*Brachyramphus marmoratus marmoratus*)
E	Nightjar, Puerto Rican (*Caprimulgus noctitherus*)
E	Nukupu'u (honeycreeper) (*Hemignathus lucidus*)
E	'O'o, Kauai (honeyeater) (*Moho braccatus*)
E	'O'u (honeycreeper) (*Psittirostra psittacea*)
T	Owl, Mexican spotted (*Strix occidentalis lucida*)
T	Owl, northern spotted (*Strix occidentalis caurina*)
E	Palila (honeycreeper) (*Loxioides bailleui*)
E	Parrot, Puerto Rican (*Amazona vittata*)
E	Parrotbill, Maui (honeycreeper) (*Pseudonestor xanthophrys*)
E	Pelican, brown (*Pelecanus occidentalis*)
E	Petrel, Hawaiian dark-rumped (*Pterodroma phaeopygia sandwichensis*)
E	Pigeon, Puerto Rican plain (*Columba inornata wetmorei*)
E,T	Plover, piping (*Charadrius melodus*)

Status	Species name
T	Plover, western snowy (*Charadrius alexandrinus nivosus*)
E	Po'ouli (honeycreeper) (*Melamprosops phaeosoma*)
E	Prairie-chicken, Attwater's greater (*Tympanuchus cupido attwateri*)
E	Pygmy-owl, cactus ferruginous (*Glaucidium brasilianum cactorum*)
E	Rail, California clapper (*Rallus longirostris obsoletus*)
E,XN	Rail, Guam (*Rallus owstoni*)
E	Rail, light-footed clapper (*Rallus longirostris levipes*)
E	Rail, Yuma clapper (*Rallus longirostris yumanensis*)
T	Shearwater, Newell's Townsend's (*Puffinus auricularis newelli*)
E	Shrike, San Clemente loggerhead (*Lanius ludovicianus mearnsi*)
E	Sparrow, Cape Sable seaside (*Ammodramus maritimus mirabilis*)
E	Sparrow, Florida grasshopper (*Ammodramus savannarum floridanus*)
T	Sparrow, San Clemente sage (*Amphispiza belli clementeae*)
E	Stilt, Hawaiian (*Himantopus mexicanus knudseni*)
E	Stork, wood (*Mycteria americana*)
E	Swiftlet, Mariana gray (*Aerodramus vanikorensis bartschi*)
E	Tern, California least (*Sterna antillarum browni*)
E	Tern, least (*Sterna antillarum*)
E,T	Tern, roseate (*Sterna dougallii dougallii*)
E	Thrush, large Kauai (*Myadestes myadestinus*)
E	Thrush, Molokai (*Myadestes lanaiensis rutha*)
E	Thrush, small Kauai (*Myadestes palmeri*)
T	Towhee, Inyo California (*Pipilo crissalis eremophilus*)
E	Vireo, black-capped (*Vireo atricapillus*)
E	Vireo, least Bell's (*Vireo bellii pusillus*)
E	Warbler (=wood), Bachman's (*Vermivora bachmanii*)
E	Warbler (=wood), golden-cheeked (*Dendroica chrysoparia*)
E	Warbler (=wood), Kirtland's (*Dendroica kirtlandii*)
E	Warbler, nightingale reed (old world warbler) (*Acrocephalus luscinia*)
E	White-eye, bridled (*Zosterops conspicillatus conspicillatus*)
E	Woodpecker, ivory-billed (*Campephilus principalis*)
E	Woodpecker, red-cockaded (*Picoides borealis*)

Reptiles

Status	Species name
T(S/A)	Alligator, American (*Alligator mississippiensis*)
E	Anole, Culebra Island giant (*Anolis roosevelti*)
T	Boa, Mona (*Epicrates monensis monensis*)
T	Boa, Puerto Rican (*Epicrates inornatus*)
E	Boa, Virgin Islands tree (*Epicrates monensis granti*)
E	Crocodile, American (*Crocodylus acutus*)
E	Gecko, Monito (*Sphaerodactylus micropithecus*)
T	Iguana, Mona ground (*Cyclura stejnegeri*)
E	Lizard, blunt-nosed leopard (*Gambelia silus*)
T	Lizard, Coachella Valley fringe-toed (*Uma inornata*)
T	Lizard, Island night (*Xantusia riversiana*)
E	Lizard, St. Croix ground (*Ameiva polops*)
T	Rattlesnake, New Mexican ridge-nosed (*Crotalus willardi obscurus*)
E,T	Sea turtle, green (*Chelonia mydas*)
E	Sea turtle, hawksbill (*Eretmochelys imbricata*)
E	Sea turtle, Kemp's ridley (*Lepidochelys kempii*)
E	Sea turtle, leatherback (*Dermochelys coriacea*)
T	Sea turtle, loggerhead (*Caretta caretta*)
T	Sea turtle, olive ridley (*Lepidochelys olivacea*)
T	Skink, bluetail mole (*Eumeces egregius lividus*)
T	Skink, sand (*Neoseps reynoldsi*)
T	Snake, Atlantic salt marsh (*Nerodia clarkii taeniata*)
T	Snake, Concho water (*Nerodia paucimaculata*)
T	Snake, copperbelly water (*Nerodia erythrogaster neglecta*)
T	Snake, eastern indigo (*Drymarchon corais couperi*)
T	Snake, giant garter (*Thamnophis gigas*)
T	Snake, Lake Erie water (*Nerodia sipedon insularum*)
E	Snake, San Francisco garter (*Thamnophis sirtalis tetrataenia*)
T(S/A),T	Tortoise, desert (*Gopherus agassizii*)
T	Tortoise, gopher (*Gopherus polyphemus*)
E	Turtle, Alabama red-belly (*Pseudemys alabamensis*)
T(S/A),T	Turtle, bog (=Muhlenberg) (*Clemmys muhlenbergii*)
T	Turtle, flattened musk (*Sternotherus depressus*)
E	Turtle, Plymouth redbelly (*Pseudemys rubriventris bangsi*)
T	Turtle, ringed map (*Graptemys oculifera*)
T	Turtle, yellow-blotched map (*Graptemys flavimaculata*)
T	Whipsnake (=striped racer), Alameda (*Masticophis lateralis euryxanthus*)

Status	Species Name
Amphibians	
T	Coqui, golden (*Eleutherodactylus jasperi*)
T	Frog, California red-legged (*Rana aurora draytonii*)
E	Frog, Mississippi gopher (*Rana capito sevosa*)
T	Guajon (*Eleutherodactylus cooki*) E Salamander, Barton Springs (*Eurycea sosorum*)
E	Salamander, California tiger (*Ambystoma californiense*)
T	Salamander, Cheat Mountain (*Plethodon nettingi*)
E	Salamander, desert slender (*Batrachoseps aridus*)
T	Salamander, flatwoods (*Ambystoma cingulatum*)
T	Salamander, Red Hills (*Phaeognathus hubrichti*)
T	Salamander, San Marcos (*Eurycea nana*)
E	Salamander, Santa Cruz long-toed (*Ambystoma macrodactylum croceum*)
E	Salamander, Shenandoah (*Plethodon shenandoah*)
E	Salamander, Sonoran tiger (*Ambystoma tigrinum stebbinsi*)
E	Salamander, Texas blind (*Typhlomolge rathbuni*)
E	Toad, arroyo (=arroyo southwestern) (*Bufo californicus (=microscaphus)*)
E	Toad, Houston (*Bufo houstonensis*)
T	Toad, Puerto Rican crested (*Peltophryne lemur*)
E	Toad, Wyoming (*Bufo baxteri (=hemiophrys)*)
Fishes	
T	Catfish, Yaqui (*Ictalurus pricei*)
E	Cavefish, Alabama (*Speoplatyrhinus poulsoni*)
T	Cavefish, Ozark (*Amblyopsis rosae*)
E	Chub, bonytail (*Gila elegans*)
E	Chub, Borax Lake (*Gila boraxobius*)
E	Chub, Chihuahua (*Gila nigrescens*)
E	Chub, humpback (*Gila cypha*)
T	Chub, Hutton tui (*Gila bicolor* ssp.)
E	Chub, Mohave tui (*Gila bicolor mohavensis*)
E	Chub, Oregon (*Oregonichthys crameri*)
E	Chub, Owens tui (*Gila bicolor snyderi*)
E	Chub, Pahranagat roundtail (*Gila robusta jordani*)
T	Chub, slender (*Erimystax cahni*)
T	Chub, Sonora (*Gila ditaenia*)
E	Chub, spotfin (*Cyprinella monacha*)
E	Chub, Virgin River (*Gila seminuda (=robusta)*)
E	Chub, Yaqui (*Gila purpurea*)
E	Cui-ui (*Chasmistes cujus*)
E	Dace, Ash Meadows speckled (*Rhinichthys osculus nevadensis*)
E	Dace, blackside (*Phoxinus cumberlandensis*)
E	Dace, Clover Valley speckled (*Rhinichthys osculus oligoporus*)
T	Dace, desert (*Eremichthys acros*)
T	Dace, Foskett speckled (*Rhinichthys osculus* ssp.)
E	Dace, Independence Valley speckled (*Rhinichthys osculus lethoporus*)
E	Dace, Kendall Warm Springs (*Rhinichthys osculus thermalis*)
E	Dace, Moapa (*Moapa coriacea*)
E	Darter, amber (*Percina antesella*)
T	Darter, bayou (*Etheostoma rubrum*)
E	Darter, bluemask (*Etheostoma sp.*)
E	Darter, boulder (*Etheostoma wapiti*)
T	Darter, Cherokee (*Etheostoma scotti*)
E	Darter, duskytail (*Etheostoma percnurum*)
E	Darter, Etowah (*Etheostoma etowahae*)
E	Darter, fountain (*Etheostoma fonticola*)
T	Darter, goldline (*Percina aurolineata*)
T	Darter, leopard (*Percina pantherina*)
E	Darter, Maryland (*Etheostoma sellare*)
T	Darter, Niangua (*Etheostoma nianguae*)
E	Darter, Okaloosa (*Etheostoma okaloosae*)
E	Darter, relict (*Etheostoma chienense*)
T	Darter, slackwater (*Etheostoma boschungi*)
T	Darter, snail (*Percina tanasi*)
E	Darter, vermilion (*Etheostoma chermocki*)
E	Darter, watercress (*Etheostoma nuchale*)
E	Gambusia, Big Bend (*Gambusia gaigei*)
E	Gambusia, Clear Creek (*Gambusia heterochir*)
E	Gambusia, Pecos (*Gambusia nobilis*)
E	Gambusia, San Marcos (*Gambusia georgei*)
E	Goby, tidewater (*Eucyclogobius newberryi*)
E	Logperch, Conasauga (*Percina jenkinsi*)

TABLE 5.2

Animal species on the federal list of endangered and threatened wildlife, by taxonomic group, 2002 [CONTINUED]

Status	Species Name
E	Logperch, Roanoke (*Percina rex*)
T	Madtom, Neosho (*Noturus placidus*)
E	Madtom, pygmy (*Noturus stanauli*)
E	Madtom, Scioto (*Noturus trautmani*)
E	Madtom, smoky (*Noturus baileyi*)
XN,T	Madtom, yellowfin (*Noturus flavipinnis*)
T	Minnow, Devils River (*Dionda diaboli*)
T	Minnow, loach (*Tiaroga cobitis*)
E	Minnow, Rio Grande silvery (*Hybognathus amarus*)
E,XN	Pikeminnow (=squawfish), Colorado (*Ptychocheilus lucius*)
E	Poolfish, Pahrump (*Empetrichthys latos*)
E	Pupfish, Ash Meadows Amargosa (*Cyprinodon nevadensis mionectes*)
E	Pupfish, Comanche Springs (*Cyprinodon elegans*)
E	Pupfish, desert (*Cyprinodon macularius*)
E	Pupfish, Devils Hole (*Cyprinodon diabolis*)
E	Pupfish, Leon Springs (*Cyprinodon bovinus*)
E	Pupfish, Owens (*Cyprinodon radiosus*)
E	Pupfish, Warm Springs (*Cyprinodon nevadensis pectoralis*)
E	Salmon, Atlantic (*Salmo salar*)
E,T	Salmon, chinook (*Oncorhynchus (=Salmo) tshawytscha*)
T	Salmon, chum (*Oncorhynchus (=Salmo) keta*)
T	Salmon, coho (*Oncorhynchus (=Salmo) kisutch*)
E,T	Salmon, sockeye (*Oncorhynchus (=Salmo) nerka*)
T	Sculpin, pygmy (*Cottus pygmaeus*)
T	Shiner, Arkansas River (*Notropis girardi*)
T	Shiner, beautiful (*Cyprinella formosa*)
T	Shiner, blue (*Cyprinella caerulea*)
E	Shiner, Cahaba (*Notropis cahabae*)
E	Shiner, Cape Fear (*Notropis mekistocholas*)
E	Shiner, palezone (*Notropis albizonatus*)
T	Shiner, Pecos bluntnose (*Notropis simus pecosensis*)
E	Shiner, Topeka (*Notropis topeka (=tristis)*)
E	Silverside, Waccamaw (*Menidia extensa*)
T	Smelt, delta (*Hypomesus transpacificus*)
T	Spikedace (*Meda fulgida*)
T	Spinedace, Big Spring (*Lepidomeda mollispinis pratensis*)
T	Spinedace, Little Colorado (*Lepidomeda vittata*)
E	Spinedace, White River (*Lepidomeda albivallis*)
T	Splittail, Sacramento (*Pogonichthys macrolepidotus*)
E	Springfish, Hiko White River (*Crenichthys baileyi grandis*)
T	Springfish, Railroad Valley (*Crenichthys nevadae*)
E	Springfish, White River (*Crenichthys baileyi baileyi*)
E,T	Steelhead (*Oncorhynchus (=Salmo) mykiss*)
E	Stickleback, unarmored threespine (*Gasterosteus aculeatus williamsoni*)
E	Sturgeon, Alabama (*Scaphirhynchus suttkusi*)
T	Sturgeon, gulf (*Acipenser oxyrinchus desotoi*)
E	Sturgeon, pallid (*Scaphirhynchus albus*)
E	Sturgeon, shortnose (*Acipenser brevirostrum*)
E	Sturgeon, white (*Acipenser transmontanus*)
E	Sucker, June (*Chasmistes liorus*)
E	Sucker, Lost River (*Deltistes luxatus*)
E	Sucker, Modoc (*Catostomus microps*)
E	Sucker, razorback (*Xyrauchen texanus*)
T	Sucker, Santa Ana (*Catostomus santaanae*)
E	Sucker, shortnose (*Chasmistes brevirostris*)
T	Sucker, Warner (*Catostomus warnerensis*)
E	Topminnow, Gila (incl. Yaqui) (*Poeciliopsis occidentalis*)
T	Trout, Apache (*Oncorhynchus apache*)
T	Trout, bull (*Salvelinus confluentus*)
E	Trout, Gila (*Oncorhynchus gilae*)
T	Trout, greenback cutthroat (*Oncorhynchus clarki stomias*)
T	Trout, Lahontan cutthroat (*Oncorhynchus clarki henshawi*)
T	Trout, Little Kern golden (*Oncorhynchus aguabonita whitei*)
T	Trout, Paiute cutthroat (*Oncorhynchus clarki seleniris*)
E,XN	Woundfin (*Plagopterus argentissimus*)

Note: E = Endangered; T = Threatened; T(S/A) = Similarity of appearance to a threatened taxon; XN = Experimental population, non-essential; EmE = Emergency listing, endangered

SOURCE: "U.S. Listed Vertebrate Animal Species Report by Taxonomic Group," in *Species Information: Threatened and Endangered Animals and Plants,* U.S. Fish and Wildlife Service, Washington, DC, 2002 [Online] http://ecos.fws.gov/webpage/webpage_vip_listed.html?&code=V&listings=0#A [accessed May 17, 2002]

FIGURE 5.16

Higgins eye, a species of pearly mussel, is listed as endangered throughout its range in the Great Lakes-Big Rivers region. The United States harbors the greatest diversity of freshwater mussel species in the world. Unfortunately, many of these species are now in danger of extinction. (*U.S. Fish and Wildlife Service*)

The Klamath River once supported the third largest salmon run in the country. However, in recent years, water diversion has caused river water levels to be too low to maintain healthy stream conditions and temperatures. Over 7,000 fishing jobs have been lost due to salmon declines. Water diversion practices also violate agreements with Native American tribes to avoid harming healthy salmon runs. Water diversion in the Klamath Basin has also caused the loss of over 75 percent of area wetlands, including portions of the Klamath Marsh National Wildlife Refuge in southern Oregon, at the headwaters of the Klamath River. This habitat supports the shortnose sucker and the Lost River sucker, which were listed as endangered in their entire ranges in California and Oregon in 1988. Both were once highly abundant in the Upper Klamath Lake, but populations have declined due to alteration of water flow patterns, habitat degradation, and water pollution. Suckerfish species live in the lake most of the year, but migrate downstream to spawn. Habitat alteration has particularly affected the survival of juvenile suckers. The Klamath Marsh National Wildlife Refuge also supports other listed species such as the bald eagle, northern spotted owl, and several species of endangered coastal dune plants.

A lawsuit regarding the distribution of Klamath Basin waters was brought against the U.S. Bureau of Reclamation by the Pacific Coast Federation of Fishermen's Associations, the Klamath Forest Alliance, the Institute for Fisheries Resources, the Oregon Natural Resources Council, and other groups. The plaintiffs argued that the Bureau of Reclamation had met farmers' demands for water, but left Klamath River flows much lower than that required for survival of the coho salmon, shortnose sucker fish, and Lost River sucker fish. Furthermore, the Bureau was charged with violating the Endangered Species Act in not consulting with the National Marine Fisheries Service regarding endangered species conservation. Farmers were also accused of wasting water.

In April 2001 the U.S. Bureau of Reclamation was found by a Federal District Court to have knowingly violated the Endangered Species Act when it allowed delivery of irrigation water required to maintain habitat of the three listed species. As a result of the court decision, federal agencies cut water to irrigation canals in order to preserve water levels in the Upper Klamath Lake for the two species of sucker fish and to increase water flow in the Klamath River for coho salmon. In April 2002, a lawsuit was filed on behalf of the farmers to remove all three species from the Endangered Species List.

THE MISSOURI "SPRING RISE" ISSUE. A similarly heated debate addresses the issue of water flow on the Missouri River. The U.S. Fish and Wildlife Service determined in 2000 that existing water flow patterns, managed to create a steady depth for barge traffic, were endangering three listed species—the pallid sturgeon, piping plover, and least tern. The U.S. Fish and Wildlife Service argued that increased water flow in the spring—a "spring rise"—was necessary for sturgeon spawning. In addition, it called for less water flow in the summer, which is necessary for exposing the sandbars used by the bird species as nesting grounds. The Fish and Wildlife Service gave the Army Corps of Engineers, which controls Missouri water flow, until 2003 to implement these changes. However, the Bush administration delayed decision on a final plan in 2002. The *Washington Post* reported that the administration had "begun an 'informal consultation' on possible changes to the wildlife service's demands." The issue has been extremely controversial in the Midwest, with environmentalists, recreation interests, and upper-basin officials favoring a spring rise, and farmers, barge interests, and Missouri leaders opposed. There have been 55,000 submitted comments on the issue, with 54,000 favoring a spring rise.

RAZORBACK SUCKER. The razorback sucker is an endangered fish species found in the lower Colorado River. It is named for the razor-like ridge on its back that helps it swim in rapid waters. The razorback sucker is in danger of extinction due to habitat loss, competition with introduced species, and predation by non-native species such as carp. Habitat destruction is largely the result of dam-building, which has affected water temperature and flooded habitat areas. Razorback suckers can live up to 45 years, and the fish that remain are generally old individuals. Over 90 percent of existing razorback suckers inhabit a single site, Lake Mojave in Arizona.

In an attempt to help razorback sucker populations recover, mature fish are collected and transported to the Willow Beach National Fish Hatchery each spring, where

they spawn. In spring 2000, for example, 80 adult fish were collected from Lake Mojave and laid a total of over 300,000 eggs. Juveniles are then returned to various Colorado River habitats when they are larger and have a better chance of survival (usually when they reach 10 inches in size and 18 months of age). It is estimated that about 9,000 razorback sucker adults remain in the population, as well as some 3,000 to 4,000 younger individuals that have been reintroduced from captivity.

THE SNAIL DARTER. The snail darter, a small fish species related to perch, was the object of perhaps the largest controversy regarding endangered species conservation prior to the conflict surrounding the northern spotted owl. The snail darter was originally listed as endangered by the U.S. Fish and Wildlife Service in 1975. At the time, it was believed only to exist in the Little Tennessee River, and this area was designated as critical habitat for the species. That same year, the Tellico Dam was near completion on the Little Tennessee River, and the filling of the Tellico Reservoir would have destroyed the entire habitat of the snail darter. A lawsuit was filed to prevent this from happening. The case went all the way to the Supreme Court, which ruled in 1978 that under the Endangered Species Act, species protection must take priority over economic and developmental concerns. One month after this court decision, Congress amended the Endangered Species Act to allow for exemptions under certain circumstances. In late 1979, the Tellico Dam received an exemption and the Tellico Reservoir was filled. The snail darter is now extinct in that habitat. Fortuitously, however, snail darter populations were later discovered in other river systems. In addition, the species has been introduced into several other habitats. Due to an increase in numbers, the snail darter was reclassified as threatened in 1984. Currently, it occurs in Alabama, Georgia, and Tennessee.

SHARKS. Sharks have been predators of the seas for nearly 400 million years. There are more than 350 species of sharks, ranging in size from the tiny pygmy shark to the giant whale shark (Figure 5.17).

Shark populations are being decimated because of the growing demand for shark meat and shark fins. Fins and tails sell for as much as $100 a pound. In the United States, some shark populations have already declined 70 to 80 percent from levels in the 1980s and 1990s due to overfishing. Overfishing is particularly harmful to sharks because they reproduce slowly. In 1997 the Fisheries Service cut quotas on commercial harvests of some shark species by half and completely banned harvest of the most vulnerable species—whale sharks, white sharks, basking sharks, sand tiger sharks, and bigeye sand tiger sharks. The annual U.S. commercial shark quota for the Caribbean, the Gulf of Mexico, and the Atlantic coast is

FIGURE 5.17

The whale shark can grow up to 50 feet in length. Numerous sharks are now being overfished for meat and fins. *(WWF/James Watt/Panda Photo)*

150,000 large coastal sharks. However, many biologists consider that number too high to be sustainable.

Fishermen in Costa Rica, where several major cartilage manufacturers operate, claim that the real cause of shark declines is trolling by large fleets from China, Japan, and other countries. In 1994 environmentalists persuaded the Convention on International Trade in Endangered Species (CITES) to study the biological and trade status of sharks. In April 2000 CITES delegates decided against CITES protection for sharks. Opposition to the proposal, which was supported by Brazil and the United States, centered on whether the United Nations Food and Agriculture Organization (FAO) or CITES should be responsible for managing threatened fish species. Opponents favored the FAO.

Coral Reefs

Coral reefs are found in coastal, tropical waters and are the largest living structures on Earth. Biologically, the richness of coral reef ecosystems is comparable to that of tropical rainforests. The reefs themselves are formed from calcium carbonate skeletons secreted by corals. Corals maintain a close relationship with certain species of photosynthetic algae, providing shelter to them and receiving nutrients in exchange.

The World Conservation Union (IUCN) reports that 30 percent of coral reefs worldwide are in critical condition—10 percent have already been destroyed. In 1997 researchers at the Florida Keys National Marine Sanctuary reported that unidentified diseases affected coral at 94 of 160 monitoring stations in the 2,800-square-mile coral reef sanctuary. Coral reefs are also threatened by coastal development that spurs the growth of unfriendly algae. Coastal development increases the danger of the reefs being trampled by divers and boat anchors. Other serious threats to reef ecosystems include marine pollution, blast fishing, and cyanide fishing. Collection of tropical reef specimens for the aquarium trade has also damaged a number of species. Perhaps the greatest immediate threat to coral reefs is rising water temperature due to global climate change. This has caused extensive coral bleaching in recent years.

Marine Mammals

Dolphins, whales, and numerous other marine mammals are threatened with extinction. Some species have declined due to centuries of hunting, while others have been harmed as a result of habitat decline or other forms of human activity.

GREAT WHALES. Whales are the largest animals on Earth. The blue whale, the largest whale species, can reach a length of 80 feet and weigh 150 tons. Its heart alone weighs 1,000 pounds and is the size of a small car. Whales are found throughout the world's oceans and are highly intelligent. Some species communicate via haunting "songs." In 2002 seven whale species had been listed for protection under the Endangered Species Act: humpback whales, sperm whales, bowhead whales, northern right whales, sei whales, fin whales, and blue whales.

Whale populations have declined due to a long history of hunting by humans. As early as the eighth century, humans hunted whales for meat and whalebone. In the nineteenth century, large numbers of whales were killed for whale oil, which was used to light lamps, as well as for baleen—the large horny plates that some species use to filter food. Baleen or "whalebone" was particularly valued for making fans and corsets. Today whales are hunted primarily for meat and for whale oil used in the manufacture of cosmetics and industrial lubricants. The Marine Mammal Protection Act, passed in 1972, made it illegal to import goods containing ingredients from whales. The International Whaling Commission (IWC) has imposed a moratorium on whale hunting since 1986, but animals continue to be killed by countries that flout its regulations or claim that the hunts are for "research."

The northern right whale is the most endangered of the great whales, with fewer than 300 individuals in existence. Once the "right" whale to hunt because it swims slowly and floats upon death, the species has been protected for several decades. However, northern right whale populations are not increasing. The primary threat to the species is continued mortality from collisions with ships. Entanglement in fishing gear and habitat decline in right whale feeding areas are additional causes of population decline. Research has also revealed that the northern right whale's huge fat reserves store an array of toxic substances, possibly affecting whales' health. The situation is so dire, says Dr. Scott Kraus, chief scientist at the New England Aquarium in Boston, that the right whale may become extinct in our lifetime. The National Marine Fisheries Service has declared an area off the coast of Georgia and northern Florida coast as critical right-whale habitat.

MANATEES. The last remaining West Indian manatees, also known as Florida manatees, swim in the rivers, bays, and estuaries of Florida and surrounding

FIGURE 5.18

Manatees, also known as "sea cows," are endangered throughout their range in Florida and the southeastern United States. *(Corbis/Brandon D. Cole)*

states (Figure 5.18). These mammals are often called "sea cows" and can reach weights of up to 2,000 pounds. Manatees swim just below the surface of the water and feed on vegetation. Females bear a single offspring every three to five years. West Indian manatees migrate north in the summer, though generally no farther than the North Carolina coast. In 1995 a manatee nicknamed "Chessie" made headlines by swimming all the way to Chesapeake Bay. Eventually biologists, concerned about his health in cooler waters, had him airlifted back to Florida.

Unlike most animals, manatees have no natural predators. The primary dangers to this species come from humans. Motorboats are the major cause of manatee mortalities—because of their large size, manatees often cannot move away from boats quickly enough to avoid being hit. Environmentalists have tried to protect manatees from boat collisions, and have successfully had several Florida waterways declared boat-free zones. There are also areas where boaters are required to lower their speeds. Because manatees do not produce young very often, their population is decreasing due to high death rates.

The manatee population has suffered severe losses in the last decade. In 1995 approximately 10 percent of Florida's manatees died suddenly, most likely from an unidentified virus. The following year 20 percent of the remaining population—a total of 415 manatees—died. Researchers attributed mortality to a variety of causes, including red tide, which occurs when toxin-producing aquatic organisms called dinoflagellates bloom in large quantities, and motorboat collisions. In 2001 the Florida Fish and Wildlife Conservation Commission and Florida Marine Research Institute reported 325 manatee deaths. Eighty-one were due to collisions with watercraft, and another 110 were due to unknown causes. The Florida Marine Research Institute reported that human-related activity accounted for 44 percent of all manatee deaths between 1976 and 2001, most from watercraft collisions.

A lawsuit by the Save the Manatee Club and other environmental and conservation organizations in 2000 successfully required the state to implement new boat speed zones and establish areas for manatee "safe havens." However, new rules were immediately challenged by individual boaters and boating organizations. The restrictions were upheld by Florida courts in 2002. As of May 2002 there are continuing discussions regarding the creation of more low speed zones.

Biologists estimate that between 2,000 and 3,000 manatees remain in the wild. An aerial survey in 2002 counted 1,796 individuals. Most of these manatees have scars on their backs from motorboat propellers—these allow individual manatees to be recognized. The National Biological Service has catalogued about 1,000 manatees using scar patterns, and maintains manatee sighting histories in a computer-based system.

DOLPHINS. Large numbers of dolphins have been killed by the tuna fishing industry. These marine mammals are often found swimming over tuna schools—in fact, tuna fishers have learned to locate tuna by looking for dolphin pods. Dolphins die when they become trapped in commercial tuna nets and drown. Many millions of dolphins have been killed this way since tuna netting began in 1958.

In 1972 more than 360,000 dolphins were killed by U.S. tuna fishermen. Congress passed the Marine Mammal Protection Act the same year partly to reduce dolphin deaths. Amendments to the law in 1982 and 1985 theoretically halted U.S. tuna purchases from countries whose fishing methods endangered dolphins. In the years after passage, however, these laws were often ignored. Public awareness of dolphin killings was critical in bringing more interest and attention to the issue. In 1988 a reauthorization of marine mammal laws required observers to be present on all tuna boats. Even this measure, however, had only limited impact. In 1990 StarKist, the biggest tuna canner in the world, declared that it would no longer purchase tuna caught in ways that harmed dolphins. Within hours of StarKist's press conference, the next two largest tuna canners followed suit. In 1991 the government established standards for tuna canners that wished to label their products "Dolphin Safe." The International Dolphin Conservation Act, passed in 1992, reduced the number of legally permitted dolphin deaths. This act also made the United States a dolphin-safe zone in 1994, when it became illegal to sell, buy, or ship tuna products obtained using methods that kill dolphins. Reputable tuna canners now label their canned tuna "Dolphin Safe."

SEALS AND SEA LIONS. In 2002 there were four species of pinnipeds—seals and sea lions—on the U.S. Endangered Species List. These were the Caribbean monk seal, Hawaiian monk seal, Guadalupe fur seal, and Steller sea lion. However, the Caribbean monk seal has not been sighted since 1952 and is believed extinct. The species was widely hunted for both blubber and meat.

Hawaiian monk seals are the only pinnipeds found on Hawaii and are endemic to those islands—that is, they occur nowhere else on Earth. Because Hawaiian monk seals have no natural terrestrial enemies, they are not afraid of humans and were once easily hunted for blubber and fur. Hunting was the primary cause of population decline. Hawaiian monk seals are also extremely sensitive to human activity and disturbance and now breed exclusively on the remote northwestern Hawaiian islands, which are not inhabited by humans. Most females give birth to a single pup every two years, a reproductive rate lower than other pinniped species. Hawaiian monk seals feed on fish, octopuses, eels, and lobsters. This species was officially listed as endangered in 1976. In 2002 seal populations were estimated at between 1,200 and 1,500 individuals.

The Guadalupe fur seal breeds on the Isla de Guadalupe and the Isla Benito del Este near Baja California in Mexico. Although populations once included as many as 20,000 to 100,000 individuals, decline and endangerment resulted from extensive fur hunting in the 1700s and 1800s. The species was believed extinct in the early twentieth century, but a small population was discovered in 1954. The species was listed as threatened in 1967. Protection of the Guadalupe fur seal under both Mexican and U.S. law has resulted in population increases, and there are now an estimated 7,000 individuals in the wild. However, some individuals continue to be killed by driftnets.

Steller sea lions are large animals, with males reaching lengths of 11 feet and weights of 2,500 pounds. Females are significantly smaller. Steller sea lions are found in Pacific waters from Japan to central California, but most populations breed near Alaska and the Aleutian Islands. Populations have declined by 80 percent in the last three decades, most likely due to the decline of fisheries that provide food for the species. Many sea lions are also killed in driftnets. In 1990 the Steller sea lion was listed as endangered in Alaska and Russia and threatened in other habitats. There are currently about 40,000 individuals in the wild.

LAWS PROTECTING AQUATIC SPECIES

The Lacey Act

The Lacey Act was originally passed in 1900 and is the oldest wildlife conservation law in the United States. The Lacey Act prohibits interstate and international trade in wildlife that has been collected or exported illegally. In 1999 the U.S. Fish and Wildlife Service processed 1,476 cases under the Lacey Act. These included illegal commerce in endangered species, illegal hunting, and illegal harvest of shellfish from closed areas.

FIGURE 5.19

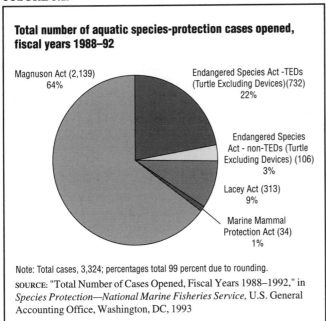

Total number of aquatic species-protection cases opened, fiscal years 1988–92

Magnuson Act (2,139) 64%

Endangered Species Act -TEDs (Turtle Excluding Devices)(732) 22%

Endangered Species Act - non-TEDs (Turtle Excluding Devices) (106) 3%

Lacey Act (313) 9%

Marine Mammal Protection Act (34) 1%

Note: Total cases, 3,324; percentages total 99 percent due to rounding.

SOURCE: "Total Number of Cases Opened, Fiscal Years 1988–1992," in *Species Protection—National Marine Fisheries Service,* U.S. General Accounting Office, Washington, DC, 1993

FIGURE 5.20

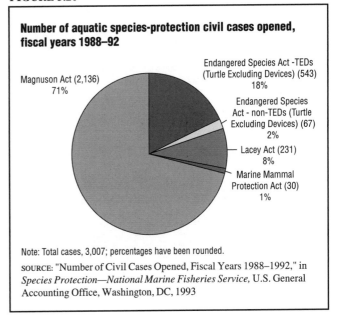

Number of aquatic species-protection civil cases opened, fiscal years 1988–92

Magnuson Act (2,136) 71%

Endangered Species Act -TEDs (Turtle Excluding Devices) (543) 18%

Endangered Species Act - non-TEDs (Turtle Excluding Devices) (67) 2%

Lacey Act (231) 8%

Marine Mammal Protection Act (30) 1%

Note: Total cases, 3,007; percentages have been rounded.

SOURCE: "Number of Civil Cases Opened, Fiscal Years 1988–1992," in *Species Protection—National Marine Fisheries Service,* U.S. General Accounting Office, Washington, DC, 1993

The Magnuson Act

The Magnuson Fishery Conservation and Management Act of 1976 established a system for fisheries management within U.S. waters. Examples of Magnuson Act violations include fishing without a permit, possessing out-of-season fish, or retaining undersized fish.

The Marine Mammal Protection Act

The Marine Mammal Protection Act (MMPA), passed in 1972, recognized that many marine mammals are either endangered or have suffered declines as a result of human activity. The MMPA prohibits the taking (hunting, killing, capturing, and harassing) of marine mammals. The act also bars importation of most marine mammals or their products. Exceptions are occasionally granted for scientific research, public display in aquariums, subsistence hunting (by Alaskan natives), and some incidental take during commercial fishing operations. The goal of the MMPA is to maintain marine populations at or above "optimum sustainable" levels. Under the MMPA, the National Marine Fisheries Service (NMFS) manages all cetaceans (whales and dolphins) and pinnipeds (seals and sea lions) except walruses. The NMFS relies on the U.S. Coast Guard and other federal and state agencies to assist with the detection of violations. The U.S. Fish and Wildlife Service (FWS) manages polar bears, walruses, sea otters, manatees, and dugongs (manatee relatives).

A Congressional Study of Violators

A 1993 congressional study examined federal enforcement of the four primary laws that address aquatic species protection—the Lacey Act, the Magnuson Act, the Marine Mammal Protection Act (MMPA), and the Endangered Species Act's (ESA) regulations on turtle-excluder devices (TEDs). The study found that 64 percent of cases arose from violations of the Magnuson Act, 22 percent from violations of the ESA's TED regulations, 9 percent from violations of the Lacey Act, and 1 percent from violations of the MMPA. (See Figure 5.19.) Another 3 percent of cases resulted from violations of other provisions of the ESA.

Both civil and criminal charges were made against violators of the four laws. Of the civil violations (90 percent of total cases), 71 percent involved Magnuson violations, 18 percent involved ESA TED violations, 8 percent involved Lacey crimes, and 3 percent involved MMPA and other ESA violations. (See Figure 5.20.) Of the total criminal cases, 60 percent were for failure to use a TED, 26 percent were for Lacey Act violations, including the illegal transport of fish across state lines for resale, 12 percent were for violations of other ESA regulations, 1 percent was for MMPA violations, and 1 percent was for Magnuson violations. (See Figure 5.21.) Punishments assessed included written warnings, fines, and, in some cases, jail time. The average fine was $2,560. The largest fines were for Lacey Act violations.

FIGURE 5.21

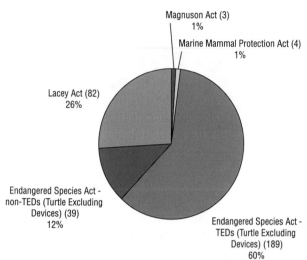

Number of aquatic species-protection criminal cases opened, fiscal years 1988–92

Magnuson Act (3)
1%

Marine Mammal Protection Act (4)
1%

Lacey Act (82)
26%

Endangered Species Act -
non-TEDs (Turtle Excluding
Devices) (39)
12%

Endangered Species Act -
TEDs (Turtle Excluding
Devices) (189)
60%

Note: Total cases, 317; percentages have been rounded.

SOURCE: "Number of Criminal Cases Opened, Fiscal Years 1988–1992," in *Species Protection—National Marine Fisheries Service*, U.S. General Accounting Office, Washington, DC, 1993

CHAPTER 6

IMPERILED AMPHIBIANS AND REPTILES

Amphibians and reptiles are collectively known by biologists as herpetofauna. At present, there are over 5,000 described amphibian species and over 6,000 reptiles. New species in both these groups are being discovered every day, particularly in remote tropical regions that are only now being explored.

Amphibians and reptiles are also among the world's most threatened groups. The World Conservation Union (IUCN) reported in its *2000 Red List of Threatened Species* that some 25 percent of surveyed reptiles and 20 percent of surveyed amphibians are imperiled. However, conservation status has yet to be assessed for numerous species—only one-fifth of reptiles and one-eighth of amphibians have been examined. The IUCN list currently includes 291 threatened reptiles and 146 threatened amphibians, up from 253 and 63 respectively in 1996. The increase in the number of listed reptiles reflects, in part, more complete examination of freshwater turtle species. Many of these are highly imperiled, particularly in Asia, where they are hunted for both food and medicine (Figure 6.1). Recent amphibian declines—part of a global pattern—have been particularly alarming to researchers and conservationists.

AMPHIBIANS

Amphibians represent the most ancient group of terrestrial vertebrates. The earliest amphibians are known from fossils and date from the early Devonian era, some 400 million years ago. The three groups of amphibians that have survived to the present day are salamanders, frogs and toads, and caecilians. Figure 6.2 shows the worldwide density of amphibian species by country. Table 6.1 describes some of the major amphibian groups in North America.

"Amphi-" means "both," and amphibians get their name from the fact that many species occupy both aquatic and terrestrial habitats. In particular, many amphibian species undergo a dramatic change called metamorphosis, in which individuals move from an aquatic larval stage to a terrestrial adult stage. In many frog species, for example, aquatic, swimming tadpoles metamorphose into terrestrial jumping frogs. In the process, they lose their muscular swimming tails and acquire forelimbs and hind limbs. Many amphibian species occupy terrestrial habitats through most of the year, but migrate to ponds to breed. However, there are also many species that are either entirely aquatic or entirely terrestrial. Whatever their habitat, amphibians generally require a moist environment. This is because their skins are formed of living cells and are prone to drying.

A large number of amphibian species are in serious decline due to factors such as habitat loss, pollution, and climate change. Amphibians are particularly vulnerable to pollution because their skin readily absorbs water and other substances from the environment. For this reason, amphibians are frequently considered biological indicator species. There are currently 28 amphibian species listed with the Fish and Wildlife Service as either threatened or endangered. The 19 U.S. species listed—11 salamanders and 8 frogs and toads—appear in Table 6.2.

Sudden Disappearances

At the end of the twentieth century, biologists uncovered growing evidence of an unexplained global decline in amphibian populations. AmphibiaWeb, a conservation organization that monitors amphibian species worldwide, reported in 2002 that at least 200 amphibian species had experienced serious population declines in the last few decades. In addition, no fewer than 32 amphibian species have gone extinct (see Table 6.3). Amphibian declines have been documented worldwide, though the degree of decline varies across regions (see Figure 6.3). Areas that have been hardest hit include Central America and

FIGURE 6.1

This Asian box turtle, native to China, is seriously threatened due to demand for trade. *(Photograph by David Northcott. Reproduced by permission of the Corbis Corporation.)*

Australia. In the U.S., amphibian declines have been concentrated in California, the Rocky Mountains, the Southwest, and Puerto Rico. Particularly disturbing is the loss of numerous populations within protected and relatively pristine wildlife refuges.

The golden toad, named for its unusual and striking orange color, is a prime example of the global amphibian decline. Over a three-year period, golden toads disappeared inexplicably from their only known habitat in the Monteverde Cloud Forest Reserve in Costa Rica. In 1987 herpetologists observed an apparently healthy golden toad population estimated at 1,500 adults along with a new generation of tadpoles. The following year, in 1988, there were only 11 toads. In 1989 only a single surviving toad was found. It was the last individual on record for the species.

Concern regarding declining amphibian populations led then–U.S. Secretary of the Interior Bruce Babbitt to meet with amphibian biologists in 1998. These scientists reported that a large number of amphibian species—particularly frogs—had become extinct over a very short period of time. They also noted that numerous other species were either declining or showing high levels of gross deformities, such as extra limbs, and that amphibians were dying out in unexpected places, such as protected national parks in the western United States. Secretary Babbitt commented:

> Many of these frogs and amphibian species have been in an evolutionary relationship with our landscape for millions of years, and when all of a sudden they start to just, in the blink of an eye, disappear, there's clearly some external cause that's probably related to something that we are doing across the broader landscape. The deformities are particularly ominous because of the potential human implications as well.

In May 1998 the Federal Task Force on Amphibian Decline and Deformities compiled a statement regarding amphibian declines and called for research into the sources of these declines. (See Table 6.4.) Since then, a number of potential causes have been identified.

HABITAT DESTRUCTION. Loss of habitat is a major factor in the decline of numerous amphibian species, as it is for many endangered species. The destruction of

FIGURE 6.2

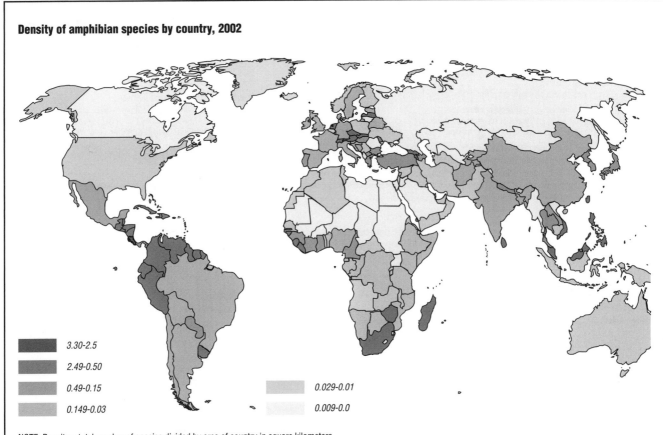

Density of amphibian species by country, 2002

3.30-2.5

2.49-0.50

0.49-0.15

0.149-0.03

0.029-0.01

0.009-0.0

NOTE: Density = total number of species divided by area of country in square kilometers.

SOURCE: Tiwari, Gross, van der Meijden, and Vredenburg, "Density of Amphibian Species by Country," in *AmphibiaWeb: Information on Amphibian Biology and Conservation,* University of California, Berkeley, Berkeley, CA, 2002 [Online] http://elib.cs.berkeley.edu/aw/amphibian/speciesnums.html [accessed May 1, 2002]. Information is updated daily. Please visit AmphibiaWeb for the latest version.

tropical forests and wetlands, ecosystems that are rich with amphibians, has done particular damage to populations. In the U.S., deforestation has caused the loss or decline of at least seven salamander species in the Pacific Northwest and 16 salamander species in Appalachian hardwood forests. Global climate change has also destroyed unique habitats such as cloud forests (forests containing large amounts of water mists), resulting in the loss of cloud forest amphibian species. In addition, some amphibians have lost appropriate aquatic breeding habitats, particularly small bodies of water such as ponds. These aquatic habitats are often developed or filled in by humans, because they appear to be less biologically valuable than larger aquatic habitats.

Finally, habitat fragmentation may be particularly harmful to amphibian species which migrate during the breeding season. These species require not only that both breeding and non-breeding habitats remain undisturbed, but also that there be intact habitat along migration routes.

POLLUTION. Pollution is a second major factor in global amphibian declines. Because amphibians absorb water directly through skin and into their bodies, they are particularly vulnerable to water pollution from pesticides or fertilizer runoff.

Air pollution by substances such as chlorofluorocarbons (CFCs) has reduced the amount of protective ozone in the Earth's atmosphere. This has resulted in increased levels of UV radiation striking the Earth's surface. Exposure to UV radiation causes genetic mutations that can prevent normal development or kill eggs. Increased UV levels particularly affect the many frog species whose eggs float on the exposed surfaces of ponds.

INVASIVE SPECIES. Many amphibian species have also been affected by the introduction of non-native species which either compete with them or prey on them. These include fish, crayfish, and other amphibians. The bullfrog, the cane toad (a very large frog species), and the African clawed frog (a species used in much biological research) are some of the invasive species believed to have affected amphibian populations. In addition, introduced trout are blamed for the extinction of several species of harlequin frogs in Costa Rica. It is hypothesized that trout consume

TABLE 6.1

Major amphibian groups

A. Completely aquatic
1. Salamanders (for example, hellbender, mudpuppy, siren, amphiuma, neotenic[1] ambystomatid salamanders).
2. Frogs (for example, African clawed frog; introduced)

B. Lentic (still water) breeding/semi-terrestrial adults
1. Salamanders (for example, ambystomatid salamanders, newts[2])
2. Frogs (for example, spotted frogs, wood frogs, treefrogs, toads)

C. Lotic (running water) breeding/semi-terrestrial adults
1. Salamanders (for example, red and spring salamanders)
2. Frogs (for example, foothill yellow-legged frog, tailed frog)

D. Completely terrestrial
1. Salamanders (for example, red-backed salamander, slender salamanders)

[1]Animals reach sexual maturity but retain the larval form.
[2]The eastern red-spotted newt (*Notophthalmus viridescens*) has an aquatic larval form that metamorphoses into a terrestrial subadult form (red eft). When the newt reaches sexual maturity (3-7 years) it makes a few more changes (morphological and physiological) and returns to the water for the rest of its life.

SOURCE: J.K. Reaser, "Major Amphibian Groups of North America," in *Amphibian Declines: An Issue Overview,* Federal Task Force on Amphibian Decline and Deformitites, Washington, DC, 2000

TABLE 6.2

Amphibians listed as endangered or threatened, May 15, 2002

Status	Species Name
T	Coqui, golden (*Eleutherodactylus jasperi*)
T	Frog, California red-legged (*Rana aurora draytonii*)
E	Frog, Mississippi gopher (Wherever found west of Mobile and Tombigbee Rivers in AL, MS, and LA) (*Rana capito sevosa*)
T	Guajon (*Eleutherodactylus cooki*)
E	Salamander, Barton Springs (*Eurycea sosorum*)
E	Salamander, California tiger (*Ambystoma californiense*)
T	Salamander, Cheat Mountain (*Plethodon nettingi*)
E	Salamander, desert slender (*Batrachoseps aridus*)
T	Salamander, flatwoods (*Ambystoma cingulatum*)
T	Salamander, Red Hills (*Phaeognathus hubrichti*)
T	Salamander, San Marcos (*Eurycea nana*)
E	Salamander, Santa Cruz long-toed (*Ambystoma macrodactylum croceum*)
E	Salamander, Shenandoah (*Plethodon shenandoah*)
E	Salamander, Sonoran tiger (*Ambystoma tigrinum stebbinsi*)
E	Salamander, Texas blind (*Typhlomolge rathbuni*)
E	Toad, arroyo (=arroyo southwestern) (*Bufo californicus (=microscaphus)*)
E	Toad, Houston (*Bufo houstonensis*)
T	Toad, Puerto Rican crested (*Peltophryne lemur*)
E	Toad, Wyoming (*Bufo baxteri (=hemiophrys)*)

Notes: E = endangered
      T = threatened

SOURCE: Adapted from "U.S. Listed Vertebrate Animal Species Report by Taxonomic Group as of 5/15/2002," U.S. Fish & Wildlife Service, Threatened and Endangered Species System, Washington, DC, May 15, 2002 [Online] http://ecos.fws.gov/webpage/ webpage_vip_listed.html?module=undefined&code=V&listings=0 [accessed May 15, 2002]

TABLE 6.3

Species of amphibians thought to have recently gone extinct, March 2002

Australia
Litoria nyakalensis (Mountain Mist Frog) (last seen April, 1990)
Litoria lorica (Armoured Mist Frog) (last seen 1991)
Taudactylus diurnus (Southern Day Frog) (last seen 1979)
Taudactylus acutirostris (Sharp-snouted Day Frog) (last seen January, 1997)
Rheobatrachus vitellinus (Northern Gastric-Brooding Frog, Northern Platypus Frog) (last seen March, 1985)
Rheobatrachus silus (Gastric-Brooding Frog, Southern Platypus Frog) (last seen 1981)
Litoria castanae (Yellow-spotted Tree Frog) (last seen 1975)
Litoria piperata (Peppered Tree Frog) (last seen 1973)

Honduras
Eleutherodactylus anciano
Eleutherodactylus chrysozetetes
Eleutherodactylus cruzi
Eleutherodactylus fecundus
Eleutherodactylus milesi
Eleutherodactylus omoaensis

Costa Rica
Bufo periglenes (Golden Toad)
Atelopus varius (Harlequin Frog)
Atelopus senex
Bufo holdrigei

Puerto Rico
Eleutherodactylus karlschmidti (last seen in 1974)
Eleutherodactylus jasperi (last seen in 1981)
Eleutherodactylus eneidae (last seen in 1984)

Ecuador
Atelopus arthuri (last seen in 1988)
Atelopus bomolochos (last seen in 1993)
Atelopus elegans (last seen in 1994)
Atelopus ignescens (last seen in 1988)
Atelopus longirostris (last seen in 1986)
Atelopus mindoensis (last seen in 1989)
Atelopus pachydermus (last seen in 1996)
Atelopus planispina (last seen in 1983)
Atelopus sp. A (de Guanujo, Provincia de Bolivar) (last seen in 1988)
Atelopus sp. B (de los pramos del Cajas, Provincia del Azuay) (last seen in 1989)
Atelopus sp. C (aff. ignescens) (last seen in 1993)

SOURCE: Adapted from "The AmphibiaWeb Watch List: A. Extinct," in *AmphibiaWeb: Information on Amphibian Biology and Conservation,* University of California, Berkeley, Berkeley, CA, 2002 [Online] http://elib.cs.berkeley.edu/aw/declines/extinct.html [accessed May 16, 2002]. Information is updated daily. Please visit AmphibiaWeb for the latest version.

fungus. This fungus attacks skin, and was first identified in 1998 in diseased amphibians. There are often no symptoms initially, but eventually individuals begin to shed skin and die. The precise cause of death is not known, though damage to the skin can interfere with respiration. The chytrid fungus is believed to be responsible for the demise of numerous species in Australia and Panama. In 2000, it was also documented in populations of the Chiricahua leopard frog in Arizona and the boreal toad in the Rocky Mountains.

HUMAN COLLECTION. Many amphibian species are vigorously hunted for food, the pet trade, or as medical research specimens.

Amphibian Deformities

Amphibian deformities (see Figure 6.4) first hit the spotlight in 1995, when middle-school students discovered

tadpoles. Similarly, introduced salmon have affected native frog populations in California.

EPIDEMICS. Amphibian diseases caused variously by bacteria, viruses, and fungi have devastated certain populations. Of particular importance in recent years is the chytrid

FIGURE 6.3

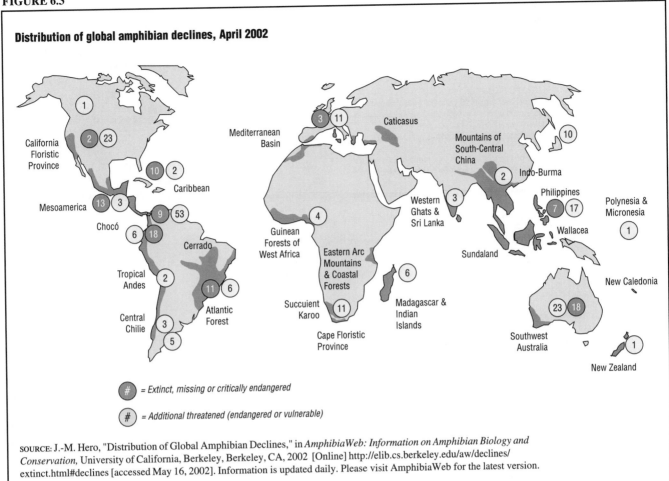

Distribution of global amphibian declines, April 2002

SOURCE: J.-M. Hero, "Distribution of Global Amphibian Declines," in *AmphibiaWeb: Information on Amphibian Biology and Conservation*, University of California, Berkeley, Berkeley, CA, 2002 [Online] http://elib.cs.berkeley.edu/aw/declines/extinct.html#declines [accessed May 16, 2002]. Information is updated daily. Please visit AmphibiaWeb for the latest version.

large numbers of deformed frogs in a pond in Minnesota. Deformed frogs have since been found in 44 states in the U.S. These include representatives of 38 different frog species and 19 different toad species. In some populations, over 60 percent of individuals are deformed.

The high incidence of amphibian deformities in U.S. species appears to have multiple causes, as no single hypothesis accounts for all the different types of deformities seen. The most common deformities include missing hind limbs and toes, missing feet, misshapen feet, missing eyes, deformed front legs, and extra legs. Some of these malformations are believed to be related to a parasitic trematode, or flatworm, which in experiments causes the development of additional limbs. Aquatic trematodes have increased in number due to human activity, via a complicated chain of events. First, fertilizer runoff increases nutrient levels in ponds, allowing more algae to grow. More algae results in more algae-eating snails, and snails host juvenile parasitic trematodes. Trematodes move on to frogs when they mature, forming cysts in the vicinity of developing frog legs. Chemical pollution and UV radiation may account for some of the other observed deformities.

Salamanders

Salamanders are tailed amphibians. The group contains over 500 described species, including the newts. The majority of salamanders are fairly small in size, most often six inches long or less. The Chinese and Japanese giant salamanders, which grow to as large as five feet long, are the largest of all amphibians. In 2002, salamanders comprised 11 of the 19 U.S. amphibians on the Endangered Species List. Some endangered salamanders, including many cave species (Figure 6.5), have highly restricted habitats. The Barton Springs salamander, for example, is only found in a single locale in and around the Barton Springs pool in Austin, Texas. The Barton Springs salamander has been the subject of contentious debate between conservationists and those who wish to guarantee free recreational use of the pool.

GIANT SALAMANDERS. There are two species of giant salamanders, the Chinese giant salamander and the Japanese giant salamander. These are by far the largest currently living amphibian species, reaching lengths of up to five feet. Both are listed with the Fish and Wildlife Service and are highly endangered. Giant salamanders are aquatic, and have folded and wrinkled skin that allows them to

TABLE 6.4

The critical issues of worldwide amphibian decline

Resolution: Declining Amphibian Populations

This resolution was drafted by participants of a 28-29 May 1998 workshop on amphibian declines sponsored by the National Science Foundation, Washington, D.C.

Whereas, there is compelling evidence that over the last 15 years there have been unusual and substantial declines in abundance and numbers of populations of various species of amphibians in globally distributed geographic regions, and

Whereas, many of the declines are in protected areas or other places not affected by obvious degradation of habitats, and

Whereas, these factors are symptomatic of a general decline in environmental quality, and

Whereas, even where amphibian populations persist, there are factors that may place them at risk, and

Whereas, some patterns of amphibian population decline appear to be linked by causative factors, and

Whereas, declines can occur on multiple scales, in different phases of amphibian life cycles, and can impact species with differing ecology and behavior, and

Whereas, there is no obvious single common cause of the declines, and

Whereas, amphibian declines, including species extinctions can be caused by multiple environmental factors, including habitat loss and alteration, global change, pathogens, parasites, various chemicals, ultraviolet radiation, invasive species, and stochastic events, and

Whereas, these factors may act alone, sequentially, or synergistically to impact amphibian populations, and

Whereas, to understand, mitigate, an preempt the impacts of these factors, a comprehensive, interdisciplinary research program must be undertaken, and

Whereas, this research program must be conducted in several regions around the globe, both in areas of known declines, and in areas where declines have not been documented, and

Whereas, this research must examine issues ranging from environmental quality of landscapes to the condition of individual animals,

NOW IT BE THEREFORE RESOLVED, the signatories hereto call for the establishment of an interdisciplinary and collaborative research program, which will specify and quantify the direct and indirect factors affecting amphibian population dynamics, and

Be it further resolved, that this program will include basic research and monitoring that will test hypotheses of causative factors and examine patterns of change through historical records, field-based correlative data, and controlled, multifactorial experiments, and

Be it further resolved, that interdisciplinary, incident response teams should be assembled in "hot spots" of amphibian decline to identify causative factors to facilitate the mitigation of these sudden declines, and

Be it further resolved that the signatories hereto call upon both public and private a agencies and institutions, to promote and support research, policies and conservation measures that will ameliorate losses and declines of amphibian populations, and

Be it further resolved that this broad-based approach to the study of amphibian population dynamics will serve as a model for study of the global biodiversity crisis.

SOURCE: J. K. Reaser, "The Critical Issues of Worldwide Amphibian Decline," in *Amphibian Declines: An Issue Overview,* Federal Task Force on Amphibian Decline and Deformitites, Washington, DC, 2000

FIGURE 6.4

A frog showing deformed and extra limbs. The high incidence of amphibian deformities in the United States is cause for concern. *(JLM Visuals)*

FIGURE 6.5

The Texas blind salamander has been listed by the Fish and Wildlife Service as endangered since 1967. It occupies subterranean streams near San Marcos, Texas. Because of its subterranean cave habitat, the Texas blind salamander has only vestigial eyes, found below the skin. *(U.S. Fish and Wildlife Service)*

absorb oxygen from their watery habitats. The Chinese giant salamander is found in fast mountain streams in western China. Despite official protection, the species is endangered partly because of hunting for food or medicine. The Chinese giant salamander is also harmed by loss of habitat and aquatic pollution. Its close relative, the Japanese giant salamander, is also endangered and protected. This species inhabits cold, fast mountain streams in northern Kyushu Island and western Honshu in Japan. Japanese giant salamanders have been successfully bred in captivity.

Caecilians

Very little is known about most species of legless, worm-like amphibians called caecilians. Some caecilians are aquatic, but most of these elusive animals are underground burrowers that are difficult to locate and to study. Caecilians generally have very poor eyesight because of their underground habitat—some have no eyes at all or are nearly blind. There are 160 described species of caecilians. All live in tropical climates. Because so little is known about this group, it is difficult for environmentalists to assess the level of endangerment of these animals. Although there are no currently listed species, the loss of tropical habitats worldwide suggests that many caecilians are likely imperiled.

Frogs and Toads

Over 5,000 species of frogs and toads have been described worldwide, making this by far the most diverse group of living amphibians. Most occupy tropical habitats, though two species are found within the Arctic Circle. Many frog species go through a swimming tadpole stage before metamorphosing into a tailless, jumping, adult frog. However, in some species, eggs hatch directly as juvenile froglets, which are miniature versions of the adults. Tadpoles are most often herbivorous, although there are some carnivorous tadpoles, including cannibalistic species. Adult frogs are carnivorous and catch prey with their sticky tongues. Altogether, eight frogs and toads were listed by the Fish and Wildlife Service as threatened or endangered in 2002.

GASTRIC-BROODING FROGS. There are two species of gastric-brooding frogs, both found in Australia. Gastric-brooding frogs are described as timid and are often found hiding under rocks in water. These species were only discovered in the 1970s, and, unfortunately, went extinct only a decade after their discovery. One species was last seen in the wild in September 1982; the other was last seen in March 1985. Gastric-brooding frogs get their name from their unusual reproductive strategy—females brood their young in their stomachs! During brooding, the mother does not eat and does not produce stomach acids. The gestation period lasts about eight weeks, and as many as 30 tadpoles may be in the brood. Juveniles eventually emerge as miniature froglets from the mother's mouth. Although it is not certain what led to the extinction of gastric-brooding frogs, one hypothesis is that populations were killed off by the chytrid fungus, which is also responsible for the decline of other frog species.

CALIFORNIA RED-LEGGED FROG. The California red-legged frog, made famous by Mark Twain's short story "The Celebrated Jumping Frog of Calaveras County," experienced a significant decline during the mid-twentieth century. By 1960 California red-legged frogs had disappeared altogether from California's Central Valley, probably due to the loss of 70 percent of their habitat. The California red-legged frog was officially listed as a threatened species by the Fish and Wildlife Service in 1996.

California red-legged frogs require riverside habitats covered by vegetation and close to deep water pools. They are extremely sensitive to habitat disturbance and water pollution—tadpoles are particularly sensitive to varying oxygen levels and siltation (mud and other natural impurities) during metamorphosis. California red-legged frogs require three to four years to reach maturity and have a normal life span of eight to ten years.

Water reservoir construction and agricultural or residential development are the primary factors in this species' decline. Biologists have shown that California red-legged frogs generally disappear from habitats within five years of a reservoir or water diversion project. The removal of vegetation associated with flood control, combined with the use of herbicides and restructuring of landscapes, further degrade remaining habitat. Finally, non-native species have also attacked red-legged frog populations. These include alien fish predators as well as competing species such as bullfrogs.

In 2002 California red-legged frogs were known to occupy 238 streams or drainages, primarily in the central coastal region of California. Only four localities are known to support substantial populations (over 350 individuals) of adult frogs. The recovery plan for the California red-legged frog includes eliminating threats in current habitats, restoring damaged habitats, and re-introducing populations into the historic range of the species. The U.S. National Park Service helped to preserve one current frog habitat by altering water flow in the Piru Creek connection between Lake Piru and Pyramid Lake, located in the Los Angeles and Los Padres National Forests about 60 miles northwest of Los Angeles. This also benefited another threatened species, the arroyo southwestern toad. The Fish and Wildlife Service has taken measures to preserve habitat in the foothills of the Sierra Nevada, in the central coastal mountains near San Francisco, along the Pacific coast near Los Angeles, and in the Tehachapi Mountains. Protected frog habitats have also been established in Marin and Sonoma Counties. The Contra Costa Water District east of San Francisco Bay has established protected habitat areas in an attempt to compensate for habitat destruction caused at the Los Vaqueros watershed and reservoir. Finally, captive breeding of California red-legged frogs is being considered for feasibility at the Los Angeles Zoo, in a coordinated effort with The Nature Conservancy.

GUAJÓN. The threatened web-footed guajón is a Puerto Rican cave-dwelling frog species. Its decline has resulted largely from introductions of alien species such as mongooses, rats, and cats, all of which eat unhatched guajón eggs. In addition the species has experienced habitat loss from garbage dumping in caves and deforestation for agriculture, roads, and dams. Deforestation also creates the potential for future environmental disasters such as flash floods, which drown adult frogs and destroy nests. Encroaching agriculture causes pollution from fertilizer runoff. Finally, the guajón, with its large white-rimmed eyes and phantom-like appearance, is frequently killed by superstitious local residents who believe the mere sight of the animal can bring disaster.

REPTILES

Approximately 6,300 species of reptiles have been described. These include turtles, snakes, lizards, and crocodilians. Birds are also technically reptiles (birds and crocodiles are actually close relatives), but have historically been treated separately. Reptiles differ from amphibians in that their skin is cornified—that is, made of dead cells. All reptiles obtain oxygen from the air using lungs.

TABLE 6.5

Reptiles listed as endangered or threatened, May 15, 2002

Status	Species Name
T(S/A)	Alligator, American (*Alligator mississippiensis*)
E	Anole, Culebra Island giant (*Anolis roosevelti*)
T	Boa, Mona (*Epicrates monensis monensis*)
E	Boa, Puerto Rican (*Epicrates inornatus*)
E	Boa, Virgin Islands tree (*Epicrates monensis granti*)
E	Crocodile, American (*Crocodylus acutus*)
E	Gecko, Monito (*Sphaerodactylus micropithecus*)
T	Iguana, Mona ground (*Cyclura stejnegeri*)
E	Lizard, blunt-nosed leopard (*Gambelia silus*)
T	Lizard, Coachella Valley fringe-toed (*Uma inornata*)
T	Lizard, Island night (*Xantusia riversiana*)
E	Lizard, St. Croix ground (*Ameiva polops*)
T	Rattlesnake, New Mexican ridge-nosed (*Crotalus willardi obscurus*)
E,T	Sea turtle, green (*Chelonia mydas*)
E	Sea turtle, hawksbill (*Eretmochelys imbricata*)
E	Sea turtle, Kemp's ridley (*Lepidochelys kempii*)
E	Sea turtle, leatherback (*Dermochelys coriacea*)
T	Sea turtle, loggerhead (*Caretta caretta*)
T	Sea turtle, olive ridley (*Lepidochelys olivacea*)
T	Skink, bluetail mole (*Eumeces egregius lividus*)
T	Skink, sand (*Neoseps reynoldsi*)
T	Snake, Atlantic salt marsh (*Nerodia clarkii taeniata*)
T	Snake, Concho water (*Nerodia paucimaculata*)
T	Snake, copperbelly water (*Nerodia erythrogaster neglecta*)
T	Snake, eastern indigo (*Drymarchon corais couperi*)
T	Snake, giant garter (*Thamnophis gigas*)
T	Snake, Lake Erie water (*Nerodia sipedon insularum*)
E	Snake, San Francisco garter (*Thamnophis sirtalis tetrataenia*)
T(S/A),T	Tortoise, desert (*Gopherus agassizii*)
T	Tortoise, gopher (*Gopherus polyphemus*)
E	Turtle, Alabama red-belly (*Pseudemys alabamensis*)
T(S/A),T	Turtle, bog (=Muhlenberg) (*Clemmys muhlenbergii*)
T	Turtle, flattened musk (*Sternotherus depressus*)
E	Turtle, Plymouth redbelly (*Pseudemys rubriventris bangsi*)
T	Turtle, ringed map (*Graptemys oculifera*)
T	Turtle, yellow-blotched map (*Graptemys flavimaculata*)
T	Whipsnake (=striped racer), Alameda (*Masticophis lateralis euryxanthus*)

Notes: E = endangered
T = threatened
T(S/A) = similiarity of appearance to a threatened taxon

SOURCE: Adapted from "U.S. Listed Vertebrate Animal Species Report by Taxonomic Group as of 5/15/2002," U.S. Fish & Wildlife Service, Threatened and Endangered Species System, Washington, DC, May 15, 2002 [Online] http://ecos.fws.gov/webpage/webpage_vip_listed.html?module=undefined&code=V&listings=0 [accessed May 15, 2002]

Most reptiles lay shelled eggs, although many species, particularly lizards and snakes, give birth to live young.

Many reptiles are in serious decline. Numerous species are endangered due to habitat loss or degradation. In addition, some reptiles are hunted by humans for their skins, shells, or meat. Global climate change has affected some reptile species, particularly turtles, in ominous ways—this is because in some reptiles, ambient temperatures determine whether males or females are produced, in some cases resulting in few or no males being born. Natural disasters may also affect reptiles, as in 1999, when tens of thousands of turtle hatchlings were lost to the fury of Hurricane Floyd.

There are a total of 78 listed endangered reptiles, including 14 U.S. species and 64 foreign species. There are an additional 37 threatened reptiles, including 22 U.S. species and 15 foreign species. Threatened and endangered U.S. reptiles are listed in Table 6.5.

Sea Turtles

Sea turtles are excellent swimmers and spend nearly their entire lives in water. They feed on a wide array of food items, including mollusks, vegetation, and crustaceans. Some sea turtles are migratory, swimming thousands of miles between feeding and nesting areas. Individuals are exposed to a variety of both natural and human threats. Because of these, only an estimated one in 10,000 sea turtles survives to adulthood.

Of the seven species of sea turtles that exist worldwide, six spend part or all of their lives in U.S. territorial waters—the loggerhead turtle, green turtle, leatherback turtle, hawksbill turtle, olive ridley turtle, and Kemp's ridley turtle. (The seventh species, the flatback turtle, occurs near Australia.) All of these are listed as either threatened or endangered with the Fish and Wildlife Service. Figure 6.6 shows leatherback turtle population trends at nesting grounds in St. Croix, Virgin Islands, over the last several decades. Conservation efforts for this species have met with some success.

THREATS TO NESTING TURTLES. Sea turtles bury their eggs in nests on sandy beaches. The building of beachfront resorts and homes has destroyed a large proportion of nesting habitat. Artificial lighting associated with coastal development also poses a problem—lights discourage females from nesting and also cause hatchlings to become disoriented and wander inland instead of out to sea. Finally, beach nourishment, the practice of rebuilding eroded beach soil, creates unusually compacted sand on which turtles are unable to nest. The sands of Tortuguero National Park in Costa Rica are believed to be the last remaining nesting ground for one species, the endangered green turtle.

SHRIMP-NET CASUALTIES. Large numbers of sea turtles are killed in shrimp nets in the Gulf of Mexico and the Caribbean. In 1990 the National Academy of Sciences reported that shrimp trawling was the greatest cause of sea turtle deaths in U.S. waters, killing 55,000 turtles every year. In 1981 the turtle excluder device (TED), which allows sea turtles to escape from shrimp nets, was invented. The use of TEDs became a requirement under the Endangered Species Act. Biologists attribute the gradual increase in some turtle species in the 1990s to the use of TEDs. In January 1996 federal courts ruled that, under provisions of the Endangered Species Act, the Commerce Department must require all nations that export shrimp to the United States to use TEDs as well. The law has been suspended by the Bush Administration, which complained that it would hurt commerce.

FIGURE 6.6

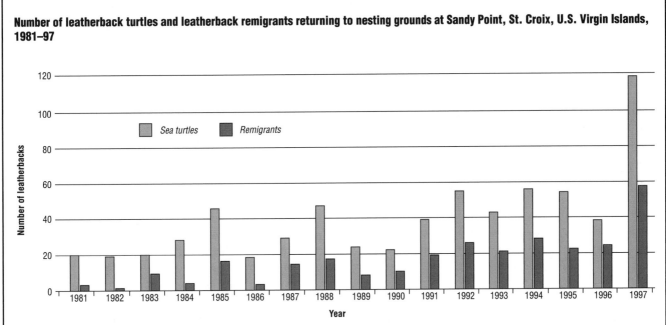

Number of leatherback turtles and leatherback remigrants returning to nesting grounds at Sandy Point, St. Croix, U.S. Virgin Islands, 1981–97

SOURCE: M.J. Mac, P.A. Opler, C.E. Puckett Haecker, and P.D. Doran,"Fig. 7. Number of leatherback turtles and leatherback remigrants (that is, a nesting female who returns to nest at a particular site in subsequent nesting seasons) returning to nesting grounds at Sandy Point, St. Croix, U.S. Virgin Islands, 1981–97," in *The Status and Trends of Our Nation's Biological Resources,* U.S. Geological Survey, Reston, VA, 1998

In April 1998 the World Trade Organization (WTO), an international trade body, ruled that the United States could not prohibit shrimp imports from countries that do not use turtle excluder devices. Experts fear that when free trade conflicts with environmental protection, the WTO is likely to favor trade over environmental protection.

KEMP'S RIDLEY TURTLE. Kemp's ridley turtle is the smallest species of sea turtle, with individuals measuring some three feet in length and weighing less than 100 pounds. Kemp's ridley is also the most endangered of the sea turtle species. It has only one major nesting site, located in Rancho Nuevo, Mexico, where it faces increasing threats from human activity. In particular, eggs and hatched juveniles are collected by people or eaten by coyotes. At Rancho Nuevo, numerous female Kemp's ridley turtles nest at the same time—this is referred to as an "arribada." Female ridleys nest in daylight, unlike other sea turtle species. Kemp's ridley populations have declined drastically over the past several decades—in 1947, approximately 42,000 females nested in one day. In 1990, only 300 females were observed. Since then, Kemp's ridley numbers have improved a little, with approximately 900 females tallied in Mexico in 1999.

The decline of the Kemp's ridley turtle is due primarily to human activities such as egg collecting, fishing for juveniles and adults, and killing of adults for meat or other products. In addition, Kemp's ridleys have been subject to high levels of incidental take by shrimp trawlers. They are also affected by pollution from oil wells, and by floating debris in

the Gulf of Mexico, which can choke or entangle turtles. Now under strict protection, the population appears to be in the earliest stages of recovery, with numbers having increased annually for several years. Population increase can be attributed to two primary factors—full protection of nesting females and their nests in Rancho Nuevo, and TED requirements for shrimp trawlers in the U.S. and Mexican waters. Prior to TED requirements, shrimp boats killed 500 to 5,000 Kemp's ridleys each year. Responsibility for conservation of the Kemp's ridley turtle is shared by the Fish and Wildlife Service and the National Marine Fisheries Service because turtles nest on land but otherwise live in the ocean.

In the late 1970s, biologists attempted to establish a second nesting site for Kemp's ridleys on the Padre Island National Seashore in Texas. In 2001, eight Kemp's ridley nests were found there. Padre Island is also the site of a captive breeding program for Kemp's ridleys—eggs are collected from nests and raised in a protected environment. After hatching, baby turtles are returned to the sea. This allows turtle hatchlings to bypass one of the most dangerous parts of the life cycle—approximately 85 percent of hatchlings survive incubation at the station, whereas only 17 percent survive in unprotected nests. In 2001, 656 eggs were incubated at the Padre Island Station, and several hundred turtles released.

Desert Tortoise

The desert tortoise (Figure 6.7) was listed in 1990 as threatened in most of its range in the Mojave and Sonoran

FIGURE 6.7

The desert tortoise is threatened due to habitat destruction, livestock grazing, invasion of non-native plant species, collection, and predation by ravens. (*U.S. Fish and Wildlife Service*)

Deserts in California, Arizona, Nevada, and Utah. Decline of this species has resulted from collection by humans, predation of young turtles by ravens, off-road vehicles, invasive plant species, and habitat destruction due to development for agriculture, mining, and livestock grazing. Livestock grazing is particularly harmful to tortoises because it results in competition for food, as well as the trampling of young tortoises, eggs, or tortoise burrows. Invasive plant species have caused declines in the native plants that serve as food for tortoises. Off-road vehicles destroy vegetation and sometimes hit tortoises.

Desert tortoise populations are constrained by the fact that females do not reproduce until they are 15 to 20 years of age (individuals can live 80–100 years), and by small clutch sizes, with only 3–14 eggs per clutch. Juvenile mortality is also extremely high, with only 2 to 3 percent surviving to adulthood. About half this mortality is due to predation by ravens, whose populations in the desert tortoise's habitat have increased with increasing urbanization of desert areas—human garbage provides food for ravens and power lines provide perches.

Protected habitat for the desert tortoise includes areas within Joshua Tree National Park and Lake Mead National Recreation Area in Nevada and Arizona. There is also a Desert Tortoise Research Natural Area on a Bureau of Land Management habitat in California. A Habitat Conservation Plan for the area around Las Vegas requires developers to pay fees for tortoise conservation.

Snakes and Lizards

There are approximately 2,400 species of snakes and 3,800 species of lizards. Although they represent the largest group of reptiles, snakes and lizards are also among the least studied. There are numerous groups of lizards, including iguanas, chameleons, geckos, and horned lizards, among many others. There are even "fly-ing" lizards found in the tropical forests of Southeast Asia—these are not capable of true flight, like birds and bats, but actually glide with "wings" formed by skin stretched over mobile and elongated ribs. Most lizards are carnivorous, although there are some herbivorous species as well, including the iguanas. Snakes are elongate reptiles that have, during the course of evolution, lost their limbs. All species are carnivorous. Most snakes are adapted to eating relatively large prey items, and have highly mobile jaws that allow them to swallow large prey. In some species, the jaw can be unhinged to accommodate prey. Several groups of snakes are also characterized by a poisonous venom which they use to kill prey.

In 2002 there were 12 U.S. snakes listed as threatened or endangered, including 3 species of boa, a rattlesnake, and several species of garter snakes. Nine U.S. lizards were threatened or endangered in 2002: the Culebra Island giant anole, Monito gecko, Mona ground iguana, blunt-nosed leopard lizard, Coachella Valley fringe-toed lizard, island night lizard, St. Croix ground lizard, bluetail mole skink, and sand skink. Among these the Monito gecko, St. Croix ground lizard, Culebra Island giant anole, and blunt-nosed leopard lizard were listed as endangered.

SAN FRANCISCO GARTER SNAKE. The San Francisco garter snake is one of the most endangered reptiles in the United States. It was one of the first species to be listed under the Endangered Species Act. The decline of this species can be attributed primarily to habitat loss resulting from urbanization. Most of the snake's habitat was lost when the Skyline Ponds, located along Skyline Boulevard south of San Francisco County along the San Andreas Fault, were drained in 1966 for development. In addition, the building of the San Francisco International Airport and the Bay Area Rapid Transit regional commuter network destroyed additional snake habitat. Pollution and illegal collection have also contributed to the species' decline. Most San Francisco garter snakes today inhabit areas in San Mateo County, south of San Francisco. The species lives close to streams or ponds and feeds mainly on frogs, including Pacific tree frogs, small bullfrogs, and California red-legged frogs, which are also endangered.

MONITO GECKO. The endangered Monito gecko is a small lizard less than two inches long. This species exists only on the 38-acre Monito Island off the Puerto Rican coast. Endangerment of the Monito gecko has resulted from human activity and habitat destruction. After World War II the U.S. military used Monito Island as a site for bombing exercises, causing large-scale habitat destruction. The military also introduced predatory rats, which eat gecko eggs. In 1982 the FWS observed only 24 Monito geckos on Monito Island. In 1985 Monito Island was designated critical habitat for the species. The Commonwealth of Puerto Rico is now managing the island for the

FIGURE 6.8

The Komodo dragon is the largest lizard in the world. One of the greatest threats to the Komodo dragon is illegal trade. *(WWF/Michel Terrettaz. Reproduced by permission.)*

gecko and as a refuge for seabirds; unauthorized human visitation is prohibited.

MONITOR LIZARDS. In contrast to the Monito gecko, monitor lizards are among the largest lizard species in existence. The Komodo dragon (Figure 6.8), native to only a few islands in Indonesia, is the world's largest lizard. It reaches lengths of as much as 10 feet and weighs as much as 300 pounds. Despite the fact that the Komodo dragon is protected under Appendix I of the CITES treaty, one of the greatest threats to this species is illegal trade. The price on delivery is approximately $30,000 for one Komodo dragon specimen. Gray's monitor, a species found in the Philippine Islands, is also prized in illegal trade, and sells for around $5,000 on the illegal market. Gray's monitor is protected under CITES Appendix II.

HORNED LIZARDS (HORNY TOADS). Horned lizards, sometimes called "horny toads," are native to the deserts of North America. There are 14 species of horned lizards. All species have flat, broad torsos and spiny scales and feed largely on ants. Although all horned lizards are reptiles, they are often referred to as horny toads because they bear some resemblance to toads in size and shape.

FIGURE 6.9

Once abundant across Texas, the Texas horned lizard has disappeared from much of its habitat. *(Corbis Corporation. Reproduced by permission.)*

The Texas horned lizard (Figure 6.9) was once abundant in the state of Texas and was designated the official state reptile in 1992. It has declined largely as a result of pesticide pollution, the spread of invasive fire ants across the state, and habitat loss. It is protected by state law in Texas.

FIGURE 6.10

Range of the American Alligator

SOURCE: "Range of the American Alligator," U.S. Department of the Interior, U.S. Fish and Wildlife Service, Washington, DC, n.d.

Crocodilians

There are 22 existing species of crocodilians, a group that includes crocodiles, alligators, caimans, and gavials. Crocodilians play a crucial role in their habitats. They control fish populations and also dig water holes, which are important to many species in times of drought. The disappearance of alligators and crocodiles has a profound effect on the biological communities these animals occupy.

Worldwide, 17 species of crocodilians are in serious danger of extinction. Illegal trade poses one of the greatest threats to crocodilians, despite CITES restrictions. Conservation efforts include enforcement of trade restrictions and habitat restoration. Captive breeding programs are also underway for several species.

The Chinese alligator is one of many species listed in CITES Appendix I. Unfortunately, this species is among those most prized by collectors, commanding a black market price of as much as $15,000. The false gavial, a crocodilian which grows to 13 feet in length and is native to Indonesia, sells for an estimated $5,000 per specimen. Like the Chinese alligator, the false gavial is protected under CITES Appendix I.

In the United States, the American alligator was once a threatened species, but has now recovered enough to qualify for delisting. Figure 6.10 shows the range of the American alligator. The elusive and reclusive American crocodile, however, remains highly endangered. Less than 500 American crocodiles remain in Florida swamps.

Tuatara

The two-foot-long, lizard-like tuatara is sometimes called a living fossil, being the sole existing representative of a once diverse group. Tuataras are native to New Zealand and the Cook Strait. Like many other reptiles, tuataras are valued by collectors. They are protected by CITES under Appendix I.

CHAPTER 7
ENDANGERED MAMMALS

The majority of threatened and endangered mammals are imperiled for the same reasons as other biological species—habitat destruction, pollution, competition with invasive species, and so on. However, many mammals have also been intentionally obliterated by humans. In the nineteenth century, two mammals in completely different parts of the world, the quagga of southern Africa and the thylacine, or Tasmanian tiger, a marsupial of Australia, were both hunted to extinction because they competed with sheep for grazing land.

Other mammals have been driven to endangerment or extinction because they are seen by humans as dangerous or threatening. Large predators of all types—including grizzly bears, wolves, mountain lions, and other species—are endangered at least partly for this reason. Changing attitudes, however, have led to interest in preserving all species, and conservation measures have allowed several predatory mammals to recover. As their populations increase, however, encounters with humans are also becoming more common. In California, following a ban on mountain lion hunting, reports of mountain lions rose through the 1990s. In Yosemite National Park in California, black bears have increasingly confronted park visitors, causing significant damage and occasional injury. In 1997 alone, there were 600 car break-ins by bears, causing over $500,000 in damage. Biologists attribute the incidents not to aggressive bears but to careless park visitors. In 2000, tragedy struck when biathlete Mary Beth Miller was mauled to death by a black bear as she ran along a wooded path during her training routine in Quebec, Canada. The tragedy ignited controversy over attempts by Canadian officials to protect the species, including the cancellation of an annual bear hunt. Bear management is still a contentious issue at Yosemite. In 2001 park officials killed a female bear, the mother of two cubs, because she was allegedly teaching her cubs to raid cars, campsites, and picnic areas for food.

LEVELS OF ENDANGERMENT

In 2002 there were a total of 342 threatened and endangered mammals listed under the Endangered Species Act. Of the endangered mammals, 65 are found in the U.S. and 251 are foreign. Of the threatened species, 9 are found in the U.S. and 17 are foreign. U.S. threatened and endangered mammals are shown in Table 7.1. Some mammalian groups that are particularly well-represented on the U.S. list include bats (9 species), bears (3 species), kangaroo rats (6 species), mice (10 species), and whales (7 species).

The 2000 *Red List* report from the World Conservation Union (IUCN) reports that 24 percent of mammal species are threatened globally, including 180 species that are critically endangered and 340 species that are endangered. Nearly all of these are imperiled because of human activity. A large majority—83 percent—are endangered due to loss of habitat. The status of mammals has worsened significantly since the last IUCN assessment in 1996, when 163 species were listed as critically endangered and 315 species were listed as endangered. The IUCN Director-General, Maritta con Bieberstein Koch-Weser, described the 2000 results as "a jolting surprise, even to those already familiar with today's increasing threats to biodiversity." The habitat types occupied by the largest numbers of threatened mammal species are lowland and tropical rainforests, both of which are being rapidly degraded. Countries that harbor the largest number of threatened mammals include Indonesia, India, Brazil, China, Thailand, Cameroon, Russia, and Tanzania.

The biggest cause of mammalian decline and extinction in the twentieth century is the same as that for many other groups—habitat loss and degradation. As humans convert forests, grasslands, rivers, and wetlands for various uses, they relegate many species to precarious existences in small, fragmented habitat patches. Primates, for example, are highly threatened partly because they are

TABLE 7.1

Mammals listed as endangered or threatened, April 23, 2002

Status	Species Name
E	Bat, gray (*Myotis grisescens*)
E	Bat, Hawaiian hoary (*Lasiurus cinereus semotus*)
E	Bat, Indiana (*Myotis sodalis*)
E	Bat, lesser long-nosed (*Leptonycteris curasoae yerbabuenae*)
E	Bat, little Mariana fruit (*Pteropus tokudae*)
E	Bat, Mariana fruit (=Mariana flying fox) (*Pteropus mariannus mariannus*)
E	Bat, Mexican long-nosed (*Leptonycteris nivalis*)
E	Bat, Ozark big-eared (*Corynorhinus (=Plecotus) townsendii ingens*)
E	Bat, Virginia big-eared (*Corynorhinus (=Plecotus) townsendii virginianus*)
T(S/A)	Bear, American black (*Ursus americanus*)
XN,T	Bear, grizzly (*Ursus arctos horribilis*)
T	Bear, Louisiana black (*Ursus americanus luteolus*)
E	Caribou, woodland (*Rangifer tarandus caribou*)
E	Deer, Columbian white-tailed (*Odocoileus virginianus leucurus*)
E	Deer, key (*Odocoileus virginianus clavium*)
E,XN	Ferret, black-footed (*Mustela nigripes*)
E	Fox, San Joaquin kit (*Vulpes macrotis mutica*)
E	Jaguar (*Panthera onca*)
E	Jaguarundi, Gulf Coast (*Herpailurus (=Felis) yagouaroundi cacomitli*)
E	Jaguarundi, Sinaloan (*Herpailurus (=Felis) yagouaroundi tolteca*)
E	Kangaroo rat, Fresno (*Dipodomys nitratoides exilis*)
E	Kangaroo rat, giant (*Dipodomys ingens*)
E	Kangaroo rat, Morro Bay (*Dipodomys heermanni morroensis*)
E	Kangaroo rat, San Bernardino Merriam's (*Dipodomys merriami parvus*)
E	Kangaroo rat, Stephens' (*Dipodomys stephensi (incl. D. cascus)*)
E	Kangaroo rat, Tipton (*Dipodomys nitratoides nitratoides*)
T	Lynx, Canada (*Lynx canadensis*)
E	Manatee, West Indian (*Trichechus manatus*)
E	Mountain beaver, Point Arena (*Aplodontia rufa nigra*)
E	Mouse, Alabama beach (*Peromyscus polionotus ammobates*)
E	Mouse, Anastasia Island beach (*Peromyscus polionotus phasma*)
E	Mouse, Choctawhatchee beach (*Peromyscus polionotus allophrys*)
E	Mouse, Key Largo cotton (*Peromyscus gossypinus allapaticola*)
E	Mouse, Pacific pocket (*Perognathus longimembris pacificus*)
E	Mouse, Perdido Key beach (*Peromyscus polionotus trissyllepsis*)
T	Mouse, Preble's meadow jumping (*Zapus hudsonius preblei*)
E	Mouse, salt marsh harvest (*Reithrodontomys raviventris*)
T	Mouse, southeastern beach (*Peromyscus polionotus niveiventris*)
E	Mouse, St. Andrew beach (*Peromyscus polionotus peninsularis*)
E	Ocelot (*Leopardus (=Felis) pardalis*)
XN,T	Otter, southern sea (*Enhydra lutris nereis*)
E	Panther, Florida (*Puma (=Felis) concolor coryi*)
T	Prairie dog, Utah (*Cynomys parvidens*)
E	Pronghorn, Sonoran (*Antilocapra americana sonoriensis*)
E	Puma (=cougar), eastern (*Puma (=Felis) concolor couguar*)
T(S/A)	Puma (=mountain lion) (*Puma (=Felis) concolor (all subsp. except coryi)*)
E	Rabbit, Lower Keys marsh (*Sylvilagus palustris hefneri*)
EmE	Rabbit, pygmy (*Brachylagus idahoensis*)
E	Rabbit, riparian brush (*Sylvilagus bachmani riparius*)
E	Rice rat (*Oryzomys palustris natator*)
E	Seal, Caribbean monk (*Monachus tropicalis*)
T	Seal, Guadalupe fur (*Arctocephalus townsendi*)
E	Seal, Hawaiian monk (*Monachus schauinslandi*)
E,T	Sea-lion, Steller (*Eumetopias jubatus*)
E	Sheep, bighorn (*Ovis canadensis*)
E	Sheep, bighorn (*Ovis canadensis californiana*)
E	Shrew, Buena Vista Lake ornate (*Sorex ornatus relictus*)
E,XN	Squirrel, Carolina northern flying (*Glaucomys sabrinus coloratus*)
E	Squirrel, Delmarva Peninsula fox (*Sciurus niger cinereus*)
E	Squirrel, Mount Graham red (*Tamiasciurus hudsonicus grahamensis*)
T	Squirrel, northern Idaho ground (*Spermophilus brunneus brunneus*)
E	Squirrel, Virginia northern flying (*Glaucomys sabrinus fuscus*)
E	Vole, Amargosa (*Microtus californicus scirpensis*)
E	Vole, Florida salt marsh (*Microtus pennsylvanicus dukecampbelli*)
E	Vole, Hualapai Mexican (*Microtus mexicanus hualpaiensis*)
E	Whale, blue (*Balaenoptera musculus*)
E	Whale, bowhead (*Balaena mysticetus*)
E	Whale, finback (*Balaenoptera physalus*)
E	Whale, humpback (*Megaptera novaeangliae*)
E	Whale, right (*Balaena glacialis (incl. australis)*)
E	Whale, Sei (*Balaenoptera borealis*)

TABLE 7.1

Mammals listed as endangered or threatened, April 23, 2002

[CONTINUED]

Status	Species Name
E	Whale, sperm (*Physeter catodon (=macrocephalus)*)
E,XN,T	Wolf, gray (*Canis lupus*)
E,XN	Wolf, red (*Canis rufus*)
E	Woodrat, Key Largo (*Neotoma floridana smalli*)
E	Woodrat, riparian (=San Joaquin Valley) (*Neotoma fuscipes riparia*)

SOURCE: "U.S. Listed Vertebrate Animal Species Report by Taxonomic Group," in *Species Information: Threatened and Endangered Animals and Plants*, U.S. Fish and Wildlife Service, Washington, DC, 2002 [Online] http://ecos.fws.gov/webpage/ webpage_vip_listed.html?&code=V&listings=0#A [accessed April 23, 2002]

dependent on large expanses of tropical forests, a habitat under siege around the globe. In regions where tropical forest degradation and conversion have been most intense, such as South and Southeast Asia, Madagascar, and Brazil, as many as 70 percent of native primate species face extinction.

The introduction of invasive species by humans has also taken a toll on mammalian wildlife. Australia is over-run with domestic cats whose ancestors were brought by settlers to the island continent 200 years ago. Stray domestic cats have multiplied in the deserts, forests, and alleys, driving indigenous species such as bandicoots, bet-tongs, numbats, wallabies, and dozens of other bird and mammal species, most of which are found nowhere else on Earth, towards extinction. Richard Evans, a member of the Australian Parliament, claims the feral cats are responsible for the extinction of at least 39 species in Australia. He has called for total eradication of cats from the island by 2020, to be achieved by neutering pets and spreading feline diseases in the wild. The Australian National Parks and Wildlife Service reports that house cats each kill some 25 native animals each year on average, and feral domestic cats kill as many as 1,000 per year.

THE BLACK-FOOTED FERRET

The black-footed ferret (Figure 7.1) is a small furrow-digging mammal and member of the weasel family. Nocturnal creatures, ferrets help to control populations of snakes and rodents, including their primary prey, black-tailed prairie dogs. Black-footed ferrets once ranged over 11 Rocky Mountain states as well as parts of Canada. They have declined drastically because of the large-scale conversion of prairie habitats to farmland, and because their primary prey, prairie dogs, have been nearly exterminated by humans. Prairie dogs are considered pests because they dig holes and tunnels just beneath the ground surface. These can cause serious injury to horses or other large animals that step into them. (Some municipalities also poison prairie dogs in city parks, where burrow holes can trip and injure humans.) Poisons used to kill prairie dogs may also kill some ferrets.

Black-footed ferret populations had declined so greatly that the species was put on the Endangered Species List in 1973. However, prairie dog poisonings continued, and by 1979 it was believed that the black-footed ferret was extinct. In 1981 a ferret was sighted in Wyoming and discovered to be part of a remnant population. Rewards were offered for more sightings, and by the end of the year a few black-footed ferret populations had been located. These typically existed in close proximity to prairie dog populations in sagebrush-heavy areas. In 1985 ferret populations were struck by disease, and by 1987, only 18 black-footed ferrets were in existence. These individuals were captured and entered into a captive breeding program.

The captive breeding of ferrets has been reasonably successful. There are now core populations of 269 breeding-age individuals in five zoos in the U.S. and Canada as well as one Fish and Wildlife Service facility. In 1999 a total of 133 kits were born. The Fish and Wildlife Service has also tried to reintroduce black-footed ferrets in several states. Studies suggest that each population of black-footed ferret requires approximately 10,000 acres of black-tailed prairie dog habitat to survive. Unfortunately, prairie dogs are also in decline due to habitat loss and episodes of sylvatic plague, which have decimated many populations. Although some reintroductions have failed, two are doing well—one in National Forest habitat in Conata Basin/Badlands, South Dakota, and another in the Charles M. Russell National Wildlife Refuge in Montana. In 2000 there were already many more wild-born than captive-born ferrets at those sites. The Fish and Wildlife Service recovery plan for black-footed ferrets hopes to move the species from endangered to threatened status by 2010. This would require that 1,500 breeding adults exist in the wild in a minimum of 10 separate locations, with a minimum of 30 breeding adults included in each population. Captive breeding and reintroductions of black-footed ferrets were organized by the Black-Footed Ferret Recovery Implementation Team, and involved 26 separate state and federal organizations, conservation groups, and Native American tribes.

THE WOLF

The wolf has played numerous roles in the popular imagination. Romulus and Remus, the mythical founders of Rome, were supposedly raised by nurturing wolves. Romantic impressions of the species originate from sources such as Jack London's novel *The Call of the Wild*. However, western culture has also demonized wolves, portraying them as ravenous man-eaters. Because people feared wolves and believed they preyed on humans and livestock, they were hunted with abandon. Wolves were not only shot, trapped, and poisoned, but also often burned alive, dragged behind horses, and mutilated. They

FIGURE 7.1

Black-footed ferrets, once thought extinct, are now being successfully bred in captivity. A few reintroduced ferret populations are doing well. *(U.S. Fish and Wildlife Service, Washington, DC)*

were also hunted for their luxurious coats. Popular notions of wolves are sometimes based on fiction rather than fact. Although wolves sometimes attack cattle or sheep, they actually prefer to prey on wild species. In addition, there have been no fatal attacks by non-rabid wolves on humans in North America. In fact, wolves are afraid of people and usually flee at the sight of them.

Wolves were once among the most widely distributed mammals on Earth. Prior to European settlement, wolves ranged over most of North America, from central Mexico to the Arctic Ocean. Their decline was largely the result of hunting. In 1914 Congress authorized funding for the removal of all large predators, including wolves, from federal lands. By the 1940s wolves had been eliminated from most of the contiguous United States. In 1973 the Endangered Species Act was signed into law. Because the wolf had all but disappeared, it became the first animal listed as endangered under the ESA. Two species of wolves exist in North America today, the red wolf and the gray wolf. Both species are imperiled.

FIGURE 7.2

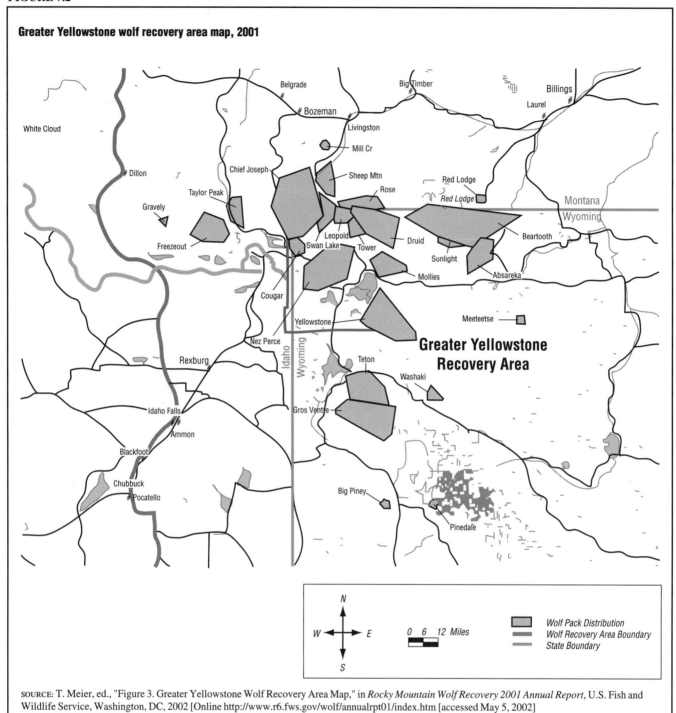

Greater Yellowstone wolf recovery area map, 2001

SOURCE: T. Meier, ed., "Figure 3. Greater Yellowstone Wolf Recovery Area Map," in *Rocky Mountain Wolf Recovery 2001 Annual Report*, U.S. Fish and Wildlife Service, Washington, DC, 2002 [Online http://www.r6.fws.gov/wolf/annualrpt01/index.htm [accessed May 5, 2002]

The Gray Wolf Reintroduction Program

In 1991 Congress instructed the Fish and Wildlife Service to prepare an environmental impact report on the possibility of reintroducing wolves to habitats in Yellowstone National Park and central Idaho. Reintroductions began in 1995, when 14 Canadian gray wolves were released in Yellowstone National Park.

Wolf reintroductions were not greeted with universal enthusiasm. Ranchers, in particular, were concerned that wolves would attack livestock. They were also worried that their land would be open to government restrictions as a result of the wolves' presence. Some ranchers said openly that they would shoot wolves they find on their land. Several measures were adopted to address ranchers' concerns. The most significant was that ranchers would be reimbursed for livestock losses from a compensation fund maintained by the Defenders of Wildlife, a private conservation group based in Washington, D.C. As of 2001 the fund had paid out $214,929 to 188 ranchers, covering the

TABLE 7.2

Greater Yellowstone wolf pack and population data, 2001

Wolf Pack	State	Pack size Jan 2002 Adult	Pup	Tot	Mortalities Natural	Human[1]	Unkn	Known Dispersed	Missing[2]	Control Killed	Moved	Confirmed losses[3] Cattle	Sheep	Dogs
Druid Peak [4]	WY	26	11	37										
Rose Creek II	WY	4	5	9										
Tower	WY	2	0	2				4	1					
Leopold	WY	10	4	14		1		2						
Swan Lake	WY	6	2	8										
Mollie's	WY	4	6	10										
Chief Joseph	WY/MT	4	7	11		1						1		
Nez Perce	WY/ID		?	18	2			1						1
Cougar Creek	WY	3	3	6										
Yellowstone Delta	WY	11	5	16										
Teton	WY	3	9	12										
Gros Ventre	WY	3-4	?	3-4								1		
Washakie	WY	6-7	4	10-11								2		1
Sunlight Basin	WY	5-7	4-5	9-12								2		
Absaroka	WY	4	4	8		1				1		8		1
Beartooth	WY	3	3	6										
Greybull River	WY		?	6										
Pinedale	WY		?	2										
Taylor Peaks	MT	3	0	3		3				2		1	2	
Freezout	MT	2	4	6		1								
Gravelly Range [6]	MT	3	0	3		1				1	8		38	
Mill Creek	MT		?	5-7		1				1		1		
Sheep Mountain	MT	1	6	7	1	1				1		1		
Red Lodge	MT		?	3-5										
Loners inside YNP	WY			1										
Loners outside YNP [5]	WY			1		3				3		5	34	1
Loners outside YNP [5]	MT												5	
Loners outside YNP [5]	ID			2									38	
Total		77	218		3	13	0	7	1	9	8	22	117	4

[1] Includes 8 wolves killed in control actions.
[2] Collared wolves that became missing in 2001
[3] Additional losses listed as "probable" or "possible" described in text.
[4] Underlined packs are counted as breeding pairs toward recovery goals.
[5] Wolf numbers indicate collared lone wolves. Lone wolves killed 5 calves, 77 sheep (plus 19 probable kills) and 1 dog, and injured 2 dogs
[6] Eight members of the Gravelly Pack (2 adults and 6 pups) were translocated to the Yaak River valley in NWMT in December 2001.

Note: YNP = Yellowstone National Park
      NWMT = Northwest Montana recovery area

SOURCE: T. Meier, ed., "Great Yellowstone wolf recovery area: Wolf packs and population data 2001," in *Rocky Mountain Wolf Recovery 2001 Annual Report*, U.S. Fish and Wildlife Service, Washington, DC, 2002 [Online] http://www.r6.fws.gov/wolf/annualrpt01/index.htm [accessed May 5, 2002]

losses of 260 cattle, 568 sheep, and 28 other animals killed by wolves.

Nonetheless, wolf introductions were legally challenged in 1997, when the American Farm Bureau Federation initiated a lawsuit calling for the removal of wolves from Yellowstone. The farm coalition scored an initial victory, but in January 2000 the 10th Circuit Court of Appeals in Denver overturned the decision upon appeal by the United States Department of the Interior, the World Wildlife Fund, and other conservation groups.

As of 2002 the FWS had reintroduced 41 wolves into Yellowstone and 35 wolves into central Idaho. Wolf packs in both Yellowstone and Idaho have thrived. A map of the Yellowstone wolf recovery area is shown in Figure 7.2, and data on Yellowstone wolf packs are shown in Table 7.2. The population currently includes some 218 wolves, including 77 pups. Since the reintroduction, there have been 13 wolf mortalities due to humans and three due to natural causes.

Despite the concern of ranchers and livestock owners, a recovered wolf population in the Yellowstone Park area has only slightly reduced populations of cattle, sheep, elk, moose, bison, and deer. In fact, wolves weed out sick and weak animals, thus improving the overall health of prey populations. Wolf predation on herbivorous species also takes pressure off vegetation and produces carrion for an array of scavengers including eagles, ravens, cougars, and foxes. Finally, the presence of wolves has increased visitor attendance to Yellowstone National Park, generating an estimated $7–10 million in additional net income each year.

In 2002 the total wolf population in the continental United States was estimated at 3,500 individuals. In July 2000 the FWS moved to downlist all gray wolves in the continental United States from endangered to threatened status.

Gray Wolves in Alaska

Gray wolves have never been listed as endangered or threatened in Alaska, where there are more than 7,000

FIGURE 7.3

The red wolf is one of the most endangered animals in the world, with an estimated population of less than 300. *(U.S. Fish & Wildlife Service)*

individuals. In Canada gray wolves also number in the thousands and are hunted legally. Because wolf prey species, particularly caribou and moose, are fewer in number, some people believe that hunting wolves will help to protect their prey species.

Until 1991 Alaskans were allowed to hunt wolves for sport. Aerial wolf-killing by state wildlife officials also occurred following a simple and highly efficient procedure—state workers trapped individual wolves in the summer, fit them with radio collars, and released them. In the winter, hunters in aircraft found the collared wolves with their packs, and wildlife agents shot non-collared wolves from the air, leaving the collared wolves to go find new packs.

In 1992 a group of tourists visiting Alaska protested the aerial shooting of wolves, threatening a boycott of the state if it continued. Additional threats of boycotts from conservation groups prompted the state to stop aerial hunting. Eventually a modified plan was adopted allowing hunters to locate wolves from the air and then land and shoot the animals from 100 yards away or more. Hunters were also allowed to snare wolves in traps. However, the trapping program was canceled in 1995 by Alaska Governor Tony Knowles when it was discovered that many moose, caribou, eagles, and red foxes had also died in the steel snares designed for wolves.

The Mexican Gray Wolf

In 1998 the Fish and Wildlife Service began to reintroduce rare Mexican gray wolves, the smallest of North America's gray wolves, into federal lands in the Southwest. This distinct subspecies once occupied habitats in central and southern Arizona, central New Mexico, western Texas, and northern Mexico. The Mexican gray wolf had been hunted to near extinction in the late 1800s and early 1900s in the United States. By 1960 only seven individuals survived in captivity. Captive breeding programs in

the U.S. and Mexico have helped to increase population numbers. Released Mexican gray wolves are being tracked using radio collars. Subsequent releases are expected to create a viable population of 100 individuals by 2005.

The Red Wolf

The red wolf (Figure 7.3) was once found throughout the eastern United States, but declined as a result of habitat loss and aggressive hunting by humans. It has been considered endangered since 1967. The red wolf is a smaller species than its relative, the gray wolf, and, despite its name, may have any of several coat colors including black, brown, gray, and yellow. In 1975, to prevent the immediate extinction of this species, the Fish and Wildlife Service captured the twenty-some remaining individuals and began a captive breeding program. The red wolf reintroduction program began in 1987, marking the first reintroduction of a species extinct in the wild. Red wolves now reside over about one million acres in North Carolina and Tennessee, including three National Wildlife Refuges, a Department of Defense bombing range, some state-owned lands, and private property (with the permission and cooperation of landowners). As of 2002 there are close to 100 red wolves in these populations, with about 90 percent of these born in the wild. There are also approximately 200 red wolves managed among captive-breeding facilities around the lower 48 states.

BEARS AND PANDAS

Bears and pandas are imperiled worldwide. In 2002 seven species were listed as in immediate danger of extinction under Appendix I of the Convention on International Trade in Endangered Species (CITES): the giant panda (China), red panda (Himalayas), Asiatic black bear, sloth bear (Asia), sun bear (Asia), spectacled bear (South America), and grizzly bear (North America). U.S. bear species listed by the Fish and Wildlife Service in 2002 included the American black bear, the Louisiana black bear, and the grizzly bear.

Many bears are endangered due to habitat loss. According to the FWS, bears have been eliminated from about 50 to 75 percent of their natural ranges. Some bears have traditionally been hunted because they are considered predatory or threatening. Others are hunted for sport. In addition, bears are killed in large numbers by poachers, who sell bear organs and body parts in the illegal wildlife trade. These organs usually end up in Asia, where they are valued as ingredients in treatments for ailments or illnesses, or to delay the effects of aging—although there is no evidence that such treatments are effective.

Grizzly Bears

The grizzly bear was originally found throughout the continental United States, but has now been eliminated from every state except Colorado, Idaho, Montana, Washington, and Wyoming. In 2002, there were an estimated 1,000 individuals in the wild, down from some 50,000 to 100,000 before human interference. The grizzly bear has declined due primarily to aggressive hunting and habitat loss. It is listed as threatened under the Endangered Species Act.

Grizzly bears are large animals, standing four feet high at the shoulder when on four paws, and as tall as seven feet when upright. Males weigh 500 pounds on average but are sometimes as large as 900 pounds. Females weigh 350 pounds on average. Grizzlies have a distinctive shoulder hump, which actually represents a massive digging muscle. Its claws are two to four inches long. They are considered more aggressive than black bears.

The federal government has established recovery zones for the grizzly bear in Yellowstone National Park, the North Continental Divide, the Selkirk and Bitterroot Mountains in Idaho, the North Cascades, the San Juan Mountains in Colorado, and the Cabinet/Yaak area on the Canadian border. (See Figure 7.4.) Recovery plans for this species are coordinated under the Interagency Grizzly Bear Committee, which was created in 1983.

Giant Pandas

Few creatures have engendered more human affection than the giant panda, with its roly-poly character, small ears, and black eye patches on a snow-white face. Giant pandas are highly endangered, with only approximately 1,000 pandas in the wild and some 100 individuals in captivity. Pandas are found only in portions of southwestern China, where they inhabit a few fragmentary areas of high altitude bamboo forest. Unlike other bear species, to which they are closely related, pandas have a vegetarian diet that consists entirely of bamboo. Pandas also have a "sixth digit" which functions like a thumb, and which they use to peel tender bamboo leaves from their stalks.

Pandas have become star attractions at many zoos, where they single-handedly draw scores of visitors. Despite tremendous efforts, pandas have proven notoriously difficult to breed in captivity. The birth of a giant panda cub, named Hua Mei, at the San Diego Zoo in 1999 was a major event, with millions of people following the cub's progress online and in the papers through its first days of life. The San Diego Zoo pays China $1 million annually for the loan of the pair of adult pandas and the cub that was born. These funds are used to support panda conservation efforts in China, including the purchase of land for refuges as well as the development of habitat corridors to link protected areas.

Red Pandas

The red panda is also called the lesser panda because it is significantly smaller than the giant panda. Red pandas are not, like giant pandas, related to bears—they are actually relatives of the raccoons. Red pandas are virtually

FIGURE 7.4

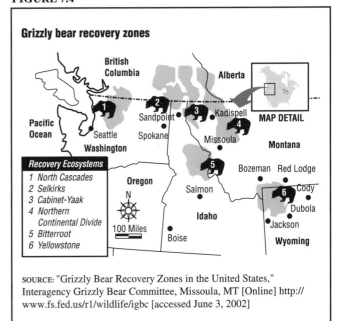

Grizzly bear recovery zones

Recovery Ecosystems
1 North Cascades
2 Selkirks
3 Cabinet-Yaak
4 Northern Continental Divide
5 Bitterroot
6 Yellowstone

SOURCE: "Grizzly Bear Recovery Zones in the United States," Interagency Grizzly Bear Committee, Missoula, MT [Online] http://www.fs.fed.us/r1/wildlife/igbc [accessed June 3, 2002]

extinct in the wild, due mostly to habitat loss and degradation. Red pandas occupy temperate forests in the foothills of the Himalayas in Nepal, Burma, and southwestern China at altitudes between 5,000 and 13,000 feet. Like giant pandas, red pandas eat bamboo, focusing on the most tender leaves. Because bamboo is not very nutritious, red pandas spend as much as 13 hours each day eating in order to acquire the nutrients they need. Because of a slow rate of reproduction, it is difficult for this species to recover from population declines. Red pandas are solitary creatures, occupying generally non-overlapping home ranges of approximately one square mile for females and two square miles for males. A captive breeding effort for red pandas is underway at zoos across the world to prevent the complete extinction of this species. Over 300 red pandas are found in captivity.

THE BIG CATS

Of the nearly 40 feline, or cat, species, only one—the domestic cat—is believed to be secure. As undeveloped land becomes harder to find, large cats, such as lions, panthers, tigers, jaguars, and cheetahs, are left with less and less natural habitat in which to live.

Mountain Lions—America's Large Cat

The mountain lion is a seven-foot-long cat that can weigh between 70 and 170 pounds. It was once found throughout North America from southern Argentina to northern British Columbia, making it one of the most widely distributed terrestrial species on the continent. It is also known as the panther, puma, or cougar, and preys on large animals, particularly deer. Mountain lions may also eat wild hogs, rabbits, and rodents. They require large home ranges for securing food. A single individual may have a home range spanning 85 square kilometers. By 1900 the species was nearly extinct due to habitat loss and hunting. Until the 1960s, many states offered monetary rewards for the killing of mountain lions. It is now found primarily in mountainous, unpopulated areas.

Conservation efforts have met with success in some portions of the country. In fact, there are now so many encounters between humans and mountain lions in California that hikers and park officials are given instruction in how to react to these large cats. Scientists attribute the increased encounter rate to more wilderness ventures by humans as well as a larger mountain lion population—an estimated 6,000 individuals. Because of these events, some people are demanding that hunting be reinstituted.

In most of the eastern United States, however, mountain lions have long been presumed extinct. If they are present, they are still extremely rare. In 1997 several sightings were reported in the Appalachian Mountains, but these have not been verified.

THE FLORIDA PANTHER. The Florida panther is one of 27 subspecies of the mountain lion. It has been considered endangered since 1967, and there are only 30 to 50 individuals surviving in the wild. The Florida panther has declined due to loss of habitat to urbanization and development, water contamination, and highway traffic. Their population size is now so small that many are victim to genetic disorders resulting from inbreeding. Ninety percent of male Florida panthers suffer from sperm abnormality, sterility, congenital heart defects, and possible immune deficiencies due to long-term inbreeding. Experts fear the species may die out in less than 20 years without aggressive intervention.

In 1994 and 1995 scientists and wildlife managers introduced Texas cougars, the Florida panthers' closest relatives, into habitats in Florida. Eight female Texas cougars were released. Biologists hoped that interbreeding would strengthen and diversify the Florida panther gene pool. "This is a very drastic measure and not one we ordinarily undertake," reported Dr. John Fay of the U.S. Department of the Interior. Dr. Fay noted that the strategy had helped save woodland caribou in Idaho and Washington in the 1980s, when individuals were interbred with Canadian caribou. In fact, Florida panthers and Texas cougars once formed a single, interbreeding population that ranged freely throughout the southeastern United States. They were eventually isolated from each other by human encroachment a little more than a hundred years ago.

Other efforts are also underway to help maintain the existing Florida panther gene pool. A captive breeding program was initiated in 1991 with ten panther cubs that had been removed from the wild. It is hoped that captive breeding will allow for the establishment of two additional pop-

ulations of 50 individuals each. Scientists are also hopeful that the habitat destruction that threatens the Florida panther has slowed. The primary issue in panther conservation today is providing large enough expanses of protected habitat for the species. This is particularly challenging not simply because the carnivores need large home ranges to feed, but because male panthers are territorial and will not tolerate the presence of other males. About half the area occupied by Florida panthers is private land, including farms, ranches, and citrus groves adjacent to protected reserves. Efforts are being made to secure the cooperation of landowners in conservation efforts.

As a result of the Florida panther's plight and public affection for the animal, in 1982 Florida declared the panther its state animal. Florida businessman Wayne Huizenga named his National Hockey League (NHL) team the Florida Panthers and has pledged many thousands of dollars to panther recovery efforts.

Jaguars

The jaguar is the largest cat in the Americas, measuring five to six feet long and weighing some two hundred pounds. Jaguars once ranged from Arizona to Argentina, but are now quite rare in the United States, where they may still occur in low numbers in Arizona, New Mexico, and Texas. Jaguars are listed as endangered throughout their range, which also includes Mexico and Central and South America. An estimated 15,000 individuals remain in the wild. Jaguars occupy a wide variety of habitats, from dense jungle and scrubland to reed thickets, forests, and even open country. They prey on wild pigs, rodents, deer, sloths, tapirs, and a variety of smaller species. They are endangered primarily due to habitat destruction and habitat fragmentation. Because they are so rare, much of what is known about the species comes from studying zoo populations.

Tigers

Wild tigers are found exclusively in Asia, from India to Siberia. Although the world tiger population surpassed 100,000 in the nineteenth century, experts fear that as few as 7,000 tigers remained in 2002. Approximately 2,000 of these are found in captivity. In addition to habitat loss, countless tigers fall victim to the illegal wildlife trade every year. Many tiger body parts are used as ingredients in traditional Chinese medicine, and the big cats are also prized in the exotic pet industry.

In 1999 the Wildlife Conservation Society reported a rebound in the world tiger population, in part because of a worldwide moratorium on tiger hunting imposed by CITES listing. However, ecologists warn that tigers, which hunt deer, wild pigs, cattle, antelope, and other large mammals, are threatened seriously by loss of prey, much of which consists of non-protected species being eliminated by hunters.

THE SIBERIAN TIGER. The Siberian tiger (Figure 7.5) is the largest cat in the world and one of the world's most endangered species, with only 500 individuals estimated to exist in the wild. There are also several hundred Siberian tigers in captivity. The Siberian tiger, also known as the Amur tiger, once occupied mixed deciduous and coniferous forest habitats in the Amur-Ussuri area in Siberia, as well as in northern China and Korea. It is now believed to be extinct, or nearly extinct, in China and Korea. Individuals reach lengths of eight to ten feet and weigh up to 800 pounds. They eat wild boars, Sika deer, and elk. Siberian tigers are territorial and require large home ranges of some 500 to 600 square miles.

Populations have suffered greatly from habitat loss caused by logging and deforestation, as well as illegal trade. The Siberian tiger is sought for its skin, bones, eyes, whiskers, teeth, internal organs, and genitals. These are used for everything from skin cures to tooth medicine. In Russia, where unemployment is high, poachers have flooded nearby Asian markets with tiger parts. In 1995 alone, poachers killed more than 65 Siberian tigers. The financially strapped Russian government can devote neither money nor time to protecting the tigers. Like the Florida panther, the Siberian tiger has also been weakened by inbreeding, which increases the possibility of reproductive problems and birth defects.

Cheetahs

The cheetah is the fastest land animal on Earth, able to sprint at speeds up to 70 mph. Cheetahs occupy grassland, shrubland, and woodland habitats. Their range once extended through most of Africa as well as southwestern Asia. Currently, cheetahs are found only in a few areas in Iran, North Africa, and sub-Saharan Africa. Cheetahs hunt small prey, particularly Thomson's gazelle. The cheetah has been listed in CITES Appendix I since 1975. In 2002 there were an estimated 10,000 cheetahs in the wild.

Cheetah populations have declined for many reasons. Much of the species' habitat has been developed for agricultural or ranching use, and many of the cats are shot by farmers who wish to protect their livestock. In addition, cheetahs are badly inbred, and many individuals are infertile. In addition, cheetahs are smaller and less aggressive than other predators that share their environment (including lions and leopards) and often have their food kills stolen or their cubs killed. Conservation biologists have determined that in order to save the cheetah, human assistance in the form of habitat protection, protection from competitor species, and measures to improve the genetic diversity of the species are required.

THE RHINOCEROS

Rhinoceros are among the largest land mammals. They weigh up to 8,000 pounds—as much as 50 average-

FIGURE 7.5

The Siberian tiger is one of the most endangered species in the world. It now occupies forest habitats in the Amur-Ussuri region of Siberia. *(Field Mark Publications)*

sized men—and are herbivorous grazers. The name rhinoceros is made up of two Greek words meaning "nose" and "horn," and rhinos are in fact the only animals on Earth that have horns on their noses. Figure 7.6 shows an African white rhinoceros with two horns. The female may be identified by her longer, more slender primary horn.

Rhinoceros have roamed the land for more than 40 million years, but in less than a century, humans—their only predators—have reduced populations to dangerously low levels. There are five species of rhinoceros—the black rhino (African), white rhino (African), Sumatran rhino (found in Borneo, Malaysia, and Sumatra), Javan rhino (found in Indonesia and Vietnam), and Indian rhino (found in both India and Nepal). Certain rhino species can be divided into distinct subspecies. For example, the Javan rhino has two subspecies, one found in Vietnam, the other in Indonesia. The Vietnamese subspecies consists of only one tiny population of five to seven individuals, and was thought extinct until this tiny population was discovered in 1999. All rhinos are close to extinction, with populations estimated in 2001 at 10,400 for the white rhino, 2,700 for the black rhino, 2,400 for the Indian rhino, 300 for the Sumatran rhino, and 60 for the Javan rhino. Some individuals are also found in captivity.

Hunting has been the primary cause of rhinoceros decline. Rhinoceros horn is highly prized as an aphrodisiac, as well as an ingredient in Chinese medicine (although its potency has never been shown). Rhinos were first listed by CITES in 1976. This banned international trade in the species and their products. In 1992 CITES also started requiring the destruction of horn caches confiscated from poachers. Nonetheless, people continue to buy and consume rhinoceros horn, and many poachers are willing to risk death to acquire it.

FIGURE 7.6

The white rhinoceros is native to Africa and can weigh up to 8,000 pounds. *(U.S. Fish and Wildlife Service)*

Indian Rhinos

Conservation efforts have improved the status of some rhino species. The Indian rhinoceros, which was reduced to fewer than 100 individuals in the mid-1970s, has experienced significant population growth in the past 25 years. In 2001 the International Rhino Foundation (IRF) reported some 2,400 Indian rhinos in the wild. Population increase resulted from habitat protection, including the designation of several national parks, as well as measures that curbed poaching.

The Royal Chitwan National Park was established in Nepal in 1973 and includes over a thousand square kilometers of protected habitat. At the time of establishment, fewer than 80 Indian rhinos were found in the park. Troops from the Royal Nepalese Army were dispatched to help prevent poaching. Indian rhinos flourished at Royal Chitwan, and individuals were later transported to a second rhino conservation area at Royal Bardia National Park, a few hundred miles from Royal Chitwan. In April 2002 the Department of National Parks and Wildlife Conservation in Nepal reported 529 rhinos at Royal Chitwan and 63 at Royal Bardia, a substantial increase from when conservation efforts began.

However, in April 2002 the Department of National Parks and Wildlife Conservation reported that 39 rhinos had died in the past 12 months at Royal Chitwan. Of these, only nine were believed to have died from natural causes. Twenty-five were almost certainly killed by poachers. Horns and other body parts had been removed from the carcasses. Two other rhinos were found electrocuted and three had been poisoned. These were found intact by park officials, who believe that they were killed by villagers whose crops were damaged by rhinos in areas adjacent to the park. The 2002 numbers represent the continuation of a disturbing pattern—42 rhinos died in 1999 and 23 were killed in 1997–1998.

African Rhinos

Africa is home to two species of highly imperiled rhinoceros, the black rhino and the white rhino. Both species have a second, smaller horn situated slightly behind the larger main horn. They are threatened primarily by poaching. Wildlife officials in Zimbabwe, Swaziland, and Namibia have gone so far as to sever rhino horns in an effort to curtail poaching. Most experts, however, discourage the practice, as animals use their horns for both digging and defense. In 2001 the IRF reported 2,700 black rhinos in the wild. Of the black rhinoceros subspecies, the northwestern variety is the most severely endangered, with only 10 currently found in the wild. Over 10,000 white rhinos were reported in 2001. Captive breeding efforts for the African rhino species have met with some success, particularly at the San Diego Wild Animal Park, and may aid in the conservation of these species.

ELEPHANTS

Elephants are the largest land animals on Earth. They are frequently described as the "architects" of the savanna habitats in which they live. Elephants dig water holes, keep forest growth in check, and open up grasslands that support other species, including the livestock of African herders. Elephants are highly intelligent, emotional animals and form socially complex herds. There are two species of elephants, African elephants and Asian elephants, both of which are highly endangered. The African elephant (Figure 7.7), which sometimes weighs as much as six tons, is the larger species. In 2002 there were an estimated 500,000 African elephants and 50,000 Asian elephants in the wild.

Elephants have huge protruding teeth—tusks—made of ivory. Ivory is valued by humans for several reasons, particularly for use in making jewelry and figurines. Piano keys were also once made almost exclusively of ivory; however, that practice has ceased. The market for ivory has had tragic consequences for African elephants. Their numbers dropped from over 10 million individuals in 1900 to only 600,000 in 1989. As a result of this decline, the UN-administered CITES banned worldwide commerce in ivory and other elephant products in 1990. However, like rhinoceros horns, elephant tusks continue to be illegally traded. Numerous elephants are poached each year. The price of poached elephant ivory is reported to be as high as $90 per pound.

Despite continued poaching, elephant populations have recovered somewhat since enjoying CITES protection. In 1997 Zimbabwe requested that CITES change the listing status of the African elephant in three South African nations—Zimbabwe, Botswana, and Namibia—from Appendix I status (a species in immediate danger of extinction) to Appendix II status (threatened in the absence of trade controls). Kenya, India, and other nations, along with many environmental organizations, opposed the downlisting, in part because they felt that a reopening of the ivory trade might cause a resurgence in demand and poaching. CITES responded by downlisting the elephant to Appendix II, while simultaneously initiating a program, the Monitoring of Illegal Killing of Elephants (MIKE) to better assess poaching. Although MIKE statistics would not be available until 2003, CITES did approve an experimental interim proposal allowing a one-time sale of stockpiled ivory from Namibia, Botswana, and Zimbabwe to Japan. This one-time ivory transaction was made in 1999 and grossed approximately $5 million.

FIGURE 7.7

Elephants are highly intelligent and social animals. Once on the verge of extinction, elephants have recovered somewhat after a worldwide ban on the ivory trade. *(Field Mark Publications)*

At the 2000 CITES Conference, South Africa, Zimbabwe, Namibia, and Botswana again petitioned CITES to authorize ivory sales. South Africa also spearheaded a movement to allow the culling of elephants, noting that its national conservation parks were overrun. At South Africa's Kruger Park, for example, 7,000 elephants occupied an area designated to support 5,000 individuals. Under the South African plan, the funding for elephant culling would be obtained through a legitimate, but limited, international trade in ivory and elephant skin. Kenya and India, on the other hand, renewed a request to relist the elephant under CITES Appendix I, as immediately endangered. In the end, the opposing factions reached a compromise in which both proposals were withdrawn—elephants remained listed under Appendix II, and the ban on ivory sales remained in effect. There is likely to be continued contention over ivory trade and the elephant's status at future CITES meetings.

Although the ivory trade has always been the largest threat to elephants, conflicts between humans and ele-

FIGURE 7.8

The orangutan is highly endangered, along with the majority of the world's primate species. *(Field Mark Publications)*

phants are an increasing issue. The ranges of many elephant herds now extend outside protected refuges, and elephants frequently come into contact with farmers, eating or otherwise destroying crops. Increasing human settlement in areas inhabited by elephants will likely result in more conflicts over time.

PRIMATES

The World Conservation Union (IUCN), in its *2000 Red List of Threatened Species*, reported that collectively, the 233 known species of primates (excluding humans) are among the most endangered mammals. Since the last IUCN assessment in 1996, the number of "critically endangered" primates increased from 13 to 19 species, and the number of "endangered" primates rose from 29 to 46. Critically endangered primate species included the Roloway monkey (lowland tropical rainforest in Ghana and Cote d'Ivoire), Mentawai macaque (Indonesia), Sclater's black lemur (lowland tropical rainforest, Madagascar), red-handed howling monkey (Brazil), and the black lion tamarin (lowland tropical rainforest, Brazil), among others. Much of the increased endangerment of primate species is due to loss of habitat and hunting.

Brazil is home to the largest number of primate species—77 at present—followed by Indonesia (33), Democratic Republic of Congo (33), and Madagascar (30). Many of the most endangered primate species are found on Madagascar, which has a diverse and unique primate fauna. The majority of Madagascar's primate species are endemic—that is, they are found nowhere else on earth.

Habitat loss, especially the fragmentation and conversion of tropical forests for road building and agriculture, contributes to the decline of nearly 90 percent of all IUCN-listed primates. In Indonesia and Borneo, for example, home to virtually all the world's 20,000 to 30,000 orangutans (Figure 7.8), deforestation has shrunk orangutan habitat by over 90 percent. Logging and extensive burning have caused many orangutans to flee the forests for the villages, where they have been killed or captured by humans. Thirty-six percent of threatened primates also face pressures from excessive hunting and poaching. Today, almost all countries have either banned or strictly regulated the trade of primates, but these laws are often hard to enforce. Many primates, such as chimpanzees and orangutans, are valued by circuses and zoos, as well as in the exotic pet trade. Large numbers of primates are also used in medical research because of their close biological relationship with humans.

Not all relationships between primates and humans are exploitative. People in some regions protect primates from harm by according them sacred status or by making it taboo to hunt or eat them. One of the rarest African monkeys, the Sclater's guenon, survives in three areas of Nigeria in part because residents regard the animal as sacred.

SYMBOLS OF THE AMERICAN WEST

The wild horse, bighorn sheep, and buffalo are icons of the American West. The buffalo was imprinted on the five-cent coin (the "Buffalo Nickel") beginning in 1913, when it was believed the species had gone extinct. But unlike many of the symbols of bygone eras, the wild horse and the buffalo are success stories. Recent efforts aim to return bighorn sheep to the West as well.

Wild Horses of North America

In 1900 approximately 2 million untamed horses and burros roamed North America, primarily in the public lands of the Western states (Figure 7.9). These wild animals came to symbolize to many people the freedom of the American spirit. In 1971, however, the Bureau of Land Management (BLM) reported that populations had dwindled to fewer than 20,000. As a result, Congress enacted the Wild, Free-Roaming Horses and Burros Act, declaring, "Congress finds and declares that wild free-roaming horses and burros are living symbols of the historic and pioneer spirit of the West; (and) that they contribute to the diversity of life forms within the Nation and enrich the lives of the American people...." Following passage of this act, populations were able to recover.

By the early 1990s, however, a concern arose that U.S. rangelands were being severely overgrazed. In 1992 the BLM implemented a selective-removal program to reduce the number of wild horses and burros. The program removed animals less than nine years old from herds, either through relocation, destruction, or placement in the care of qualified individuals and agencies. The Adopt-A-Horse Program made about 1,200 horses available each year at affordable prices. In 2002 adoptions occurred

FIGURE 7.9

Once considered threatened, wild horse populations in the American West have since recovered. The Bureau of Land Management manages wild horse herds. *(Corbis Corporation)*

through an online auction system, with bids beginning at $125 for single animals or $250 for mares with foals. Adoptions could also be made in person. Despite these costly control efforts, new foals quickly replaced the horses removed. Mountain lions are the only natural predator of these species, and only have a significant impact on a small number of populations. In 1996 the BLM started to vaccinate mares with contraceptives to reduce the birthrate, in hopes that the West's 42,000 wild horses and 5,000 wild burros could live out their lives in the wild.

The American Horse Protection Association and the Colorado Horse Rescue believe that estimates of wild horse populations are inflated and that herds will not be able to withstand population-control measures. In addition, they claim that adopted animals often end up in the wrong hands and are either abused by their new owners or sold to meat-packing plants.

Bighorn Sheep

A hundred years ago, desert bighorn sheep were commonly seen climbing the mountains of the West. The species is named for the large, curved horns, which males use to battle for access to females, wrestling with horns interlocked. Some battles may take as long as 24 hours. Overhunting and disease have decimated bighorn sheep populations across the U.S. In Texas, for example, the number of bighorn sheep had fallen to 500 by 1903, and hunting was banned. In 1945 the state set aside 11,625 acres for bighorn sheep habitat in the Sierra Diablo Wildlife Management Area near Sierra Blanca in the Big Bend area of the state. As populations continued to decline, Texas began to import desert bighorns from other states for captive breeding. Despite these efforts, the last native bighorn in Texas is believed to have died in the 1960s. Captive breeding efforts were continued in hopes of reintroducing the species into areas of its original range but were abandoned in 1997.

Since then, however, new management efforts have met with some success. Private landowners have donated thousands of acres of mountainous terrain for breeding grounds for reintroduced bighorns. Unlike other subjects of restoration efforts, such as wolves, bighorns pose no threats to ranchers—they do not prey on livestock, and they graze in remote areas, where they do not compete with livestock. Bighorn sheep also offer landowners potential income through the sale of hunting permits—

FIGURE 7.10

Bison are the largest terrestrial animals in North America. *(Field Mark Publications)*

conducted in fall 2000 estimated that some 400 peninsular bighorn are found in the U.S.

The Bison

Sixty million bison (Figure 7.10)—also called buffalo—once roamed the grasslands of America. Historical accounts describe herds stretching as far as the eye could see. Although Native Americans hunted bison, it was not until European settlers came with firearms that their numbers fell drastically. Many shot the animals for fun, while others sold the hides. Their numbers were eventually reduced to fewer than 1,000. Today bison are found in the Great Plains from Mexico to Canada. The bison's close relative, the European bison, a taller but lighter species, is nearly extinct; only a few individuals survive in parks and zoos.

The bison is the largest terrestrial animal in North America. It is characterized by short, pointed horns and a hump over the front shoulders. The head, neck, and front parts of the body are covered by a thick, dark coat of long, curly hair; the rear has shorter, lighter hair. Adult males can weigh as much as 1,800 to 2,400 pounds; the female is smaller. The adult male also has a black "beard" about a foot long. Bison are social animals and usually travel in herds. Considering their size and weight, bison are remarkably light on their hooves—unlike cattle, they love to run and are surprisingly fast. Bison stampedes are a wonder to behold. Before the arrival of European settlers, bison were central to the existence of Plains Native Americans, who used them for food, made clothing from their hides, and tools from their bones. The dried dung, called buffalo chips, was used for fuel.

Bison first received protection from the U.S. government in 1872, with the establishment of Yellowstone National Park in Wyoming and Montana. However, the welfare of the small herd of bison was largely ignored until 1901, when it was discovered that only 25 remained in the park. The herd was restored to 1,000 by 1930 with bison imported from the Great Plains. As the herd multiplied, the park service shot animals to keep the population under control. This practice was unnecessary, however, because the harsh Wyoming and Montana winters caused the herd to dwindle naturally. The park service stopped shooting bison in the 1960s, and by 1994 the population of the Yellowstone herd had reached a peak of 4,200 animals. Over 3,000 individuals were documented in April 2002.

However, conflict over bison management continues at the park. Many bison are carriers of a cattle disease called brucellosis. In domestic cattle, it can cause miscarriage in pregnant cows. Although there is no evidence that the disease can be transmitted from bison to livestock, ranchers are nonetheless wary. Bison that leave Yellowstone are generally checked for disease and shot if they test positive.

when biologists determine the sheep population has surplus rams, the state may issue a limited number of permits for hunting. The permits are rare and are very expensive, frequently commanding five-figure prices. They are issued only to landowners participating in the restoration effort. The first Texas permit sold for $61,000. In 1993 a hunter paid more than $300,000 at auction for an Arizona permit. All the money raised from hunting permits is put back into bighorn sheep restoration. In 1998 experts estimated the population of bighorn sheep in Texas at 320 and at almost 30,000 nationwide. The Texas Parks and Wildlife Department hopes to increase the number of bighorns in that state to 600 by 2002.

In 1998 the FWS proposed an emergency endangered listing for the California peninsular bighorn sheep, a subspecies of the common bighorn. In July 2000 the FWS proposed critical habitat for these sheep. Estimated at 1.5 million in the early 1800s, the population size had dwindled due to disease, overhunting, loss of habitat, fragmentation of habitat, and predation. A helicopter survey

FIGURE 7.11

Three quaggas now run at a national park in South Africa, the result of a program to rebreed this zebra subspecies from other subspecies. *(AP/Wide World Photos)*

Today some populations of bison are managed more like livestock than as wildlife because they have become a food source for humans. Bison are a source of high-protein, low-fat, low-cholesterol meat. The National Bison Association estimates that 150,000 bison are slaughtered for food each year, producing 7.5 million pounds of meat. Bison meat is not expected to replace beef, but some people think it might become an alternative red meat source. In *Bring Back the Buffalo!* (Island Press, Washington, D.C., 1996), researcher and writer Ernest Callenbach argues that bison will gradually gain support as a food source, as it becomes more evident that bison are better adapted to grasslands and require much less human management than cattle. There are even bison ranchers abroad, including in Canada, Southern France, Switzerland, and Belgium.

By the end of the twentieth century, the National Bison Association reported a total of over 350,000 bison in the 48 continental United States, Alaska, and Canada—344,000 bison were privately owned, and 13,000 lived in public herds. Native American herds numbered 7,000 bison. Approximately 1,000 lived in zoos or outside of the United States and Canada.

REBIRTH OF THE QUAGGA

Why do zebras have stripes? Nobody knows for sure. Although scientists have proposed a variety of theories, none has proved conclusive. What is known is that among the varieties of African plains zebras, those that are native to southern Africa display less striping than zebras that inhabit the northern regions. Perhaps the most uniquely striped variety of zebra was the quagga, or Burchell's zebra. The quagga, a lightly browned zebra, displayed virtually no striping on its hindquarters and legs (Figure 7.11). In the nineteenth century, sheep and goat herders who settled within the quagga's grazing range hunted the odd-looking animal literally to extinction. When the last living quagga died at the Amsterdam Zoo on August 12, 1883, all that remained of the oddly colored zebras were 23 preserved animal skins.

Approximately 100 years later, scientists analyzed tissue from an old quagga skin and discovered that, genetically, the quagga was nearly identical to other zebras—it was therefore likely to be a subspecies of zebra and not a separate species, as had originally been thought. A selective breeding project was undertaken in 1987 in an attempt to breed zebras that had the striping traits of the extinct quagga. South African taxidermist Reinhold Rau spearheaded the project. He hypothesized that the genes that code for the distinctive color and striping patterns of quaggas existed recessively in South African zebras of the late twentieth century. Quagga project members assembled a collection of zebras that most closely resembled the extinct quagga in striping and coloring and began the slow process of breeding successive generations that increasingly resembled the quagga. By 2000 the project had pro-duced a number of individuals that resembled the preserved quagga skins in pattern, and others that resembled the skins in color. However, no individuals resembled the extinct animal in both striping and coloring. The project received public funding for the first time in June 2000, as breeding attempts continued.

A similar project was underway to rebreed the endangered Mongolian Przewalski horse and another to rebreed the tarpan, a European wild horse.

CHAPTER 8

THE STATUS OF BIRD SPECIES

Birds have always been among the best-studied biological groups, in part because of the enthusiasm of numerous amateur ornithologists. As a result, birds were the first group to be comprehensively surveyed for endangerment status. Scientists estimate that 121 bird species have gone extinct in the past 400 years. The rate of extinction has increased every 50 years. The majority of bird species have died out because of habitat destruction, hunting and collection, pollution, and predation by non-native species. The rate of disappearance of bird species is alarming not only because of the irrevocable loss of each species but also because of implications for the health of entire ecosystems. Figure 8.1 shows the Nene, or Hawaiian goose, an endangered species first listed in 1967. It is found only in Hawaii.

Long before the passage of the Endangered Species Act, the United States government recognized the importance of bird biodiversity and promoted habitat conservation for bird species. In 1929 the U.S. Congress passed the Migratory Bird Conservation Act. This law established the Migratory Bird Conservation Commission, which works with the Secretary of the Interior to designate and fund avian wildlife refuge areas. The U.S. Fish and Wildlife Service (FWS) is responsible for acquiring necessary lands through direct purchase, lease, or easement (agreement with landowners). Since that time, the FWS has procured over 4 million acres of land for bird refuges.

Birds received considerable attention in the *2000 IUCN Red List of Threatened Species*. A total of 1,183 bird species were considered threatened—this represents one of every eight described species. Another 727 bird species were considered "near threatened." There were 182 bird species categorized as "critically endangered," a significant increase from 168 listed species only four years earlier. Of these critically endangered species, a large majority—89 percent—have been harmed by loss of habitat. The number of "endangered" birds listed by the IUCN also increased dramatically, from 235 to 312 species.

Certain groups of birds have declined particularly. The number of IUCN-listed albatross species increased from three to sixteen, due largely to numerous deaths from long-line fishing. Four of the remaining five albatross species are considered near-threatened. The number of threatened penguin species has also jumped, increasing from five to ten. Finally, rapid deforestation in Southeast Asian rainforests has increased the number of threatened doves, parrots, and perching birds.

Less than 5 percent of Earth's land area is home to 75 percent of the world's threatened bird species. The largest numbers of endangered birds are found in Indonesia, the Philippines, Brazil, Columbia, China, Peru, India, and Tanzania. New Zealand and the Philippines have the highest proportion of threatened species, with 42 percent and 35 percent respectively.

WHAT ARE THE MAJOR THREATS TO BIRDS?

Habitat Loss and Environmental Decline

The driving force behind current declines in many bird species is the destruction, degradation, and fragmen-

FIGURE 8.1

The Nene, or Hawaiian goose, is one of numerous endangered birds endemic to Hawaii. *(Dr. H. Douglas Pratt)*

tation of habitat due to increasing human population size and the wasteful consumption of resources. The leading cause of habitat destruction in the United States is agricultural development. Large corporate farms cause environmental damage by clearing out native plant species, planting only one or a few crops, and draining wetlands. Natural habitats are also lost to urban sprawl, logging, mining, and road building.

Tropical bird species are threatened by large-scale deforestation worldwide. In Asia, for example, a 2001 study by BirdLife International suggested that one in four bird species is threatened, the majority due to loss of forest habitat. Populations have declined especially sharply in the last two decades, coincident with what BirdLife International calls "habitat loss or degradation resulting from unsustainable and often illegal logging, and land or wetland clearance for agriculture or exotic timber plantations." Large species, such as the Philippine eagle, are most quickly harmed by deforestation—these require large areas of undisturbed forest to hunt and breed.

Many Arctic bird species are threatened by habitat loss due to global warming. In April 2000 the World Wildlife Fund released a report indicating that a world climate change as small as 1.7 degrees centigrade (about 3.3 degrees Fahrenheit) would significantly reduce tundra habitat—the frozen arctic plain that serves as a breeding ground for many bird species. Among the tundra species already threatened are the red-breasted goose, the tundra bean goose, and the spoon-billed sandpiper.

Island species are also particularly vulnerable to habitat destruction because their ranges are usually very small to begin with. In addition, because many island birds evolved in the absence of predators, there are a large number of flightless species—these are highly vulnerable to hunting or predation by introduced species, including humans, cats, dogs, and rats. At one time some 75 percent of all bird extinctions occurred on islands. It is estimated that two-thirds of Hawaii's original bird fauna is already extinct. Of the remaining one-third, the large majority are imperiled. Habitat destruction in Hawaii has been so extensive that all the lowland species now present are non-native species introduced by humans.

Pesticides

During the latter half of the twentieth century, pesticides and other toxic chemicals were recognized as a major cause of avian mortality and a primary factor in the endangerment of several species, including the bald eagle and peregrine falcon. While the U.S. Environmental Protection Agency (EPA) regulates the manufacture and use of toxic chemicals generally, the Fish and Wildlife Service (under the Federal Insecticide, Fungicide, and Rodenticide Act [Amended 1988]) is responsible for preventing and punishing the misuse of chemicals that affect wildlife.

Many chemicals harmful to birds, such as DDT and toxaphene, have been banned. Other chemicals, such as endrin, the most toxic of the chlorinated hydrocarbon pesticides, are still legal for some uses. Endrin was responsible for the disappearance of the brown pelican from Louisiana, a population that once numbered 50,000 individuals.

Oil Spills

Oil spills constitute a major threat to birds (Figure 8.2). One of the worst and most infamous spills in history occurred on March 24, 1989, when the *Exxon Valdez* tanker released 11 million tons of crude oil into Alaska's Prince William Sound. To many Americans, it still exemplifies the disastrous effects oil spills have on wildlife. Thousands of birds died immediately after coming in contact with the oil, either from losing the insulation of their feathers or by ingesting lethal amounts of oil when they tried to clean themselves. Exxon personnel burned untold piles of birds; others were saved in cold storage under orders from the Fish and Wildlife Service. A complete count was never obtained, but Wildlife Service biologists estimated that between 250,000 and 400,000 sea birds died.

Approximately 40 percent of the region's entire population of common murres—estimated at 91,000—was eliminated. The yellow-billed loon population was also seriously depleted, as was the population of Kittlitz's murrelet, a species found almost exclusively in Prince William Sound. Other affected bird species included the bald eagle, black oystercatcher, common loon, harlequin duck, marbled murrelet, pigeon guillemot, and the pelagic, red-faced, and double-crested cormorants. Of these, the common loon, the harlequin duck, the pigeon guillemot, and the three species of cormorants have not increased in population size since the spill and are considered "not recovered" in 2002. In addition, the Kittlitz's murrelet appears to be suffering from continued population decline, and its future prospects appear bleak.

The detergents used to clean up oil spills can also be deadly to waterfowl—detergents destroy feathers, which leads to fatal chills or trauma. Research has shown that even after careful rehabilitation, birds that have been returned to nature after a spill often die in a matter of months. In 1996 Dr. Daniel Anderson, a biologist at the University of California at Davis, found that only 12 to 15 percent of rehabilitated pelicans survived for two years, compared to the 80 to 90 percent of pelicans not exposed to oil. For many ornithologists, these dismal results raise the issue of whether avian rescue efforts are worthwhile. Could money spent on rehabilitation be better used for spill prevention and habitat restoration? Oregon ornithologist Dr. Brian Sharp argues that the cleanup effort might ease the conscience of the public and of politicians, but in reality, does very little to benefit birds. However, new methods of treating oiled birds and of controlling spills have increased the bird survival rate from 5 percent to between 60 and 80 percent for some species. Under the Clean Water Act, the oil industry pays a tax that helps fund cleanups after spills.

Lead Shot

Lead is a serious threat to all wildlife. Used lead pellets settle on marsh and river bottoms and linger to contaminate the environment. Ducks and other birds sometimes inadvertently, and fatally, consume spent lead shot. Other waterfowl are killed gradually through lead accumulation. Wildlife managers have been aware of the lead shot problem since the 1940s, but it was only in 1976 that the Department of the Interior mandated the use of steel shot in numerous areas. In 1993 the use of lead shot was banned throughout the nation for hunting waterfowl. However, the use of lead for other forms of hunting continues to affect numerous species.

Domestic Cats

Studies in the United States and Britain have shown that house cats kill millions of small birds and mammals every year, a death toll that contributes to declines of some rare species. The University of Wisconsin reported that in that state alone, cats killed 19 million songbirds and 140,000 game birds in a single year. The British study reported that Britain's 5 million house cats account for an annual prey toll of some 70 million animals, 20 million of which are birds. The study also found that cats were responsible for a third to half of all the sparrow deaths in England. Both studies determined that factors such as whether a cat was well-fed at home, wore a bell collar, or was declawed made no difference to its hunting habits.

Domestic cats do so much damage in part because there are so many of them—more than 35,000 are born every day. Americans keep an estimated 60 million cats as pets. If each cat kills only one bird a year—and the number is likely far higher—over 60 million birds would succumb to cat predation each year. This is far greater than the number affected by oil spills. Many cat victims are plentiful urban species, but Fish and Wildlife studies show that cats also kill hundreds of millions of migratory songbirds annually. In addition, cats are believed to have contributed to the declines of several grassland species.

Trade in Exotic Birds

Birds are among the most popular pets in American homes today. An estimated 6–10 percent of American households own pet birds. Many of these are common finches, canaries, or parakeets, all of which are raised in captivity in the United States. However, wild birds are owned and traded as well, including numerous species of passerines (song birds) and psittacines (parrots and their relatives).

FIGURE 8.2

A bird is cleaned of oil after the disastrous *Exxon Valdez* spill in Prince William Sound, Alaska in 1989. An estimated 250,000–400,000 sea birds died in the spill. *(AP/Wide World Photos)*

Passerines include any of the approximately 4,800 species of song birds. The most commonly traded passerines include warblers, buntings, weavers, finches, starlings, flycatchers, and sparrows. Passerines are regarded as low-value birds, and few passerines are endangered due to trade.

The 333 species of psittacines, however, are generally rarer, and thus much more valuable, than passerines. The most commonly traded psittacines are macaws, Amazons, cockatoos, lovebirds, lories, and parakeets. In addition to their vivid colors and pleasant songs, many of these birds possess the ability to "talk," which makes them particularly appealing to some owners. Between 1975 and 2002, bird dealers created a new demand for an ever-increasing variety of birds, including diverse species of parrots, macaws, cockatoos, parakeets, mynahs, toucans, tanagers, and other tropical species.

Exotic talking birds—parrots, macaws, and cockatoos—comprise about 15 percent of the pet bird market in the United States. Laws in Mexico, Guatemala, and Honduras ban trade in parrots, and U.S. law bars importation of birds taken illegally from other countries. Some countries still allow exports, however, and there is also a great deal of smuggling. Legislation passed in 1992 to halt the legal importation of parrots is, ironically, believed to have increased smuggling. In 1998 customs officials announced the arrest of more than 40 people for smuggling hundreds of rare parrots and other wildlife across the Mexican border. The animals seized were believed to be worth hundreds of thousands of dollars in the pet trade, although some were considered nearly priceless because of their rarity in the wild.

The illegal bird trade has severely harmed many threatened species. New York Zoological Society bird curator Don Bruning believes that species such as the scarlet macaw are now practically extinct throughout Central America due to illegal trade. Over the past 20 years, smuggling has reduced red crown parrot populations by 80 percent and yellow-headed parrots by 90 percent in Mexico. In 2000 the World Wildlife Fund (WWF) identified the horned parakeet as one of the 10 species most threatened by illegal trade.

Invasive Species—The Case of Guam

Invasive species have damaged bird populations in some parts of the world, particularly those that occupy islands. Guam's unique bird fauna has been all but wiped out by the brown tree snake, an invasive species. The brown tree snake is believed to have been introduced from New Guinea via ship cargo in the 1950s, and had spread throughout the island by 1968. The snakes have no natural enemies on the island and plentiful prey in the form of forest birds. There are now believed to be as many as 13,000 snakes in a single square mile in some forest habitats. Twelve bird species have already gone extinct on Guam, including the Guam flycatcher, the Rufus fantail, the white-throated ground dove, and the cardinal honeyeater. Several other Guam bird species are close to extinction. Many of these birds are or were unique to Guam. Measures have been implemented to try to keep this destructive snake from invading other islands, including careful inspection of all cargo arriving from Guam. The removal of the brown tree snake in select habitat areas on Guam (which is a high effort project, requiring the constant trapping of snakes) allowed the reintroduction of one bird species, the flightless Guam rail, in 1998. The Guam rail had gone extinct in the wild, but a population is maintained in captivity.

Other particularly destructive invasive species include several associated with humans, including cats, dogs, and rats, which often prey on birds and their eggs. In fact, the World Conservation Union (IUCN) reports that invasive species represent the single most frequent cause of bird extinctions since 1800. Invasive species are currently estimated to affect 350, or 30 percent, of all IUCN-listed threatened birds.

Salton Sea Deaths

The Salton Sea, located 150 miles southeast of Los Angeles in the Sonora Desert, is a 35-mile-long expanse of salt marsh and open water encompassing 35,484 acres and situated 227 feet below sea level. The sea formed from a salt-covered depression known as the Salton Sink in 1905, when a levee on the Colorado River broke, filling the depression with water. Subsequently, the area has received additional water, primarily from agricultural runoff. Because the Salton Sea has no outlet, water is lost only through evaporation, leaving dissolved salts behind. The salinity (the amount of salt in the water) has increased gradually over time. The Salton Sea serves as habitat for migrating birds and provides winter habitat for waterfowl. The area is second only to the Texas coastline in the number of bird species sighted, and nearly 400 species had been reported by 2002. The Salton Sea National Wildlife Refuge was established in 1930 by presidential proclamation.

In the last decades of the twentieth century the Salton Sea entered a rapid and initially inexplicable decline that resulted in the deaths of countless birds and fish. The first unusual avian deaths were reported in 1987, and a task force was created by the California Department of Fish and Game in 1988 to study the problem. However, the epidemic continued, and in 1992 a massive die-off occurred in which officials reported the deaths of over 150,000 birds, including many eared grebes and ruddy ducks. Some of the fatalities were attributed to avian cholera, but experts remained baffled by the majority of casualties. At that point, the Department of the Interior initiated a $10 million Salton Sea project aimed at combating rising salinity and other environmental problems. The Salton Sea Authority was established in 1993 to coordinate activity. In 1996 there was another mass epidemic in which over 14,000 birds died, including 1,400 brown pelicans, an endangered species. This time, the cause was identified as avian botulism. The same year, thousands of tilapia fish were also killed by botulism. Authorities tentatively attributed the avian deaths to botulism from consuming tainted fish. Throughout 1997 a variety of initiatives were proposed in an effort to combat high salinity and other problems at the Salton Sea. Nonetheless, in May of that year 2,400 grebes and thousands of tilapia died. Causes of death included avian botulism, Newcastle disease, avian cholera, and poisoning by toxic algae.

Scientists have so far failed to establish a precise link between water quality and bird die-offs, but suspect a combination of natural and man-made contaminants. Evaporation and agricultural runoff have increased the salinity of the Salton Sea to levels 25 percent higher than in the Pacific Ocean. Experts fear that high salt levels increase the susceptibility of fish to disease. Birds are impacted when they consume affected fish. Another suspected cause of environmental deterioration is the defunct Salton Sea Test Base (SSTB), which served as a center for arms testing and weapons research during World War II. The U.S. Army Corps of Engineers initiated a clean-up project to decontaminate the SSTB, which occupied over 20,000 acres of land and water in the southwest corner of the Salton Sea. Environmentalists also believe that agricultural runoff from California's Imperial Valley, one of the most productive farmlands in the United States, encourages algae blooms that are deadly to fish. The Salton Sea is also polluted by additional agricultural runoff from Mexico and by untreated sewage from rivers

TABLE 8.1

Birds listed as endangered or threatened, April 23, 2002

Status	Species Name
E	Akepa, Hawaii (honeycreeper)(*Loxops coccineus coccineus*)
E	Akepa, Maui (honeycreeper) (*Loxops coccineus ochraceus*)
E	Akialoa, Kauai (honeycreeper) (*Hemignathus procerus*)
E	Akiapola'au (honeycreeper) (*Hemignathus munroi*)
E	Albatross, short-tailed (*Phoebastria (=Diomedea) albatrus*)
E	Blackbird, yellow-shouldered (*Agelaius xanthomus*)
E	Bobwhite, masked (quail) (*Colinus virginianus ridgwayi*)
E	Broadbill, Guam (*Myiagra freycineti*)
E	Cahow (*Pterodroma cahow*)
T	Caracara, Audubon's crested (*Polyborus plancus audubonii*)
E,XN	Condor, California (*Gymnogyps californianus*)
E	Coot, Hawaiian (*Fulica americana alai*)
E	Crane, Mississippi sandhill (*Grus canadensis pulla*)
E,XN	Crane, whooping (*Grus americana*)
E	Creeper, Hawaii (*Oreomystis mana*)
E	Creeper, Molokai (*Paroreomyza flammea*)
E	Creeper, Oahu (*Paroreomyza maculata*)
E	Crow, Hawaiian (*Corvus hawaiiensis*)
E	Crow, Mariana (*Corvus kubaryi*)
E	Crow, white-necked (*Corvus leucognaphalus*)
E	Curlew, Eskimo (*Numenius borealis*)
E	Duck, Hawaiian (*Anas wyvilliana*)
E	Duck, Laysan (*Anas laysanensis*)
T	Eagle, bald (*Haliaeetus leucocephalus*)
T	Eider, spectacled (*Somateria fischeri*)
T	Eider, Steller's (*Polysticta stelleri*)
E	Elepaio, Oahu (*Chasiempis sandwichensis ibidus*)
E	Falcon, northern aplomado (*Falco femoralis septentrionalis*)
E	Finch, Laysan (honeycreeper) (*Telespyza cantans*)
E	Finch, Nihoa (honeycreeper) (*Telespyza ultima*)
E	Flycatcher, southwestern willow (*Empidonax traillii extimus*)
T	Gnatcatcher, coastal California (*Polioptila californica californica*)
E	Goose, Hawaiian (*Branta (=Nesochen) sandvicensis*)
E	Hawk, Hawaiian (*Buteo solitarius*)
E	Hawk, Puerto Rican broad-winged (*Buteo platypterus brunnescens*)
E	Hawk, Puerto Rican sharp-shinned (*Accipiter striatus venator*)
E	Honeycreeper, crested (*Palmeria dolei*)
T	Jay, Florida scrub (*Aphelocoma coerulescens*)
E	Kingfisher, Guam Micronesian (*Halcyon cinnamomina cinnamomina*)
E	Kite, Everglade snail (*Rostrhamus sociabilis plumbeus*)
E	Mallard, Mariana (*Anas oustaleti*)
E	Megapode, Micronesian (*Megapodius laperouse*)
E	Millerbird, Nihoa (old world warbler)(*Acrocephalus familiaris kingi*)
T	Monarch, Tinian (old world flycatcher) (*Monarcha takatsukasae*)
E	Moorhen, Hawaiian common (*Gallinula chloropus sandvicensis*)
E	Moorhen, Mariana common (*Gallinula chloropus guami*)
T	Murrelet, marbled (*Brachyramphus marmoratus marmoratus*)
E	Nightjar, Puerto Rican (*Caprimulgus noctitherus*)
E	Nukupu'u (honeycreeper) (*Hemignathus lucidus*)
E	'O'o, Kauai (honeyeater) (*Moho braccatus*)
E	'O'u (honeycreeper) (*Psittirostra psittacea*)
T	Owl, Mexican spotted (*Strix occidentalis lucida*)
T	Owl, northern spotted (*Strix occidentalis caurina*)
E	Palila (honeycreeper) (*Loxioides bailleui*)
E	Parrot, Puerto Rican (*Amazona vittata*)
E	Parrotbill, Maui (honeycreeper) (*Pseudonestor xanthophrys*)
E	Pelican, brown (*Pelecanus occidentalis*)
E	Petrel, Hawaiian dark-rumped (*Pterodroma phaeopygia sandwichensis*)
E	Pigeon, Puerto Rican plain (*Columba inornata wetmorei*)
E,T	Plover, piping (*Charadrius melodus*)
T	Plover, western snowy (*Charadrius alexandrinus nivosus*)
E	Po'ouli (honeycreeper) (*Melamprosops phaeosoma*)
E	Prairie-chicken, Attwater's greater (*Tympanuchus cupido attwateri*)
E	Pygmy-owl, cactus ferruginous (*Glaucidium brasilianum cactorum*)
E	Rail, California clapper (*Rallus longirostris obsoletus*)
E,XN	Rail, Guam (*Rallus owstoni*)
E	Rail, light-footed clapper (*Rallus longirostris levipes*)
E	Rail, Yuma clapper (*Rallus longirostris yumanensis*)
T	Shearwater, Newell's Townsend's (*Puffinus auricularis newelli*)
E	Shrike, San Clemente loggerhead (*Lanius ludovicianus mearnsi*)
E	Sparrow, Cape Sable seaside (*Ammodramus maritimus mirabilis*)

TABLE 8.1

Birds listed as endangered or threatened, April 23, 2002 [CONTINUED]

Status	Species Name
E	Sparrow, Florida grasshopper (*Ammodramus savannarum floridanus*)
T	Sparrow, San Clemente sage (*Amphispiza belli clementeae*)
E	Stilt, Hawaiian (*Himantopus mexicanus knudseni*)
E	Stork, wood (*Mycteria americana*)
E	Swiftlet, Mariana gray (*Aerodramus vanikorensis bartschi*)
E	Tern, California least (*Sterna antillarum browni*)
E	Tern, least (*Sterna antillarum*)
E,T	Tern, roseate (*Sterna dougallii dougallii*)
E	Thrush, large Kauai (*Myadestes myadestinus*)
E	Thrush, Molokai (*Myadestes lanaiensis rutha*)
E	Thrush, small Kauai (*Myadestes palmeri*)
T	Towhee, Inyo California (*Pipilo crissalis eremophilus*)
E	Vireo, black-capped (*Vireo atricapillus*)
E	Vireo, least Bell's (*Vireo bellii pusillus*)
E	Warbler (=wood), Bachman's (*Vermivora bachmanii*)
E	Warbler (=wood), golden-cheeked (*Dendroica chrysoparia*)
E	Warbler (=wood), Kirtland's (*Dendroica kirtlandii*)
E	Warbler, nightingale reed (old world warbler) (*Acrocephalus luscinia*)
E	White-eye, bridled (*Zosterops conspicillatus conspicillatus*)
E	Woodpecker, ivory-billed (*Campephilus principalis*)
E	Woodpecker, red-cockaded (*Picoides borealis*)

SOURCE: "U.S. Listed Vertebrate Animal Species Report by Taxonomic Group," in *Species Information: Threatened and Endangered Animals and Plants*, U.S. Fish and Wildlife Service, Washington, DC, 2002 [Online] http://ecos.fws.gov/webpage/webpage_vip_listed.html?&code=V&listings=0#A [accessed April 23, 2002]

that flow across the Mexican-U.S. border. Contamination from DDT, DDE (a byproduct of DDT), and selenium also were documented as contributing to the decline.

The Salton Sea Task Force, the U.S. Bureau of Reclamation, and the California State Legislature have combined forces in the enormous undertaking of restoring the Salton Sea to health. However, another outbreak of botulism was reported in 2000. The endangered brown pelican suffered greatly in the recent outbreak, with 717 individuals dying. Another 600 brown pelicans were rehabilitated and released in December 2000. Avian botulism is not fatal if treatment is begun early, but birds do not show symptoms and are hard to catch until the disease has progressed. In addition to the brown pelican, 35 other species were affected in the 2000 outbreak. All affected species eat tilapia. Fish and Wildlife Service employees, along with California Department of Fish and Game, helped to round up sick birds and transport them to an open-air bird hospital built in 1997 from funds raised by volunteers. Recovered birds were released near the Tijuana Slough and Seal Beach national wildlife refuges, both located in Southern California.

ENDANGERED BIRD SPECIES

There are 273 birds on the Endangered Species List. Of these, 253 are endangered, including 78 U.S. species and 175 foreign species. In addition, 20 birds are threatened, including 14 U.S. species and 6 foreign species. Threatened and endangered U.S. bird species are shown in Table 8.1. This list includes many types of birds, including sparrows, albatrosses, terns, plovers, hawks, and woodpeckers. There are also a disproportionate number of Hawaiian bird species listed. Several threatened and endangered species will be discussed below.

Migratory Songbirds

Every year, more than 120 songbird species migrate between North America and tropical areas in Central and South America. Although many are appreciated by humans for their beautiful songs and colorful plumage, migratory songbirds also play a vital role in many ecosystems. During spring migration in the Ozarks, for example, some 40 to 50 migratory bird species arrive and feed on the insects that inhabit oak trees, thereby helping to control insect populations. Migratory species are particularly vulnerable because they are dependent on suitable habitat in both their winter and spring ranges. In North America, real estate development has eliminated many forest habitats. Migratory songbird habitats are also jeopardized in Central and South America, where farmers and ranchers have been burning and clearing tropical forests to plant crops and graze livestock. Some countries, including Belize, Costa Rica, Guatemala, and Mexico, have set up preserves for songbirds, but improved forest management is needed to save them.

The 1997 North American Breeding Bird Survey

The 1997 *North American Breeding Bird Survey* was a continent-wide study begun in 1966. It was conducted by the Biological Resource Division (BRD) of the United States Geological Survey. This survey provided encouragement on some fronts. For example, it found that, contrary to expectations, many North American forest species were either stable or growing in population size. Despite catastrophic regional declines, numerous species had successfully left developed areas and colonized intact forest areas. In particular, large, intact chunks of North American forest provided crucial breeding habitat for many species. The report concluded that a major conservation priority therefore must be preservation of large-tract forests. A second priority is to maintain important stopover and rest areas used by migratory species on their journeys between North America and the tropics.

North American grassland species, however, were shown to be in serious decline. One species, the bobolink, suffered a catastrophic population decrease of 90 percent when its grassland habitat was converted to cropland. These results were supported by a separate study carried out at the Sutton Avian Research Center in Bartlesville, Oklahoma between 1992 and 1996. The study, the largest undertaking of its kind in the United States, included observations of approximately 3,000 nests and 4,500 banded birds belonging to 30 species. Grassland species are being dramatically affected by loss of habitat and other threats. Some researchers believe that invasive fire ants, which kill insects and small animals, have depleted food supplies. Pesticides may also have destroyed much

of the insect base. Mark Howery of the Oklahoma Department of Wildlife Conservation concluded that as many as 30 percent of all grassland species could become threatened or endangered if current trends continue.

The Black-Capped Vireo and Golden-Cheeked Warbler

The black-capped vireo and golden-cheeked warbler are among the threatened songbirds listed with the Fish and Wildlife Service. Both species nest in central Texas and other locations in the U.S. and winter in Mexico and Central America. Both species have declined largely due to loss of habitat caused by land clearing for development. Another factor in the decline of the black-capped vireo is harm from "brood parasites"—bird species that lay their eggs in the nests of other species. In certain areas, more than half the black-capped vireo nests contain eggs of brood parasites called brown-headed cowbirds. The black-capped vireo was placed on the Endangered Species List in 1987, the golden-cheeked warbler in 1990.

Much of the critical nesting habitat for black-capped vireos and golden-cheeked warblers lies in the Hill Country of central Texas. The Texas Hill Country is characterized by diverse habitats and a high concentration of rare bird species. In the last decade, however, increased water demand by metropolitan areas has caused the local Edwards Aquifer to drop by 30 feet, resulting in a 15 to 45 percent decrease in available bird habitat. In an effort to balance development with wildlife preservation, the city of Austin, Texas invited The Nature Conservancy to formulate a plan to protect Hill Country habitats while enabling some development. The result was the Balcones Canyonlands Conservation Plan, which includes a 75,000-acre preserve in the Texas Hill Country.

Fort Hood, Texas, a heavy artillery training site for the U.S. Army, was designated essential nesting habitat for the golden-cheeked warbler and black-capped vireo in 1993. With the help of The Nature Conservancy, the Army currently manages some 66,000 acres of habitat for these species. Control of brown-headed cowbird populations has been a major part of the conservation efforts. Brown-headed cowbirds parasitize the nests of over 200 species of songbirds, and have caused declines in many of these species. Nest parasitism rates for the black-capped vireo were as high as 90 percent before control measures were begun. They are now at less than 10 percent. In 2000, surveys at Fort Hood documented 236 male black-capped vireos and 229 vireo territories, which produced an average of 1.75 fledglings each. Many other bird species also use habitat at Fort Hood, including threatened and endangered species such as the bald eagle, peregrine falcon, and whooping crane.

Shrikes

In 1993 scientists from 20 countries met at the first International Shrike Symposium in Boise, Idaho, to consider the plight of shrikes, a robin-sized predatory bird species. There are approximately 70 shrike species worldwide, many of which are imperiled. The once common U.S. species, the loggerhead shrike, has suffered significant decline, similar to many other bird species that occupy North American grasslands. The San Clemente loggerhead shrike was listed as endangered across its entire range in 1977. In addition to losing large portions of their former habitat, shrikes may be particularly sensitive to pesticide accumulation in the environment because they are carnivorous. (Shrikes hunt insects and small birds, often impaling them on thorns.) Scientists have found that the addition of fence posts for use as hunting perches may help support shrike populations.

THE CALIFORNIA GNATCATCHER. The California gnatcatcher is a small, gray and black songbird known for its "kitten-like" mewing call. Gnatcatchers are non-migratory, permanent residents of California coastal sage scrub communities, one of the most threatened vegetation types in the nation. Estimates of coastal scrub loss in the United States range from 70 to 90 percent of historic levels.

Fewer than 2,000 pairs of California gnatcatchers are estimated to remain in the United States. The plight of the species has emphasized the importance of preserving coastal sage scrub habitat, which supports many other distinctive species as well. The California gnatcatcher was listed as threatened across its entire range in California and Mexico in 1993.

Woodpeckers

Red-cockaded woodpeckers are named for the red patches, or cockades, of feathers found on the heads of males. This species is found in old pine forests in the southeastern United States, where family groups—consisting of a breeding male and female as well as several helpers—nest within self-dug cavities in pine trees. Tree cavities serve as nesting sites in addition to providing protection from predators. Because red-cockaded woodpeckers rarely nest in trees less than 80 years old, heavy logging has destroyed much of their former habitat. The red-cockaded woodpecker was first placed on the Endangered Species List in 1970. It is currently found in fragmented populations in the southeastern seaboard westward into Texas. The total population size is estimated at 10,000–14,000 individuals.

In March 2001 the U.S. Fish and Wildlife Service was forced to rescue several red-cockaded woodpeckers from habitat areas in Daniel Boone National Forest in Kentucky. Fifteen woodpeckers in six family groups were relocated to the Carolina Sandhills National Wildlife Refuge in South Carolina and the Ouachita National Forest in Arkansas. Daniel Boone National Forest had become uninhabitable for the woodpeckers after a 1999 infestation of southern pine beetles. The beetles quickly destroyed 90 percent of local woodpecker habitat despite valiant efforts by Forest Service officials and volunteers to control the insect's spread. The removal of this red-cockaded woodpecker population from Kentucky means that the species is now absent from the state.

The ivory-billed woodpecker, the largest woodpecker species, has long been thought extinct. A century ago, the species was found throughout the southeastern United States as well as in Cuba. The last confirmed sightings in the U.S. were reported in the 1970s. However, tantalizing hints that the ivory-billed woodpecker may yet survive in North America persist. Hunters occasionally report seeing it or, more often, hearing its characteristic double-rap sound deep in the Louisiana bayou. Several groups of ornithologists have devoted significant effort to relocating this species, particularly since a hunter reported seeing one on April Fool's Day in 1999. As of 2002 there have been no definitive sightings. The Cuban subspecies of the ivory-billed woodpecker was also rediscovered in 1986 after being presumed extinct. However, populations had reached such a low point by then that measures to help save the group were ineffectual.

Spotted Owls

The northern spotted owl has dark brown feathers with round white spots on the head, neck, and back. It weighs about 10 pounds, is about 18 inches high, and has a wingspan of up to 48 inches. The northern spotted owl occupies old-growth forests in the Pacific Northwest, where it nests in the cavities of trees 200 years old or older. It does not seem afraid of humans and in fact appears to be curious about humans and human activity. Its primary prey include the nocturnal northern flying squirrel, mice, and other rodents and reptiles. Owl pairs may forage across areas as large as 2,200 acres. There are about 2,000 breeding pairs in California, Oregon, and Washington, and another hundred pairs in British Columbia, Canada.

The northern spotted owl has declined primarily due to habitat loss. Most of the private lands in its range have been heavily logged, leaving only public lands, such as National Forests and National Parks, for habitat. Because logging has also been permitted in many old-growth National Forest areas, the species has lost approximately 90 percent of its original habitat. In 1990 the Fish and Wildlife Service placed the northern spotted owl on its list of threatened species. Court battles began over continued logging in National Forest habitats. In March 1991 U.S. Federal District Court Judge William Dwyer ruled in favor of the Seattle Audubon Society and against the U.S. Forest Service, declaring that the Forest Service was not meeting its obligation to "maintain viable populations." The Forest Service had argued that the Fish and Wildlife Service was responsible for the management and recovery of this species. However, Dwyer pointed out that the Forest Service had its own

FIGURE 8.3

Captively-bred condors

Zookeepers use hand puppets that look like adult condors to feed captively-bred condor chicks.

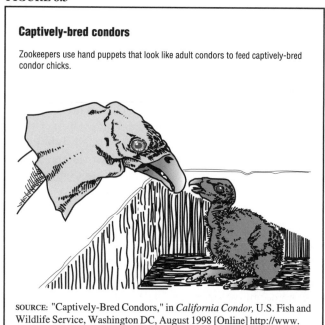

SOURCE: "Captively-Bred Condors," in *California Condor,* U.S. Fish and Wildlife Service, Washington DC, August 1998 [Online] http://www.nctc.fws.gov/library/Pubs/condor.pdf [accessed May 13, 2002]

FIGURE 8.4

The whooping crane is highly endangered. Each year, whooping cranes migrate from breeding grounds in Canada to wintering grounds in south Texas. The Fish and Wildlife Service has introduced captive-bred whooping cranes to new habitats in recent years. *(Field Mark Publications)*

distinct obligations to protect species under the Endangered Species Act, and that courts had already reprimanded the FWS for failing to designate critical habitat for the northern spotted owl. In 1992 the FWS set aside 7 million acres as "critical habitat" for the species. The Northwest Forest Plan was established in 1993. This plan reduced logging in 13 National Forests by about 85 percent in order to protect northern spotted owl habitats. However, the northern spotted owl has continued to decline by 7 to 10 percent per year—this despite the unanticipated discovery of 50 pairs of nesting adults in California's Marin County, just north of the Golden Gate Bridge.

In 1993 the Mexican spotted owl, a species native to the Southwest, was also placed on the list of threatened species. As with the northern spotted owl, the prime threat to this group is poorly managed timber harvesting. The Mexican spotted owl has a wide range, and is found in Utah, Colorado, Arizona, New Mexico, and Texas, as well as in central Mexico. Both northern and Mexican spotted owls remained threatened in 2002.

The California Condor

California condors, whose wingspans exceed nine feet, are among the continent's most impressive birds. Ten thousand years ago, this species soared over most of North America. However, its range contracted at the end of the ice age, and eventually individuals were found only along the Pacific Coast. Like other vulture species, the California condor is a carrion eater, and feeds on the carcasses of deer, sheep, and smaller species such as rodents. Random shooting, egg collection, poisoning, and loss of

habitat decimated the condor population. The species was listed as endangered in 1967.

An intense captive breeding program for the California condor was initiated in 1987 (see Figure 8.3). The first chick hatched in 1988. In 1994, after a series of deaths in the wild in which seven condors perished in rapid succession, the eight remaining wild condors were also captured and entered into the captive breeding program. The breeding program was successful enough that California condors were released into the wild beginning in 1992. The total condor population is now at 197, including 68 individuals in the wild. In April 2002, for the first time in 18 years, a condor egg laid in the wild hatched in the wild. The parents of this chick had been captive-bred at the Los Angeles Zoo and the San Diego Wild Animal Park respectively and released into the wild in 1995 at the age of one. Wild condors now inhabit parts of California as well as Nevada, Utah, and Arizona, where a population was introduced in the vicinity of the Grand Canyon in 1996, providing spectacular opportunities to view the largest bird in North America.

The Great White Whooping Crane

Standing five feet, the whooping crane (Figure 8.4) is North America's tallest bird and among the best known endangered species in the United States. Its name comes from its loud and distinctive call, which can be heard for miles. Each year, whooping cranes fly 2,500 miles from nesting grounds in Canada to south Texas for the winter before returning north in March to breed. Whooping cranes return to the same nesting site each year with the same mate. The birds were once heavily hunted, for meat as well as for their beautiful, long white feathers. In addi-

FIGURE 8.5

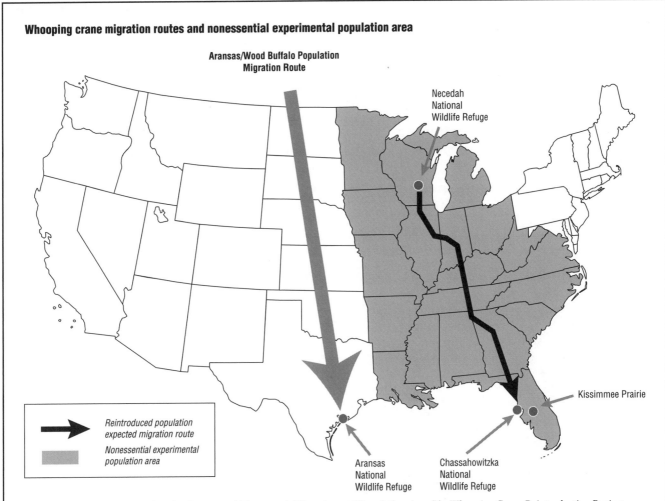

Whooping crane migration routes and nonessential experimental population area

Aransas/Wood Buffalo Population
Migration Route

Necedah
National
Wildlife Refuge

Kissimmee Prairie

Reintroduced population
expected migration route

Nonessential experimental
population area

Aransas
National
Wildlife Refuge

Chassahowitzka
National
Wildlife Refuge

SOURCE: "Whooping Crane Migration Routes and Nonessential Experimental Population Area," in *Whooping Crane Reintroduction Project*, U.S. Fish and Wildlife Service, Washington, DC, 2002 [Online] http://midwest.fws.gov/whoopingcrane/nep_map.html [accessed May 13, 2002]

tion, the heavy loss of wetland areas in the U.S. deprived whooping cranes of much of their original habitat. In 1937 it was discovered that fewer than 20 whooping cranes were left in the wild. That same year, the Aransas Wildlife Refuge was established in South Texas to protect the species' wintering habitat. Conservation efforts for the whooping crane are coordinated with the Canadian government, which manages its breeding areas.

Captive breeding programs have helped to increase the worldwide whooping crane population. As of 2002, 188 whooping cranes inhabited the traditional territory, migrating from Canada to Texas yearly. In addition, an introduced population of captive-bred individuals has been established in the Kissimmee Prairie in Florida. This population contains about 50 individuals, and has bred with success in its new habitat. A second introduced population breeds in Wisconsin on the Necedah National Wildlife Refuge and winters in Florida on the Chassahowitzka National Wildlife Refuge. Introduced cranes were led to their Florida wintering grounds along the migration

route by ultralight aircraft in 2001, and successfully made the return trip on their own in April 2002. Figure 8.5 shows the migration routes and locales of all three whooping crane populations. In addition to these wild populations, another 100 whooping cranes are found in captivity.

Hawaiian Honeycreepers

The Hawaiian honeycreepers are a group of songbirds endemic to Hawaii—that is, species in this group are found there and nowhere else on Earth. Hawaiian honeycreepers are believed to have radiated (formed many separate species, each adapted to a particular lifestyle) from a single species that colonized the Hawaiian Islands thousands of years ago. The honeycreepers are named for the characteristic "creeping" behavior some species exhibit as they search for nectar. The Hawaiian honeycreepers are extremely diverse in their diet—different species are seed-eaters, insect-eaters, or nectar-eaters. Species also differ in the shapes of the beaks and in plumage coloration. Hawaiian honeycreepers are found in forest habitats at

FIGURE 8.6

The bald eagle was once endangered due to habitat destruction and pollution by pesticides such as DDT. Its populations have recovered with protection and a ban on DDT. *(Field Mark Publications)*

high elevations. There were some 50 or 60 Hawaiian honeycreeper species originally, but a third of them have already gone extinct.

Twelve species of Hawaiian honeycreepers are currently listed with the Fish and Wildlife Service as endangered. Some honeycreeper species are among the most endangered animals on earth, with only a few individuals left. One of the primary factors involved in honeycreeper endangerment is loss of habitat. The Hawaiian Islands are estimated to retain a mere 20 to 30 percent of their original forest cover. In addition, the introduction of predators that hunt birds or eat their eggs, such as rats, cats, and mongooses, has contributed to the decline of numerous species. The introduction of bird diseases, particularly those spread by introduced mosquitoes, has also decimated honeycreeper populations. The success of mosquitoes in Hawaii has been dependent on another introduced species, pigs. The rooting activity of pigs creates pools of water where mosquitoes lay their eggs. In fact, the greater the number of pigs in a habitat, the more bird disease will be prevalent. Finally, competition with introduced bird species for food and habitat has also been a significant cause of decline.

The Po'ouli is the most endangered Hawaiian honeycreeper and probably the most endangered bird species in the world. Along with many other endangered native species, it occupies the Hanawi Natural Reserve Area, which has been aggressively rehabilitated and cleared of invasive species. There are three Po'ouli individuals left, two females and one male. The Maui Forest Bird Recovery Project and the Fish and Wildlife Service worked together in May 2002 to mate one of the Po'ouli females with the single remaining male. Unfortunately, the attempts were unsuccessful.

BACK FROM THE BRINK—SUCCESS STORIES

The Peregrine Falcon

Many falcon species have declined with the spread of humans. Like other predatory species, falcons were often hunted, either for sport or because they were considered a threat to chickens or livestock.

The peregrine falcon is the fastest bird on Earth. It achieves diving speeds of over 200 miles per hour. Like the bald eagle, much of the species' decline was due to the pesticide DDT. Populations sank to approximately 325 nesting pairs during the 1930s and 1940s. The recovery of this species was made possible by the banning of DDT as well as the establishment of special captive breeding centers on several continents. Between 1974 and 1999 more than 6,000 peregrine falcons were released into the wild. Federal and state agencies contributed to the conservation effort, as did private organizations such as the Peregrine Fund, Santa Cruz Predatory Bird Research Group, and Midwestern Peregrine Falcon Restoration Project.

In 1996 the Fish and Wildlife Service declared the peregrine falcon "officially recovered" and began the process to remove the species from the Endangered Species List. The American peregrine falcon was delisted in 1999 across its entire range, although it will be monitored for the next five years to assure that its recovery continues. By August 1999 about 1,650 breeding pairs of peregrine falcons inhabited the lower 48 states and Canada, with additional populations surviving in Mexico. The Arctic peregrine falcon, which recovered on its own after DDT was made illegal, was delisted in 1994. However, as of 2002 the Eurasian peregrine falcon, which occurs in Eurasia south to Africa and the Middle East, is still listed as endangered across its entire range.

The Bald Eagle

Almost everyone recognizes the bald eagle (Figure 8.6). Symbol of honor, courage, nobility, and indepen-

FIGURE 8.7

Peak counts of Aleutian Canada geese on wintering areas in California, 1975–2000

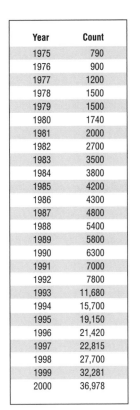

Year	Count
1975	790
1976	900
1977	1200
1978	1500
1979	1500
1980	1740
1981	2000
1982	2700
1983	3500
1984	3800
1985	4200
1986	4300
1987	4800
1988	5400
1989	5800
1990	6300
1991	7000
1992	7800
1993	11,680
1994	15,700
1995	19,150
1996	21,420
1997	22,815
1998	27,700
1999	32,281
2000	36,978

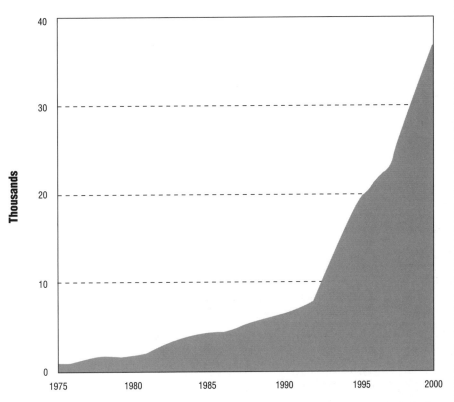

SOURCE: "Return of the Aleutian Canada Goose: Population Trends, 1975 to Present," U.S. Fish and Wildlife Service, Washington, DC, 2000 [Online] http://www.r7.fws.gov/media/acg.htm [Accessed June 5, 2002]

dence (eagles do not fly in flocks), the bald eagle is found only in North America, and its image is engraved on the official seal of the United States of America. There were an estimated 100,000 bald eagles in the Unites States in the late eighteenth century when the nation was founded.

The bald eagle nests over most of the United States and Canada, building its aerie, or nest, in mature conifer forests or on top of rocks or cliffs. Its nest is of such a grand size—sometimes as large as a small car—that a huge rock or tree is necessary to secure it. The birds use the same nest year after year, adding to it each nesting season. It is believed that eagles mate for life. Bald eagles prey primarily on fish, water birds, and turtles.

Bald eagles came dangerously close to extinction in the twentieth century, largely due to the pesticide DDT, which was introduced in 1947. Like other carnivorous species, bald eagles ingested large amounts of DDT from poisoned prey. DDT either prevents birds from laying eggs or causes the eggshells to be so thin they are unable to protect eggs until they hatch. The Bald Eagle Protection Act of 1940, which made it a federal offense to kill bald eagles, helped protect the species. However, numbers

continued to dwindle and the bald eagle was listed as endangered in 1967.

Bald eagle populations started to recover with the banning of DDT in 1972. The species also benefited from habitat protection and attempts to clean up water pollution. In 1995 the bald eagle was moved from endangered to threatened status on the Endangered Species List. In 2000, surveys showed that there were about 5,800 breeding pairs in the 48 contiguous states. The species was proposed for delisting in 1999, and that proposal is still awaiting action in 2002.

Aleutian Canada Goose

The Aleutian Canada goose was first placed on the Endangered Species List in 1966, when there were an estimated 800 individuals. The species had been thought extinct for several decades until a remnant population was discovered in 1962 by Fish and Wildlife biologists on a remote Aleutian island. Deterioration of habitat and the introduction of predators such as Arctic foxes and red foxes were blamed for the animal's decline. The goose population rebounded to 6,300 in 1991, and there were

TABLE 8.2

Decline and recovery of the Aleutian Canada goose population

1750	First known introduction of foxes onto Aleutian Islands.
1750-1936	Arctic foxes and red foxes introduced to at least 190 islands within the breeding range of the Aleutian Canada goose in Alaska.
1811	First complaints from Aleut Natives that foxes had caused severe declines in birds that had once been numerous.
1938-1962	Aleutian Canada geese were not found on any of the islands where they historically nested; thought to be extinct.
1962	Fish and Wildlife Service biologist found remnant population on remote Buldir Island in the western Aleutian Islands. Population estimated at between 200 and 300 birds.
1963	Goslings captured to start first captive flock for propogation.
March 1967	The Aleutian Canada goose was officially declared an endangered species under the Endangered Species Protection Act of 1966 (law that preceded the Endangered Species Act).
1971-1991	Captive-reared and translocated wild Aleutian Canada geese released on fox-free islands.
1973	Passage of the Endangered Species Act.
1973-1984	Hunting closures implemented for Aleutian Canada geese on wintering and breeding grounds.
1975	Recovery team begins developing formal recovery program. Spring population estimate 790 birds.
	Recovery actions implemented including the removal of foxes from breeding grounds on the Aleutian Islands and translocation of geese to unpopulated islands.
1984	Geese began to breed successfully on the islands. Foxes removed from four islands.
1990	Populations reached 6,300 geese.
December 1990	The Aleutian Canada goose was reclassified from endangered to the less imperiled threatened status. Recovery plan was revised, establishing objectives for measuring recovery and indicating when delisting was appropriate.
1990-1998	Recovery plans continue to be implemented. Population averages 20% annual growth rate.
1999	Populations reach more than 30,000 geese, over four times the original goal for delisting.
July 1999	The U.S. Fish and Wildlife Service proposed to delist the species, opening a 90 day public comment period.
	Fish and Wildlife Service evaluates comments.
March 2001	Fish and Wildlife Service removes the Aleutian Canada Goose from the list of endangered and threatened species. The goose will be managed and protected by the Migratory Bird Treaty Act.
	The FWS will continue to monitor the Aleutian Canada goose with the help of the states for five years.
	If populations decline significantly, the species can be relisted.
2005	If the status remains stable or improves, monitoring is no longer required under the ESA.

SOURCE: "Aleutian Canada Goose Road to Recovery," U.S. Fish and Wildlife Service, Washington, DC, 2001 [Online] http://www.r7.fws.gov/media/acg.htm [Accessed June 5, 2002]

well over 35,000 geese by 2002. Conservation efforts included captive breeding, removal of foxes, and relocation and reintroduction of geese to unoccupied islands. The Aleutian Canada goose was officially delisted by the Fish and Wildlife Service in 2001. A graph of population growth over time for this recovered species is shown in Figure 8.7. Table 8.2 shows some of the important events contributing to the recovery of this species.

CHAPTER 9
ENDANGERED INSECTS AND SPIDERS

Insects are the most diverse group in the animal kingdom, with close to a million named and described species and countless species yet to be discovered. However, insects have not been nearly as thoroughly studied as the vertebrate groups, and so there are likely to be many more endangered insects whose desperate state remains unrealized. Nonetheless, there are many insect species listed with the U.S. Fish and Wildlife Service under the Endangered Species Act. There are a total of 39 endangered (35 U.S., 4 foreign) and 9 threatened (all U.S.) insects. There are also 12 endangered arachnids (all U.S. species), a group related to insects that includes spiders, ticks, and mites. Some of the listed U.S. threatened and endangered insects and spiders are shown in Table 9.1.

There are also 555 threatened insect species listed in the *2000 IUCN Red List of Threatened Species* from the World Conservation Union. Most of the IUCN-listed species are butterflies, dragonflies, and damselflies, which are among the better-examined insect groups.

BUTTERFLIES

Like amphibians, many butterflies and moths are considered by scientists to be "indicator species" because they are particularly sensitive to environmental degradation. The decline of these species serves as a warning to human beings about the condition of the environment. Part of the reason butterflies are sensitive to many aspects of the environment is that these species undergo a drastic metamorphosis, or change, from larva to adult as a natural part of their life cycles. Butterfly larvae are generally crawling, herbivorous caterpillars, whereas butterfly adults fly and are nectar-eating. Butterfly species thrive only when intact habitats are available for both caterpillars and adults. Consequently, healthy butterfly populations tend to occur in areas with healthy ecosystems. Because many species are extremely sensitive to changing environmental conditions, the 20,000 known species of

moths and butterflies are carefully monitored by scientists and conservationists around the world.

Butterflies and moths have alerted scientists to numerous habitat changes. In southern Florida, for example, the sharp decline of swallowtail butterflies alerted biologists to the harm caused by mosquito sprays, as well as to the fact that pesticides had contaminated the water. In 1996 scien-

TABLE 9.1

Some of the insects and arachnids listed as endangered or threatened, April 23, 2002

Status	Species Name
E	Beetle, American burying (*Nicrophorus americanus*)
E	Beetle, Coffin Cave mold (*Batrisodes texanus*)
E	Beetle, Comal Springs dryopid (*Stygoparnus comalensis*)
E	Beetle, Comal Springs riffle (*Heterelmis comalensis*)
T	Beetle, delta green ground (*Elaphrus viridis*)
E	Beetle, Hungerford's crawling water (*Brychius hungerfordi*)
E	Beetle, Kretschmarr Cave mold (*Texamaurops reddelli*)
E	Beetle, Mount Hermon June (*Polyphylla barbata*)
E	Beetle, Tooth Cave ground (*Rhadine persephone*)
T	Beetle, valley elderberry longhorn (*Desmocerus californicus dimorphus*)
T	Butterfly, bay checkerspot (*Euphydryas editha bayensis*)
E	Butterfly, Behren's silverspot (*Speyeria zerene behrensii*)
E	Butterfly, callippe silverspot (*Speyeria callippe callippe*)
E	Butterfly, El Segundo blue (*Euphilotes battoides allyni*)
E	Butterfly, Fender's blue (*Icaricia icarioides fenderi*)
E	Butterfly, Karner blue (*Lycaeides melissa samuelis*)
E	Harvestman, Bee Creek Cave (*Texella reddelli*)
E	Harvestman, Bone Cave (*Texella reyesi*)
E	Harvestman, Robber Baron Cave (*Texella cokendolpheri*)
E	Pseudoscorpion, Tooth Cave (*Tartarocreagris texana*)
E	Spider, Government Canyon cave (*Neoleptoneta microps*)
E	Spider, Kauai cave wolf or pe'e pe'e maka'ole (*Adelocosa anops*)
E	Spider, Madla's cave (*Cicurina madla*)
E	Spider, Robber Baron Cave (*Cicurina baronia*)
E	Spider, spruce-fir moss (*Microhexura montivaga*)
E	Spider, Tooth Cave (*Neoleptoneta myopica*)
E	Spider, [unnamed] (*Cicurina venii*)
E	Spider, Vesper cave (*Cicurina vespera*)

SOURCE: "U.S. Listed Invertebrate Animal Species Report by Taxonomic Group," in *Species Information: Threatened and Endangered Animals and Plants,* U.S. Fish and Wildlife Service, Washington, DC, 2002 [Online] http://ecos.fws.gov/webpage/webpage_vip_listed.html?module=undefined&code=l&listings=0#I [accessed April 23, 2002]

tists in Michigan and England reported in the *Journal of Heredity* (September/October 1996), that during the 1960s, darker-colored moths began to predominate over light, white-and-black-flecked moths in polluted areas. This was seen in both England and the United States and was probably due to the fact that darker moths were better able to "blend in" to the dingy environment and hide from predators. In both countries, clean air laws were passed and decreases in pollution resulted. Now, in both countries, lighter-colored moths are again predominant. Dr. Douglas Futuyma, a biologist at the State University of New York at Stony Brook, reported that other insect species have shown increases in the proportion of darker-colored individuals in industrialized areas, a phenomenon called "industrial melanism." In those species, as well, the proportion of dark specimens drops as air quality improves.

In many cases, butterflies also help conservationists decide where to locate parks and nature refuges. Generally, the more varieties of butterflies that exist in an area, the more species of other animals and plants will live there too. Unfortunately, many butterfly species are disappearing around the world.

Monarch Butterflies

Historically, monarch butterflies migrated by the millions on a 3,000-mile journey up and down the North American continent. Over time, monarch butterfly populations have also become established in Australia and on the Pacific islands of Samoa and Tahiti. Other monarch populations have appeared in Hawaii and New Zealand.

For many years, naturalists sought to pinpoint the location where monarchs hibernate in January and February in preparation for their mating season and northward migration in March. In 1975, following an arduous search, a serene and delicate monarch hibernation area was located in the high altitude forests of the Michoacán Mountains in Mexico. Mexico declared the impoverished region a protected area. The inhabitants of the area turned the site into an ecotourist attraction in order to generate income for the economy. However, ecotourism not only failed to generate sufficient money to support the people of the area, but also caused severe habitat disruption. The onslaught of tourists affected habitats by introducing excessive noise, tobacco smoke, fire, and pollution. Monarch butterflies are now considered endangered by the IUCN. The U.S. Fish and Wildlife Service and the Mexican government have since attempted to nurture a self-sustaining economy in the monarch hibernation area by introducing fish breeding and horticulture.

In January 2002 a massive die-off of monarch butterflies in their wintering grounds in Mexico became major news worldwide. An estimated 250 million butterflies froze to death following a winter storm. As many as 80 percent of monarch colonies may have succumbed. While the storm may have been directly responsible for the deaths, deforestation and logging near the butterfly habitat are believed to have played a significant role. In particular, a fuller and healthier forest canopy would have better protected individuals from extreme weather. Despite the fact that butterfly hibernation areas are in protected reserves, logging continued there until recently. Although the massive die-off was a huge blow to monarch populations, many individuals did survive and it is hoped that the population will bounce back.

MONARCHS AND THE BIOPESTICIDES DEBATE. Monarch butterflies have also played an unwitting role in the recent debate regarding genetically modified foods. In an effort to reduce the amount of pesticides in the environment, plant geneticists have developed novel hybrid plants that are genetically altered to produce substances called biopesticides. These plants repel pests without additional application of pesticides. In order to create biopesticide-producing plants, scientists splice DNA for pesticidal proteins directly into plant genomes. The introduction of biopesticides generated great controversy in the 1990s, continuing into the 2000s. Proponents argued that biopesticides were much less toxic than chemical pesticides, and also claimed that biopesticides affected only targeted plant pests without affecting other consumer organisms. Opponents, however, feared that any genetically altered species posed potential unknown threats.

These fears were substantiated when researchers discovered that one genetic hybrid of corn, called Bt corn, is poisonous to monarch butterflies. Bt corn is genetically modified to include genes from a known pesticidal bacterium, *Bacillus thuringiensis*. Pesticidal proteins were genetically spliced into the corn genome to create a hybrid that repelled an important pest, the European corn borer. Bt corn was believed to be safe for the environment because it lacked toxins. Researchers reported, for example, that Bt corn had no effect on honeybees, ladybugs, or other organisms that inhabit cornfields. However, a new study reported in 1999 that in laboratory tests involving monarch caterpillars, as many as 44 percent of the caterpillars died after exposure to Bt corn.

Sacramento Mountains Checkerspot Butterflies

The Sacramento Mountains checkerspot butterfly has a highly specialized habitat—it occurs only in meadows at elevations of between 8,000 and 9,000 feet in southern New Mexico. Furthermore, the species is only found where there are native flowering plants, and is absent from meadows where invasive species have taken over. This is because Sacramento Mountains checkerspot caterpillars feed solely on native plant species such as the New Mexico penstemon. The Sacramento Mountains checkerspot is characterized by brown, red, orange, and white checked wings.

The Sacramento Mountains checkerspot is currently proposed for listing as endangered in its entire range. The species was first petitioned for listing by the Center for Biodiversity in 1999. Surveys of population sizes took place between 1997 and 2000 and revealed that the species occurs only in fragmented populations within a 33-square-mile area in New Mexico. The butterfly was officially proposed for listing in 2001. It is threatened primarily by loss of habitat due to urban development and destruction of habitat by off-road vehicles and overgrazing. In addition, several invasive plant species are taking over meadows once occupied by native plant species used by Sacramento Mountains checkerspot caterpillars. Finally, over-collection of specimens has harmed populations. A critical habitat of 5,000 acres is being proposed for the species, half of which is on federal property and half of which lies on private property.

OTHER ENDANGERED INSECTS

Zayante Band-Winged Grasshopper

Insects, like numerous other species, suffer from diminished habitat as a result of encroaching development, industrialization, and changing land use patterns. In California's Santa Cruz Mountains, the tiny Zayante band-winged grasshopper, barely half an inch long, occupies areas containing abundant high-quality silica sand, known as Zayante or Santa Margarita sand. This sand is valuable for making glass and fiberglass products, and several businesses have entered the area in the hope of capitalizing on this. The Zayante band-winged grasshopper joined the ranks of listed endangered species in January 1997. In 2000, as a result of a lawsuit filed by the Center for Biological Diversity, the Fish and Wildlife Service proposed the establishment of critical habitat for the grasshopper.

Hine's Emerald Dragonfly

The Hine's emerald dragonfly has been listed as an endangered species since 1995 and is found in federal and state preserves and National Forest lands in Illinois, Wisconsin, Michigan, and Missouri. In earlier times, its range extended through portions of Ohio, Alabama, and Indiana as well. The Hine's emerald dragonfly has a metallic-green body and emerald-green eyes. It is considered a biological indicator species because it is extremely sensitive to water pollution. The decline of this dragonfly species has resulted primarily from loss of suitable wetland habitat, such as wet prairies, marshes, sedge meadows, and fens occurring over dolomite rock. (The lakeside daisy is another species damaged by the decline of these habitats—it is listed as threatened.)

Wetland habitats support dragonflies during their aquatic larval period, which lasts some three to four years. Adult dragonflies occupy open areas and forest edges near wetland habitats, where they feed on invertebrate species such as mosquitoes. Hine's emerald dragonflies also serve as prey for a variety of bird and fish species. The recovery plan for the dragonfly includes measures to protect current habitat as well as reintroduction of the species to portions of its former range. Private companies that own land supporting dragonfly populations have aided conservation efforts by monitoring populations and preserving important habitat areas.

Ohlone Tiger Beetle

The Ohlone tiger beetle was listed as endangered in October 2001. The species was discovered in 1987 and is found only in Santa Cruz County, California. The Ohlone tiger beetle is a small species, about half an inch long, with spotted metallic green wings and copper-green legs. Both adults and larvae hunt invertebrate prey. The Ohlone tiger beetle occupies a total of less than 20 acres of remnant native coastal prairie habitat on state land, private land, and property belonging to the University of California at Santa Cruz. The species declined due to habitat loss and habitat fragmentation resulting from urban development, as well as over-collection, pollution from pesticides, and the increasing encroachment of invasive plant species. The petition to list the Ohlone tiger beetle with the Fish and Wildlife Service was originally made by a private citizen in 1997.

ENDANGERED SPIDERS

Kauai Cave Wolf Spider

The Kauai cave wolf spider is a blind species found only in special caves on the southern part of the island of Kauai in Hawaii. Several cave areas were proposed as critical habitat for this and other endangered cave species, including the Kauai cave amphipod, in 2002. Caves occupied by the Kauai cave wolf spider and Kauai cave amphipod are formed by young lava flows.

Unlike most other spiders, the Kauai cave wolf spider hunts prey directly. Its prey includes the (also highly endangered) Kauai cave amphipod. Both species were originally listed as endangered by the Fish and Wildlife Service in January 2000. Female cave wolf spiders lay some 15 to 30 eggs per clutch, and carry young on their backs after hatching. Cave species are extremely sensitive to changes in temperature and light. It is feared that official designation of critical habitat by the Fish and Wildlife Service will make the delicate cave systems more prone to human use, resulting in damage from activity including light pollution, garbage (which may attract new species to the caves), and cigarette smoke.

Spruce-fir Moss Spider

The Spruce-fir moss spider is an endangered spider related to the tarantula. It was placed on the Endangered Species List in 1995. Spruce-fir moss spiders live in moss mats found only in the vicinity of Fraser fir trees. Its populations have declined largely due to the introduction in the United States of an invasive European insect species, the balsam-wooly adelgid. The balsam-wooly adelgid infests Fraser fir trees, causing them to die within a time period of two to seven years. With the death of numerous fir trees, other forest trees have also blown over. The resulting increase in light level and temperature causes the moss mats on which spruce-fir moss spiders depend to dry up. The Fish and Wildlife Service designated critical habitat for the species in 2001, including areas in the Great Smoky Mountains National Park and the Pisgah and Cherokee National Forests, as well as a preserve managed by The Nature Conservancy. This designation of critical habitat followed a lawsuit against the Fish and Wildlife Service, which had previously deemed designating critical habitat "not prudent" because it believed the spider would be more vulnerable to collectors.

CHAPTER 10

COMMERCIAL TRADE OF WILDLIFE

Humans have used wild animal and plant products for a variety of purposes since prehistoric times. Clothing was often made from animal skins, and tools from bones. In many societies, products from rare species symbolized wealth and success. For example, flashy feathers from South American birds were given as a tribute to Inca chiefs by their subjects. Coonskin caps crowned American explorers, while women in nineteenth-century Europe sported ostrich feathers in their hats. East Asians have long used powders and ointments prepared from animal parts as medicines and aphrodisiacs. Exotic species have also been kept as pets—cheetahs and falcons, for example, were kept for hunting. In addition, many species, including dogs, cats, apes, monkeys, frogs, guinea pigs, rats, and mice, are commonly used for scientific research.

Sadly, overexploitation of wild species for commercial gain is the second most important cause of animal extinction, after habitat loss. According to the World Conservation Union's *2000 IUCN Red List of Threatened Species*, hunting, collection, and trade affect 37 percent of all bird species, 34 percent of mammals, and 8 percent of surveyed plant species. Once non-domesticated animal species are considered to be commodities, they have an extremely high likelihood of becoming endangered. A small subset of endangered species currently affected by trade include whales hunted for meat and blubber; exotic birds captured for the illegal pet trade; rhinos poached for their horns; minks killed for their pelts; snakes, alligators, and lizards hunted for their skins; and elephants slaughtered for their ivory tusks. The argalis (Figure 10.1) is a species of wild sheep endangered because trophy hunters seek its massive horns. Figure 10.2 shows numerous confiscated products made from endangered species.

THE FUR, FEATHERS, AND LEATHER TRADE

Numerous wild animal species are hunted for their fur pelts or leather hides. These are used to make coats, hats, shoes, gloves, belts, purses, and other accessories. This has led to the near extermination of mammalian and reptilian species such as minks, foxes, beavers, seals, alligators and crocodiles, chinchillas, otters, and wild cats. Birds were once hunted for fashion as well—species of egrets, herons, spoonbills, and songbirds were slaughtered by the thousands to supply plumes for women's hats during the nineteenth century.

Beginning in the nineteenth century, the fur industry turned increasingly to domestically raised animals, finding it too economically risky to leave the acquisition of pelts to chance. Fur farms opened on Prince Edward Island in Canada in 1887 and quickly spread across the country. At their height, there were well over 10,000 fur farms. By 1939, however, rising costs, the loss of European markets, and changes in fashion reduced fur demand. Canadian fur farms were reduced to less than 2,000 primarily mink farms by the middle of the twentieth century. In August 1998 animal rights activists in England, unhappy with fur farm practices, released thousands of minks from cages. The minks escaped into the district of New Forest, where they wrought havoc on natural habitats and attacked chicken farms. Many were eventually trapped and killed.

In 2000 the world market for shahtoosh, the wool of the Tibetan chiru antelope, came under scrutiny by both the U.S. Fish and Wildlife Service and the Convention on International Trade in Endangered Species of Wild Fauna and Flora (CITES). Measures were adopted at the CITES meeting in Nairobi, Kenya that year to reduce chiru poaching. The Fish and Wildlife Service also proposed listing the chiru as an endangered species, but this had yet to happen in 2002. The chiru is listed as vulnerable by the IUCN.

Crocodilian Leathers

Among the most biologically costly of fashion trends is the use of reptilian hide for leather shoes, belts, wallets,

FIGURE 10.1

The argalis is prized by hunters for its massive horns. *(Corbis Corporation)*

and other accessories. High fashion has never tired of the look and feel of tanned crocodilian leather, with alligator skin the most popular of all reptile hides. Louisiana's Department of Agriculture estimates that 90 percent of alligator hide originates in the United States, particularly from the bayou regions of Louisiana. The skins are exported to France for tanning; most are then shipped to Italy, where alligator hide accounts for more than half of the reptilian skins used by fashion designers. During its first year of operation in the mid-1990s, Roggwiller Tannery of Louisiana (RTL) shipped 20,000 tons of crocodilian hide to its parent company in Vivoin, France. RTL estimates that it ships 25 percent of all hides harvested in Louisiana. French tanners, in turn, ship an estimated 63,000 tons of processed hides to Italy every year—including alligator, crocodile, and caiman—of which 70 percent originates in the United States. Finished products are costly, with alligator purses selling for $200–$1,000 apiece.

Largely because of the demand of European designers for alligator hide, the American alligator was first listed as an endangered species in 1967. It was reclassified as threatened in the 1970s as populations recovered in response to conservation efforts. The American alligator was finally delisted after recovery in 1987. As a result of

their one time endangerment, Fish and Wildlife representatives continue to monitor the egg harvesting and hunting, particularly in Louisiana.

Huia Birds—Plucked to Extinction

Unlike American alligators, which were brought back from endangerment, the fate of the Huia bird was more tragic. The beautiful Huia, native to New Zealand, was hunted to extinction during the 1920s, mostly because of demand for adornments made from its luxurious feathers. The species was characterized by black plumes with striking white tips. In addition, Huia feathers figured prominently in the native Maori culture of New Zealand, and Maoris hunted the species as well. The Huia was declared extinct in 1930.

COLLECTORS OF RARE AND EXOTIC SPECIES

A wide variety of wild species are valued by collectors, including spiders, insects such as beetles or butterflies, and plants, particularly orchids and cacti. Rare species are particularly sought after. For that reason Fish and Wildlife biologists are sometimes reluctant to reveal the critical habitats of threatened and endangered species in the United States. Despite strict prohibition under the

FIGURE 10.2

Many species are endangered primarily because human beings value their hides or other body parts. This photo shows a number of items that were made out of endangered species. *(Environmental Investigation Agency)*

Endangered Species Act, however, the poaching of numerous imperiled species thrives.

Exotic species including wild birds, reptiles, and mammals are also valued in the illegal pet trade. According to CITES, for example, approximately 40,000 primates were illegally traded annually in the 1990s. Animal smuggling is an extremely lucrative business, and international efforts to halt it have not been successful. This is attributed in large part to shoddy or nonexistent inspection due to lack of funds and manpower.

The Reptile Trade

The reptile trade is extremely lucrative, with large profits and low transport costs. In addition, trade in reptiles is less closely controlled and monitored than that of mammals and birds. Illegally collected reptiles are used primarily for food, although some species also bring in huge sums in the pet trade.

In 1998 decades of effort by U.S. and Mexican agents culminated in the apprehension of a Malaysian reptile smuggler in Mexico City. He was convicted of heading a large smuggling operation that procured live threatened and endangered reptiles from the wild for sale as exotic pets. Animals were transported from Asia into North America via Mexico. Between 1995 and 1998 this smuggling ring was estimated to have brought in over 300 protected animals worth about $500,000. These included a Chinese alligator that sold for $15,000 on the black market, monitor lizards that brought in $3,000 apiece, and a 10-foot Komodo dragon from Indonesia that sold for $30,000.

In March 2001 the Malaysian Department of Wildlife and National Parks and the Royal Customs and Excise announced the interception of two large shipments of threatened reptiles. The first included 1,100 animals, and the second included 61 rare snakes, tortoises, and spiders.

Some exotic reptiles, including green iguanas and boa constrictors, can be legally obtained and kept as pets. However, many of the owners who acquire these animals fail to realize the responsibilities involved. Giant green iguanas, a favorite of reptile collectors, may grow to six feet in length, a size many owners find unmanageable. Giant green iguanas are also particularly susceptible to metabolic bone disease (MBD), which results from calcium deficiency and causes severe deformity or death. Although MBD can be cured, treatment is costly, and pet

FIGURE 10.3

Many tropical birds, including this scarlet macaw, are sought as exotic pets. *(Field Mark Publications)*

owners frequently decide to get rid of their pets rather than seek veterinary care. In addition some owners dispose of overgrown or diseased reptilian pets in sewers or other public conduits, creating dangers for native species. (This is the source of long-time rumors that alligators inhabit New York City sewers.)

Illegal Trade of Wild Birds

Human desire for exotic pets is emptying the skies of some of Earth's most colorful creatures. (See Figure 10.3.) Numerous bird species, particularly parrots, are endangered due to overexploitation for the illegal pet trade. Approximately 75 percent of the exotic birds sold as pets in the United States were caught in the wild rather than bred in captivity. Demand for exotic pets results in very high prices, as much as $10,000 or more for certain species. In the United States, a single parrot can easily command a thousand dollars or more. Table 10.1 shows some of the potential profits to be made in the rare bird trade.

Illegal trade in birds is thriving worldwide. Due to a lack of financial resources, most countries are only rarely able to enforce laws designed to control trade. The European community has no enforcement agency to deal with the issue, and the Fish and Wildlife Service is grossly underfunded in this respect. Illegal traders often use legal trade as a cover, relying on falsification of documents, under-declaration of the number of birds in a shipment, concealment of illegal birds in legal shipments, capture in excess of quotas, and misdeclaration of species. The United States, the largest importer of wild birds in the world, legally brings half a million exotic birds into the country each year. An estimated 100,000 more may be smuggled into the country, with as many as 60 percent of the birds dying in transit because of the frequently terrible shipping conditions. Illegal smuggling continues despite the passage of the Wild Bird Conservation Act in 1992, which banned the import of ten species of threatened birds. In 1993 the law was expanded to include almost all CITES-listed bird species.

Bird trapping methods vary from country to country. Most are indiscriminate and result in the capture of untargeted species. In liming, a "teaser" bird lures other birds to trees, where they become stuck on limes, or glued sticks. Liming causes great stress to captured birds. In addition, limes are sometimes set and left, with the result that birds break legs or wings struggling to get loose. Nets are also used to capture wild birds in Latin America and Africa. Decoy birds are used to attract the target species. In night capture, birds are immobilized using a bright light and caught. Nylon loops are sometimes strung around perches to entangle birds. As with liming, nylon loops are indiscriminate in their capture of birds, and many birds are seriously injured attempting to escape. In fact, in Indonesia 10 to 30 percent of cockatoos caught with nylon loops are rendered commercially nonviable because of injuries to their legs and feet. In wing shooting, pellets are shot into a flock, rendering some birds unable to fly and easy to capture. More birds are killed than captured in the process, and many of the captured individuals die later. Finally, young birds are sometimes taken from the nest. This method, also called tree-felling, is used to acquire parrots from the wild because pet dealers prefer young birds that can more easily be trained to "talk." The parrots' nesting tree is often cut down or hacked apart, rendering it useless as future habitat. Consequently, this is one of the most environmentally destructive methods of capture.

Tropical Fish

Collection of tropical fish species for the aquarium trade has harmed numerous species. In Hawaii, a major supplier of saltwater species for the aquarium market, fish depletion has led to conflicts between tropical reef fish collectors, scuba diving operations, and subsistence fish-

TABLE 10.1

Profits to be made in the rare-bird trade

Country and species	Price for trapper	Exporter declared value	Exporter price list	Retail value in importing country
Senegal				
Quelea	$0.09	N/A	0.50	22
Senegal parrot	$1.82	4	2.70	115
Tanzania				
Meyer's parrot	$2.10	7	17.25	105
Guyana				
Blue and Gold macaw	$5.00	175	325	750
Orange-winged Amazon	$2-3.00	25	32	298
Argentina				
Blue-fronted Amazon	$1.20-3.50	23	70-136	340
Red lory	$2.52	18	15-20	230
White cockatoo	$6.50	85	100	800-900

SOURCE: "Profits to be Made in the Rare-Bird Trade," in *Flight to Extinction—The Wild-Caught Bird Trade,* Animal Welfare Institute and Environmental Investigation Agency, Washington, DC, 1997

ers. Lisa Choquette, the owner of a scuba tour business, explains that "areas that we take divers to all the time, and that once had rivers of fish swimming in and out of the corals, are now quite barren." In addition, several tropical species collected as tiny juveniles for the aquarium trade ultimately grow into large fish sought by subsistence fishermen. Exploitation of reef fish for trade has increased over the past decades, from 90,000 fish taken in 1973 to over 423,000 in 1995. Aquarium species collected most commonly in Hawaii include the yellow tang, kole, Achilles tang, longnose butterfly fish, Moorish idol, orangespine unicornfish, and Potter's angelfish. Fish populations have declined significantly in locations where aquarium collection occurs. For example, the Achilles tang has declined by 63 percent and the longnose butterfly fish by 54 percent.

In response to these declines, Hawaii passed a bill establishing several Fish Replenishment Areas where collecting is prohibited. Biologists are also trying to develop captive breeding programs, so that aquarium species can be raised in captivity rather than collected from the wild.

HEALTH REMEDIES AND FADS

Numerous populations of both animals and plants are being depleted for medicinal purposes. At the top of wildlife contraband lists are aphrodisiacs and arthritis cures made from rhinoceros and tiger parts (none of which has been shown to be effective). In 1992 the Fish and Wildlife Service seized over $500,000 worth of East Asian medicines containing endangered species parts at the Port of Newark in New Jersey. According to a 1996 report from the Environmental News Network, illicit trade in medicinal substances is a booming business in Hong Kong, where there is little that money can't buy. Table 10.2 shows a list of endangered animal parts found in a single market in Golden Rock, Myanmar during a brief study in 2000. The study was conducted by TRAFFIC, a wildlife advocacy

and monitoring organization sponsored jointly by the World Wildlife Fund and the World Conservation Union (IUCN). Table 10.2 also lists the reasons why these animal products are valued by locals. Most of the documented animal products at Golden Rock were from mammals, though some were derived from reptiles or birds.

Threats to African Wildlife

Numerous African species are seriously threatened by demand for medicinal ingredients. Of East African and South African wildlife alone, a total of 131 plant and animal species required attention by conservation management organizations in 1998.

Over 100 African plant species were cited by TRAFFIC as overexploited and in need of conservation management. This included the Sudanese *Aloe sinkatana*, whose leaves and leaf excretions are used for treating skin disorders and diseases of the digestive system. *Adansonia digitata*, a tree, is also in decline because its fruit and bark are used in treating dysentery. The bark of the afromontane tree species, *Prunus africana*, is also overexploited for treatment of prostate gland diseases. Over one thousand tons of *P. africana* bark were exported from Kenya between 1990 and 1998. France imported four tons of *P. africana* extract from Madagascar. CITES initiated international trade control of this tree species in 1994.

At least 100 animal species are used in traditional medicine in eastern and southern Africa. Among the animals most threatened by medicinal trade is the African rock python, whose skin contains an agent used in the treatment of sexually transmitted diseases and back pain. The Cape pangolin, a rare species of horny "scaled" mammal, is prized by shamans who use the scales to make charms and talismans. The African wild ass is exploited for blood, meat, and fat, all of which are valued for a variety of curative powers by the Eritreans of

TABLE 10.2

Observations during survey of Golden Rock, Myanmar, April 16–17, 2000

Species		Part	Quantity	Use	Price	National law	Cites
Asiatic Black Bear	*Ursus thibetanus*	skins	5			P	I
		paws	29	Oil for treating aching joints	K 2000 each		
		rendered fat	numerous	To improve hair condition and white skin patches	K 600/bottle		
		skulls	8	Drink made from the paste to treat childrens'mouth diseases			
Cat	*Felis sp?*	gall bladder	5	Oil for treating aching joints	K 5000 each		I/II
Leopard	*Panthera pardus*	small skulls	numerous				I
		paws	20				
		head	2				
		skin	1				
Leopard or Clouded Leopard	*Panthera pardus* *Neofelis nebulosa*	penis and testes	1	Stimulate sex hormones		TP TP	I I
Tiger	*Panthera tigris*	skeleton	5	To protect the home	K 2500 each	TP	
		canines	2	unknown			
		bone pieces	4				
		horns	2				
		skins	7				
Common Palm Civet	*Paradoxurus hermaphroditus*	head	13	Oil for treating aching joints		P	III
		skin	1				
		stuffed	1	Ornament			
Civet?		skin	4				
Dolphin	*Cetacea*	skin with fins and fat layer	2	Oil for treating aching joints		?	I/II
Elephant	*Elephas maximus*	sole of foot	6	Paste applied to skin to cure hernias		*TP	I
		skin (pieces)	25	To cure fungal skin infections			
		tail hair	numerous	Rings worn to protect against supernatural attack/to attract women			
		tail	2	Hung in the home to bring business success			
		leg bones	1.5	Carving material. Paste to cure piles			
		bones	numerous	Carved into beads for Buddhist prayer necklaces	K 100 each		
		molars	5	Carved into figurines			
			22				

TABLE 10.2

Observations during survey of Golden Rock, Myanmar, April 16–17, 2000 [CONTINUED]

Species		Part	Quantity	Use	Price	National law	Cites
Macaque	*Macaca* sp.	skull	33	Oil/ornamental purposes			II
Otter	*Lutra* or *Aonyx* sp.	charred body	1	Oil for treating aching joints		TP	I/II
		head	1	Oil for treating aching joints			
Pangolin	*Manis* sp.	skins	3	Treatment for children's diseases: scales hung on a string around a child's neck		TP	II
Porcupine	*Hystrix* sp.	quills	numerous	Quills dipped in lime are used in light acupuncture (without breaking skin) on back of neck to cure headaches			
Serow	*Capricornis sumatraensis*	heads	34	Manufacture of traditional buttons		not protected	III
		skulls	10	Oil for treating aching joints		TP	I
		legs	4	Oil for treating aching joints			
Wild Pig	*Sus* sp.	skull	3	Oil for treating aching joints			
Squirrel		tails	20	Ornament and possibly medicine			
Squirrel	*Callosciurus* sp.	stuffed	1	Key-chains			
Giant Flying Squirrel	*Petaurista* sp.	charred body	2	Ornament		not protected	–
Treeshrew	*Tupia* sp.	stuffed	3	Oil for treating aching joints		not protected	–
Giant squirrel	*Ratufa* sp.	stuffed	2	Ornament		P	II
Reticulated Python	*Python reticulatus*	skins	26	Ornament		not protected	II
Rock Python	*Python molurus*	skins	8	Sold to visiting middlemen for onward sale to leather factories	Approx. K 700/metre	TP	II
Python	*Python* sp.	meat	15	As above		P	
				Oil for treating aching joints			
Elongated Tortoise	*Indotestudo elongata*	shell	1	Manufacture of combs according to dealer, although this is questionable		P	II
Great Hornbill	*Buceros bicornis*	head	4	Ornament		TP	I
		skin	2	Ornament			
		shell	1	Oil applied to white skin blotches			

TP: totally protected; P: protected; SP: seasonally protected; *unless a domesticated elephant
K: Kyat (currency)

SOURCE: "Table 1. Observations during survey of Golden Rock, 16–17 April, 2000," in "Observations on Wildlife Trade at Golden Rock, Myanmar," *TRAFFIC Bulletin*, Vol. 19, num. 1, 2001

northeastern Africa. The green turtle, found in Kenya, is illegally traded for the pharmaceutical effects of its oil and genitalia.

Traditional Chinese Medicine

Numerous Chinese medicines are made from the parts of endangered species. The true extent of this trade is unknown—however, informed sources estimate that the industry is worth several billion dollars a year. In Taiwan, for example, rhinoceros horns are twice as valuable as gold. Although no studies have ever demonstrated the medicinal value of rhinoceros horn, numerous Asians believe it has magical curative powers. Rhino populations have declined worldwide as a result of poaching for the medicinal trade.

In the United States, at least 430 different East Asian medicines containing body parts of endangered or threatened species have been documented. According to a study by the World Wildlife Fund, such products are in fact more readily available on store shelves in the United States than in China. The products seen most frequently are tiger bone-containing remedies for arthritis and other muscular ailments. In 1994 the United States passed the Rhinoceros and Tiger Conservation Act to curtail trade of these products. A 1998 amendment to the act, the Rhino and Tiger Labeling Law, closed a loophole in the original legislation by empowering the Fish and Wildlife Service to remove products from store shelves based solely on labeling claims and without forensic proof that the content included tiger or rhinoceros parts. The revised statute also established prison terms of up to six months and fines of up to $12,000 for violations. Additionally, the amendment called for the establishment of outreach programs to promote public awareness of this issue.

BUSH MEAT

"Bush meat" refers to meat obtained from wild species. Trade in wild meat threatens numerous species in Africa, South America, and Asia. According to a 2001 report by TRAFFIC, wild meat in Africa is obtained from species such as "elephants, gorillas, chimpanzees and other primates, forest antelopes (duikers), crocodiles, porcupines, bush pigs, cane rats, pangolins, monitor lizards, and guinea fowl." Most of the trade occurs on a regional to national scale. However, some meat is exported, particularly to European countries. Officials have seized several illegal shipments at European airports including meat from protected monkeys, pangolins, tortoises, and antelopes. In addition, two London shopkeepers were convicted in 2001 for selling meat from CITES-listed species such as monkeys, savanna monitors, and African pythons. At the 2000 CITES meeting, a group was established to address the issue of unsustainable bush meat exploitation.

ANIMALS USED FOR RESEARCH

The use of animals for scientific and medical research is both common and controversial. Under the Animal Welfare Act (AWA) of 1966 and its amendments, the Animal and Plant Health Inspection Service (APHIS) of the U.S. Department of Agriculture is responsible for reporting on species used in research. APHIS reported that in 2000 over 1.4 million animals were used for research purposes in the United States. (See Figure 10.4.) This figure does not include the large numbers of rats, mice, and birds used in research, however, as the AWA does not require that these be tracked.

The AWA requires that animals kept for research purposes be treated humanely. However, it does not place restrictions on how animals can be used in valid experiments. It does call for the limitation of pain and suffering if doing so will not interfere with the experiment. However, many research animals experience pain or distress nonetheless. (See Figure 10.5.)

For decades, some animal rights organizations have protested the use of animals in research. Activists argue that the vast majority of animal research, if not all of it, is cruel and unnecessary. Activists also argue that, despite laws like the AWA, many research animals live in inhumane environments. Although large-scale animal research continues, animal rights and anti-cruelty organizations have had some successes. Many businesses have stopped testing their products on animals and advertise them as "cruelty-free."

Most animal research is conducted on domesticated species, whose numbers are adequate to support this use. A major exception, however, is the primates.

Research and the Primate Trade

The primate trade dates back thousands of years. Mesopotamians used monkey bones to make drugs, and Egyptians trained baboons to harvest figs. Today, however, primates are particularly valued by medical researchers because they are closely related to humans. Because of this, primates such as chimpanzees and rhesus monkeys are regularly used for medical, chemical, and even nuclear testing. In 2000 scientists in the United States used 57,518 primates for research. (See Figure 10.4.)

According to CITES, 40,000 primates are traded internationally every year for biomedical research. Most of this takes place in industrial nations—the United States, United Kingdom, and Japan are the top primate-importing countries. While the results of this research are sometimes of medical value, numerous animals suffer, and many primate populations are in severe decline. All non-human primate species are listed under either CITES Appendix I (Species in Danger of Extinction) or Appendix II (Species Threatened in the Absence of Trade Controls).

FIGURE 10.4

FIGURE 10.5

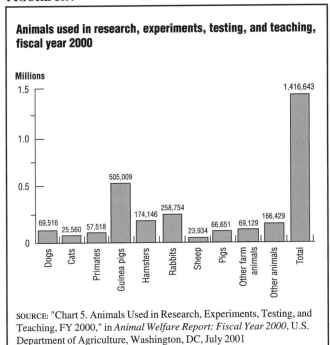

Animals used in research, experiments, testing, and teaching, fiscal year 2000

SOURCE: "Chart 5. Animals Used in Research, Experiments, Testing, and Teaching, FY 2000," in *Animal Welfare Report: Fiscal Year 2000*, U.S. Department of Agriculture, Washington, DC, July 2001

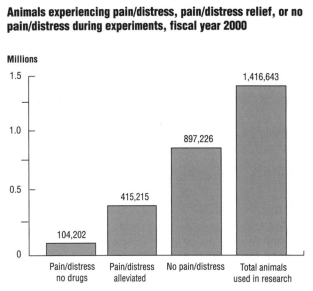

Animals experiencing pain/distress, pain/distress relief, or no pain/distress during experiments, fiscal year 2000

SOURCE: "Chart 6: Animals Experiencing Pain/Distress, Pain/Distress Relief, or No Pain/Distress During Experiments, FY 2000," in *Animal Welfare Report: Fiscal Year 2000,* U.S. Department of Agriculture, Washington, DC, July, 2001.

The discovery of acquired immunodeficiency syndrome (AIDS) in the 1980s made primates, particularly chimpanzees, even more valuable to the medical research industry. Pressure on chimpanzee populations due to collection for medical research prompted primatologists to petition the Fish and Wildlife Service to upgrade chimpanzees from threatened to endangered. Fearing opposition from the medical community, the Fish and Wildlife Service compromised, declaring in 1990 that wild chimpanzees in their natural range in Central and West Africa would be listed as endangered, while captive populations outside the natural range would be listed as threatened.

BREEDING PRIMATES FOR SCIENCE AND RESEARCH. Since the 1970s most countries harboring wild primate populations have restricted the export of these animals. Indonesia and the Philippines, which once supplied 50 to 80 percent of all internationally traded primates, adopted export bans in 1994. These bans have helped restore native populations. As a result, the demand for primates for medical research is increasingly being met through captive breeding. China has been a major source of captive-bred rhesus monkeys for the United States and Europe since 1988. Barbados, which has the largest monkey colony in the Northern Hemisphere, supplies a steady flow of primates for research purposes. Vietnam has also developed as an export center for captive-bred primates. However, some officials claim that many primates shipped from Vietnam were actually caught in the wild.

In the United States, many of the 1,800 chimpanzees used for research were owned and bred by Dr. Frederick Coulston at the Coulston Foundation in Alamogordo,

New Mexico. The foundation is federally funded in part and uses chimpanzees to study aging and the diseases of age, including arthritis, Alzheimer's disease, diabetes, senility, and Parkinson's disease. With some 650 chimpanzees, the Coulston Foundation colony is the largest of its kind in the world.

WORLD "LEADERS" IN WILDLIFE TRADE

The United States—A Consuming Giant

In 1994 the Fish and Wildlife Service reported that U.S. wildlife trade represented a $20 billion market, including an estimated $5 billion in illegal trade—this is despite U.S. claims to leadership in the protection of threatened plant and animal species. Although the U.S. undeniably has some of the most promising legislation in the world regarding wildlife trade, the insatiable demand of American consumers, plus inadequate resources for law enforcement, has created a booming trade. The most alarming aspect of this trade is Americans' desire for exotic birds—particularly Amazonian parrots, African gray parrots, and Indonesian cockatoos—precisely those bird species most endangered by trade.

Bird smuggling is a particular problem along the Texas-Mexico border. In 1994 federal officials uncovered what they believed to be one of the nation's largest parrot-smuggling operations and seized $70,000 worth of smuggled birds from a Mexican gang. However, this represented only a tiny part of a huge smuggling market responsible for the illegal importation of between 25,000 and 150,000 birds each year. In 1996 a parrot expert named Tony Silva was convicted of smuggling $1.4 million worth of endangered parrots. This included the highly endangered hyacinth macaw, of which only 2,000–5,000 individuals remain in the wild. Because of their rarity, hyacinth macaws are valued at $12,000 each by unscrupulous collectors. In 1997 Adolph Pare of Miami, Florida was sentenced to a year in prison and fined $300,000 for attempting to smuggle 4,000 African gray parrots illegally collected in the Democratic Republic of Congo (formerly Zaire) into the United States. He had obtained fake CITES permits for the parrots.

In 1996 the Fish and Wildlife Service also uncovered an illegal trade operation involving bald eagles. The investigation culminated in the arrest of eight men. Citations were also issued against eight tourist shops in the Four Corners region of Arizona, Colorado, New Mexico, and Utah, where bald eagle carcasses were being sold for $1,000 apiece. FWS also reported that more than 60 bald and golden eagles were shot or trapped that winter to feed the demand for feathers, wings, tails, and talons. Numerous tourist centers were fined for selling eagle feathers, prohibited under the Bald and Golden Eagle Protection Act. This law, originally passed in 1940, prohibits all trade in bald and golden eagle parts without a permit. A 1972 amendment to the act raised the maximum fine for some crimes to half a million dollars.

Asia and the Pacific Rim—A Black Hole for Endangered Species

The failure of some Asian countries—particularly China, Japan, South Korea, and Taiwan—to curtail illegal trade has combined with economic growth in the Far East to produce a huge demand for numerous endangered species and their products. Although some effort has recently been made to enforce CITES regulations within Asia, officials have had difficulty combating entrenched organized crime networks. Nor are cultural habits, such as the use of endangered species products in many traditional Chinese medicines, easily changed.

CHINA. With a population in excess of 1.26 billion in 2002, China has become one of the world's largest consumers of wildlife and endangered species. The massive growth in wildlife consumption in China is matched by growth in the export and import of endangered species, their parts, and medicines derived from them. Despite the threat of sanctions by CITES and the United States, the Chinese government has largely turned its back on the growing illegal trade. Furthermore, corruption is widespread. A number of investigations have revealed the involvement of government stores and officials in the sale of restricted products.

INDONESIA. Indonesia legally exports between 58,000 and 91,000 birds each year, primarily cockatoos, lories, and other psittacines (birds belonging to the parrot family). Countless others are exported illegally. Approximately 126 avian species native to Indonesia are threatened because of trade or habitat destruction.

JAPAN. With a population in excess of 127 million in 2002, Japan has one of the highest per capita levels of wildlife consumption in the world. Japan also persists in aggressively campaigning for increased consumption of some types of endangered wildlife. At the 2000 meeting of the International Whaling Commission (IWC), for example, it joined forces with Norway in an effort to eliminate bans against commercial whaling. Moreover, Japan has lobbied CITES for increased wildlife trade. Japan's population of black bears is listed on CITES Appendix I, and its brown bear on Appendix II. Domestic trade in bears (not regulated by CITES, which only deals with international trade) is nonetheless both legal and completely unregulated. Up to one-fifth of Japan's black bear population is killed each year.

VIETNAM. In the late 1990s Vietnam was one of the worst offenders in the trade of rare and endangered species. Although the country joined CITES in 1994, little change resulted in the absence of rigid enforcement policies. As other countries in Southeast Asia tightened controls on wildlife smuggling, Vietnam welcomed trade and turned itself into the largest endangered species market in the world. In market stalls in Ho Chi Minh City, a wide variety of wildlife, both dead and alive, fills the streets.

The Americas

ARGENTINA. Argentina is the largest world supplier of wild psittacines (birds related to parrots), shipping between 63,000 and 183,000 individuals each year and threatening the continued survival of numerous species. The extent of illegal traffic is difficult to determine. In addition, tree-felling, a method for collecting young birds from nests, is causing extensive habitat destruction. The blue-fronted Amazon parrot accounts for 27 percent of the country's bird trade.

GUYANA. Guyana officially exports between 15,000 and 19,000 birds each year, including some valuable macaws. The country ranks, along with Senegal, Tanzania, Argentina, and Indonesia, among the top five exporters of wild birds for the international market. National legislation in Guyana allows for the capture of any species, regardless of its conservation status, and inspectors have documented the trade of dozens of rare scarlet macaws.

Africa

NIGERIA. Poachers trap or shoot gorillas for their heads, which are sold as trophies to tourists, and their hands, which are sold as ashtrays. In Nigeria, more lowland gorillas are being killed each year than are being born, creating an imminent threat of extinction for this species.

NAMIBIA. Despite protests from animal rights groups, commercial sealing endures as a flagship industry in Namibia, where the penises of baby seal pups are sold as aphrodisiacs to markets in the Far East. Sealskin is also used for shoes, wallets, and accessories. Large-scale sealing, a successful industry in the job-starved Namibian economy, brings approximately $500,000 into that country each year.

SENEGAL. Senegal exports between 1 and 10 million birds each year and derives approximately 65 percent of the value of its bird exports from a single species, the African gray parrot. This species does not occur naturally in Senegal but is imported from other African countries for trading with third parties.

TANZANIA. Tanzania supplies the international market with a variety of songbirds, including the popular Fischer's lovebird, a native species whose numbers have declined drastically. Tanzania exports somewhere between 200,000 and 3 million birds per year. Despite government attempts to control trade, protected species are routinely exported.

UNITED STATES TRADE POLICIES

The Lacey Act

In the United States, the indiscriminate slaughter of wildlife in the nineteenth century brought about the extinction of numerous species. The Lacey Act was passed in 1900 and represented the first national conservation law. The Lacey Act prohibited interstate transport of wildlife killed in violation of a state law, and also allowed individual states to prohibit import of wildlife or their products even if killed lawfully. For example, egret plumes taken in a state where the bird was protected could not be shipped to other states; in addition, a state could outlaw entry of the plumes even if collection was legal in the exporting state. In 1908 the scope of the Lacey Act was expanded to include wildlife imported from abroad. The Lacey Act contributed to the elimination of the meat markets where the last Labrador ducks were sold, and of the plume trade that nearly led to extinction for the snowy and common egrets as well as other water birds.

Two comprehensive amendments to the Lacey Act in 1981 and 1988 added important new restrictions and increased the fines for illegal trade of wildlife. The amended Lacey Act now covers all CITES- and state-protected species. Its regulations apply to species, their parts, and products made from them. Illegal import or export of wildlife-related contraband is now a federal crime. The amended Lacey Act also makes it illegal to provide guide or outfitting services for would-be poachers. The Lacey Act authorizes fines and jail time for offenders. Fines and penalties, authorized at $10,000 maximum by the amendment of 1981, were increased more than tenfold by the

Criminal Fines Improvement Act of 1987, with penalty limits now as high as $250,000 for misdemeanors and $500,000 for felonies. Lacey Act enforcement agents are authorized to carry firearms under the amended act, and rewards are authorized for those who provide tips to law enforcement.

Trade Sanctions

In April 1994 the U.S. government deployed trade sanctions for the purpose of protecting endangered wildlife for the first time. The 1994 sanctions banned all wildlife-product imports from Taiwan in an effort to reduce illegal smuggling, particularly of tiger bones and rhinoceros horns. At the time, Taiwanese wildlife exports to the United States amounted to an estimated $25 million a year, including coral and mollusk-shell jewelry, snake-, lizard-, and crocodile-skin shoes, and other leather products. The import embargo reiterated the importance of considering the environmental consequences of global trade.

INTERNATIONAL FREE TRADE AGREEMENTS

The North American Free Trade Agreement (NAFTA) was signed in 1993 by the United States, Mexico, and Canada. Its goal was to remove trade barriers among the three nations by eliminating most tariffs, investment restrictions, and quotas. Conservationists feared that the passage of NAFTA would weaken U.S. species and environmental protection laws. This had resulted earlier from the signing of another free trade agreement, the General Agreement on Tariffs and Trade (GATT). Under GATT, laws for wildlife protection were sometimes judged to be "technical barriers to trade." For example, in 1991, Mexico used GATT to successfully challenge U.S. tuna-import restrictions intended to protect dolphins. Similarly, U.S. loggers successfully sued under GATT to prevent the British Columbian government from subsidizing the replanting of forests, arguing that it was an unfair subsidy for Canadian loggers.

The Environmental Investigation Agency, a watchgroup for environmental issues, concluded that NAFTA's elimination of trade barriers would stimulate the already high demand for wildlife products from Mexico. It added that trade liberalization among the U.S., Mexico, and Canada would result in increased border crossings, facilitating illegal trade and placing an even greater burden on overworked FWS inspectors and agents.

Impact of the World Trade Organization

The World Trade Organization (WTO) is a global trade association that promotes trade among nations and possesses broad authority to rule on trade disputes. The original WTO agreements were signed at Marrakech, Morocco in April 1994. As of January 2002 the organization included 144 member nations.

Environmentalists have frequently been critical of the WTO, charging that it is unconcerned about environmental issues when these conflict with trade and development. Conservationists also fear that the WTO could force the U.S. to back down on environmentally-friendly laws that restricted trade, just as GATT had done. This fear was realized when India, Thailand, Pakistan, and Malaysia petitioned the WTO on U.S. shrimp import legislation. In particular, these countries objected to U.S. laws prohibiting importation of shrimp from countries without turtle excluder device (TED) regulations for the protection of endangered sea turtles. In April 1998 the WTO ruled that the U.S. laws were discriminatory. Conservation groups called on the U.S. government to defy the WTO decision, fearing the environment would take a back seat whenever a direct conflict arose with free trade. The United States attempted a compromise, requiring environmentally friendly fishing practices from foreign nations only when shrimp was earmarked for export to the United States.

A similar compromise was proposed with regard to dolphin-safe tuna fishing, and the federal government agreed to disregard its own policy in order to maintain its standing in the WTO. Critics alleged that the United States had placed the fate of the American environment in the hands of other nations. Many critics considered the move a serious blow to environmental protection.

In the wake of these decisions, a series of WTO meetings held in Seattle, Washington from November 29 through December 4, 1999, erupted in massive civil unrest. Over 50,000 protesters from around the globe participated, protesting vehemently against diverse policies of the WTO, including its attitudes towards the environment, human rights, sweatshops, labor unions, wages, and the price and quality of food. Special-interest groups engaged in the protests included the Humane Society, the Sierra Club, the Center for Science and the Public Interest, Global Exchange, the United Auto Workers, and numerous others. An estimated $6 million in damages resulted from the demonstrations, and over 600 protesters were arrested. The WTO meeting was entirely shut down, if only temporarily.

THE CONVENTION ON THE INTERNATIONAL TRADE IN ENDANGERED SPECIES (CITES)

The Convention on International Trade in Endangered Species of Wild Fauna and Flora (CITES) is an international treaty established to regulate commerce in wildlife. CITES, first ratified in 1975, was developed to block both the import and export of endangered species as well as to regulate trade in vulnerable species. CITES maintains three levels of control. Appendix I, the most stringent, includes species that are in immediate danger of extinction. CITES generally prohibits international trade of these species. Appendix II lists species that are likely to become in danger of extinction without strict protection from inter-

national trade. Permits may be obtained for the trade of Appendix II species only if trade will not harm the survival prospects of the species in the wild. Appendix III includes species identified by individual countries as being subject to conservation regulations within its borders.

CITES is generally regarded as the most important legislation regulating trade in endangered or vulnerable species. The treaty nations hold a meeting, called a Conference of Parties, approximately every two to three years. The CITES conference of 2000 was attended by delegates from 151 member nations. The next CITES conference will take place in Chile in November 2002.

Among the most hotly contested topics at the 2000 CITES meeting was the listing status of the African elephant. The African elephant population, which stabilized during the 1990s after a drastic 20-year decline, served as an example of the beneficial nature of CITES protection. Indeed, some wildlife experts surmised that the market for ivory products in North America and Western Europe evaporated after CITES imposed a ban on ivory trafficking in 1989, and that the Japanese market for these products dropped by 50 percent. The error of that assumption was exposed, however, following the 1997 CITES conference in Harare, Zimbabwe. When delegates at that conference authorized the export of 60 tons of stockpiled ivory from three African countries—Zimbabwe, Botswana, and Namibia—the ivory sold for over $5 million on the international market. This occurred in 1999. Soon after, ivory poaching increased more than fourfold in Kenya. Tanzania and Zimbabwe reported increases in illegal elephant slaughter as well.

In 2000 South Africa, Zimbabwe, Namibia, and Botswana once again petitioned CITES for authorization to sell stockpiled ivory. In addition, these nations declared that they were now overrun by elephants because of the ivory ban and petitioned for the approval of a culling system in which elephants from overpopulated areas would be moved to less populated regions. The South African contingency requested an allowance for some trade, both in ivory and in elephant leather. In the ongoing debate, India and Kenya responded by petitioning for a total ban on elephant ivory trade. India and Kenya also proposed that the elephant be moved to CITES Appendix I. In the end, the opposing factions reached a compromise in which both proposals were withdrawn—elephants remained listed under Appendix II, and the ban on ivory sales remained in effect.

CITES has a number of shortcomings. First, many countries lack the funds and expertise to determine the endangerment status of their species. As a result, numerous species that require protection have yet to be listed with the convention. Some experts also argue that CITES listing serves to advertise a species' rarity, thereby boosting its trade. However, the primary criticism of CITES is that its regulations are notoriously difficult to enforce.

Wildlife protection organizations such as TRAFFIC estimate that 30 percent of the total value of the global wildlife trade occurs in violation of either CITES or national laws. Other problems include the absence of laws to implement CITES, weak penalties for violators, and widespread corruption among public officials. Many nations are not even party to the CITES convention, making them potential wildlife bazaars where animals and plants illegally exported from CITES nations can be "laundered." Numerous biologically rich nations have not signed the CITES treaty, including Laos, South Korea, and Taiwan. Finally, CITES addresses only trade across international borders. It does not address the problem of trade within countries, which is detrimental to many endangered and vulnerable species.

THE INTERNATIONAL WHALING COMMISSION

The campaign to save endangered whales has perhaps made greater progress than any other international effort to protect endangered species. In 1946, long before the creation of CITES, the International Whaling Commission (IWC) was established to regulate whaling. The IWC, a loosely governed consortium, currently includes 48 nations. Its 54th meeting was held in Shimonoseki, Japan in May 2002. The primary function of the IWC is to conserve whale stocks through measures such as: the complete protection of endangered whale species; designation of whale sanctuaries; limiting of the numbers and sizes of whales that can be taken; designation of open and closed seasons for whaling; and prohibition of takes of whale calves as well as females accompanied by calves. Unfortunately, the IWC is powerless to enforce its resolutions, and depends largely on international pressure and the enforcement policies of individual nations. Member countries that are unwilling to comply with restrictions imposed by any IWC agreement may refuse to participate or may simply quit the IWC.

In order to protect dwindling whale populations, the IWC began by setting quotas on whale kills. As populations continued to decline, however, the IWC declared a moratorium on commercial whaling in 1986, with certain exceptions. In 1994 the IWC banned whaling within the 11 million square miles around Antarctica, an area called the Southern Ocean Sanctuary. The sanctuary, which must be reauthorized at 10-year intervals, is intended to create a safe harbor for the 90 percent of world whales that feed there. There is also an IWC whale sanctuary in the Indian Ocean, originally established in 1979. At the IWC conference in 2002, Mexico, which boasts a large whale watching industry, declared it would establish a 1.15 million square mile whale sanctuary along Mexican coastal waters in the Atlantic and Pacific Oceans.

Despite international pressure to obey the moratorium on commercial whaling, Japan, Norway, and Russia, among other nations, continue to whale. Iceland has quit the IWC altogether. Additionally, although the IWC has condemned whaling for research purposes, it nonetheless tolerates a self-allocated annual kill for research. Japan, which, along with Norway, continues to campaign for the reinstatement of commercial whaling, has killed numerous whales under the auspices of research. In 2002 Japan allocated itself a research quota of 700 whales, including 590 minke whales, 10 sperm whales, 50 Bryde's whales, and 50 sei whales. Selling the whale meat, Japan claims, is required by a commission rule prohibiting the waste of research byproducts. The IWC condemned this as a thinly veiled ruse to continue commercial whaling. Moreover, some environmentalist groups charge that this "research" trade provides a cover for illegal trade in whale meat. In 1997, Earthtrust, a conservation group based in Hawaii, announced the results of several years of tests on whale meat obtained from Japanese markets and restaurants. DNA tests revealed that a large proportion were from endangered species such as humpback and blue whales, rather than from "research" specimens. The Earthtrust project involved conservation biologists Steve Palumbi of Harvard University and C. Scott Baker of the University of Auckland. The illegal trade in whale meat—which brings in as much as $300 per pound—is hypothesized to involve large organized crime groups in Japan. At the IWC meeting in 2002, Japan also argued that whales deplete fisheries, a claim not substantiated by patterns of fish catch in recent years. Norway has also objected to the IWC moratorium on commercial whaling and killed 675 whales in 2001. In addition, Japanese and Taiwanese companies have been caught smuggling large amounts of whale meat.

Subsistence Whaling

In response to the IWC's moratorium on whaling, several groups—including the Makah of Washington State, the Inuits of Alaska (formerly known as Eskimos), and the Chukchi of Siberia—requested a special exemption to hunt bowhead whales, arguing that whales were necessary for their subsistence, in addition to being a significant part of their culture and tradition. These hunts have occurred for over 8,000 years, and no part of the whale is wasted. Critics of the exemptions argued that these groups were no longer dependent on whaling for food. Furthermore, critics charged that traditional whaling in these cultures had involved spears—resulting in a much smaller kill than is possible today with harpoon guns. The IWC granted permission for aboriginal subsistence whaling in 1997 but also established quotas to limit the annual take. In particular, only 280 whales could be taken in a five-year period, with no more than 67 takes in a single year. Since then, subsistence hunting permits have also been issued to Greenlanders (for fin whales and minke whales) as well as inhabitants of St. Vincent and the Grenadines (for humpback whales).

In 2002 subsistence whaling was dealt a blow when the IWC rejected the United States' request that Alaskan Inuits be allowed to continue their whale hunts. The U.S. had requested 55 bowhead whales over a period of five years. This was the first time aboriginal hunting quotas were denied. The decision was attributed in the U.S. press to Japanese retaliation—the U.S. had led efforts against allowing Japanese coastal whaling towns to hunt a total of 50 minke whales.

AFRICA'S LUSAKA AGREEMENT

On December 10, 1996, the African nations of the Congo, Kenya, Lesotho, Uganda, Zambia, and the United Republic of Tanzania entered into a pact called the Lusaka Agreement. The agreement, formally titled the Lusaka Agreement on Cooperative Enforcement Operations Directed at Illegal Trade in Wild Fauna and Flora, was conceived in 1994 under the auspices of the United Nations Environmental Program (UNEP). In addition to the six core-member nations, representatives from Ethiopia, South Africa, and Swaziland also signed the treaty. The Lusaka Agreement Task Force was established on June 1, 1999, to define policies, missions, and operations for the member nations. The goal of Lusaka is to establish a multilateral police force for controlling illegal trade in wildlife that includes as many nations as possible.

CHAPTER 11
WILDLIFE AS RECREATION

One of the reasons frequently given for conserving wildlife and habitat is the aesthetic and recreational value of natural places. Human beings derive pleasure from natural places in large numbers, and in a wide variety of ways.

NATIONAL SURVEY OF FISHING, HUNTING, AND WILDLIFE-ASSOCIATED RECREATION

Americans have a rich tradition of enjoying nature. In fact, several of the country's most popular recreational activities involve wildlife and wild places. As part of its effort to conserve species and natural habitats, the U.S. Fish and Wildlife Service publishes a periodic report on how Americans use these natural resources. The data come from interviews conducted by the U.S. Bureau of the Census. The most recent FWS report is the *2001 National Survey of Fishing, Hunting, and Wildlife-Associated Recreation*. The FWS found that over 80 million Americans over the age of 16—39 percent of the population—participated in some form of wildlife-related activity in 2001. They spent a total of $110 billion on those activities—about 1.1 percent of the nation's Gross Domestic Product.

During 2001, 34 million people in the United States fished, 13 million hunted, and over 66 million enjoyed some form of wildlife-watching recreation, including photography and feeding or observing animals. Many participants in one of these wildlife-related activities engaged in the others as well. Total participant numbers have changed slightly since the last survey, conducted in 1996—the numbers of fishers and hunters have dropped, whereas the number of wildlife-watchers has increased.

In 2001, 16 percent of the U.S. population, or 34 million people, fished. A majority of these—28 million—engaged in freshwater fishing (see Figure 11.1). Nine million people saltwater fished. The average expenditure on trips, equipment, and licenses was $1,046 per person.

Over 13 million people hunted in 2001. A large majority of hunters—84 percent or 10.9 million people—hunted big game, including species of deer and elk (see Figure 11.2). Five million hunted small game, including species such as squirrels, rabbits, quail, and pheasant. Three million hunters pursued migratory bird species such as ducks, geese, and doves. The average expenditure per hunter in 2001 was $1,581.

Wildlife watching attracted over 66 million Americans in 2001, 31 percent of the total population (see Figure 11.3). These included residential participants who took a "special interest" in wildlife near their homes (65 million) as well as nonresidential participants who went on a trip the "primary purpose" of which was wildlife-watching (22 million). (See Figure 11.4 and Table 11.1.) A large majority of wildlife-watchers were primarily interested in birds—46 million people, or 69 percent of the total (Figure 11.5 and Table 11.2). However, other animal groups, such as mammals and fish, also drew wildlife-watchers (Table 11.3). Of the wildlife-watching

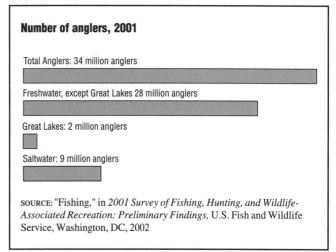

FIGURE 11.1

Number of anglers, 2001

Total Anglers: 34 million anglers

Freshwater, except Great Lakes 28 million anglers

Great Lakes: 2 million anglers

Saltwater: 9 million anglers

SOURCE: "Fishing," in *2001 Survey of Fishing, Hunting, and Wildlife-Associated Recreation: Preliminary Findings*, U.S. Fish and Wildlife Service, Washington, DC, 2002

FIGURE 11.2

FIGURE 11.3

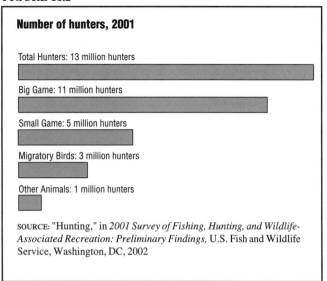

Number of hunters, 2001

Total Hunters: 13 million hunters

Big Game: 11 million hunters

Small Game: 5 million hunters

Migratory Birds: 3 million hunters

Other Animals: 1 million hunters

SOURCE: "Hunting," in *2001 Survey of Fishing, Hunting, and Wildlife-Associated Recreation: Preliminary Findings,* U.S. Fish and Wildlife Service, Washington, DC, 2002

Wildlife watching is a popular activity among Americans. Over 66 million Americans watched birds or other wildlife in 2001. *(Field Mark Publications)*

participants, 54 million people fed wildlife, 42 million people observed wildlife, and 14 million people photographed wildlife. A significant number—11 million—engaged in their wildlife-watching activities in public parks and natural areas.

ECOTOURISM

Tourism is one of the largest industries worldwide, generating 200 million jobs globally. The World Tourism Organization (WTO) estimated that there were some 663 million international travelers in 1999, and that these spent a total of more than $453 billion. Nature tourists perhaps account for 40–60 percent of all international tourists, with 20–40 percent focusing on wildlife in particular. In addition, nature tourism is increasing at an annual rate of 10–30 percent.

Ecotourism is a special form of nature travel that The International Ecotourism Society (TIES) defines as "responsible travel to natural areas which conserves the environment and sustains the well-being of local people." The World Conservation Union (IUCN) defines ecotourism as "environmentally responsible travel and visitation to relatively undisturbed natural areas, in order to enjoy and appreciate nature (and any accompanying cultural features—both past and present) that promotes conservation, has low negative visitor impact, and provides for beneficially active socioeconomic involvement of local populations."

The United Nations General Assembly designated 2002 the International Year of Ecotourism. Programs run collaboratively by United Nations Environment Programme (UNEP), the WTO, and TIES will educate authorities and the public regarding ecotourism's capacity to aid in the conservation of natural and cultural heritage, promote the exchange of ideas in ecotourism management, and allow for exchanges of experiences in ecotourism.

According to TIES, ecotourists are most often between the ages of 35 and 54, are evenly split between males and females, and are usually college graduates (82 percent). However, recent increases in ecotourism among people with less education suggest that ecotourism is expanding into more mainstream markets. The majority of ecotourists (60 percent) prefer to travel as a couple, though others like to travel either with their families (15 percent) or alone (13 percent). In surveys, ecotourists ranked their top priorities as "wilderness setting," "wildlife viewing," and "hiking/trekking."

TIES' list of popular ecotourism destinations and activities includes hiking and camping in U.S. National Parks (more than 424 million visitations in 2001), visiting nature reserves in South Africa (5,898,000 visitors in 1998), going on safari in Kenya (826,000 visitors in 1993), visiting national parks in Australia (1.7 million visitors in 1998), birdwatching in Peru (642,336 visitors in 1999), visiting national parks in Brazil (3.5 million visi-

FIGURE 11.4

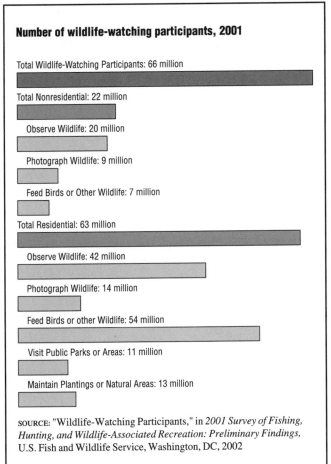

Number of wildlife-watching participants, 2001

Total Wildlife-Watching Participants: 66 million

Total Nonresidential: 22 million

Observe Wildlife: 20 million

Photograph Wildlife: 9 million

Feed Birds or Other Wildlife: 7 million

Total Residential: 63 million

Observe Wildlife: 42 million

Photograph Wildlife: 14 million

Feed Birds or other Wildlife: 54 million

Visit Public Parks or Areas: 11 million

Maintain Plantings or Natural Areas: 13 million

SOURCE: "Wildlife-Watching Participants," in *2001 Survey of Fishing, Hunting, and Wildlife-Associated Recreation: Preliminary Findings,* U.S. Fish and Wildlife Service, Washington, DC, 2002

TABLE 11.1

Wildlife-watching participants 16 years and older, by primary activity, 2001

(U.S. population 16 years old and older. Numbers in thousands)

	Number	Percent
Total participants	**66,105**	**100**
Nonresidential (away from home)	**21,823**	**33**
Observe wildlife	20,080	30
Photograph wildlife	9,427	14
Feed wildlife	7,077	11
Residential (around the home)	**62,928**	**95**
Observe wildlife	42,111	64
Photograph wildlife	13,937	21
Feed wildlife	53,988	82
Visit public parks or areas*	10,981	17
Maintain plantings or natural areas	13,072	20

Note: Detail does not add to total because of multiple responses and nonresponse.
*Includes visits only to parks or publicly held areas within one mile of home.

SOURCE: "Table 5. Wildlife-Watching Participants 16 Years Old and Older, by Primary Activity: 2001," *2001 Survey of Fishing, Hunting, and Wildlife-Associated Recreation: Preliminary Findings,* U.S. Fish and Wildlife Service, Washington, DC, 2002

tors in 1998), trekking in Nepal (50,708 international trekkers in 1997), visiting parks and reefs in Belize, and viewing wildlife in the Galapagos Islands (60,000 visitors per year on average).

A nationwide survey conducted by TIES in 1998 asked the question, "What type of nature-based activities did you participate in during your last nature-based vacation?" The top 12 answers in order were: visiting parks, hiking, exploring a preserved area, observing wildlife (non-birds), walking nature trails in ecosystems, viewing unique natural places (sinkholes, dunes), participating in environmental education, birdwatching, biking, freshwater fishing, snorkeling or scuba diving, and exploring a major protected swamp or marsh.

BIRDING

Birding is a wildlife-related recreational activity that enjoys worldwide appeal—there are countless national and regional birding organizations. More than 46 million Americans engage in birdwatching every year. Important conservation studies such as the U.S. Breeding Bird Survey rely largely on volunteer birders to help document long-term population trends and distributions of over 400 North American breeding bird species.

The American Birding Association (ABA) is the largest association of amateur birders in the U.S. Membership has grown steadily since its founding in 1968 and was well over 20,000 in 1998. In terms of birding activity, a 1997 ABA survey showed that 16 percent of members bird more than 80 days a year, and 24 percent bird between 40 and 80 days a year. In addition, 17 percent of members traveled more than 10,000 miles to go birdwatching, while another 20 percent traveled between 5,000 and 10,000 miles. Birdwatchers see diverse species on their outings—21 percent reported identifying 401 species or more in the last year, 17 percent identified 301–400 species, 25 percent identified 201–300 species, and 22 percent identified 101–200 species. A large majority—over 80 percent—of members maintain a "life list" of all the bird species they have ever seen. Among other activities, 82 percent feed birds in their backyards, 67 percent participate in bird counts, 36 percent photograph birds, 6 percent record bird songs, and 41 percent are active with a local bird club.

WHALE WATCHING

Whale watching (Figure 11.6) has become increasingly popular in recent years, contributing to coastal economies worldwide. In 1995 the Whale and Dolphin Conservation Society, based in Bath, England, estimated the industry's value at $504 million. In August 2000 the International Fund for Animal Welfare reported that the industry had grown to $1.049 billion by 1998. It also reported that over 9 million people in 87 countries went on whale-watching expeditions in 1998—an increase of over 3.5 million people since 1994 and more than double the figure of 4 million people in 1991. According to the report, the number of whale watchers increased by an average of more than 12 percent each year during the late 1990s. In 1998 nearly 48 percent of all whale watching occurred in the United States, with an estimated 4.3 million people participating.

A few American cities—Provincetown, Massachusetts, and Lahaina, Hawaii, in particular—reap significant economic benefits from whale watching. Countries such as Canada, New Zealand, South Africa, Argentina, Iceland, and Mexico have also developed lucrative whale-watching industries. Smaller nations, including St. Lucia, Namibia, Oman, and the Solomon Islands, also run profitable whale-watching operations. By 1998 whale-watching programs featured not only the most popular species—humpback whales, fin whales, minke whales, and pilot whales—but

83 additional cetaceans, including orcas, or killer whales, and highly endangered northern right whales. The California gray whale, recently removed from the Endangered Species List, is the star of the whale-watching industry on the U.S. West Coast. In addition, commercial whale-watching vessels frequently serve as forums for educational outreach and scientific research.

CANNED HUNTING

In the 1980s a controversial form of hunting known as "canned hunting" swept the United States. Originating in Texas, canned hunting now occurs in most states.

FIGURE 11.5

Number of bird observers, 2001

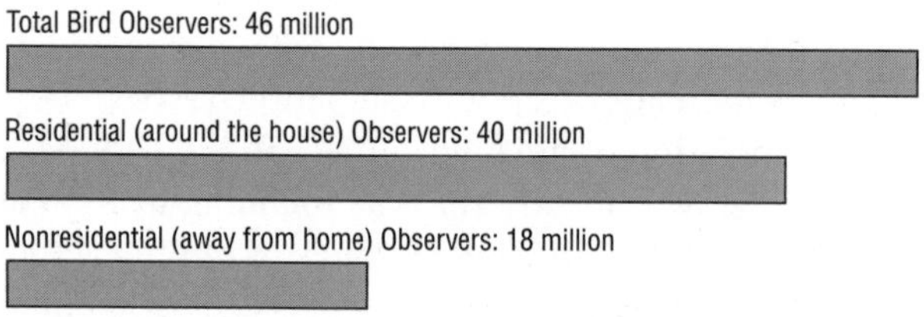

Total Bird Observers: 46 million

Residential (around the house) Observers: 40 million

Nonresidential (away from home) Observers: 18 million

SOURCE: "Bird Observers in the U.S.," in *2001 Survey of Fishing, Hunting, and Wildlife-Associated Recreation: Preliminary Findings,* U.S. Fish and Wildlife Service, Washington, DC, 2002

TABLE 11.2

Wild bird observers and days of observation, 2001

(U.S. population 16 years old and older. Numbers in thousands)

	Number	Percent
OBSERVERS		
Total Bird Observers	**45,951**	**100**
Residential (around the home) observers	40,306	88
Nonresidential (away from home) observers	18,342	40
DAYS		
Total Days Observing Birds	**5,467,841**	**100**
Residential (around the home)	5,159,259	94
Nonresidential (away from home)	308,583	6

Note: Detail does not add to total because of multiple responses and nonresponse.

SOURCE: "Table 7. Wild Bird Observers and Days of Observation: 2001," in *2001 Survey of Fishing, Hunting, and Wildlife-Associated Recreation: Preliminary Findings,* U.S. Fish and Wildlife Service, Washington, DC, 2002

TABLE 11.3

Primary nonresidential participants by wildlife observed, photographed, or fed and place, 2001

(U.S. population 16 years old and older. Numbers in thousands)

	Total participants		Total in U.S.		Participation by place			
					In state of residence		In other states	
	Number	Percent	Number	Percent	Number	Percent	Number	Percent
Total, All Wildlife	**21,823**	**100**	**21,823**	**100**	**18,041**	**83**	**6,570**	**30**
Total Birds	**18,580**	**85**	**18,580**	**100**	**16,150**	**87**	**5,855**	**32**
Songbirds	12,878	59	12,878	100	11,182	87	3,860	30
Birds of prey	12,495	57	12,495	100	10,596	85	4,060	32
Waterfowl	14,432	66	14,432	100	12,384	86	4,258	30
Other water birds (shorebirds, herons, etc.)	10,314	47	10,314	100	8,474	82	3,229	31
Other birds (pheasants, turkeys, etc.)	7,907	36	7,907	100	6,640	84	2,248	28
Total Land Mammals	**15,506**	**71**	**15,506**	**100**	**13,207**	**85**	**4,844**	**31**
Large land mammals (deer, bear, etc.)	12,226	56	12,226	100	10,047	82	3,784	31
Small land mammals (squirrels, prairie dogs, etc.)	12,958	59	12,958	100	10,911	84	4,200	32
Fish	6,330	29	6,330	100	5,019	79	2,000	32
Marine mammals	3,013	14	3,013	100	1,982	66	1,233	41
Other wildlife (turtles, butterflies, etc.)	9,409	43	9,409	100	7,929	84	3,071	33

Note: Detail does not add to total because of multiple responses. Columns showing percent of total participants are based on the "Total, All Wildlife" row. Participation by place percent columns are based on the total number of participants in the U.S. for each type of wildlife.

SOURCE: "Table 6. Primary Nonresidential Participants by Wildlife Observed, Photographed, or Fed and Place in the U.S.: 2001," in *2001 Survey of Fishing, Hunting, and Wildlife-Associated Recreation: Preliminary Findings,* U.S. Fish and Wildlife Service, Washington, DC, 2002

FIGURE 11.6

A humpback whale, seen off the coast of Massachusetts. Whale-watching tours have become a popular way to make a profit from whales. *(AP/Wide World Photos)*

In a canned hunt, the hunter pays a set fee and steps onto private property where an animal—most often a boar, ram, bear, lion, tiger, zebra, buffalo, rhinoceros, or antelope—is confined. The hunter then kills the animal with the weapon of his or her choice. The animals are easily cornered—some have been domesticated or raised in facilities where they've become friendly to humans. A 1994 Humane Society investigation found that there may be several thousand canned-hunting facilities in the United States.

There are no federal laws restricting canned hunts. As of 1999, only California, Indiana, Maryland, Nevada, New Jersey, New York, North Carolina, Oregon, Rhode Island, Texas, Wisconsin, and Wyoming had laws prohibiting or regulating canned hunts. Investigations revealed that zoos frequently sell "surplus" animals either directly to canned-hunt facilities or to dealers who then sell animals at auctions attended by canned-hunt organizers. Some pressure has been exerted on zoos to acknowledge their responsibility for the animals they discard.

IMPORTANT NAMES AND ADDRESSES

American Association of Zoological Parks and Aquariums
8403 Colesville Rd., Suite 710
Silver Spring, MD 20910-3314
(301) 562-0777
FAX: (301) 562-0888
URL: http://www.aza.org

American Ornithologists' Union
Smithsonian Institution
Washington, DC 20560-0116
(202) 357-2051
FAX: (202) 633-8084
E-mail: aou@nmnh.si.edu
URL: http://www.aou.org/

American Rivers
1025 Vermont Ave. N.W., Suite 720
Washington, DC 20005
(202) 347-7550
FAX: (202) 347-9240
E-mail: amrivers@amriverslorg
URL: http://amrivers.org

AmphibiaWeb
3101 VLSB #3160
Berkeley, CA 94720
URL: http://amphibiaweb.org

Animal Protection Institute
P.O. Box 22505
Sacramento, CA 95822
(916) 731-5521
URL: http://api4animals.org

Animal Welfare Institute
P.O. Box 3650
Washington, DC 20007
(202) 337-2332
FAX: (202) 338-9478
URL: www.awionline.org

Biological Resources Division (BRD)—USGS
U.S. Dept. of the Interior

Office of Public Affairs
12201 Sunrise Valley Dr.
Reston, VA 22092
(301) 317-3819
E-mail: biologywebteam@usgs.gov
URL: http://biology.usgs.gov

BirdLife International
Wellbrook Court
Girton Rd.
Cambridge, CB3 ONA, UK
44(1) 223 277 318
E-mail: birdlife@birdlife.org.uk
URL: http://www.birdlife.net

Center for Plant Conservation (CPC)
P.O. Box 299
St. Louis, MO 63166-0299
(314) 577-9450
E-mail: cpc@mobot.org
URL: http://www.mobot.org/CPC/welcome.html

Coral Reef Alliance (CORAL)
2014 Shattuck Ave.
Berkeley, CA 94704-1117
(510) 848-0110
FAX: (510) 848-3720
Toll-free: 1-888-CORAL-REEF
E-mail: info@coral.org
URL: http://www.coral.org

Declining Amphibians Populations Task Force (DAPTF)
Department of Biological Sciences
The Open University, Walton Hall
Milton Keynes MK7 6AA, UK
(202) 357-2620
FAX: (202) 786-2934
E-mail: DAPTF@open.ac.uk
URL: http://www.open.ac.uk/daptf/

Defenders of Wildlife
1101 14th St. NW, Suite 1400
Washington, DC 20005

(202) 682-9400
FAX: (202) 833-3349
E-mail: info@defenders.org
URL: http://www.defenders.org

Desert Tortoise Preserve Committee, Inc.
4067 Mission Inn Ave.
Riverside, CA 92501
(909) 683-3872
FAX: (909) 683-6949
URL: http://www.tortoise-tracks.org

Duke University Primate Center
3705 Erwin Rd.
Durham, NC 27705
(919) 489-3364
FAX: (919) 490-5394
E-mail: primate@duke.edu
URL: http://www.duke.edu/web/primate

Environmental Defense Fund
257 Park Ave. S
New York, NY 10010
(212) 505-2100
FAX: (212) 505-2375
E-mail: Contact@environmentaldefense.org
URL: http://www.edf.org

Florida Panther Society, Inc.
Rt. 1 Box 1895
White Springs, FL 32096
(386) 397-2945
E-mail: coolcat@atlantic.net
URL: http://www.atlantic.net/~oldfla/panther/panther.html

Friends of the Earth
1025 Vermont Ave. NW, 3rd Floor
Washington, DC 20005-6303
(202) 783-7400
FAX: (202) 783-0444
Toll-free: 1-877-843-8887
E-mail: foe@foe.org
URL: http://www.foe.org

Greenpeace U.S.A.
702 H St. NW
Washington, DC 20001
FAX: (202) 462-4507
Toll-free: 1-800-326-0959
E-mail: gp1@sharewest.com
URL: http://www.greenpeaceusa.org

Human Ecology Action League (HEAL)
P.O. Box 29629
Atlanta, GA 30359-0629
(404) 248-1898
FAX: (404) 248-0162
E-mail: HEALNatnl@aol.com
URL: http://members.aol.com/HEALNatnl/
index.html

Humane Society of the United States
2100 L. St. NW
Washington, DC 20037
(202) 452-1100
FAX: (202) 778-6132
URL: http://www.hsus.org

**Intergovernmental Panel on
Climate Change**
IPCC Secretariat
C/O World Meteorological Organization
7bis Avenue de la Paix
CH-1211
Geneva 2, Switzerland
41 (22) 730-8208
FAX: 41 (22) 730-8025
E-mail: ipcc_sec@gateway.wmo.ch
URL: http://www.ipcc.ch

Izaak Walton League of America
707 Conservation Ln.
Gaithersburg, MD 20878
(301) 548-0150
FAX: (301) 548-0146
Toll-free: 1-800-453-5463
E-mail: general@iwla.org
URL: http://www.iwla.org

National Audubon Society
700 Broadway
New York, NY 10003
(212) 979-3000
FAX: (212) 979-3188
URL: http://www.audubon.org

National Wildlife Federation
11100 Wildlife Center Dr.
Reston, VA 20190-5362
(703) 438-6000
URL: http://www.NWF.org

Natural Resources Defense Council
40 West 20th St.
New York, NY 10011
(212) 727-2700
FAX: (212) 727-1773

E-mail: nrdcinfo@nrdc.org
URL: http://www.nrdc.org

Nature Conservancy
4245 North Fairfax Drive, Suite 100
Arlington, VA 22203-1606
(703) 841-5300
FAX: (703) 841-1283
Toll-free: 1-800-628-6860
URL: http://www.tnc.org

Ocean Conservancy
1725 DeSales St., Suite 600
Washington, DC 20036
(202) 429-5609
FAX: (202) 872-0619
E-mail: info@oceanconservancy.org
URL: http://www.oceanconservancy.org

**People for the Ethical Treatment of
Animals (PETA)**
501 Front St.
Norfolk, VA 23510
(757) 622-7382
FAX: (757) 622-0457
E-mail: info@peta-online.org
URL: http://www.peta-online.org

Rachel Carson Council
8940 Joans Mill Rd.
Chevy Chase, MD 20815
(301) 652-1877
FAX: (301) 451-7179
E-mail: rccouncil@aolcom
URL: http://members.aol.com/rccouncil/
ourpage/index.htm

Sierra Club
85 Second St., 2nd Floor
San Francisco, CA 94105-3441
(415) 977-5500
FAX: (415) 977-5799
E-mail: information@sierraclub.org
URL: http://www.sierraclub.org

TRAFFIC International
219c Huntingdon Rd.
Cambridge, CB3 0DL, UK
(44) 1223 277427
FAX: (44) 1223 277237
E-mail: traffic@trafficint.org
URL: http://www.traffic.org

**TRAFFIC North America—
Regional Office**
1250 24th St. NW
Washington, DC 20037
(202) 293-4800
FAX: (202) 775-8287
E-mail: tna@wwfus.org
URL: http://www.traffic.org

Union of Concerned Scientists
2 Brattle Square
Cambridge, MA 02238
(617) 547-5552
E-mail: ucs@ucsusa.org
URL: http://www.ucsusa.org

**U.S. Fish and Wildlife Service
Division of Endangered Species**
U.S. Department of the Interior
4401 N. Fairfax Dr., Rm. 420
Arlington, VA 22203
E-mail: contact@fws.gov
URL: http://endangered.fws.gov

United Nations Environment Programme
United Nations Avenue, Gigiri
P.O. Box 30552
Nairobi, Kenya
(254-2) 621234
FAX: (254-2) 624489/90
E-mail: info@unep-wcmc.org
URL: http://www.unep.org

The Wilderness Society
1615 M St. NW
Washington, DC 20036
Toll-free: 1-800-843-9453
URL: http://www.wilderness.org

Wildlife Management Institute
1101 14th St. NW, Suite 801
Washington, DC 20005
(202) 371-1808
FAX: (202) 408-5059
URL: http://www.wildlifemanagement
institute.org

World Conservation Union
Rue Mauverney 28
Gland, 1196, Switzerland
41 (22) 999-0000
FAX: 41 (22) 999-0002
E-mail: mail@hq.iucn.org
URL: http://www.iucn.org

World Wildlife Fund
1250 24th St. NW
P.O. Box 97180
Washington, DC 20090-7180
(202) 293-4800
FAX: (202) 293-9211
Toll-free: 1-800-225-5993
URL: http://www.wwf.org

Worldwatch Institute
1776 Massachusetts Ave. NW
Washington, DC 20036-1904
(202) 452-1999
FAX: (202) 296-7365
E-mail: worldwatch@worldwatch.org
URL: http://www.worldwatch.org

RESOURCES

A first source of information on endangered species is the U.S. Department of the Interior's Fish and Wildlife Service. Their Endangered Species Program Web site (http://endangered.fws.gov/) includes news stories on threatened and endangered species, information about laws protecting endangered species, regional contacts for endangered species programs, and a searchable database with information on all listed species. Each listed species has an information page that provides details regarding the status of the species (whether it is listed as threatened or endangered and in what geographic area), federal register documents pertaining to listing, information on Habitat Conservation Plans and National Wildlife Refuges pertinent to the species, and, for many species, links to descriptions of biology and natural history. The Fish and Wildlife Service also maintains updated tables of the number of threatened and endangered species by taxonomic group, as well as lists of U.S. threatened and endangered species. Finally, the Fish and Wildlife Service publishes the bimonthly *Endangered Species Bulletin* (available online at http://endangered.fws.gov/bulletin.html), which provides information on new listings, delistings, and reclassifications, in addition to news articles on endangered species.

The World Conservation Union (IUCN) has news articles on a wide array of conservation issues at its Web site (http://www.iucn.org). Information from the *2000 IUCN Red List of Threatened Species* is also available online at http://www.redlist.org. This site includes an extensive database of information on IUCN-listed threatened species. Species information available includes Red List endangerment category, the year the species was assessed, the countries in which the species is found, a list of the habitat types the species occupies, major threats to continued existence, and current population trends. Brief descriptions of ecology and natural history and of conservation measures for protecting listed species are also available. Searches can also be performed by taxonomic group, Red List categories, country, region, or habitat.

The Convention on International Trade in Endangered Species of Wild Fauna and Flora (CITES) has information on international trade at http://www.cites.org. This includes a species database of protected fauna and flora in the three CITES appendices, as well as information on the history and aims of the convention and its current programs.

Aside from the above three rich sources of species information, numerous organizations are dedicated to the conservation of particular listed species. Readers with interest in a particular endangered species are advised to conduct Internet searches to locate these groups. The Save the Manatee Club (http://www.savethemanatee.org), which focuses on West Indian manatees, and the Save Our Springs Alliance (http://www.sosalliance.org), which focuses on protection of the endangered Barton Springs salamander, are only two of many examples.

Information on federal lands and endangered species management can be found at the National Wildlife Refuge Web site (http://refuges.fws.gov), the National Park System Web site (http://www.nps.gov), and the National Forest Service Web site (http://www.fs.fed.us/). National Wildlife Refuge brochures are available at http://library.fws.gov/refuges/index.html.

The Intergovernmental Panel on Climate Change has a wealth of global warming-related resources available online at http://www.ipcc.ch. Particularly valuable are periodic "Summary for Policymaker" reports, which summarize the extent of global warming as well as predicted impacts. The U.S. Environmental Protection Agency (EPA) also maintains a site dedicated to global warming issues at http://www.epa.gov/globalwarming. Finally, the "GLOBAL WARMING: Early Warning Signs" Web site is a joint production of the Environmental Defense Fund, Natural Resources Defense Council, Sierra Club, Union of

Concerned Scientists, U.S. Public Interest Research Group, World Resources Institute, and World Wildlife Fund, and can be found at http://www.climatehotmap.org. This site provides a graphical interface for examining the numerous documented effects global warming has already had on the world. Early warning signs are divided into "fingerprints"—"direct manifestations of a widespread and long-term trend toward warmer global temperatures," and "harbingers"—"events that foreshadow the types of impacts likely to become more frequent and widespread with continued warming." Fingerprints include heat waves, sea level rise, coastal flooding, melting glaciers, and Arctic and Antarctic warming. Harbingers include spreading disease, earlier arrival of spring, plant and animal range shifts and population declines, coral reef bleaching, downpours, heavy snowfall, flooding, droughts, and fires.

"Endangered Ecosystems of the United States—a Preliminary Assessment of Loss and Degradation," a 1995 publication from the National Biological Service, remains the most up-to-date assessment of U.S. ecosystems. Information on water quality in the United States is available at the EPA Web site, http://www.epa.gov/water. Information on wetlands can be found at the Fish and Wildlife Service's "National Wetlands Inventory" page at http://www.nwi.fws.gov.

The World Conservation Union's *1997 IUCN Red List of Threatened Plants* is a valuable resource on threatened plant species.

BirdLife International (http://www.birdlife.net) provides diverse resources on global bird conservation. It is an association of non-governmental conservation organizations that has over 2 million members worldwide.

AmphibiaWeb (http://amphibiaweb.org) provides detailed information on global amphibian declines. It maintains a watch list of recently extinct and declining species, discusses potential causes of amphibian declines and deformities, and also provides detailed information on amphibian biology and conservation. AmphibiaWeb also sponsors a discussion board where readers can submit questions regarding amphibians. The U.S. Geological Survey's National Biological Information Infrastructure runs "FrogWeb: Amphibian Declines and Deformities" at http://www.frogweb.gov/.

TRAFFIC (http://www.traffic.org) was originally founded to help implement the CITES treaty but now addresses diverse issues in wildlife trade. It is a joint wildlife trade monitoring organization of the World Wildlife Fund (WWF) and the World Conservation Union (IUCN). The TRAFFIC Web site contains articles on current topics related to wildlife trade. In addition, TRAFFIC also publishes several periodicals and report series on wildlife trade, including the *TRAFFIC Bulletin, TRAFFIC Online Report Series*, and *Species in Danger Series*. These publications are available online at http://www.traffic.org/publications/index.html.

The International Whaling Commission has a Web site at http://www.iwcoffice.org/. Information on whaling regulations, whale sanctuaries, and other issues associated with whales and whaling can be accessed there.

The *National Survey of Fishing, Hunting, and Wildlife-Associated Recreation* provides extensive data on wildlife recreation in the United States. It is published by the Fish and Wildlife Service using data collected by the U.S. Bureau of the Census. Preliminary results from the 2001 survey were reported here. The full publication will be available in late 2002.

Information Plus sincerely thanks all of the organizations listed above for the valuable information they provide.

INDEX

rhinoceros, 127
wolves, 121, 123–124
Hyacinth macaws, 160

I

Ice core data, 44, 45*f*
Iceland, 163
Indian rhinoceros, 128
Indonesia, 130
    trade in animals/animal products, 160
Infectious diseases, 50
Insects
    with critical habitat under the
      Endangered Species Act (1973), 21*t*
    diseases carried by, 50
    endangered, 147–150, 147*t*
    in National Wildlife Refuge System, 35*t*
    proposed additions to the Endangered
      Species Act, 18*t*
    reasons contributing to endangerment, 10*t*
    spruce bark beetles, 56
Intergovernmental Panel on Climate Change
    (IPCC), 44, 48
The International Ecotourism Society
    (TIES), 166
International efforts/trade agreements,
    35–36, 39, 161–164
    Convention on International Trade in
      Endangered Species (CITES), 15, 36
    Convention on Migratory Species of
      Wild Animals (CMS), 36, 39
    General Agreement on Tariffs and Trade
      (GATT), 161
    Lusaka Agreement of Africa, 164
    North American Free Trade Agreement
      (NAFTA), 161
    See also Convention on International
      Trade in Endangered Species (CITES)
International Whaling Commission, 15,
    163–164
Invasive species, 8*f*, 8*t*
    amphibians endangered by, 107–108
    Asian eels, 91
    balsam-wooly adelgids, 150
    brown tree snakes in Guam, 138
    domestic cats in Australia, 120
    forests endangered by, 72
    plants endangered by, 59
    zebra mussels, 7, *91*, *92f*, 93
Iowa
    National Wildlife Refuge Systems in, 33*t*
IUCN. *See* World Conservation Union
    (IUCN)
IUCN Red List of Threatened Species, 2, 3
    amphibians and reptiles, 105
    birds, 135
    fish, 94
    insects and spiders, 147
    invasive species, 7
    mammals, 119
    plants, 59, 65
    primates, 130
    on the trade of animal products, 151
Ivory-billed woodpeckers, 141
Ivory trade, 129, 162

J

Jaguars, 126
Jamaica
    endangered plant species in, 65
Japan
    trade in animals/animal products, 160
    whaling practices, 163
Jessica (ship), 83
Journal of Heredity, 148

K

Kauai cave wolf spiders, 149
Kazakhstan, 88
Kemp's Ridley Turtles, 113
Kennebec River, ME, 87
Kentucky
    Daniel Boone National Forest, 141
Klamath Basin, CA-OR, 95, 98–99
Knowles, Tony, 124
KochWeser, Maritta con Bieberstein, 119
Komodo dragons, *115*
Kublai Khan, 15
Kyoto Protocol, 57, 58

L

Lacey Act (1900), 102, 103, 161
Lambert, Thomas, 23
Larsen B ice shelf, Antarctica, 49–50, *51*
Lead shot, 137
Leatherback turtles, 113*f*
Legislation
    Animal Welfare Act (1966), 158
    Bald Eagle Protection Act (1940), 145
    Clean Water Act (1972), 137
    Endangered Species Act (1973), 3, 16–24
    Endangered Species Conservation Act
      (1969), 15
    Endangered Species Preservation Act
      (1966), 15
    Lacey Act (1900), 102, 103, 161
    Magnuson Act (1976), 90, 103
    Marine Mammal Protection Act (1972),
      101, 103
    Migratory Bird Conservation Act (1929),
      135
    Wild Bird Conservation Act (1992), 154
Livestock ranching, 122, 132–133
Lizards, 114–115
    See also Reptiles
Loggerhead shrikes, 141
Logging, 3–4, 6
    clear cutting, 72
    within national forests, 26
    See also Deforestation
Longline fishing, 90
Lost River sucker fish, 96, 98
Louisiana, 152

M

Magnuson Act (1976), 90, 103
Maine
    Kennebec River, 87
Malawi, Lake, 94
Mammals, 119–134
    bears, 124–125
    big cats, 125–127

bighorn sheep, 131–132
bison, 132–133
black-footed ferrets, 120–121, *121*
with critical habitat under the
    Endangered Species Act (1973), 20*t*
elephants, 129–130
endangered or threatened, 96*t*, 119–120
extinct, 2*t*
marine, 101–102
in National Wildlife Refuge System, 35*t*
primates, 130–131
proposed additions to the Endangered
    Species Act, 18*t*
reasons contributing to endangerment,
    10*t*
rhinoceros, 127–129
wild horses in American west, 130–131,
    131
wolves, 121–124
Manatees, *101*, 101–102
Mangrove forests, 54, 75–76, *76*
Marine Mammal Protection Act (1972), 101,
    102, 103
Marine species, 81–104
    See also Aquatic species
Mass extinctions, 1–2
Massachusetts
    National Wildlife Refuge Systems in, 33*t*
Mauritius
    endangered plant species in, 59
Medicines derived from plants, 77, 79
Merck pharmaceutical company, 79
Mercury, 85, 86*f*, 87*f*
Methane (CH_4), 43
    as greenhouse gas, 44, 46
    Greenland ice core data, 45*f*
Mexican gray wolves, 124
Mexican spotted owls, 142
Mexico
    monarch butterflies, 148
    whale watching in, 163
Michigan
    National Wildlife Refuge Systems in, 33*t*
Migratory Bird Conservation Act (1929),
    135
Migratory birds
    songbirds, 140
    whooping cranes, 143*f*
    See also Birds
Milankovitch Cycles, 43
Miller, Mary Beth, 119
Minnesota
    Boundary Waters Canoe Area, 28
Mississippi
    National Wildlife Refuge Systems in, 33*t*
Missouri
    National Wildlife Refuge Systems in, 33*t*
Missouri River, 99
Mojave, Lake, AZ, 99
Mojave Desert, California, 28
Monarch butterflies, 148
Mongolian Przewalski horse, 134
Monito geckos, 114–115
Monitor lizards, *115*
Montana
    Charles M. Russell National Wildlife
      Refuge, 121